Discard MICKLEOVER

KEDLESTON ROAD

D0277746

Race, Class, and Community in Southern Labor History

Race, Class, and Community in Southern Labor History

Edited by
Gary M Fink
Merl E. Reed

THE UNIVERSITY OF ALABAMA PRESS
Tuscaloosa and London

Copyright © 1994
The University of Alabama Press
Tuscaloosa, Alabama 35487–0380
All rights reserved
Manufactured in the United States of America

∞

The paper on which this book is printed meets the minimum
requirements of American National Standard for Information
Science-Permanence of Paper for Printed Library Materials,
ANSI Z39.48-1984.

Library of Congress Cataloging-in-Publication Data

Race, class, and community in Southern labor history / edited by
Gary M Fink, Merl E. Reed.
   p.   cm.
Includes bibliographical references and index.
ISBN 0-8173-0719-2 (alk. paper)
   1. Textile workers—Southern States—History.   2. Afro-Americans—
Employment—Southern States—History.   3. Women—Employment—
Southern States—History.   4. Labor movement—Southern States—
History.   5. Working class—Southern States—History.   6. Southern
States—Social conditions.   I. Fink, Gary M   II. Reed, Merl Elwyn,
1925–   .
HD9877.A13R33   1994
331'.0975—dc20   93-32301

British Library Cataloguing-in-Publication Data available

UNIVERSITY OF DERBY

LIBRARY

Acc. No: 3045754

Class: 331.0975 RAC

Contents

Tables

Associate Editors

LESLIE S. HOUGH
  Director, Archives of Labor and Urban Affairs
  Wayne State University

CLIFFORD M. KUHN
  Associate Director, Georgia Government
  Documentation Project
  Georgia State University

JOE W. TROTTER, JR.
  Professor of History
  Carnegie-Mellon University

ROBERT H. ZIEGER
  Professor of History
  University of Florida

Preface

The essays in this volume were selected from the papers read at the Seventh Southern Labor Studies Conference held in Atlanta, Georgia, 10–13 October 1991. As in previous publications from the Southern Labor Studies Conferences, the editors looked for originality in the use of methodology, sources, content, and interpretation.

At least two referees read each of the papers submitted by conference participants. Based on these critiques and their own evaluations, the editors made their selections. For the most part, the essays that follow are closely similar to the conference versions, although the authors sometimes added material where appropriate; in a few cases substantial revisions occurred.

The editors greatly appreciate the efforts of the associate editors; without their expertise and comments this undertaking would have proven far more difficult and less certain in results. Special thanks goes to Christine Lutz, who painstakingly assembled the numerous editorial comments into a fresh text. She also entered manuscripts that came on hard copy into the computer and almost miraculously, it seemed, managed the transfer of essays submitted on several different kinds of software to the program used by the editors.

Finally, the editors congratulate the contributors for their scholarship and dedication without which neither the conference nor this volume of essays would have been possible.

Gary M Fink and Merl E. Reed
Atlanta, Georgia

Introduction

The unfortunate scholarly neglect of southern labor history, noted in the introductions of two earlier volumes of essays drawn from previous Southern Labor Studies Conferences, clearly appears to be at an end. Indeed, as evidenced by the quality and range of essays in this collection, the field may well have come into its own during the past decade. Not only does research interest seem to be peaking, but the practitioners are overwhelmingly younger scholars, and much of their work emphasizes the new social and political history. While the topics covered usually reflect that methodology, their chronology ranges from the antebellum period to the 1970s, a fact that suggests the variety of sources and changing research approaches that can be used in rendering new meaning to the past. Although the subject of gender was generally a minor theme in these sessions, work now being done in the field leaves no doubt that at some future conference, and in its resulting publication, gender also will attract a commanding amount of attention.

In introducing and describing their respective areas, the associate editors, Robert H. Zieger (textile workers), Joe W. Trotter, Jr. (African Americans), and Clifford M. Kuhn (labor politics), have provided a rich historiographical background. So too have some of the essays, including Bess Beatty's article on gender relations, political scientist Michael Goldfield's sweeping conceptualization of the significance of Operation Dixie, and David L. Carlton's review of paternalism in the southern textile industry.

It is not surprising that paternalism and its effect on southern workers also appear in other essays in this collection. Gary R. Freeze notes how industrial paternalism replaced the rural patriarchy as fiercely independent farmers in the late nineteenth century were forced off the land, migrating to the towns and usually becoming wards of the "Big Daddies" who owned the textile mills. Through court action, James D. Schmidt's plantation overseers sometimes were able to liberalize labor contracts that bound them tightly to the wills and whims of paternalistic planters. In Suzanne Schnittman's antebellum Richmond, slaves hired out to tobacco processors and managed a partial escape from the paternalism of the plantation.

In addition, both Schnittman and Dernoral Davis, another essayist on African-American workers, illustrate how using conventional source material created primarily by a white elite can provide insight into the lives of both antebellum slaves and postbellum freedmen. Davis uses Civil War and Freedmen's Bureau records to show how deeply former Memphis slaves yearned for their own land and how decisively they rejected attempts to revive the gang labor system. On the other hand, using oral histories, Michael Honey points to the gaps in knowledge that occurred when contemporary participants lacked direct input into the historical process in his study of Memphis's black industrial workers in the 1930s and 1940s.

Just as themes such as paternalism and race touch many of the essays, so does the role of the state and the political process. Both Alex Lichtenstein's study of Georgia's convict lease system and Bryant Simon's work on depression and New Deal politics illustrate the conflicting role that the state sometimes played, both in sanctioning worker exploitation in the mines and mills and in extending the possibility of tentative and grudging protection from such abuses. James A. Hodges's study of the J. P. Stevens strike describes that industry's brazen disregard of laws designed to protect individual workers in their union activity and the seeming inability of federal agencies to mete out retribution.

Political demagoguery was alive and well in the period after World War II, as Alan Draper demonstrates when describing how Alabama's Governor George C. Wallace battled and nearly destroyed that state's central labor body while seeking the presidency and projecting the doctrine of white supremacy. Meanwhile, Douglas Flamming relates the use of McCarthyite techniques by local demagogues to defeat union attempts to organize the carpet industry in Dalton, Georgia.

Curiously, in this postwar saga of worker defeats and union decline, the federal legislative role is mostly ignored. Yet the Taft-Hartley Act of 1947 was passed shortly after the start of Operation Dixie. By outlawing secondary boycotts, by endorsing employer-satisfying worker individualism over union collectivism, by permitting employer intimidation of workers in the name of free speech, by blurring the boundaries between state and federal jurisdiction in labor disputes, and by allowing state criminal and nuisance statutes to become substitutes for solid labor law, among its other features, Taft-Hartley certainly hampered union organizing activity in the southern and other nonindustrial states. The rapid appearance of more than two score of state right-to-work laws that Taft-Hartley made possible illustrates the popularity of such anti-union measures. With this federal sanction, was it merely coincidental that the southern model of labor relations, which brought the decline of unionism and worker power, began to assume nation-wide acceptance during the forty-five years since Taft-Hartley's passage, twenty-eight of which fell under the tutelage of administrations hostile to organized labor? Indeed, by the 1990s had the South finally prevailed in a manner totally unanticipated by its traditionalist champions?

The essays in this volume could not be expected to deal with all of the issues confronting workers and their unions. Nevertheless, the editors trust and hope that these selections will enlighten the reader on many important aspects of the history of southern labor and will raise new questions to be explained by other scholars and future conferences.

Part I.

Southern Textiles: Toward a
New Historiographical Synthesis

ROBERT H. ZIEGER

Introduction

Until the 1980s, southern textile workers were the neglected stepchildren of social and labor historiography. True, historians widely acknowledged their presence as a component of the labor force and commonly imputed to them a key role in the South's failure to join the labor-liberal political mainstream. Yet they rarely underwent the scrutiny of professional historians. As late as the mid-1980s, the list of historical works on this central element of the twentieth-century southern labor force consisted mainly of dissertations by Robert R. R. Brooks and Herbert Lahne, appearing in 1935 and 1944, respectively, the "Revolt in the Piedmont" section of Irving Bernstein's *The Lean Years* (1960), and sections of Ray Marshall's *Labor in the South* (1967) and George Brown Tindall's *The Emergence of the New South, 1913–1945* (1967). In the 1960s and 1970s some dissertations were taking shape, and there had always been a historically informed political literature relating to textiles, as exemplified by W. J. Cash's 1941 characterizations in *Mind of the South* and Harry Boyte's sweeping 1972 article in *Radical America*. Still, the South's hundreds of thousands of textile operatives and their families seldom intruded into the central arenas of labor and social historiography.[1]

Yet even as historians neglected the Piedmont, social scientists forged a classic literature of description and analysis. From the early 1920s onward, sociologists, social workers, economists, and social psychologists subjected the textile workers and their communities to detailed and often insightful analysis. Beginning with Broadus Mitchell's 1921 study of labor relations in cotton textiles and extending through recent investigations of the impact of racial and technological change, social scientists generated a rich and evocative literature. Works by participant observers such as Harriet Herring and Lois MacDonald, more formal sociological studies such as Liston Pope's

Millhands and Preachers (1942) and John Morland's *Millways of Kent* (1957),
and more recent examinations of race, technology, and occupational disease
activism by Rhonda Zingraff and Michael D. Schulman, Bennett M. Jud-
kins, and John Gaventa and Barbara Smith have brought three generations of
mill workers vividly to life. Gastonia, North Carolina, site in 1929 of one of
American labor's epic confrontations, has been particularly well served. In
1930 Jennings J. Rhyne published *Some Southern Cotton Mill Workers and
Their Villages*, which contains rare survey data about Gastonia's workers in
the period before the strike. Pope's study, a mainstay for historians writing
about the textile industry, focused on the role of religion in shaping workers'
acquiescence and protest in the North Carolina community. A 1976 work,
Spindles and Spires, was a "re-study" of religion and social change, providing intimate perspectives on a new generation of Piedmont workers, stereo-
typically anti-union but now leavened by an infusion of black workers into
the mills.[2]

Reasons for historiographical neglect spring readily enough to mind.
Historians interested in the South traditionally have had items other than
industrialization at the top of their agendas. The fact that the textile labor
force was overwhelmingly white made its workers seemingly peripheral
to race, the central problem of southern history and historiography. The
repeated failure of union organizing among textile workers resulted in
a paucity of institutions through which workers' behavior and activities
might be systematically studied. Textile workers had the reputation of
being diffident and inarticulate and thus left few of the written records on
which standard historical literature ordinarily rests. Moreover, northern-
based unions, whose focus and records lay outside Dixie, largely inspired
whatever union organization that did take place. Perhaps the vigor and
repute of the social science literature, seemingly preempting the field,
discouraged historians from invading the turf; after all, Rhyne, MacDonald,
Herring, Pope, John Dollard, and Moreland dealt face-to-face with workers
and left little in the way of a paper trail behind them.

The neglect of southern textile workers ended in the 1980s. Studies of the
historical experiences of Piedmont workers have become, in the words of
one of its practitioners, something of a cottage industry. Works such as
C. Vann Woodward's *Origins of the New South, 1877–1913* (1951) and
Marshall's and Tindall's books helped to legitimate industrialization and
labor relations as central concerns of twentieth-century southern histo-

riography. The founding of the Southern Labor Archives in Atlanta in 1970 helped end the neglect of labor activism in the region. The collecting of business records at the University of North Carolina, the Georgia Institute of Technology, and elsewhere helped shed light on the contentious and problematic nature of labor relations in southern factories, including the textile mills. And the revolution in oral history gave historians, eager to follow the new social history's injunction to study the people and to write the history of the inarticulate, new ways of investigating the lives of mill workers.

The result has been an outpouring of vigorous scholarly literature. In every respect, it has challenged the conventional historiographical and social scientific wisdom. Thus, for example, David L. Carlton's pioneering examination of South Carolina mill workers, *Mill and Town in South Carolina, 1880–1920* (1982), finds not docile and downtrodden denizens of the mill villages but rather a lusty and aggressive political culture of mill life—one based on deep feelings of racial hierarchy and precise notions of moral economy. James Hodges's study of the fate of mill workers in the New Deal period, *New Deal Labor Policy and the Southern Cotton Textile Industry, 1933–1941* (1986), works against the standard, union-centered accounts of scholars such as Bernstein. Carefully documenting the weakness of industrial unions and the frailty of federal labor relations machinery, Hodges sees a strong and resilient mill village culture that led to shrewd and realistic assessments of the balance of power, not the tragic and dominated mass of lethargic or mindless southern proles that Bernstein and many disappointed union organizers perceived. More recently, I. A. Newby has produced an acute reexamination of mill village life and culture. In *Plain Folk in the New South: Social Change and Cultural Persistence, 1880–1915* (1989), he stresses the struggle for cultural and familial autonomy that pitted mill workers against blacks, union organizers, schoolteachers, and social reformers more often that it did against their employers and clergymen.[3]

In an insightful 1982 article, Mary Frederickson challenged one of the staples of social investigation relating to southern textile workers, namely, the belief that cotton textiles had a virtually all-white labor force. Frederickson showed that blacks always composed at least a small portion of the mill working population. Even though they were usually relegated to janitorial and rough maintenance work, blacks worked episodically in the production process, often as informal fill-ins or replacements for white workers. During times of strike or labor shortage, they drifted into the factories in substantial numbers. Through much of the century, the presence in or near the mills of this experienced labor supply helped employers keep white workers in line, even if open recruitment or employment of large numbers of black workers invariably led to vigorous, and often violent, resistance by white workers in the mills and in the villages. In the wake of the civil rights agitation of the 1950s and 1960s, increasing numbers of black workers made their way into the mills and surged to the fore in a spate of organizing campaigns that in the 1970s gave labor partisans new hope that at last organized labor could gain a sustained presence in southern textiles.[4]

By 1988, mill workers had come so far from their historiographical invisibility as to serve as the subject of the winning entry in that year's Philip A. Taft Prize competition, which recognizes the outstanding work in labor history. *Like a Family: The Making of a Southern Cotton Mill World* (1987), by Jacquelyn Dowd Hall, James Leloudis, Robert Korstad, Mary Murphy, Lu Ann Jones, and Christopher B. Daly, grew from hundreds of oral histories of mill workers and family members. This impressive volume was a kind of living embodiment of the values of the looser version of the new social history that emerged in the 1960s.[5] In asserting for mill workers an impressive degree of cultural autonomy and human agency, *Like a Family* drastically revised the traditional picture of a victimized and passive folk. Piedmont workers' letters to Franklin and Eleanor Roosevelt, written in the wake of the disastrous NRA experiment and the tragic General Strike of 1934, poignantly document the inability of customary unionism and government programs to assist them in their efforts to give cohesive substance to their often courageous, localized protests against the stretch-out and other community and workplace injustices.

Like a Family used gender as a key theme. Mill women, in their capacity both as workers and as homemakers and mothers, stood at the center of the kin and village networks that gave the Piedmont its distinctive work and community culture. Hall has expanded upon these insights in imaginative and provocative articles, notably "Disorderly Women: Gender and Labor Militancy in the Appalachian South" (1986) and "Private Eyes, Public Women: Class and Sex in the Urban South" (1991). Here she deploys gender to defamiliarize the standard accounts of well-known early twentieth-century strikes and thus to reconceptualize the nature of labor conflict. Her

1929 women strikers of Elizabethton, Tennessee, were not the quaint, ana-
chronistic mill girls depicted by contemporaries and historians but rather
shrewd, self-directed young women. Embracing modern culture as exhibited
in the movies, radio programs, and magazines, they exploited the traditionalist views of women held by town elites, employers, and the soldiers
who patrolled the town. In imaginative and revealing episodes of public
theater they asserted their rights and undermined gender and class hierarchies. In Hall's telling, the sobersided and bureaucratic labor organizers and
government investigators constituted the anachronisms in Elizabethton,
while young mill women tested and exploited the possibilities offered by
modern culture. In her 1991 article, Hall moves into the realm of discourse
theory, using the life of a female photographer-activist during an Atlanta
textile strike as a window through which to observe the dialectic between
subversive modernist notions of female possibility and tenacious Victorian
values at a critical moment in the history of the New South.

The new social history and the more recent focus on gender have transformed the historiography of southern textiles, but the new economic
history has been less evident. Our understanding of the economic characteristics of the industry and its labor force remains rudimentary. As yet, Cathy
McHugh's sharply focused *Mill Family: The Labor Systems in the Southern
Cotton Textile Industry, 1880–1915* (1988) remains the only book-length
effort to reconceive such themes as paternalism, female and child labor, and
general labor force recruitment and retention in an econometric context.
Gavin Wright's acute analyses, both in *Old South, New South* (1986) and in
detailed journal articles, however, have suggested a reshaping of our understanding of the political economy of southern textiles as dramatic as that of
the industry's social dynamics. Thus, Wright documents the economic
imperatives underlying managerial changes that triggered the strike waves
of 1919–1921 and 1929–1932, all the while reminding his fellow econometri-
cians that notions of moral economy and cultural autonomy, so enthusiastically invoked and documented by the social historians, were a crucial
part of the textile workers' calculations of their interests.[6]

The essays in this section well reflect the merging stream of textile
historiography. Bess Beatty's contribution gives an overview of gender,
stressing its role as a basic shaping factor in the textile workers' experience
and in the effort to understand the character of the industry and its labor
force. David Carlton's reexamination of class and paternalism as themes

in textile history underscores the extent to which recent historiography forces us into complex new understandings of once familiar staples of interpretation. Gary Freeze's detailed examination of paternalism in a late nineteenth-century North Carolina mill focuses on the mill workers' strategies of survival, reinforcing the theme of paternalism as a reciprocal relationship defined by time and place. Bryant Simon's study of the political behavior of South Carolina mill workers in the interwar years adds forcefully to the theme of the agency of workers as it broadens our understanding of their political values and behavior. James Hodges provides a dose of more traditional labor history, along with a reminder that, whatever the insights and contributions of newer questions and techniques, the issue of unionization remains relevant and significant. Even here, though, the mill workers are pioneers, for Hodges's emerging work on the J. P. Stevens controversy is one of the few full scholarly historical studies to subject post-1960 workers to sophisticated historiographical treatment. As with his examination of their counterparts in the 1930s, his study of textile workers of the 1960s and 1970s fuses institutional and social history.[7]

There is little doubt as to the continued vigor of the historiographical recasting of southern textile workers. In addition to the papers here presented, new and forthcoming works by Linda Frankel, Gary Fink, Douglas Flamming, Janet Irons, and Philip Holleran, among others, ensure that the breakthroughs of the past decade will continue. Perhaps as the contours of the textile labor force become more clearly mapped and as its changing circumstances are more precisely charted, we will gain a fuller understanding of the textile workers' impact on the South's sociopolitical trajectory over the course of the twentieth century.[8]

Gender Relations in Southern Textiles
A Historiographical Overview

As industry began moving into the South by the late antebellum period, textile men in the Piedmont looked upon female workers as a wholly dependent and exploitable group. Thus did George Makepeace, a northern mill man who had followed the industry south, enjoin his southern peers to "get all the widow women that has got a family of girls or other families that are mostly girls as we do not want many boys."[1] Makepeace's advice continued to appeal to southern textile employers well into the twentieth century, because they believed that female workers in the mills and largely female families in the mill communities would be less independent and thus a more stable and tractable labor force. The precarious nature of survival on the land helped attract such families as well as individual girls and women. Women sought mill work because they "got tird of the farm" and wanted jobs "lighter and unaffected by the vicissitudes of weather."[2] Bertha Awford Black spoke for her four sisters and undoubtedly thousands of other girls and women when she recalled, "we were all anxious to go to work because . . . we didn't like the farming. It was so hot and from sunup to sundown. . . . Mill work was better. It had to be."[3]

Until recently, however, historians largely ignored these southern women. As late as the mid-1980s, Anne Scott still placed them among the ranks of the "all but invisible."[4] Moreover, what little attention they had received from historians presented contradictory images. Labor historians usually describe southern textile workers as particularly individualistic; yet writers of women's history commonly portray southern white women as largely unaffected by nineteenth-century individualism. On the one hand, according to Jean Friedman, an enclosed circle confined southern women, binding them to kin, place, and tradition.[5] On the other hand, David Carlton noted a "backwoods individualism" in South Carolina's mill workers.[6] How did the enclosed circle and this backwoods individualism extend beyond the homes and communities of these workers to the work positions at the looms and spindles of the southern textile industry?

Making white southern, working-class women more visible and reconciling contradictory images necessitates rethinking the different categories used in defining them. Studies of the South usually concentrate on what is peculiarly southern. Consequently, historians of the South infrequently raised questions about gender and class, which were central concerns to the new social history that emerged in the 1960s. Social historian Jacquelyn Dowd Hall, in describing the wealth of revisionist southern history published in the 1960s and 1970s, noted that "race, not class or gender, was the new scholarship's obsession."[7] Another characteristic of this generation of historians became stereotyping by region. What Catherine Clinton has called the "New Englandization" of women's history largely held true for white working-class history as well.[8]

Anne Firor Scott's pioneering work *The Southern Lady: From Pedestal to Politics, 1830–1930* (1970) revealed the great potential for research on southern women, but it stood almost alone for nearly a decade.[9] In the 1980s, however, an impressive literature began to appear on plantation women, black women, and the relationship between black and white women. Still, most historians of southern women studied subjects who were categorically southern. Catherine Clinton chose the archetypically "southern" woman, the plantation mistress, as the focus of her study. Elizabeth Fox-Genovese did likewise, but she gave enslaved black females a role in the story. Non-slaveholding white women have a bit part in Fox-Genovese's narrative, but the difficulties of including them became apparent in a footnote referring readers to the sources in which Fox-Genovese could identify only books largely or exclusively about northern working-class women. Dolores Janiewski, one of the first historians to publish a book on working-class women in the South, focused her attention on Durham, North Carolina, primarily in the period prior to the 1960s. Although Durham employers offered black women wage work in the tobacco industry, they more typically excluded these women from textiles. Fortunately, Janiewski's study brought questions about class and gender into a southern setting while still focusing on race. The determination of these authors of some of the best work on southern women—Janiewski, Fox-Genovese, Jean Friedman, Suzanne Lebsock, and Jacqueline Jones—to make their studies biracial is commendable.[10] But the tradition of race that remains at the core of any study of the South has prompted historians to approach black and white women primarily in their relationship to race.

In the last two decades historians have paid much greater attention to relationships between gender and class. But most of the resulting studies, even those focusing specifically on American women, either largely ignore southern women or specifically exclude them. Leslie Woodcock Tentler's work, *Wage Earning Women: Industrial Work and Family Life in the United States, 1900–1930* (1979), for example, concludes that "urban working-class women, save perhaps in the South, entered essentially the same world of low-skill jobs whether garment makers in New York or packinghouse workers in Chicago."[11] With southern working-class women thus excluded from the national mainstream, historians of the South face the task of explaining the world in which southern working-class women labored and the extent to which their experiences reinforce or challenge theories about women and work.

Scholars, primarily sociologists and economists, began studying the southern textile industry in the early twentieth century. Most recognized that women worked in the mills and that, when combined with children, both groups became victims. Yet Broadus Mitchell, who wrote the first important historical study of the industry, *The Rise of the Cotton Mills in the South* (1921), rejected the sociological theory of victimization while maintaining the conflation of women and children. In this setting, he insisted, the textile industry was "a boon especially because it gave means of livelihood to women and children." Mitchell, primarily responsible for the long entrenched and still influential portrayal of mill owners as paternalistic and mill workers as docile and grateful, used class rather than gender analysis. Mill owners always knew, he wrote, "that employer and employee were of the same origin, the same blood, and not remotely, the same instincts." While recognizing the large female component in the workforce, Mitchell ignored the question of whether men and women shared these values and characteristics.[12]

Liston Pope's *Millhands and Preachers: A Study of Gastonia* (1942) stands between Mitchell's work and the scholarship of the 1970s as a major historical study of southern workers. Pope as adroitly as Mitchell saw without seeing. His typical southern worker "retained an individualism which leads him to resent encroachment upon his 'personal liberties' in his job, and a 'chivalry' which causes him to resent even more deeply such efficiency studies as timing his wife while she goes to the toilet." For Pope, the "southern worker" remained in the male category even though he acknowledged that textile mills employed many women.[13]

In 1971 Melton McLaurin published *Paternalism and Protest: Southern Cotton Mill Workers and Organized Labor, 1875–1905*, which launched a reassessment of the history of the southern textile industry. Although McLaurin acknowledged the presence of women and girls in the southern mills, he did not make gender a major theme of his work. Like Pope and Mitchell, McLaurin sometimes generalized without regard to gender differences. For example, he wrote, "simple, independent, poor, uneducated, and culturally homogeneous, the people of the Piedmont willingly abandoned the land in droves." Unlike earlier historians, however, McLaurin questioned whether the word "independent" would describe equally well the many women who left the land, and he raised questions about the relationship of women to organization and protest.[14]

The next major historical study of the southern cotton industry, David Carlton's *Mill and Town in South Carolina, 1880–1920* (1982), skillfully blended a class and race analysis. But Carlton paid less attention to gender roles and conflict than did McLaurin a decade earlier. Like Pope and McLaurin, Carlton described the "backwoods individualism" of southern workers, tracing it to their yeomen, "poor white trash," or mountaineer origins.[15] Carlton did not include as a distinct source of mill workers the families that George Makepeace described as the "widow women that has got a family of girls or other families that are mostly girls."

Not surprisingly, *Norma Rae*, the popular, late 1970s movie about female workers fighting for unionization in the South, offered a more realistic portrayal of southern textile women workers than did the scholarly studies bound by assumptions of docility or individualism. The acknowledgment of the gendered nature of the labor force in the mid-1980s, however, forced scholars interested in the southern textile industry to reassess older views.

In 1984 Linda Frankel's "Southern Textile Women: Generations of Survival and Struggle" analyzed women's lives in the Harriet-Henderson Cotton Mills of North Carolina across three generations. This article and an essay by Frankel in *Hanging by a Thread: Social Change in Southern Textiles* (1991) emphasized the importance of putting women and gender roles at the center of any analysis on southern textile workers. Frankel's study of a mill convulsed by two strikes within twenty years led to the conclusion that "the history of women textile workers in the South belies a simplistic image of passivity while at the same time it attests to the powerful forces limiting the autonomy of women workers in southern mill villages."[16]

A short time later, Mary Frederickson's " 'I Know Which Side I'm On': Southern Women in the Labor Movement in the Twentieth Century" appeared in a volume about working women. Like Frankel, Frederickson also challenged the image of southern docility, concluding that "the courage of women workers in the south has matched that of women anywhere."[17]

Continuing this line of inquiry, Jacquelyn Dowd Hall in 1986 published "Disorderly Women: Gender and Labor Militancy in the Appalachian South" in the *Journal of American History*. The essay gave southern white working women a visibility previously experienced only through *Norma Rae*. Hall's "disorderly women" actively participated in the 1929 strike in Elizabethton, Tennessee, a conflict earlier detailed in Tom Tippett's *When Southern Labor Stirs* (1931). Tippett, noting the German ownership of the mills, described Elizabethton's streets as "bristling with soldiers, armed and fighting on the side of the Germans against the native sons of Tennessee." He described a constantly changing leadership in the union as "one man after another came and went." Hall wrote about the same strike, but not about "native sons," nor the men who "came and went." Convinced that "with gender at the center of analysis, unexpected dimensions would come into view," Hall recast the history of the Elizabethton strike. She demanded more than contributory history, such as adding the names of Trixie Perry and Texas Bill beside those of the native sons of Tennessee. She also interjected "a female angle of vision" and "a close look at women's distinctive forms of collective action, using language and gesture as points of entry to a culture."[18]

Between 1987 and 1989 three books on the southern textile industry appeared that put "gender at the center of analysis." *Like a Family: The Making of a Southern Cotton Mill World* (1987), by Hall and a team of writers at the University of North Carolina, weaves analysis based on gender throughout the book. The work is not about women but, significantly, about workers, both male and female. Indeed, the index entry "men" is almost as lengthy as the entry "women." The assumptions about workers are routinely analyzed from a perspective of gender difference. The authors reject broad generalizations about independence or docility in favor of more nuanced arguments examining the way mill work more or less empowered workers, depending on whether they were male or female. In discussing the creation and organization of the workforce, they investigated why employers preferred hiring women, and they analyzed the social significance of the job differentiation those women encountered. It was no surprise that "the greatest barrier women faced in the mill was the male monopoly on machine-fixing and supervisory jobs." The authors concluded that only in the weave room did "women as well as men [enjoy] a rare independence."

The book also raises less familiar questions, such as ones about the nature of the conflict created between men and women by industrialization and the ways women coped with being child bearers and nurturers as well as industrial workers. Popular new methods of considering the southern folk, such as their sense of mutuality, are explored with gender as a central focus.

Sometimes the authors point out what is often seen but not recognized. For example, researchers asking questions about cotton mill people and political power first need to grapple with the reality that until 1920 none of the women workers could vote, and even after that date many were too young. *Like a Family* concludes by contrasting the lives of Spencer Love, a male mill builder, and Icy Norman, a female worker. Norman recalled the attention and encouragement that Love and his father gave her as a young worker, the very kind of relationship that the designation "paternalistic" has long evoked. The book's poignant epilogue, however, reveals Norman's ambivalent feelings after a lifetime of laboring for Burlington Industries. The company denied her request to work a few extra months in order to participate in a new profit-sharing plan. Clearly, the complexity of the relationship between powerful men and the women who worked for them cannot be adequately explained simply by the word "paternalistic."[19]

In 1989 I. A. Newby published *Plain Folk in the New South: Social Change and Cultural Persistence, 1880–1915.* The introduction places little emphasis on the interaction of class formation and gender roles. Newby described the majority of plain folk as "agricultural laborers, sharecroppers, tenant farmers, . . . small and insecure landowners[,] . . . hunters, fishermen, or herdsmen," many of whom from time to time "worked in logging, lumbering, sawmilling, rail-splitting, mining, turpentining, gristmilling, cotton ginning or railroad construction." Such observations seemed to suggest that Newby, like many earlier scholars interested in southern textile workers, would acknowledge the presence of females and then discuss men.

But this impression is deceptive. Although male-centered phrasing is scattered throughout the book, overall Newby's work added impressively to scholarship that places gender at the center of analysis. Similar to the authors of *Like a Family,* Newby used extensively the resources of the Southern Oral History Project, which Hall directed. Approximately two-thirds of the interviews Newby cited are of women. Their stories appear frequently throughout the book and offer a fresh perspective on the "independent" southern worker. Newby concluded that textile mills "promised what many women sought—security and perhaps even a kind of emancipation." The independence Newby described here differs significantly from the ill-tempered male variety that interested many earlier historians.[20]

Also in 1989 Allen Tullos published *Habits of Industry: White Culture and the Transformation of the Carolina Piedmont,* a third study based primarily on the Southern Oral History Project interviews. Tullos juxtaposed the stories of male and female workers beside those of powerful men. The most telling and poignant memoir, which makes up one-sixth of the book, is that of Ethel Hilliard. Tullos used her life history to suggest "the contours of temperament and moral choice that were faced by many in her generation of white, working-class Piedmont women." Hardly a touchy individualist, Hilliard dutifully responded to the needs of ten children and the demands of an abusive husband. She accepted the dominant power of men, both in the factory and in the home, as God decreed. But as an old woman, she concluded, "I'd love to live my life over if I knowed some things."[21]

These three books bring gender analysis to the fore in southern textile history. Meanwhile, other scholars continue to explore the lives of southern textile women workers using gender roles and a variety of other approaches. Several essays in *Hanging by a Thread* suggest that this analysis can be enhanced by comparing southern workers to those in the North and in other countries. Gay Gullickson, for example, paired the South with Normandy to conclude that "shared assumptions about gender, childhood and work, and technological stagnation between the 1840s and 1920s produced remarkably similar work experiences for women and men and girls and boys on both sides of the Atlantic." An essay by Gary Freeze in the same volume focuses on cotton mill women prior to 1880 and successfully demonstrates that, although historians interested in this period do not have access to the rich oral testimony so valuable in re-creating the lives of contemporary working men and women, a creative search will yield telling sources for these earlier years as well. Jacquelyn Hall's recent work on labor activist Ola Delight Smith furthers our understanding of the relationship between gender roles and protest in the textile South. An article by Lee Ann Whites, "The De Graffenried Controversy: Class, Race, and Gender in the New South," published in the *Journal of Southern History* in 1988, explores the relationships of cotton mill women and elite women. In *Hard Times Cotton Mill Girls*, published in 1986, Victoria Byerly presented personal stories that complement the more analytical approach taken by Janiewski, Frederickson, and others in describing gender and race relations in mills that began integrating in the mid-twentieth century.[22]

When Anne Scott assessed scholarship on southern women in 1982, she could point only to several dissertations that mentioned the lives of women who worked in the textile mills. The subsequent decade saw an outpouring of important work dealing with women and with gender roles. In this pursuit, Victoria Byerly interviewed Crystal Lee Sutton, the real Norma Rae. Sutton recalled her hatred of school "because of the way the teachers treated the working-class kids." She remembered learning about southern workers only in her economics book, which "had three little pages on unions." But once becoming experienced in the fight for the dignity of working people, both men and women, Sutton stated, "I understand the importance of history."[23]

2

DAVID L. CARLTON

Paternalism and Southern Textile Labor
A Historiographical Review

If the central theme of southern textile labor history is the question, "Why is there no unionization in the South?," in all likelihood the most common answer to that question has been "paternalism." In the eyes of most observers, the ability of southern workers to act, and sometimes even to think, as a class has been inhibited by a social order imbued with notions of intrinsic human inequality, hierarchy, and deference, an order sharply divergent from what is ideally/typically viewed as the "American" pattern.

Yet beneath the surface of the traditional "paternalist" consensus has lain widespread disagreement, even confusion, over the character of the regime prevailing in the mill villages. To the earliest scholarly observers of the southern textile industry, Broadus Mitchell and Holland Thompson, paternalism had a benign face. In their view, the rise of the mills was a broadly social, as well as economic, movement; in building factories industrialists had the uplift of their workers as much in mind as the making of profits, and the workers in response understood and appreciated their efforts. Paternal concern stemmed from a tradition, derived from the "plantation aristocracy," of noblesse oblige on the part of the elite, and the uncritical acceptance by the white masses of rule by the "better sort."[1]

In the eyes of most observers, though, southern industrial paternalism has been far less beneficent an institution. The simplest and most common version of the hostile view regards the region's industrial relations as a manifestation of what has commonly been regarded as the central feature of southern social structure—the concentration of power in the hands of a small, unchallengeable elite. The notion of the mill village as an analogue to the slave plantation, and accordingly of mill workers as "white slaves," predates Frank Tannenbaum's dire portrait in his 1924 book *Darker Phases of the South*, but became especially popular in the crisis years of the 1920s and 1930s and entered the consciousness of generations of southern history undergraduates through W. J. Cash's *Mind of the South.* According to this still-popular view, the mill village was a mild sort of "total institution" at best, a prison or police state at worst, an enveloping, stifling environment that left workers little or no independent space. Moreover, the power of the industrialists extended well beyond the village, effectively controlling local and even state governments. Political institutions were undemocratic and oligarchical, the nonindustrial middle class was weak or dependent on the ruling grandees. Thus unopposed in their control of the levers of state power, industrialists could pull them at will, bringing all the crushing weight of "legitimate" armed force to bear whenever the normally cowed workers threatened revolt.[2]

In recent years some social scientists have offered more sophisticated versions of this scheme, adding Gramscian (or perhaps more appropriately Genovesean) notions of "cultural hegemony" to the mix. To them, the traditionally patriarchal shape of southern society imbued millhands, even before their entry into the mill, with habits of dependence and deference to authority that posed basic cultural and psychological barriers to the development of class consciousness. Notable among these scholars are Dwight B. Billings and, most recently, I. A. Newby.[3] If pressed far enough, this version of the "left" argument bends so far back on itself as to come suspiciously close to the "right" argument; both versions depict southern class relations as structurally and culturally determined and the South as a fundamentally different place from modern, enlightened, democratic, egalitarian America.

In short, the traditional view of southern textile paternalism has been of a piece with the traditional insistence that the South is a place apart from the American mainstream. In recent years, however, the case for southern exceptionalism in labor relations, as in other realms, has eroded considerably. On the one hand, many southern "peculiar institutions"—segregation, disfranchisement, one-party politics, the mill village itself—have been swept away in a torrent of change. On the other hand, the larger American labor movement has become increasingly beleaguered; as Robert Zieger has pointed out, one can even argue that southern employers have been more "advanced" than their counterparts in other regions of the country in the sheer sophistication of their union-busting.[4] Nonetheless, paternalism in one or another guise retains its hold on southern historians' imaginations. Accordingly, in order to appreciate how labor historians have in recent years sought to understand the dynamics of class in southern textile history, a study of the evolving interpretations of mill paternalism is necessary.

The paternalist model of southern textile labor relations has long had its detractors. In 1951 C. Vann Woodward, in *Origins of the New South*, ironically remarked on the quintessentially capitalist rates of profit earned by "paternalistic" mill owners. More recently, Bess Beatty and Paul Escott have contended that such industrialists as the Holts of North Carolina viewed, and treated, their employees in strictly instrumental terms, and David L. Carlton has suggested that much of what passed for paternalism was a public relations mirage.[5] These assaults, however, have been directed less at the structure of labor relations per se than at the more restricted notion that industrialists were *benevolent* paternalists. If paternalism is understood more generally as a combination of workplace authority with other forms (e.g., familial or political), the basic picture remains intact. Even Woodward, determined to show that the "New South" was truly "American" and thus meaner than the "Old South," falls back on plantation, even "feudal," analogies in his depiction of mill villages.[6]

A more important challenge, if not to the existence of paternalism, then at least to its peculiar identification with the South, has come from the breakdown of the old dichotomies that have for so long neatly opposed "North" and "South," "modern" and "traditional," "liberal capitalist" and "Prussian Road." To begin with, research into labor relations in the early nineteenth-century Northeast, notably work by Anthony Wallace, Jonathan Prude, and Barbara Tucker, has excavated a form of textile paternalism in the North strikingly similar to that appearing later in the southern Piedmont, but owing nothing either to the plantation or to the vast Boston Associates' developments so commonly regarded as setting the northern pattern. With these findings has come an increasing realization that industrial paternalism has deep American, not just southern, roots and that, far from being associated with "retrograde" social institutions such as the slave plantation, it was intertwined with the origins of modern capitalism itself.[7]

In particular, the noneconomic authority of the factory master over his workers increasingly has been seen as an extension of the authority of a household head over his family or of a master over his apprentices. The household analogy is reinforced by the ubiquity of the family labor system, which appeared first in Samuel Slater's Rhode Island enterprises, and by the predominance of those "natural dependents," women and children, in the workforces and villages of Slater-type mills, North and South. The confusion of capitalistic and more traditional social relations imparted religious and moral authority to mill masters as well. Michael Shirley's investigations of the mill in antebellum Salem, North Carolina, show strong links between efforts at moral uplift of its operatives and the strictly ordered, pious Moravian community that brought them there. Gary Freeze has even suggested recently, perhaps a bit too extravagantly, that the model for the paternalistic mill village was not the plantation but the Methodist chapel (Allen Tullos would say the Presbyterian congregation).[8]

The widespread appearance in nineteenth-century America of paternalistic forms sometimes thought peculiarly southern, along with analogous forms in other countries, suggests that they served an economic function important to early capitalist firms, especially those pioneering in regions without well-developed supplies of skilled, experienced labor external to the firm. Thus Philip Scranton, writing in the *American Quarterly*, identifies a form of paternalism he calls "familiar paternalism," which was closely tied to small, undercapitalized rural firms seeking to gather and hold a workforce while conserving scarce capital through such devices as scrip payment and the company store. More broadly, according to the economic historian Cathy McHugh, paternalistic relations served the functions of developing the workforce and encouraging its long-term stability, goals similar to those animating the later "welfare capitalist" movement.[9] Finally, and not negligibly, familiar paternalism served functions of economic, as well as social, control of the workforce; not only did it allow employers to cull "undesirables" and block "subversive" influences, but it also encouraged in workers a sense of personal loyalty to the owner, inhibiting any consciousness of an adversarial relationship to factory authority or common interest with other workers.

That last point was the theory; but what was the reality? How did southern textile workers respond to paternalism? Were they, in fact, "docile," as the old formula would have it? Although I. A. Newby has recently renewed the argument that mill workers were deeply ingrained with deference to personal authority, the general verdict of historians has been "No." While the turmoil of the 1930s refuted the docility argument, the pioneering work of George S. Mitchell clearly has pushed the genealogy of southern labor conflict back to the 1880s, and more recently Melton McLaurin has documented at some length the uprisings of late nineteenth-century mill workers.[10]

Generally, though, pre-World War I conflict was sporadic and evanescent and with some telling exceptions was suppressed with ease by employers; no enduring institutional embodiment of class consciousness appeared at the time. That being the case, some historians of the mill workers have sought evidence of worker autonomy in the sort of day-to-day resistance recovered by historians of the slave experience. But day-to-day resistance was resistance *within* a structure of subjection; even McLaurin's militants could be easily cowed by the concentrated power of "the paternalistic mill village system."[11]

More recently, historians have argued that workers had far more autonomy than the paternalist paradigm would suggest and that they had the cultural and social resources to be active participants in their world. David L. Carlton, for instance, has questioned the "industrial plantation" analogy so often used to describe mill villages. After all, they were free labor (not slave) institutions, and the workers were white, a point of no mean significance in a region that identified independence and citizenship with white skin. Mill workers could not be bound against their will to an employer, and the evidence on absenteeism and turnover shows that they were not. Moreover, they voted. Although disfranchisement limited their electoral clout in some places, in others, notably South Carolina, they became a force in state politics. Their membership in the "ruling race," along with their political and consumer power, gave them considerable leverage with a public, and a state, whose relationship to the industrial elite was far more ambiguous than theorists of paternal hegemony would have it. Progressive reformers operated in the South along with political leaders (such as Richard Manning and Olin Johnston in South Carolina and Thomas W. Bickett in North Carolina) whose roles in labor relations, if falling well short of labor advocacy, hardly qualified them as handmaidens to employers. Finally, mill workers, at least the males among them, were heirs to a cultural heritage almost obsessed with the maintenance of personal honor; they were people with little tolerance for being pushed around.[12]

The most elaborate case for an autonomous, even incipiently class-conscious worker culture has been made by Jacquelyn Hall, James Leloudis, Robert Korstad, Mary Murphy, Lu Ann Jones, and Christopher Daly in what has become the central work in the canon of southern textile labor history, *Like a Family*. Hall and her North Carolina associates draw on a broad range of research in women's history, working- and lower-class history, and rural history to argue for the existence of a strong, vital culture arising among mill villagers. This culture was based on a traditional rural ethos of mutuality and an old-republican sense of personal rights, but was differentiated from the preindustrial world by increasingly intricate community relations and a dawning sense, especially among second-generation workers, that their destiny was wedded to the new industrial society they or their forebears had joined. Their emergent sensibility, furthermore, transcended local boundaries, as both the relative freedom of movement permitted by the village system and the widespread demand for experienced hands generated by a rapidly expanding industry created among the workers a community of affection and interest spanning the entire Piedmont cotton mill region.

The story the North Carolina historians tell, then, is one of "the making of the southern working class" and, significantly, a story effectively denying that mill paternalism had any positive meaning to workers. They insist, for instance, that workers resisted the frequently condescending "welfare work" programs, in much the same fashion, as Stuart Brandes has suggested, that workers generally resisted the blandishments of welfare capitalism.[13]

In stressing the autonomy of the worker community, the authors offer a corrective to earlier views of village life that emphasized the domination of worker lives by management and its agents. Unfortunately, in their effort to assert both worker autonomy and class solidarity, the *Like a Family* historians tend to reduce the mill to an irrelevance, except for its role as aggressor and repressor. The mill, though, was not an irrelevance; it called the community into being, and it sustained the community with the wealth it produced and its intrinsic power over community life. Much like Tamara Hareven found at the Amoskeag Mill of Manchester, New Hampshire, mill and community in the South interpenetrated each other in a web of relationships. Kinship and community ties recruited workers and maintained discipline; in turn, the subcultures formed on the factory floor created friendships and romances that spilled out into the village. Mill employment policies affected the moral tone of the community, giving working-class folk concerned for the welfare of their children a vested interest in the moral controls so offensive to present-day civil libertarian sensibilities.[14]

Thus, it would be wrong to throw out paternalism altogether or to reduce it to a mere concentration of brute power. Like Gerald Zahavi's workers at Endicott Johnson, southern millhands were not simply co-opted by paternalism, but used it to their advantage and even participated in shaping its outlines.[15] This reciprocal model of paternalism is especially relevant because it bears on what remains the great half-developed historiographical frontier in understanding class relations in southern textiles from the onset of the Great Depression until the early 1950s. In this period southern labor conflict peaked, providing focus for the enduring hope that southern workers might obtain a better deal than they have historically received. The General Strike of 1934, in particular, gathers considerable attention in *Like a Family*, in James A. Hodges's work on New Deal labor policy and the industry, and in a recent dissertation by Janet Irons. At the same time, though, the story of the 1930s, and of the 1940s as told in Barbara Griffith's recent book on Operation Dixie, is in the end one of largely unrelieved failure to achieve institutionalized worker power; at this time southern employers decisively established their region as the great anti-union bastion in the age of the industrial union.[16]

For this failure we have as yet no good explanation. Irons, Griffith, and Paul Richards in his dissertation on the Textile Workers Union of America point to obtuseness and strategic failure on the part of union leadership as contributing factors, but the favorite explanation remains "repression," whether through employer control of the village or through the automatic, massive use of state power to crush all worker self-assertion.[17] Repression there was; but it was far worse in industries, such as coal mining, that were more successful at organizing. Moreover, the work of Irons, Linda Frankel, and others suggests that there was much ambiguity and variability in state and local governmental responses to the turmoil. The state's interest, while indubitably expressing, in Leon Fink's words, "the voluntaristic assumptions, individual sovereignty, and respect for property embedded in the law," was nonetheless separate from the particular interests of even an industry as powerful as cotton textiles. In any case the argument begs the question. The persistence of employer dominance is not the explanation; it is what needs to be explained.[18]

It is with respect to this question that paternalism needs to be taken seriously, particularly insofar as it affects a phenomenon of the 1930s that has been more explained away than explained, namely, conflict among the workers themselves. While Hall and associates account for worker divisions primarily as products of employers' use of "green hands" from the countryside as strikebreakers, abundant evidence, including oral testimony and recent research by Douglas Flamming and others, indicates that labor conflict rent the established worker communities themselves. Nor was it simply a division between the docile and the undocile; nonunion workers were often aggressive and, as Flamming's work indicates, sometimes even willing themselves to attack employers.[19]

Thus far scholars know very little about these divisions, which have been dismissed as simple products of company intimidation or manipulation. However, the importance of complaints about arbitrary foremen and shop-floor favoritism in worker grievances of the time would seem to suggest that the divisions were in origin independent of company inspiration; rather, they arose from a crisis in the personalistic labor relations system that lay at the heart of "familiar paternalism."

As textile entrepreneurs in the crisis years of the 1920s and 1930s were pressed to cut costs and then to cut work time, they not only offended the "moral economy" of the mill worker but disarranged the whole web of understandings that simultaneously undergirded shop-floor and community culture. As David Brody and John Bodnar, among others, have suggested of industrial workers generally, the resulting chaos drove many workers to seek a new means, the union, of protecting their security and restoring their sense of control; but others still clung to the old system, especially if they could use it to their personal advantage. After all, they knew the old system; unions were untried and might not work equitably. More important, workers had reason to doubt that a union could become strong enough to provide a viable alternative to the old system; cotton textiles had always been a difficult industry to organize, and the region in its development generally managed to avoid those branches with the strongest traditions of worker militancy. Perhaps it was short-sighted to cling to the old paternalism at a time when the industry was beginning to dismantle it, but for workers it was an age of hard choices.[20]

What choices did workers make, and what dictated their decisions? How rigid were their internal divisions? What roles were played by company manipulation and repression and by state and local governments? How did the balance of power, and shifts in that balance, vary by mill, by community, by subregion? To what degree did workers experience the conflicts of the 1930s as a national class conflict and to what degree as a series of local clashes, as James Hodges has suggested was true even of 1934? More close studies of worker communities and factory floors can provide answers. Evidence for such studies is notoriously difficult to find, but some scholars—notably

Flamming on the Crown mill of Dalton, Georgia; Frankel and Daniel James Clark on the Harriet-Henderson mill of Henderson, North Carolina; and Bryant Simon on the Cone mills in Greensboro, North Carolina—have made pioneering efforts.[21] The oral history explosion of recent years has generated considerable raw material; moreover, the dramatic restructuring of the textile industry over the past fifteen years has had at least one happy by-product in the release of a treasure trove of corporate records to the burgeoning textile archives of Duke, the University of North Carolina at Chapel Hill, Clemson University, the University of South Carolina, and the Georgia Institute of Technology.

To be sure, historians should not expect too much of such local studies. Worker conflict may be understood as a debate over options, but those options were limited by forces transcending the mill community. The authors of *Like a Family* notwithstanding, southern mill workers have never had effective control in the workplace; indeed, it is arguable that the celebrated process of "deskilling," which occurred first and went farthest in cotton textiles, was a major precondition for the rise of the southern textile industry.[22] Thus, employers in an industry with a low capital-to-worker ratio confronted a workforce whose skill counted for little and whose cost and reliability counted for much. In the early stages of southern textile development, a compensating restraint on employer power was imposed by the same poorly developed labor market that gave rise to paternalistic labor institutions, forcing managers to accommodate employees in the interest of "holding their force together." As labor and capital markets integrated, though, even those tenuous bonds between mill and community progressively weakened, first by erosion from within and then by the increasing liberation of southern textile enterprises from all community ties. The mill village itself, the bedrock institution of the old regime, began to lose its grip on the industry in the 1920s, and between the late 1930s and the 1950s textile firms largely divested themselves of what had become a troublesome property. With the end of the village, and indeed the end of the "paternalistic age" in southern industry, employers began shifting assets about with ever greater freedom. In later years, especially, they have been aided by a permissive national political economy and, most recently, by economic globalization, which pits workers not only against their neighbors but also against the vast armies of underemployed in less developed regions of the world.[23]

Too great a focus on locality can blind scholars to those decisive attributes of southern textile labor relations beyond community control, attributes that have survived the end of paternalism, of mill villages, of political oligarchies, of all those old marks of southern peculiarity. Yet, too great a focus on the "big picture" can easily result in a bleak determinism. If the great weakness of community studies lies in the villages' ultimate subjection to larger constraints, their great strength lies in their ability to clarify the choices people have made within the larger constraints imposed upon them and through that clarification to explore the possibilities for creative change in southern industrial relations. Through local studies, more can be learned about how workers, and managers too, understood what was happening to them and what they thought could be done about it. Perhaps, more can also be learned about what their counterparts in the present "post-paternal age" can do about it as well.

3

Patriarchy Lost
The Preconditions for Paternalism in the Odell Cotton Mills of North Carolina, 1882–1900

Holland Thompson knew the type well. Middle-aged, a Confederate veteran or the son of one, burdened by the crop lien, the man had long been a farmer but recently became a millhand. His family had made a postbellum South journey from the cotton field to the cotton mill. These people, Thompson observed, came into the mill with "the tang of the soil" on their minds as well as on their feet. The switch from an agrarian to an industrial world, always difficult, was particularly traumatic for the fathers. Many never adjusted to the regimen. Some returned to the land. Those who stayed found adapting to the factory exhausting and depressing. In the evening, after twelve hours under "the overseer's nod," the typical operative wanted only "to sit in his shirt sleeves" on the front steps and "be left alone."[1]

During the 1890s Thompson, the first scholar of southern textiles, studied men in Concord, North Carolina, whose patriarchal misfortunes on the land had forced them to accommodate a paternalistic future in the factory. In Forest Hill, the mill village of the Odell Manufacturing Company, lived victims of the cultural as well as the commercial dislocations of the New South. The decline of agrarian autonomy, followed by the difficulties of adjustment to the mill environment, particularly stigmatized the fathers. Their agrarian traditions had accorded them the respectful title of "Mister" among their kin and kith. Now, in the mill, many spent their latter days as everyone's "Uncle" in an affective but not an authoritative way. The avuncular attribute was both a cause and an effect of the paternalistic ethos then being established in Forest Hill. As a reexamination of Thompson's casework shows, the loss of patriarchy became a key precondition for the managerial imposition of a new form of paternalistic community.[2]

The idea that men bred to rural rhythms found mill work difficult is not new to southern labor history. Recent revisionism, however, has yet to assess the full impact of these obstacles on the emerging pattern of paternalism in some postbellum mills.[3] Farmers who found their traditional status diminished suffered more than personal and family problems. Their experiences, in Concord at least, reoriented an already existing rationale that mill workers needed what local manufacturers paternalistically called "uplift." The emargination of older male mill migrants in the Odell cotton mills helped to capture the loyalty and support of younger men and to legitimate the hierarchical, evangelical community sought by the owners. For paternalism to be an effective means of organization and control, a rationale for intervention and direction first had to be developed, then sustained. The transformation of respect for older men from paternal to avuncular, based upon the juxtaposition of their social conditions, was built upon mill traditions as old as the mills themselves.

Southerners migrated to the mills for a variety of reasons, but most came out of the absence of a better alternative. This perception, Thompson found, typified the mill experience for North Carolinians. It contributed to the persistent myth that millhands were among the lost souls of a regenerated South. "They become imbued with the idea," Thompson learned from recent migrants in Concord, that "the hand of everyone is against them."[4] This perception of alienation, so prevalent in a Victorian culture obsessed with the dichotomy of sin and salvation, augmented what Thompson called "the cotton mill stigma." Mill people, as a Charlotte minister put it in 1899, were commonly believed to be suffering earthly "afflictions" of one sort or another.[5] The mill migrants of Concord knew that their image sprang from a family history marked by agrarian decline. In contrast, the local mill proprietors, renowned for their paternalistic policies, proffered what many at the time regarded as a refuge from that past, a sanctuary for those supposedly needing one.

Paternalism and cotton mills had always gone hand in hand in the Odell family. John Milton Odell, the principal proprietor, and his brother, James Alexander Odell, a Greensboro merchant, managed and then owned some of North Carolina's earliest mills. The Odells first clerked during the Civil War in what they told Thompson were "somewhat peculiar" conditions. At that time, in Cedar Falls on the Deep River in Randolph County, widows and orphans seeking a way to make ends meet literally filled the mill village. In these mills the Odells became protégés of the first demonstrable paternalists, "mill managers [who] felt themselves to stand in parental relation to the operatives." When the Odells dedicated their first Concord factory in 1882, more than half their workers remained female, teenaged, and living with widowed mothers. To these workers the Odells pledged paternalistic involvement. Before two thousand witnesses they promised "to be true to the interests of those who would be in their employ, that they might be led to regard them as their protectors." After they took the vow, a prominent Methodist minister charged the owners with teaching "the boys and girls to respect themselves, to do honest work, to save the pennies, to look for brighter manhood and womanhood." This exhortation drew deeply from an evangelical, agrarian world view familiar to both owners and operatives. The demographic structure in North Carolina's early mill villages had long engendered a perception that factories, as one visitor observed, were places to which people came who "might otherwise be wretched."[6]

The Old South's perception of the mill as an asylum grounded in cultural assumptions about gender and benevolence underwent a reorientation in the New South. A different kind of "widow" came to the mill, accompanied by another type of "orphan." Labor demand in the postbellum Odell mills outstripped the supply of traditionally "afflicted" families. The old factory the Odells reopened in 1877 became the nucleus for the six plants that existed by 1900. The mill, the first in the state to be valued at more than $500,000, employed almost one thousand workers. Correspondingly, Piedmont farmers succumbed to a crisis of overproduction and overcrowding, creating a previously unavailable source of labor. A surplus population left the land as mill owners beckoned individuals as well as whole families with promises of steadier if not higher income. Farmers broken by postbellum conditions moved with their families into the mill village. As a result, the Odell workforce became increasingly male. In June 1900, men comprised 61 percent of Odell operatives. Of these 499 employees, 286 were over the age of 21.[7] Each of these workers, particularly the older ones, came into the mill with a stigma associating his action with patriarchal failure. Like the women who preceded them, the men who took refuge in the mill village brought with them blemishes that contributed to the rationalization of a New South paternalism.

In large measure this perception of patriarchy was grounded in the strong traditions of self-reliance that for generations had been integral to most North Carolinians. As Bill Cecil-Fronsman has shown, the dedication to an egalitarian male autonomy was strong in the rural Piedmont, particularly in areas long isolated from the direct effects of market forces. Although gender and generational relationships varied among families, each male head expected to exercise the burdens of leadership, authority, and control that were integral to his assumptions of independence. The widespread availability of land, however marginal, throughout much of the Piedmont continued until the Civil War. The link of patriarchy and land kept alive the yeomanry ethos. Few men had to contemplate becoming a "wage slave" to the factory. Cotton mills remained places, as one visitor noted, for "poor girls."[8]

Many Odell operatives came from areas like Stanly County, in the Uwharrie hills to the east of Concord where a yeomanry culture largely self-contained by geography persisted through Reconstruction. Visitors used words like "sparing," "poor," and "scarcity" to describe antebellum Stanly. The area lay largely outside the Piedmont plantation belt. Barely a third of the county came under cultivation in the 1850s, and cotton was "rarely attempted" on its "uplands," one area politician recalled. By 1859, the year of the Old South's largest cotton crop, only 14 percent of Stanly farmers grew any of the staple, and most of those lived in one small neighborhood. About 5 percent of farmers worked as tenants before the war, and only about one-fifth of adult males were landless, an indication that surplus farm labor was not needed. Stanly depended so heavily on the patterns of self-reliance that no manufactured blankets could be procured there for the Confederacy. Only handmade quilts were available. As Forest Hill millhands later recalled, Stanly farmers took pride in their autonomy. In 1895 Elizabeth Swearingen returned to celebrate her father's one hundredth birthday. Joshua Hudson was said to "have never seen a sewing machine, a cotton factory, or a train, and once bought a horse for $95 in small change gained from selling eggs." Andrew Honeycutt, another resident, claimed that Hudson "never spent but one dollar in all his life for a doctor[,] . . . never bought but two sacks of flour, though he always has flour bread, and only once has he ever bought corn."[9]

As Stanly recovered slowly from the war, the children of men like Joshua Hudson found it almost impossible to replicate their fathers' lives. Hundreds of young men, born in the 1840s and 1850s but unable to go west as easily as had their forebears, came of farming age around the time of the 1873 financial panic. The subsequent demand for start-up capital dramatically changed local farming. By the end of the decade the number of farms in the county had almost doubled, and tenantry had grown at a faster rate. Almost 80 percent of farmers grew cotton in 1879, compared to 10 percent a decade before, as lenders sought to protect their investments by requiring cotton as collateral. The intensification of cotton production continued into the 1880s, even as prices fell and farmers increasingly worked marginal soil augmented by expensive fertilizer. "Our lands do not suit cotton," one area farmer lamented in 1887; "still we plant it and fail to make it pay every year." With increased cotton cultivation came declining self-sufficiency. Stanly farmers were growing per capita half as much wheat and one-third as much corn in 1890 as in 1860. Year by year more farmers became caught in the vise of the New South market. By the subsequent depression of 1893, as a local newspaper editor lamented, "the chattel mortgages given for fertilizer" put an end to a time of self-sufficiency based on "corn, wheat, meat, possums, potatoes, and turnips."[10]

Instead of returning to the old ways, many Stanly families took a new option: the mill. This change became increasingly evident after 1890 when the Odell mills were doubled in capacity and employment. By 1894 residents were "leaving the county almost daily for want of employment. They are going to the manufacturing towns." One resident in northern Stanly noted in 1895: "If you don't see a man for two weeks, you can just say he has gone to Concord's cotton mills." Emigration became so widespread that tax collectors began to mark "gone to Concord" in the tax books next to the names of delinquents.[11]

The Stanly migrants to the mills as well as their neighbors in nearby counties brought with them personal experiences very different from the self-reliant traditions of their elders. Most migrants who had started farming during the 1870s hailed from areas too marginal to grow for the market without substantial amounts of guano. The crop liens needed to buy fertilizer broke freeholder and sharecropper alike. Thomas H. Hall, despite immediate postwar hopes, met a fate after the Panic of 1873 that exemplified the plight of others. Hall's 156 acres seemed secure during the 1870s, but a lien of seventy dollars in spring 1881 pledging his cotton could not be paid. After harvest that year Hall borrowed eighty dollars from a second merchant to pay off the first, this time pledging his winter wheat crop, "now sown." The next season went by without difficulty, but in 1883 Hall went to a third local merchant and borrowed to pay the continuing debt, putting up his land as collateral. By 1884 the desperate Hall convinced a fourth Stanly merchant to pay off the debts in return for the land. Hall continued to borrow for crops "raised on John L. Palmer's land" for several years, but by 1890 he joined the emigration to Concord.[12]

Some of Hall's neighbors were already there. Others would follow. Almost all shared similar experiences. John C. Fry, too, lost his property. In 1865 Fry took up family lands willed to him by a brother killed at Gettysburg. Through the 1870s Fry became increasingly dependent on the crop liens provided by J. O. Ross, a local merchant. Until 1882 Fry paid his debts, but that year he borrowed two hundred dollars to settle his brother's estate and gain clear title to the land, pledging "one mare, one philly, two cows, five pigs, [my] household furniture, and my crop of cotton, corn, and wheat." Fry renewed the loan the following year, using the eighty acres as collateral. The Stanly tax rolls listed Fry as a landless tenant by 1885. The following year he and his family moved to Concord.

Aaron G. Hathcock, the son of one of Stanly's few antebellum tenants, in 1870 bought land in the south central area of the county. To pay for the land he borrowed from the local firm of Bennett and Barnett. By 1875 Hathcock was taking out crop liens to secure his payments, and within three years the land appeared for the first time as collateral when Hathcock had problems paying out in the tight economy. In 1879, to stop foreclosure, Hathcock resold the land to the previous owner, paid off the merchants, and then sharecropped the same land. He moved to the Forest Hill mill village the same year the Frys did. Although not every migrant to Forest Hill was landless upon arrival, most had gone through some version of the sequence of acquisition, struggle, and decline.[13]

Most migrants viewed their demise as a personal loss of heritage. To the end, men bred to autonomy stuck to their cherished self-reliance. One Stanly County sharecropper in 1887 promised that "with reasonable health and soberness" he expected to "continue to maintain my family as I have in the past in good condition." Some could and others could not. The vagaries of Piedmont farming after 1880 seemed a Victorian melodrama, where the tension lay between assumed strengths and weaknesses of character. Personal inadequacy best accounted for the common crisis. One prominent Stanly farmer in 1887 claimed, "none but he who is an everyday watcher of the strokes of the farm can possibly succeed in tilling the soil." Too often, the observer claimed, his poorer neighbors did "not vie with the progress and improvement" demanded in the New South. "It is hard," he noted, "to reach and awaken to energetic work this class of small farmer." Too many farmers "follow the old practices," a resident of nearby Montgomery County observed, "without trying to improve them. . . . [They] depend solely upon cotton to better their condition." Too often, it seemed, those who failed to better themselves, "the common laborer[s] . . . depressed in spirits," ended up in the mills.[14]

The diminished status that plagued the migrants in the country, the sense that they were "very low in humility," followed them into the mill village. Holland Thompson, who watched the Stanly families move into town, shared the impression of one local editor that "the old men, old women, young men, and young women" bound for Forest Hill were like "living freight."[15] Once, they had chopped the cotton that widows and orphans made into cloth. Now they were to make the cloth themselves.

The transition frightened many. The same editor noted after visiting an Odell factory addition in 1888, "The continuous clacking and humming of pulleys, belting, looms and so forth made us dizzy." Many individuals could not accept the new regimen. The tax rolls of Concord contained the names of scores of men who came and went during the 1890s. Further, few of those who stayed had skills or backgrounds highly valued by the Odells. With each expansion of the factories J. M. Odell, the chief proprietor, repeated the apology that "raw help" would take time to train. Mill work, the Odell overseers told Holland Thompson, was not "irregular" as had been the case "in the country." The new hands had to accept the condition that "loss of wages and the displeasure of the overseer" followed "any departure from absolute regularity."[16] As evidenced by their employment practices, the Odells believed that failed farmers in particular would be burdens as millhands.

The demographics of employment in Forest Hill indicated the continuing frustrations of the former patriarchs. At the time of the 1900 census, men headed 250 of the 288 households in the Odell mill village. Within this group, only half of the 60 men who were over age 50 worked in the factory. In contrast, two-thirds of the 93 men aged 36 to 49 were operatives. Among the 97 men under the age of 35 who headed a household, 95 percent held factory jobs.[17] Age and experience clearly worked in reverse when it came to rewards in the Odell factory system. Although the children of the migrants, especially young adult sons, readily found employment,the fathers found little offered to them.

The cultural assumptions of the paternalists to a large extent drove the dynamic of age and employment. The Odells believed that too many ex-farmers, whose preindustrial values were deeply ingrained, were "drones" living off the family's wages. Odell company policies indicate an innate hesitation to use the older men for central roles in the factory. Holland Thompson heard that "this class of idlers" had "the conscious purpose of living a life of ease through the labor of [their] children."[18] In truth, some self-imposed idlers lived around Forest Hill as in most southern mill villages. Some, as Jeremiah D. McLester, a widower with three daughters working in the mill, clearly had reached retirement age. A few, like William Freeze or Obediah Baucum, stayed home and put their grandchildren to work, indicating they may have been exemplars of the Odells' harsh judgment.[19] Many, however, seemed to be disabled, reinforcing the commonly held notion that the infirm and maimed took refuge in the mill. Both Joseph M. Mabry, former keeper of the Stanly County poorhouse, and Eli Forrest, a former Stanly merchant, at times were described as "a crippled man." Jacob Simpson, the one-armed local preacher in the Odells' Methodist station, put his children in the mill. Yet, Wiley T. Caudle, 42, a widower with six of his nine children in the factory, alone among the older men claimed that he "was not able to work."[20]

Most older men worked somewhere, an indication of both their need and desire to remain gainfully employed. For many it meant taking the most menial jobs the mill offered. In 1900, 278 men over the age of 21 toiled in the factories. Only 43 men surpassed the age of 50. Only one of those, John Dent, 51, was a weaver. The remainder labored in the preparation and packing areas. John A. Clayton and Solen Fisher, both 50, worked as picker tenders. Fisher had once been a common school committeeman in a rural township outside Concord. Howell Farris and John Propst, both in their 60s, were card grinders. James A. Goodman, 59, who had gone to Texas as late as 1896 to seek better fortunes, swept floors. So did Virginia native James J. Dillon, age 80. John R. Hinson, 61, who fought in the Army of Northern Virginia, carried water. Albert W. Morgan, 53, once owner of a farm in nearby Montgomery County, tended the water closets. In contrast, the majority of the overseer, loom fixer, and weaver positions were filled by men too young ever to have sown a crop or owed a crop lien. Of 115 male weavers employed in June 1900, 104 were under the age of 35. Eleven of the fourteen loom fixers were in the same age range. Only one of the twenty-three overseers,

Thomas P. Ivey, the son of a prominent Stanly County merchant, was over age 50.[21]

Employment among the younger men was more frequent and more remunerative. The younger the man, the more likely he could make a significant portion of his family's income. Odell workers, as millhands elsewhere in the New South, depended on the family wage to make ends meet. The average Odell mill family made about $2 per working day in 1900. The amount roughly equaled the wage of a local carpenter, but it represented in most cases the wages of two or three family members. According to figures computed from a wage model, male heads of the households earned an average of 59 percent of all wages. Many male operatives, however, failed to make that mean, since it was weighted upward by including the wages of overseers. Eighty of the 198 household heads working in the factory but not as overseers earned less than half their family's income. A clear association between age and wage level appears when this group is subdivided. Men over age 50 averaged about 39 percent of their family's wage; men under age 35 contributed considerably more.[22] Almost all of the 78 men earning their family's sole means of support were under the age of 35. Hardly any of these younger men had ever farmed on his own before coming to the factory. They were either the sons of migrants or of men who remained on the farms.

The traumas of adjustment for many mill families included more than the financial uncertainty occasioned by the diminished earning power of the fathers. For one thing, few men worked in close contact with or supervised their children, as on the farm. Although most operative households depended on the family wage to survive, in only 29 of 177 households with three or more members in the mill did all family members have identical jobs. An exception was the 40-year-old weaver Thomas McCollum whose children worked with him at the same task. McCollum's background was in textiles, not farming, however, and he came from the same locality as the Odells. McCollum's exceptional status testified further to the problems most former farmers experienced. A father likely had little to say about keeping his children together, even had he wanted such an arrangement. Only Pleasant G. Cook, a nearby farmer whose six children worked as spinners while he maintained his traditional livelihood, seemed to have had the leverage to have all of his children working together.

The lessened authority of the patriarch also appeared in the evolving social patterns of mill village young people. Some children certainly resisted working in the factory. Some cried and feigned illness; others ran away. In October 1893 the residents of the Odell village learned that John Troutman and John Deaton, both age twelve, "have skipped for parts unknown." After reporting for work about eight o'clock, they allegedly "asked some other boys to leave with them, but the other boys would not do it." The two returned after spending several days in nearby Charlotte. Similar episodes appeared in the local press throughout the 1890s. Older offspring also left with their parents' knowledge, but they, too, often returned. In February 1893 about a half dozen young men left to seek jobs in Danville, Virginia, "where they expected to make big money." Three weeks later they began to drift back, as "things were not as they expected." Similar exoduses were reported in 1897 and 1899.[23]

Young men leaving to search for better opportunities occurred in most social settings whether in the mill village or on the farm. It cannot be proved that the youth of the Odell village left more frequently than did their counterparts in other rural and industrial settings. Yet, the way their elders recounted the young men's stories hinted at a continuing local pattern of generational conflict. One overseer, posing the same question that fathers might have asked, queried in a local news column: "Why do the boys leave . . . and return in such a short time? Why do some of them leave in a first-class car and beat their way back on a freight train?"[24] The question itself seemed to communicate a sense of futility. In the country a young man could leave and return, perhaps comforted with the thought that a landed father would consent to set him up for an agrarian future. Most mill fathers could not do so, but likely they tried to retain some sort of control over the family's wealth and security. Jobs elsewhere represented one aspect of a possible freedom of choice that the older patriarch could no longer offer or oppose.

The fact that so many young couples in the mill village eloped also signaled lessened control. As with job seeking, elopements commonly occurred in the country, but seldom did they engender the tensions recounted in the mill village news columns. The local gossips reported in June 1897 that "considerable excitement prevailed . . . when it became known that Mr. John Ballard, a youth of eighteen, and Miss Laura Dunn, daughter of Mr. and Mrs. John R. Dunn, had eloped." That account revealed no animosity, but other flights appeared to many residents as open acts of rebellion against paternal control. In 1898, on a "Friday evening, just when the mill closed, a young man could be seen helping the one he loved from a window at the Odell mills." The two left town to be married, because the local ministers, knowing both fathers objected, refused to perform the ceremony. Sometimes the father of the intended bride threatened violence. More than once older millhands, like John H. Swearingen, a former Stanly sharecropper, caught their daughters in the train station as they attempted to elope to South Carolina. In one case the prospective husband spent time in jail after fighting with the girl's father. Other fathers took more preventive steps. In December 1895 Zillie Griffin, daughter of a migrant from nearby Union County, attempted to run off with her boyfriend, William Snider. Although the father and a brother kept close watch over Zillie in the mill, she slipped out with Snider during work hours. The brother followed the pair down the street and "at pistol point" ordered Zillie back home, where she was locked in her room. When Zillie returned to work (the next day, by the way) she waited for Snider to appear with a horse and wagon, then bolted out the door before the family could catch her. The two were married in a nearby town.[25]

Obviously, parents in the mill village did not oppose every marriage. Still, the pattern is clear that the offspring of the migrants to the mill married earlier than had their parents. Since the young couple could work in the factory and rent a house, the wait for land and patriarchal sanctions was no longer necessary. This fact becomes obvious when dividing the mill village's married adults into two groups: those who had married before 1890, presumably back on the land, and those who married after 1890, presumably after coming to the mill, since 1890 was the year the workforce doubled. The age of first marriage for those wed after 1890 was significantly lower than for those who married earlier. Only 9 percent of the older men and 39 percent of the older women had been married before the age of twenty, in keeping with findings in much of preindustrial America. In contrast, 22 percent of younger men and 52 percent of younger women were teenagers at the time of the ceremony.[26]

The conflicts among the generations at best provide only conjectures about how life in the mill undermined the traditional patriarch's sense of authority and self-worth. Similar to most southerners undergoing the transition to factory work, older men seldom expressed themselves directly. Yet on at least two occasions they voiced dissatisfaction, revealing a sense of alienation. Their diminished control over wages, coming on the heels of the lien system, rankled severely. Some of the farmers who brought their families into the mill in 1890 complained that the mill owners "keep back one month's pay" to "compel the hands to trade in the company's store." Most galling, according to "two old men," was "living without vegetables," since they had "no money to buy fresh from wagons" brought in by folks still farming outside town.[27] In addition, the lack of opportunity for decent work led to "much grumbling," according to J. M. Odell. In 1894 the company announced it had "adopted a rule to hire as many old men as possible" in order to "avoid" so many complaints.[28] The complaintants were likely new hands off the farm just learning what the mill offered and what it did not. Soon after arriving in 1895, Holland Thompson found signs that newcomers were unsettled and unhappy in the mill village houses. "Some windows shine from constant scrubbing," Thompson observed, "but usually you may look through dirty glass at dirtier curtains and on interiors where people eat and sleep and work. . . . Such are the homes of those come lately to the mill." All in all, he concluded, "the manner of life" in the mill village was unlike "the rural independence" left behind.[29]

The cumulative nature of discouragement and frustration diminished the role of the older men within the emerging structure of the mill village community. Forest Hill during the 1880s was transformed from a center of women and orphans to a neighborhood catering to the needs of younger men who cast their loyalties with the Odells and the mill environment. In the various church and civic groups sponsored by the Odells, the younger men came to the fore. When the Odells organized the local Methodist station into classes as a way to foster discipline, nine of the twelve class leaders were under the age of thirty-five. The Odells particularly pressured younger men to come forward "to give the preacher his hand" during frequent revival meetings. According to Thompson, who attended some of the services during the 1890s, the class leaders would circle the sanctuary during the altar calls to solicit the young men. "A chorus of ejaculations" arose when the more resistant gave in. Once the young men became serious Methodists they seem also to have become part of the inner element of the mill workforce. The young leaders of the church often received promotions at the mill. Leadership in the Forest Hill community found its basis in a matrix of church, baseball, civic clubs, and political involvement. Only seldom did one of the elders of the community emerge with widespread responsibilities. Even J. M. Odell, the chief owner and seventy years of age in 1901, gave way during the 1890s to his son Will. Clearly evident in Forest

Hill by 1900 were those who looked to the promises of a paternalistic future. Men over the age of thirty-five who had several school-aged children were three times more likely to keep all of them out of the Odell-sponsored school than were their younger counterparts.[30]

This sense of age and involvement also showed itself in local politics. At election time the younger men in their voting patterns more easily allied themselves with the mill owners. In numerous ways, the older generation of millhands newly arrived from the farm were kept at arm's length from the locus of community that developed in the mill village. Although many preferred to remain aloof, to some extent their very marginality aided in the formation of the community. As visiting drummers from Charlotte noted, mill village residents increasingly thought of the owners, not the patriarchs, as the "Big Daddies."[31]

In their fringe status the former agrarian patriarchs were not totally left out of the emerging community. Rather, in many cases, affection replaced the traditional respect rendered them by families and neighbors. The older men assumed the role of a favorite uncle who represented the best of the past but somehow seemed unfit in the present. The transition from patriarchy to paternalism made these marginal mill workers revere the world lost, yet resign themselves to the life around them. This ritual played itself out in the last days of John C. Fry. Records show that Fry never worked for the Odells once he moved to the mill village. Four sons had become millhands by 1900; all married and settled into the life and work of Forest Hill. Fry belonged to the local Methodist church but held no positions of leadership. He also fitted the asylum image of the maimed and infirm taking refuge in the mill. The old man suffered from asthma and often was ill in the 1890s. In retirement he lived in the mill village but remained an agrarian in spirit and habit. In 1897, shortly before his death, he discovered a swarm of bees near the factory, collected them in a hive, and took it home. He died of asthmatic complications soon afterward, unable, as he expressed the wish, to "return to Stanly for a rest and a change." The mourning for "Uncle John Fry," as he was "familiarly known," seemed as "sincere and widespread" as any felt throughout the increasingly close-knit mill village.[32]

William C. Robbins, who eulogized Fry, had been a doffer as a boy in a mill in Randolph County. He followed the Odells to Concord, working his way up to mill supervisor. His leadership in the Methodist congregation in the early 1900s also brought local political prominence. In 1901 a Charlotte labor newspaper, which aimed at a readership of skilled textile hands, named Robbins one of the finer cotton mill bosses of the Piedmont. Folks in Forest Hill, despite Robbins's relative youth (thirty-two in 1900), always referred to him as "Mister Billy."[33]

The process of socialization of a new element into the workforce at the Odell cotton mills loomed large in the shaping of the southern cotton mill world. Through the 1890s the Odell mills provided a model as to how paternalism could succeed. But contemporary observers often failed to note the extent to which a new frame of reference slowly developed a rationale for managerial direction. A new sort of "widower," bereft of the husbandry of his fathers, replaced the "widow" as a precondition for owner intervention. What Holland Thompson called "a class in the making, unlike any other we have," in the early 1900s looked more to the millways of the future than to the farmways of the past.[34]

4

Prelude to the New Deal
The Political Response of South Carolina Textile Workers to the Great Depression, 1929–1933

Greenwood, South Carolina, mill workers huddled around their radios on 16 July 1933. After hearing the news reports, they contacted family and friends in the nearby mill hamlets of Ninety-Six and Ware Shoals and those from as far away as Newberry. The next evening fifteen hundred women and men frolicked in the streets of Greenwood. Throughout the night and into the morning hours, they sang, square-danced, and made "merry in front of the local cotton mill office." Several days later, Greenville and Spartanburg textile laborers paraded through the streets of their home-towns. President Franklin Delano Roosevelt's approval of the Cotton Textile Code of the National Industrial Recovery Act sparked this revelry.[1] For the seventy-five thousand mill workers of South Carolina, this decree, which seemed to ensure shorter hours, higher wages, and reduced work loads, represented an "industrial declaration of independence." It was a "new deal" worthy of celebration.

The dances of South Carolina textile workers did not reflect an overnight conversion to the faith of government activism but stemmed from their struggles to deal with the Great Depression. In the bleak economic winter leading to Roosevelt's ascent to the White House, millhands felt the sting of layoffs, the bite of wage cuts, and the burn of an escalation of the pace of labor. Numerous accounts of the Great Depression chronicle the inventive private strategies formulated by working-class families to cope with the hard times, documenting how they canned vegetables, doubled up to save on rent, wore tattered garments, and postponed marriage. Yet these narratives often overlook laborers' political responses to the economic crisis.[2] Unfortunately, this pattern of neglect holds true for South Carolina, where the politics of labor, not just during the depression but throughout the state's history, have been largely ignored.[3] Between 1929 and 1933, South

Carolina textile workers asserted themselves in the political arena. They called on their elected representatives to implement a host of measures aimed at spreading employment, controlling the actions of the mill owners, and establishing economic stability. This activity represented a break with the workers' long-standing antistatism and set the stage for their embrace of the New Deal.

Emphasizing workers' public rather than their private responses to the depression can, in addition, serve as a modest historic corrective. While the "new" southern labor history has exposed hidden pasts of industrial militancy and cultural resistance to wage labor, it has neglected the subject of politics.[4] Politics, nevertheless, shaped the identities of South Carolina textile workers. Their political thoughts and actions, moreover, echoed through the larger public dialogue about the meaning and distribution of state power. This essay focuses on the Great Depression in the southern cotton mill world, shifting political concerns from the historic periphery to the core.

An economic crisis gripped the South Carolina Piedmont five long years before the stock market crash signaled the beginning of the Great Depression across the rest of the nation. The wartime boom that had thrust textile production to new heights during the 1920s went bust. Falling demand and changing fashions at home along with the emergence of cotton manufacturing industries in India and Japan cut deeply into profits. Rejecting production cutbacks, southern mill owners responded by churning out more cloth and yarn in frantic bids to grab part of the dwindling market. Company officials simultaneously pored over their ledgers looking for ways to slash costs, particularly labor costs. Seeking to spur productivity, many enlisted the services of industrial engineers. Dressed in white coats and armed with stopwatches, calibrators, and clipboards, these "minute men" came to the mill, preaching the gospel of scientific management. They shadowed workers around the factory, making cryptic notations while timing their every move, even how long it took to eat lunch, gulp a glass of water, or visit the bathroom. Behind closed doors the engineers compiled their data and presented mill officials with stacks of recommendations, diagrams, and order forms for equipment.[5] Managers, in turn, rearranged the shop floor, pushing older machines closer together and introducing faster and more dependable electrical looms and spindles rigged with production monitors. With new machines came a new generation of supervisors. College-educated bosses with few ties to the communities in which they worked replaced overseers who had risen through the ranks. They lorded over the shop floor, closely watching laborers, making sure they performed their tasks with the unremitting ceaselessness of the machines.[6]

Prior to the introduction of the new industrial order, mill work was hard. The heat was suffocating and the dust could be deadly, but the machines ran at a relatively relaxed pace.[7] In 1927, for example, Charles Putman, a weaver at Spartanburg's Saxons Mills, oversaw twenty-eight looms. "Now [that] . . . was a fair job," he determined. Putman took an occasional break, and during the frequent shutdowns, he wandered around the plant, talked to friends, listened to local gossip, wrangled about politics, or swigged a Coca-Cola near a "dope" cart. Three years later the weaver's work load tripled, and he found himself tending machines "by the acre." If he left his looms for more than a few minutes, he fell too far behind to catch up. At the end of his shift, Putman's hands quivered, his feet ached, and his eyes burned with exhaustion. "Too tired to even play ball in the afternoon," he lamented; "used to play two or three hours nearly every afternoon." The maddening pace of labor, he cried out, "is killing [us] faster than the World War did."[8] Extra work did not mean that Putman received more pay. In fact, in 1932, he earned less than half his 1920 wage rate.[9] Still, Putman felt lucky to have a job at all. After 1929, a third of his coworkers in the weave room lost their positions altogether; others worked on short-time or became spare hands who labored only during the busy seasons. The changes experienced by Putman and his coworkers were shared by millhands across the state.[10]

Hardship had always been part of life in the mill towns, but times got tougher with the spread of unemployment and wage cuts. Families had to get by with less than before, and much of the work fell to women. The story of Clinton's Mrs. C. M. Hogan and her family of eight was typical. Before 1928, four of them worked in the weave room of the local mill. Following an invasion of minute men, only Hogan's husband had a job, and he earned just eleven dollars a week. Out of his check, Mrs. Hogan needed to feed and clothe her family, pay the rent, and meet all other expenses. Debts mounted. She owed money to the grocer and the doctor, yet what troubled her most was her inability to buy clothes to keep her "children in school or church."[11]

In 1929, the Ware Shoals Manufacturing Company invested in hundreds of high-speed looms. Soon after, W. H. Riddle lost his job in the weave room. For the next several months, he searched for work, but he wore out his only pair of shoes before he found another job. Battling to support his family of five, he spent all of their savings and tapped every source of credit available. When the first chill of winter struck, Riddle became a desperate man. "My family is almost on starvation," he reported. "[I] have always been honest hard working and lawabidin'[.] I am down and out[;] . . . it would be a fine time for me to blow my brains out."[12]

Millhands tagged the cumulative changes of the postwar period the "stretch-out." They associated the stretch-out with the industrial engineers, the stop watches, the new supervisors, the frenzied pace of production, the constant escalation of work loads, and the drop in wages. Stretch-out also captured the way workers felt when they walked away from their jobs— trembling all over and feeling so drained that they could "hardly get rested for the next day." Finally, workers equated the stretch-out with the desperation of the era and the gnawing uncertainty of not knowing from day to day whether they would have a job or enough money for food, clothes, and fuel.[13]

Most South Carolina workers argued that the stretch-out, by "taking three mens [sic] jobs and putting it on one," created unemployment; and joblessness, they believed, represented not only the most conspicuous mark of hard times but the source of the depression itself.[14] "The 'Stretch-out System' is the cause of the whole trouble," avowed one wage earner; "we wouldn't have the depression if it were not for it." "The Stretch-out system is what is wrong," agreed another worker, who wrote his views on the back of a print showing French peasants praying in a field of hay. Few linked the surge in joblessness with the chaos of international markets or the rhythmic undulations of the business cycle. Laborers, instead, blamed it on greedy mill owners. Selfish manufacturers grabbing for profits, the workers charged, had installed the stretch-out, sinking mill folks into the depths of despair.[15]

In order to dramatize their hardships and highlight their grievances, workers compared the stretch-out to slavery: "The most damnable system ever put on free people" was how one worker described the new work regime. According to a weaver from Langley, in 1930, working in a mill was like being "chained . . . to bondage." "I ask you," wrote another laborer with reference to the Old Testament, "to read of the Pharaoh's treatment of the Israelites to get a comparison." "The cotton mills," he and others insisted, "are not as different as . . . people think." "The stretch-out system is worse than Roman slavery," alleged a Greenville resident. "If our government had surrendered their arms to the Kaiser of Germany in 1918," maintained another millhand, "our textile people would be better off."[16]

The image of slavery produced an arresting picture of injustice.[17] Since the birth of the nation, industrial workers across America invoked both slavery and wage slavery as metaphors for cruel and callous treatment at the hands of their bosses.[18] Millhands who used this idiom did not perceive of themselves as slaves but rather sought to stress the deterioration of their working conditions, the decline of their material status, and their dependency on the will of others. Rarely, if ever, did white laborers during the depression era liken themselves to African Americans once held in bondage. Instead, mill people discussed slavery either in vague terms or with an allusion to the ancient civilizations of Egypt and Rome. Interestingly enough, national trade union leaders were the only group to fashion an analogy between white workers and African-American slaves. "We do not believe that any man who had sworn to support the Constitution of the United States," wrote John Peel, "can honestly and sincerely say that such action upon the part of any employer is less than slavery for the abolition of which a war was fought more than sixty years ago."[19] In the end, the metaphor of slavery served as a call to arms and united workers in the fight against the oppressive new industrial order.

Initially, small groups led the battle against "the abominable conditions of servitude in the textile mills." By the close of the 1920s, loosely organized resistance gave way to an unprecedented round of collective action. In the spring of 1929, wage earners across the Piedmont protested the stretch-out as industrial unrest shook the communities of Elizabethton, Tennessee, and Gastonia and Marion, North Carolina. The Palmetto State stirred as well. According to the U.S. Bureau of Labor Statistics, in 1929 fourteen strikes rocked South Carolina, involving twelve thousand textile employees or one-sixth of the state's full-time millhands. Trade unions played only minor roles in the protests; most workers opted instead to petition mill owners directly for emancipation from the stretch-out.[20] In nearly every case, strikers gained modest pay hikes and slight adjustments in their work loads, yet within months, sometimes weeks, many managers simply "stretched-out the stretch-out."[21]

Having failed to "abolish" the onerous work regime on the picket line, many laborers shifted the struggle to the political arena. It had happened before. Earlier in the century, mill workers, particularly those of the Horse

Creek Valley, had endorsed state action. After a 1902 dispute, for instance, valley laborers sent to the state capital a union organizer who proposed legislation aimed at outlawing lockouts.[22] After 1929, political mobilization once again appeared to be a substitute for industrial protest, a way in which millhands could band together to counterbalance the power of the manufacturers. South Carolina's constitution, enacted in 1895, and to a lesser extent the nineteenth amendment, provided the vehicle for workers' maneuvers. By the start of the third decade of the century, virtually every adult white resident of the state could vote. Therefore, millhands and their families, who represented almost a quarter of the state's white population, had tremendous potential political leverage, especially in the heavily industrialized counties of the upcountry.

Spartanburg County provides a good illustration of the local power situation. In 1930, the population of the county was 116,323, just over 30,000 of whom were African American and therefore almost certainly ineligible to vote. Meanwhile, the textile industry employed 15,795 people, and approximately 40,000 people lived in the mill villages.[23] Between 1929 and 1933, laborers in Spartanburg and elsewhere made their voices heard as they tried to use their electoral clout as a weapon against their employers and as an instrument for economic stability. As textile workers looked to politics for redress of their grievances, they articulated, in a flurry of speeches, marches, letters, petitions, and proclamations, their own ideas about what caused the Great Depression and what would solve the economic collapse.

"I cant live," cried out Rinnie Bishop in 1930. She shared a house with her parents and sister. All of them had lost their jobs in the local textile mill, and none found any openings elsewhere. Yet, Bishop complained, some families still had two and three people on the payroll. To her mind, this discrepancy was unfair. "If one in the family was working we could keep something to eat and keep wood and coal," Bishop argued.[24] Many concurred, believing that the pernicious effects of the depression could be eradicated by a more equitable distribution of employment. But how could it be accomplished? Some called for stiff restrictions on access to the labor market by minorities. Although few African Americans vied with whites for jobs inside the mills and foreign-born residents comprised less than one-half of 1 percent of all South Carolinians, legislation to keep these groups out of the mills won a smattering of support.[25]

Long before the dark days of depression, moreover, pundits identified a woman's place as in the home. Prohibiting women from public work thus became a relatively popular scheme both in South Carolina and across the nation for curbing male unemployment.[26] Robert Battle expressed this view: "Simply fire the women, who shouldn't be working anyway, and hire the men. Presto! No unemployment. No relief rolls. No depression."[27] Some wanted to bar women as well as children from night work. Others expressed hostile views toward married women.[28] "Why," asked a Clinton man, "are mill owners of this state allowed to work married women?"[29] An Anderson woman called for the passage of a statute banishing married women from the state's cotton mills. "There are men living [near] me that really needs work," she disclosed, "but they don't work at public work now. . . . [I]f every married women was cut off public work I am sure times would be better, it would end this awful depression."[30] Weathering public scorn, most women stayed at their factory posts. Even if they had wanted to leave, practically none could have managed it financially. From 1925 to 1937, in fact, the percentage of women engaged in mill labor in South Carolina actually rose slightly.[31]

While tributes to traditional gender roles, paeans to white supremacy, and harangues on the evils of immigration certainly soothed some anxious souls amid economic catastrophe, most millhands concentrated their political passions on the stretch-out.[32] The elimination of this onerous new industrial regime, many workers predicted, would solve the job crisis. "If the stretch-out system was abolished, unemployment would be erased," asserted a Jonesville worker. P. M. Mooney from Columbia added: "My recommendation is to abolish the Stretch-Out-System completely and restore every man and woman to their job, give them a living wage, and watch business hum."[33] "It's work . . . ," Old Man Dobbin declared, "that needs government regulating."[34] "We want some law made to help us, we want the stretch-out abolished," ordered a group of wage earners in 1930.[35] All of these workers pressed for state intervention into the productive process and thereby seemed to have had few qualms about challenging management's self-declared "right to operate their plants as they saw fit."[36]

Between 1929 and 1933, millhands persuaded, insisted, and cajoled elected officials to pass an "anti-stretch-out bill" or a law restricting the number of looms that an employer could legally assign an individual weaver.[37] When a caravan of candidates for state office barnstormed through the mill districts of Spartanburg in 1932, laborers turned out in force to declare that the thirty-two-loom limit law, defeated in the General Assembly the previous year, would be their electoral litmus test. Candidates championing the measure won the electoral support of the textile workers, while those who refused had difficulty garnering votes in the mill precincts.[38]

The next year a similar bill came before the South Carolina House of Representatives. During the debate over the measure, millhands filled the galleries. Echoing the views of labor, member after member from textile districts stepped forward to urge its passage. Each predicted it would ease unemployment. Some depicted the horrors of "industrial slavery," while a few charged that excessive work loads killed laborers. Still others pointed to the strikes a few years earlier and warned of continued upheaval. "Unless something is done . . . a cotton mill [will] be blown up," forecast one representative. Another accused the mill owners of "inviting Communism." Meanwhile, the bill's opponents cautioned that its implementation would prolong the depression and unleash an exodus of industry from the state. Throughout the deliberations, mill workers waited tensely, cheering the plan's supporters and hissing its detractors.[39]

The campaign for shorter hours went hand in glove with the fight for reduced machine loads. Despite extensive underemployment and unemployment, mill owners defied a state statute, passed at the behest of reformers a decade earlier, fixing fifty-five hours as the maximum work week. Instead, they operated their factories on the basis of twelve-to-fourteen-hour shifts, sometimes without the customary fifteen-minute break. "I want to explain to you about the Kershaw Cotton Mill is not abiding by the Labor Law," wrote A. P. Dewitt; "they hold the night hands in 12 hours every night." A Pelham textile worker complained: "This mill is a running day and night and a workin' the same hands 14½ hours each day."[40] "Thousands [are] out of work," grumbled a group of millhands, "and we who have work have too much."[41] Instead of two stints a day, Paul Clark suggested, "they could have 3 shifts at 8 hours each and the jobless would have jobs." Not only would this check on hours create openings in the mills, but according to Clark it would be a "blessing in Christ's name."[42] Many rallied to the banner of the eight-hour day, and some pushed for the six-hour day. By governing the hours of labor, South Carolina textile workers sought to organize a massive job-sharing program in the state.[43]

Despite the concerted efforts of mill workers and some of their representatives, none of the so-called anti-stretch-out bills made it through the General Assembly. In 1929, 1930, and 1931, these measures either died in committee or on the floor of the state House of Representatives. In 1932 and 1933, proposals to limit weavers' work loads to thirty-six looms passed the House. Each time, however, the Senate crushed these bills. Hours legislation met a similar fate. Support from upcountry politicians fed by grassroots agitation gained momentum until an eight-hour measure finally passed in the House only to succumb to conservative opposition in the less representative Senate.[44]

Although legislative agitation failed, it indicated a political departure for South Carolina textile workers. Between 1908 and 1929, most of the state's mill laborers backed the political campaigns of Coleman Livingston Blease, or "Coley" as his fervent supporters called him. Refusing to stand on an activist platform, the self-proclaimed champion of the millhands rejected calls for reduced hours, opposed child labor restrictions, and lambasted compulsory school legislation. Workers endorsed the candidate's antistatist stance largely because he pledged to keep the reins of government out of the hands of their class enemies, the uptown reformers.[45]

Merchants, lawyers, clergymen, and doctors greeted the mill-building crusade of the late nineteenth century with ardor that bordered on religious zeal. Industrialization directed by benevolent and civic-minded manufacturers, they predicted, would pull "failed farmers" out of poverty and convert them into "peaceful and contented workers." By the second decade of the century, however, many middle-class citizens had concluded that, rather than "civilizing" these "clay-eaters" and "sand-loppers," the mill villages unleashed the most debased passions and lawless tendencies of poor whites. Editors and academics began to talk openly of "the cotton mill problem." The crux of the dilemma, as they saw it, was neither capitalism nor proletarianization but the textile workers themselves, particularly the parents. Mill mothers and fathers, they charged, had inculcated their children with values and habits that threatened social stability. Reformers turned to the state to stifle these insidious influences. Through child labor restrictions and compulsory school attendance legislation, they sought to "uplift" mill children by intervening in their upbringing.

Textile workers, meanwhile, already edgy about how the process of industrialization had eroded their economic independence, did not welcome the notion of ceding control over their families to the state. Mill people, moreover, bristled when town folks portrayed them as "shiftless" and "immoral" and described them as in need of drastic and coercive reform. After all, they noted, this kind of language was usually reserved for African Americans. White mill people refused to allow their uptown neighbors to put restrictions on their lives or to place them in the same category as their black neighbors, at least not without a fight.[46]

Blease understood South Carolina textile workers' distrust of state action, and throughout his campaigns he shaped and gave voice to their fears. "Compulsory education," the candidate declared in 1910, "means disrupting the home, for it dethrones the authority of the parents." "Of course I am opposed," Blease assured a mill crowd, referring to the same legislation two years later. "[I]t comes from some narrow-minded bigot who was a failure in raising his own children and now wants to attempt to raise someone elses." Lashing out at both the reforms and the reformers, Blease stood up for the rights of mill folks to control their own lives and those of their families. At the same time, he assailed "aristocrats" inclined to "place . . . cotton mill people on the same basis as a free negro." He vowed never to let that happen. By supporting Coley's campaigns, therefore, workers engaged in class politics aimed at obstructing almost all state actions except those that safeguarded white supremacy.[47]

Between 1929 and 1933, South Carolina textile workers took their first tentative ideological steps away from Bleasism, especially in the election of 1930. In the fall of that year, as the upcountry slipped deeper into the mire of the depression, Blease kicked off his Senate reelection campaign. His chief opponents were Leon Harris and James F. Byrnes, the Spartanburg attorney and former member of the United States House of Representatives who six years earlier had finished a close second to Blease in the Senate race. Harris assailed the incumbent on the stump. He charged Blease with betraying the textile workers by becoming an agent of the cotton mill executives. Byrnes, it seems, was the chief beneficiary of Harris's attacks. While Blease clowned around the stump and ranted about "liquor and niggers"—"negroes," he said, "pray for [my] defeat"—Byrnes spoke quite seriously of the need to wrest the region from the grip of economic chaos. He talked vaguely of government action. "There can be no improvement in the cotton mill situation," Byrnes argued, "as long as the farmers are in need." He pledged to loosen international trade restraints so that South Carolina's textile mills and cotton growers could increase their export business.[48] Byrnes's strategy of raising economic questions and hinting at government solutions seemed to work. As returns drifted in on election night, Blease supporters must have noticed a drop in the candidate's margin of victory in many mill districts. This shift was critical because Blease lost the contest by the slimmest of margins.[49]

Shop floor changes, unemployment, wage cuts, and industrial action seemed to have jostled the thinking of mill workers. Cultural and racial concerns lost some of their saliency as economic issues loomed with pressing urgency. Workers, as a result, began to reexamine their ideas about state power. The expansion of governmental power and an end to the suffering of the stretch-out appeared inseparable to a growing number of millhands. Only the government, more and more laborers came to believe, had enough power to counter the rapacity of the mill owners, end injustice at the workplace, and guarantee the freedoms of workers. Only the government had the authority to regulate the economy. The government, moreover, remained the only route to prosperity available to laborers armed with the ballot yet unorganized at the workplace.

When the New Deal dawned in 1933, a tidal wave of optimism passed over the mill hills of South Carolina. Workers celebrated the novelty of federal intervention on their behalf, both on the shop floor and in the community. While FDR's recovery programs pledged something new, they resonated with the laborers' pasts as well. Workers heard in the Roosevelt administration's class-tinged rhetoric confirmation and legitimization of their own analysis of the economic calamity. When New Dealers blamed the depression on the greed of a few, textile laborers must have thought of the mill owners and nodded their heads in agreement. By pegging recovery, at least in part, to minimum wages, maximum hours, and reduced output, the National Industrial Recovery Act must have sounded to workers like a repetition of their own views.[50]

Mill laborers translated the symbols and programs of the New Deal into their own language of struggle. Most notably, they extended the metaphor of slavery to reach the New Deal. Laborers believed that the New Deal guaranteed the "abolition of the stretch-out system." Roosevelt, in the minds of many, was "God-sent," a "modern-Moses," who "by his mighty hand" would deliver them to a promised land of justice.[51] The New Deal, in other words, did not just happen to South Carolina textile workers. Instead, they made it in their own image, and the rendition that they constructed reflected changes in their ideological and political outlook triggered by the Great Depression.

J. P. Stevens and the Union
Struggle for the South

From 1963 to 1980 the Textile Workers Union of America (TWUA) and its successor, the Amalgamated Clothing and Textile Workers Union of America (ACTWU), targeted J. P. Stevens for a special organizing effort. Because of ACTWU's adroit publicity effort and the continuing importance of the textile industry in the Southeast, the campaign became a national symbol of militancy and hope for organized labor in its long quest to create a more significant presence in the South. The special push to organize Stevens took on an importance far beyond its individual economic significance as the nation's second largest textile company, one of over eighty plants and 44,000 workers in 1976. To secure collective bargaining at Stevens would demonstrate that the textile industry could be significantly and perhaps permanently unionized, thus breaking the pattern of defeat that characterized the history of textile labor organization in the South. The Stevens campaign symbolized for unionists everywhere the struggle to organize the region. Throughout the dispute textile unionists struggled to create a winning strategy that would eventually lead to unionization of this industry and to greater unionization in other southern industries. Ironically, the union did create an innovative and compelling strategy to attack Stevens; sadly for the union, however, the campaign did not bring the desired results of good faith collective bargaining at Stevens and the rapid unionizing of the textile industry elsewhere.

The textile industry continued to dominate the South's manufacturing base after World War II almost as much as it had from 1880 to 1945. By 1950 the basic southeastern textile mill production industry still employed 509,100 workers, and the apparel industry, just beginning to relocate to the South, employed another 154,200. A decade later, on the eve of the Stevens campaign, the basic textile labor force grew to 589,500, and apparel workers had more than doubled to 308,500.[1] In both North Carolina and South Carolina, textiles dwarfed all other industries. For example, in 1970 at the peak year of employment in South Carolina, textile and apparel employment reached 193,100 workers, accounting for 57 percent of all manufacturing jobs. The same year in North Carolina, 280,000 basic textile millhands accounted for nearly one-third of all textile jobs in the nation, and a decade later, despite growth in other industries, the industry still provided over 30 percent of all manufacturing jobs in the state.[2] In the 1980s over 72 percent of the nation's basic textile millhands worked in the South, and by that decade apparel workers grew from 17 percent of the industry's labor force to well over 50 percent.[3]

Organizing this mass of workers in the post-World War II years became imperative to unionize the region. Textile unionists had mounted the first extensive organizing effort during the New Deal era. From 1933 to 1941, three successive union efforts by the United Textile Workers (UTW), the Textile Workers Organizing Committee (TWOC), and the TWUA, formed in 1939, brought only limited success. By 1941 the TWUA had negotiated only twenty-three active contracts in the South representing 17,000 workers. During the war years, however, TWUA managed to expand in the very small segment of the industry it occupied, and by 1945 some 20 percent of southern textile workers had union contracts, a historic high.[4] When the war ended and the War Labor Board disappeared, the union came under attack throughout the South, and its locals fell apart. One historian wrote, "The union's war-time experiences in the South gave them little to encourage hope. . . . The TWUA was . . . out on a limb. The ending of government controls promised to sever that limb from its tree—the southern textile industry."[5]

The union hoped that Operation Dixie, the CIO's postwar southern drive that began in 1946, would bring gains in membership and bargaining contracts. Operation Dixie attempted early that year to organize the giant Cannon Mills complex at Kannapolis, North Carolina, which employed 24,000 workers in twenty-one plants. The effort failed miserably. By its end in 1953 Operation Dixie had netted the TWUA only 10,805 new southern workers over its total of 70,200 covered under contract when the drive began.[6] The campaign collapsed for diverse reasons—the failure to overcome the debilitating effect of racial division in the South, the failure to create a regionally targeted drive with a southern face for southern workers, and the inability to assault the South with enough resources. But above all else, the failure to organize textiles ensured Operation Dixie's demise.[7]

Wisely, the TWUA invested little emotionally in Operation Dixie. Although at the 1948 Biennial Convention southern workers reported that the "South is tough, but we'll win," George Baldanzi, the director of the southern organization, warned that the story was not one of "romance and magnolia blossoms," and he spoke of "bloodshed and hatred aroused by the anti-union forces."[8] As early as 1947 the TWUA had given up hope in Operation Dixie. Emile Rieve, TWUA president, argued that his union would create its own "permanent drive." "I am not predicting that it will be done in a year or two," he said, "but I know it will be done no matter how long it will take."[9] Although the union never wavered from its understanding that the struggle for the South held the key to significant industry-wide unionism, it often acknowledged being overmatched in the South. Operating from a small membership base, it faced strong employer and community opposition and a history of past failures, which made it difficult to attract workers. In the 1950s TWUA president William Pollock talked darkly of a diabolic conspiracy by the southern "power structure" to keep the union out, and as late as 1978 his successor, Sol Stetin, spoke of a "vast Dixie plot."[10]

The TWUA strategy embodied a prudent, low-risk approach of using its limited resources on targets of opportunity to create little bunkers of unionism in a hostile land, a strategy suggested as early as 1939 by the union's director of research, Solomon Barkin. But the bunker strategy slowly failed in the 1950s. Boyd Payton, the new southern director, saw this failure in 1953 and argued, in a precursor to the Stevens campaign, for concentration of resources "in large, pattern-setting companies rather than small marginal ones which even if organized would have no impact on others."[11] In 1958 Payton wrote, "we are quite busy, but I have the feeling sometimes that we are just 'spinning our wheels.' There must be a brighter day coming—somewhere—sometime."[12] That day never came for the union in the 1950s. A disastrous strike at Danville, Virginia, and at other cotton mill centers in 1951; a bruising internal fight for the union presidency in 1952; a conspicuous inability in 1956 to prevent Deering-Miliken from "chilling" the union by closing a plant in Darlington, South Carolina, after a union victory; and a nationally noticed strike, marred by violence, at the Harriet-Henderson Cotton Mills in Henderson, North Carolina, 1958–1961, left the union weaker and even more burdened by a pattern of defeat. The TWUA still lacked a winning strategy in the South, but help was on the way.

In 1955, after the AFL-CIO merger, the CIO lived on in labor's house with the creation of the Industrial Union Department (IUD), which was dedicated to continuing organizing drives along the old CIO model. In the early sixties the IUD began coordinating multi-union drives in several places across the nation, one of them in the Spartanburg and Greenville, South Carolina, area, the heart of the textile country. That effort spawned an agreement in 1962 between IUD and the TWUA to conduct a joint campaign to organize in the textile industry, and on 23 January 1963, a TWUA committee selected J. P. Stevens as "the organizational target for an IUD textile drive." The TWUA executive committee approved the report at its April 1963 meeting. J. P. Stevens, then the second largest textile company in the country with fifty-three plants and 36,000 workers, traced its founding to the year 1813 in Massachusetts, but in 1946 it began a massive relocation to the South, particularly to the Carolinas.

The TWUA targeted Stevens because it was a profitable company that concentrated large numbers of workers in three centers of operation. In the Rock Hill, South Carolina, area the company had eleven plants with 6,500 workers, and in Spartanburg and Greenville, South Carolina, fourteen plants employed 12,650 workers. The Roanoke Rapids, North Carolina, complex had six plants employing 3,600. The IUD already fielded twenty-two full-time organizers in the Spartanburg and Greenville area. "With the same amount of manpower available," said the TWUA committee, "a larger part of Stevens, about 60 percent, can be tackled as against about 25 percent of Burlington"—a reference to a failed, half-hearted effort to organize Burlington Industries.[13] Sol Stetin, later a TWUA president, remembered feeling that "conditions were worse" at Stevens and that the firm's northern roots made it more vulnerable to unionization.[14]

The TWUA-IUD Stevens campaign began slowly and with little publicity, as the TWUA tried to avoid the mistake of the over-publicized Operation Dixie. The campaign was very conventional. In the early summer of 1963 the TWUA shifted twelve of its fourteen Deep South organizers to Stevens, and the IUD also assigned twelve organizers to the drive with Jim Pierce of the IUD in charge. Later, Harold McIver replaced Pierce until the Stevens campaign ended in 1980.[15] By 1964 the staff had grown only by one, and progress was slow—1,062 cards of the 3,600 workers at Roanoke Rapids, 619 of 2,325 at Rock Hill, 948 cards of 4,385 at Greenville.[16] Sol Stetin remembered the campaign always being in a "difficult position." "We weren't getting anywhere . . . [because] we didn't have the resources to tackle a big company like Stevens."[17]

Stevens also surprised them by its vigorous anti-union activities. The company had come South, in part, seeking lower costs, having succumbed to the unionization of five of its ten northern plants in 1941. A company executive remembered that CEO Robert Stevens determined early "to fight like hell[;] . . . he was upset that the union thought he was a patsy . . . and now he decided to prove himself."[18] The company effectively closed the TWUA-IUD campaign for the minds, hearts, and votes of the workers, first by using blatantly illegal tactics—the firing, coercing, and intimidation of pro-union workers—and then by a well-engineered, lengthy legal contest before the National Labor Relations Board (NLRB) and the federal courts. Their anti-union argument was no more original than the TWUA's campaign, but the company used its resources with fierce tenacity.

In captive audience speeches, letters to each employee, and pamphlets, Stevens argued that the union threatened the communities because, as one official put it, the union would bring "friction, terrorism, and fear." The core of the company's appeal was that a "direct relationship" with employees worked to the "best interests of the employees themselves" and that a "union presence has historically led to strife and discord over issues that can be settled amicably when the relationship is based on mutual respect."[19]

At heart, the TWUA-IUD campaign failed before the plant gates. Prior to three victories in 1979–1980, TWUA brought only twelve of the more than forty Stevens sites to election and lost eleven of the twelve, although federal officials set aside five of the elections because of unfair labor practices. By 1967 the campaign, mired in a legal struggle and facing stiff company and worker resistance, proceeded only on a "modest scale."[20] The overwhelming number of Stevens workers at its numerous plants remained unaffected by the campaign. At the Estes plant in Piedmont, South Carolina, one anti-union worker remembered that before the losing election there in 1965 the union "really made a push," but the company said, in his words, "We feel like we can work better with you than you can with the union. We are going to treat you all right." "That was the gist" of the company argument, and he believed it.[21]

The immediate firing of pro-union employees at the most vulnerable plants created a legal struggle that consumed the union's energies and derailed the actual organizing campaign. Reed Johnston, the NLRB's regional director at Winston-Salem, North Carolina, said: "It was like nothing we ever had at the board. Every day the union was filing a new charge of unfair practices—you know, discriminatory firings—against Stevens. Hell, this company was firing people the same day they signed the union card. Doing it blatantly." Johnston eventually began to lump the cases arbitrarily, labeling the first group "Stevens I." Eventually, by the end of the struggle, the unified case files ran to XXVI. Stevens I took three years and ten months from the start in 1963 until the U.S. Supreme Court denied certiorari four years later on a Stevens appeal. The case involved seventy-one workers fired at twenty plants in North Carolina and South Carolina, and the NLRB field hearings involved 384 witnesses testifying sixty-five days. The printed record numbers over twelve thousand pages.[22]

Stevens I set a pattern. The union's staff spent an inordinate amount of time assembling the witnesses; then came days of testimony and the long delay of month on month awaiting a decision and the setting of remedies. The NLRB found Stevens guilty in twenty-one of twenty-two decisions, but the company soon violated the NLRB remedies, and eventually the NLRB successfully took the company to court for contempt. (At one time the court found the company in contempt of its contempt remedy!) Something of the mounting sense of Stevens as the "number one labor outlaw," as Sol Stetin branded the company, appears in the NLRB's trial examiners' comments. In Stevens I, Horace Ruckel said in 1967, the company was "flagrantly guilty." During the same year, in Stevens II, he argued that Stevens set out "to destroy the unions root and branch by discharging its most active members." Thomas Ricci in 1969 found Stevens's violations to be "massive and deliberate, . . . an unbroken pattern runs through them." Federal judges concurred. Chief Judge John Brown of the Fifth Circuit Court wrote in 1969 that Stevens employed "a massive multi-state campaign to prevent unionization of its southern plants." The Second Circuit Court in 1973 found that Stevens officials "have continued to resort to . . . unlawful tactics—including surveillance, interrogation of employees, threats and discharges to keep employees from joining TWUA." In 1977 administrative law Judge Bernard Ries, in Stevens XVI, summed up the company's policy. Finding Stevens guilty of refusing to bargain in good faith at Roanoke

Rapids, he said that the company had approached union negotiations "with all the tractability and open-mindedness of Sherman at the outskirts of Atlanta."[23]

The lengthy legal imbroglio with its costs in money and staff time brought a series of bittersweet victories for the TWUA. The union won eventually, and it properly proclaimed victory and carefully totaled back pay. It gained some path-breaking remedies from the NLRB, such as use of bulletin boards, direct access to workers in the plants, and company admission of guilt to all workers.[24] "We won," remembered Joel Ax, TWUA and ACTWU attorney, "but we didn't consider it a success, because while we were getting people reinstated and we were getting citations we weren't getting people organized." With ironic humor he noted: "Our object was not to get people fired and reinstated."[25] In its first election victory at Roanoke Rapids in 1974, TWUA won 1,685 to 1,448. The well-known film *Norma Rae* fictionalized the Roanoke Rapids campaign and triumph. A North Carolina unionist on the day of victory proclaimed: "It was a new day in Dixie—first J. P. Stevens, then the textile industry, then the South."[26] The reality of Roanoke Rapids, however, differed from the upbeat romantic ending of the film, which concluded with the workers chanting "unionism, unionism" and the organizer leaving town, his job done. Actually, Stevens refused to bargain in good faith; the refusal became Stevens XVI, creating another laborious legal maze for the union. Soon the recession in 1974–1975 depressed all organizing work, and the union had to lay off one-third of its organizers. At one time Harold McIver was the only IUD worker on the campaign.

The TWUA-IUD campaign had failed by the mid-seventies, although not in the usual way. The union avoided dramatic high-profile public relations at the beginning, and it averted failed strikes and militant acts. By drawing attention to Stevens's hard-nosed and illegal tactics, it had brought liberal support to the union. But the key goal was union memberships and union contracts. In 1976 the TWUA represented only 129,208 workers in 1,077 plants nationally, and in the South it represented only 33,227 workers in 58 plants.[27] That left more than 500,000 nonunionized basic textile workers in the South.

A sharp sense of crisis did not inspire the TWUA decision to merge with the Amalgamated Clothing Workers (ACW) in 1976, but rather it came from the belief that a small union could not win the struggle for the South. The

TWUA and the ACW recognized the imperative need to organize the South together if they hoped to grow and affect the lives of most workers in the industry. Stetin called the merger "the brightest day in our union history" because it would "defuse the anti-union campaign in the South which has prevented more than one million working men and women from enjoying the fruit of union."[28] Although the TWUA and IUD had discussed closing down the campaign after the failure to capitalize on the Roanoke Rapids victory in 1974, Stetin asserted that his primary merger objective, which he received, was an ACW commitment to carry on the Stevens campaign as the merged union's top priority. Scott Hoyman, a southern director and later senior vice-president, remembered the commitment: "It became such a spectacle and challenge, that there was no way you could get off the tiger's back."[29]

The ACTWU, claiming over 400,000 members, immediately pursued the campaign with enthusiasm and new strategies. Although the IUD's Harold McIver remained as director, ACTWU's Paul Swaity and Richard Rothstein increasingly managed the effort. By 1977 ACTWU had twenty-six staff assigned to the campaign—seventeen paid by the ACTWU, six from IUD, and three directly from the AFL-CIO. They conducted active campaigns in Wallace, South Carolina, Milledgeville, Georgia, and Montgomery, Alabama, as well as card-signing activities at Tifton, Georgia, and Ferrum and Stuart, Virginia. The ACTWU also held together the union members at Roanoke Rapids and conducted a six-year bargaining effort there. By the beginning of 1979 the Stevens organizing staff had grown to forty-five members, thirty-one of them on the ACTWU payroll.[30] The ACTWU had virtually created a second Stevens campaign. Eventually the increased field activity paid dividends in election victories in 1979 at High Point, North Carolina, and Allendale, South Carolina, and in early 1980 at Montgomery, Alabama.

The TWUA's dogged pursuit of Stevens via federal labor law began to produce dividends as well. The Stevens cases with their back pay awards and negative publicity took their toll, and by 1978 Stevens's management tried to avoid such confrontations. The enlarged ACTWU legal groups filed a criminal case against Stevens for bugging organizers' motel rooms in Wallace, and it aggressively pursued anti-trust suits against Stevens. Although unsuccessful, the effort annoyed the company because of the threatened potential for damages. The ACTWU sought and gained new remedies and supported the NLRB's contempt cases that, because of the possibility for criminal punishment rather than the relative low cost of reinstatement and back wages of the NLRB decisions, really closed down the company's anti-union activities. A most important step was that the ACTWU pressed the NLRB to seek a federal court injunction ordering the company to bargain at all of its more than eighty plants.

The national boycott of Stevens's products announced at the merger convention in 1976 became the best-known part of the new ACTWU campaign. The boycott became a major union project with a large staff in New York. The union gained support from every sector of the labor community and from liberal activists throughout the nation. Such support multiplied the union's own advertising effort that pummeled Stevens as a corporate outlaw. "Don't sleep with J. P. Stevens," the union's well-known cry, may not have hurt sheet sales deeply, but the corporate image took a beating.[31] The boycott literature was accompanied by exceptionally well-done "fact sheets" that in various ways highlighted the struggle with Stevens and expressed workers' hopes for fair wages, a pension plan, better and safer working conditions, and self-representation and self-identity. The ACTWU financed Southerners for Economic Justice, a lobbying effort, to attract intellectual and institutional support for the campaign. It produced the film documentary "Testimony" that gave sharp relief to Stevens "union workers" grievances. The television program "60 Minutes" aired a story that negatively portrayed Stevens, and in 1980 the ACTWU exploited the popularity of *Norma Rae* by sending the real Norma Rae, Crystal Lee Sutton, on a national tour of twenty-two cities. Invited audiences viewed the film and talked with Sutton. She also appeared in local television and radio interviews. In addition to the tour, the ACTWU prepared a boycott leaflet entitled "The Real Norma Rae" that tied the movie to the union's campaign, trumpeted by the leaflet as "the 16 year battle for justice against J. P. Stevens and Company—the nation's second biggest textile firm and one of the most notorious anti-union busters and labor scofflaws in history."[32]

The ACTWU also created in 1977 a "corporate campaign," which consisted of attending and picketing Stevens's shareholders meetings and putting pro-labor resolutions on the agenda in order to harass Stevens's management and attract press coverage of the labor dispute. The corporate campaign also identified outside directors on the Stevens board, some of them CEOs of companies with union ties. The ACTWU wanted to embarrass them and create investor unhappiness. The campaign worked; two directors resigned from the Stevens board. But it was more important that the corporate campaign kept the spotlight on Stevens, and by 1980 its new CEO, Whitney Stevens, wanted that spotlight off.[33] According to Bruce Raynor, current ACTWU southern director, Whitney Stevens felt the weight of the union's recent NLRB election victories in 1979 and the "accumulated weight" of the legal battle and publicity setbacks. "It was a tired old company," said Raynor, and "they had allowed the union to dominate them." Whitney Stevens wanted the struggle to end.[34]

Private talks for a settlement began in 1980 involving ACTWU's president Murray Finley, secretary-treasurer Jack Sheinkman, vice-presidents Sol Stetin and William DuChessi, and Stevens officials led by Whitney Stevens. They announced an agreement on 19 October 1980. J. P. Stevens accepted two-and-a-half-year contracts at Roanoke Rapids, Allendale, and High Point with dues checkoff and arbitration of disputes, terms that former CEO James Finley had said he would never accept. The company agreed also to pay about three million dollars to the Roanoke Rapids workers who had lost wage increases during the protracted bargaining period since the 1974 election victory.

The ACTWU promised to call off the boycott and corporate campaign and to refrain from citing Stevens as its "primary target," although organizing at Stevens would continue. In its press release the union quietly proclaimed victory and hoped for "harmonious and productive" relationships with Stevens. A *Charlotte News* editorial argued that "the agreement was clearly a victory" for the union, and all it had won was "a new toehold—but a toehold in a large mountain in an extensive range."[35] The ACTWU failed to expand the "toehold" in the coming months, primarily, Sol Stetin later argued, because of Ronald Reagan's aggressive anti-unionism policies and the 1981–1982 recession.

Three years later, on 20 October 1983, the ACTWU closed down the Stevens campaign by agreeing with Stevens and the NLRB to accept $1.2 million for the union and some workers in exchange for terminating all pending unfair labor practices cases. In addition, Whitney Stevens agreed to write a letter to the NLRB General Counsel promising that he would "not tolerate" unfair labor practices and personally would be responsible for preventing them.[36] Thus the war ended. J. P. Stevens itself would disappear as a corporate identity in 1988, split three ways in the leveraged eighties.

Harold McIver called the 1980 agreement "a foot in the door at least," but he was chagrined that the campaign virtually stopped: "We had the table set, we could have organized more workers" if Stevens had remained top priority.[37] Sol Stetin, present at the beginning and at the end, deemed the campaign a "success in part" and a "step in the right direction," but "it hurt" when "we got Reagan" and the union could not move ahead in the South. Joel Ax and Scott Hoyman praised the Roanoke Rapids workers and considered the 1980 agreement "a win," because the workers there got a contract. Some labor scholars demurred. Economist Richard Rowan thought the Roanoke Rapids contract ordinary, and he viewed the struggle as "a victory for management." Other scholars, Terry Mullins and Paul Leubke, echoed Stetin's line soon after the 1980 settlement. The company did agree to a contract, and thus the union gained a symbolic victory. But Mullins and Leubke predicted accurately that ACTWU's Stevens settlement would not have a multiplying effect in the southern region: "It was not," they wrote in 1982, "a watershed for the southern labor movement."[38] In the late 1980s Bruce Raynor disagreed, claiming he never felt that a Stevens settlement would create a flood of textile unionism. "Southern textile workers were never going to flock to the unions even if *every* Stevens' mill had gone union," he said. The victory to him lay in the limited gain at Roanoke Rapids and the symbolic sense that the industry could be organized. Stevens was "not a partial failure," because many other companies in the South by the late 1980s accepted the "Stevens model." "No way should we win, but we did," Raynor said.[39]

Old continuities lay behind the union's inability to attract more Stevens workers and to exploit the settlement. Despite the changing nature of the workforce since the end of World War II and its growing similarity to other blue-collar factory workers, southern textile worker culture, according to some scholars, still impeded unionization. Generalized anti-unionism had softened considerably during the period of the Stevens campaign, and the employment of black workers, more accepting of unionism, began in the sixties. Black workers ensured union victory at Roanoke Rapids in 1974 after election defeats in 1959 and 1965 with a larger white workforce. Increased numbers of female workers, particularly black women in the apparel plants, also shifted the odds in favor of the union. But as two sociologists, Michael Schulman and Jeffrey Leiter, wrote in 1991, summarizing a decade of recent scholarly work on southern textile workers, "many of the vestiges of the past paternalism seem to persist."[40] The failure of the Stevens workers to heed the call of the union can also be explained more by new realities in the nature of the industry and its economic organization than by the sociological and ideological belief structure of its workers. Declining employment in the industry in the 1970s and 1980s because of technological changes, foreign imports of apparel goods, and economic uncertainty, particularly for the manufacturing sector, also helped keep in place the industry's persistent anti-unionism.

Publicly, the ACTWU's leadership never second-guessed itself. The union needed a victory and saw enough in the Stevens settlement to claim one. Against all odds the TWUA had persevered and pursued the campaign, adhering to an identifiable strategy. By any reckoning the union had carried out an inspired organizing campaign, and the settlement gave it a sense of victory and competence that overcame the legacy of defeat that had characterized past high-profile conflicts. True, the union failed to gain significant new southern members during the Stevens campaign. Its pattern in the eighties had been strong efforts at limited targets, particularly in small apparel plants where aggressive management made angry workers more likely to join a union. What remained was something that had to be seen as "permanent enclave unionism." After the Stevens campaign the union had become a potential force in the neighborhood that could disrupt the usual pattern of nonunion industrial relations for careless management.

In the early 1980s the union thought that it had put together a viable southern strategy and created by its own efforts a winning image to attract southern textile workers. Nationally, however, unionism fared poorly. Throughout the decade the unions lost membership, and the movement's national influence declined. Bruce Raynor was right. The Stevens campaign did create a symbolic model in the struggle for the South, but the national trend against unionism made that model for the ACTWU, if not obsolete, certainly unusable in the 1980s.

Part II.

The Place of Black Workers in Southern Labor History

JOE W. TROTTER, JR.

Introduction

The development of the black working class in the South is closely intertwined with the growth of black America. Although efforts to record and interpret the black experience expanded during the late nineteenth and early twentieth centuries, it received little attention in white academe. Pioneering black scholars like Carter G. Woodson and W. E. B. DuBois placed black Americans at the center of their research and commentary on American history, but they received little support from their white counterparts. To be sure, a small number of white allies undertook the study of blacks, but they invariably emphasized race relations, usually defined as white attitudes and behavior toward blacks. Until the 1960s and 1970s, few scholars treated the experience of blacks—even educated elites, much less members of the black working class—from the vantage point of African Americans. The following essays focus on a variety of issues in the development of the black working class. They suggest the interrelationship between changes in African-American history and the gradual rise of black labor history as a subfield.

Under the impact of the modern civil rights and black power movements, African-American history, particularly slavery studies, emerged and expanded as perhaps the most energetic segment of historical research in U.S. history. Yet until the onset of World War II and its aftermath, historians continued to rely upon U. B. Phillips's *American Negro Slavery* (1918) as the principal authority on black life under bondage. Based primarily upon records left by the planter class, Phillips depicted slavery as a paternalistic institution, one that introduced "primitive" Africans to the fruits of the modern world, although through the use of coercion. While studies by post-World War II historians like Kenneth Stampp and Stanley Elkins overturned

Phillips's racist portrait of black life, their integrationist paradigm largely denied slaves the benefit of a culture of their own.[1]

Only during the early 1970s did scholars gradually place slaves at the center of their analyses of the peculiar institution. Supplementing and even supplanting the records left by planters with those left by slaves, the new scholarship emphasized the rise of a vibrant slave community and cultural life. Accenting the slave's family and religion, songs and folk tales, dances and oral traditions, the new scholarship reinforced the conclusion that "however oppressive or dehumanizing the plantation was, the struggle for survival was not severe enough to crush all of the slave's creative instincts."[2]

The emergence of ground-breaking research on emancipation and Reconstruction closely followed the appearance of the slavery scholarship. Detailed studies of black life in the transition from slavery to freedom now vie with scholarship on antebellum slavery, especially for understanding the rise of the black working class. Studies by Nell Painter, Thomas Holt, Leon Litwack, Barbara Fields, Armstead Robinson, and Eric Foner, to name a few, all document the dynamic role of blacks in shaping and giving meaning to their own emancipation and Reconstruction experience. These studies show that blacks did not wait for whites to organize and direct their lives in the quest for freedom. Former slaves and former free blacks struck out on their own: influencing the interracial alliance that underlay the Republican party; effecting the transition from slavery to sharecropping to wage labor; reconstituting family units; and, perhaps most important, building new and more cohesive African-American communities, replete with a variety of churches, fraternal orders, social clubs, and business, professional, civil rights, and political organizations.[3]

Several scholars resurrected the experiences of blacks in bondage and the early years of emancipation, while others investigated the processes that stimulated the increasing migration of blacks to American cities during the late nineteenth and early twentieth centuries. As with scholarship on slavery and emancipation, research on black urban history reversed an earlier emphasis on race relations and treated the ways that rural blacks brought their own traditions to the cities and helped to transform their own lives in the new environment. Recent studies by Earl Lewis, Darlene Clark Hine, James Grossman, and Peter Gottlieb show how southern blacks developed elaborate kin and friendship networks, shared information and resources, and organized their own migration and resettlement in the industrializing city.[4]

New scholarship on the African-American experience exposed significant socioeconomic, political, and cultural divisions within the group. It demonstrated that the black working class and poor, especially in the wake of emancipation, urbanization, and industrialization, often voiced goals and aspirations at odds with the aims of nascent black elites. Indeed, closely intertwined with the development of African-American historiography has been a growing effort to capture the distinctive experiences of the black working class. African-American scholars like Charles Wesley, Abram Harris, Carter G. Woodson, and others had studied black workers during the inter-World War years, and the late Herbert Gutman and his students helped revive interest in the subject during the 1960s.[5]

The new working-class agenda unfolded in several overlapping sections. First, Gutman called for a fresh look at the largely forgotten tradition of interracial unionism, which characterized facets of the labor movement during the late nineteenth and early twentieth centuries. In addressing this issue, several scholars turned to the history of the United Mine Workers of America and the Knights of Labor. Others developed biographical studies of individual black workers in both rural and urban settings. And still others explored the connections among work, culture, and community in the lives of black workers. In recent years, as Robert Zieger suggests in a larger context, African-American labor history, like southern labor history, appears to be in transition between an "'old' new labor history and an even newer gender-conscious labor history."[6]

Essays in this section reinforce recent research on black workers in American, southern, and African-American labor history. Focusing primarily on black workers in the urban South, they illuminate incipient proletarianization in the antebellum years; the gradual rise of a black wage-earning working class during the emancipation era; and the urban industrial transformation of workers' lives during the twentieth century. Suzanne Schnittman documents the transformation of slave labor in Richmond's tobacco industry during the antebellum period. Noting the growing use of hired rather than "personally owned" slaves in tobacco manufacturing firms, she illustrates how urban slavery departed from an earlier paternalistic pattern and took on "a more impersonal," commercial, and even "industrial" character by the 1850s. Through such practices as the boarding and bonus systems, which provided cash payments to slaves and allowed them to secure their own lodging away from the watchful eye of employers, the tobacco industry enabled slaves to approximate the development of a working class. Unlike most slaves, tobacco workers influenced the terms of their labor at the point of hiring, on the shop floor, and in the larger community.

Supplementing Schnittman's careful study, James Schmidt reminds us that antebellum class and race relations mirrored changes in the legal system. Focusing on the nature of contractual relations between plantation owners and overseers, Schmidt argues that "the dominant Southern experience with free labor contracts and the modern wage relation came from suits involving plantation owners and their overseers." At the same time that tobacco manufacturers hired rather than owned slaves in growing numbers, new contract labor laws emerged to supplant the old system of common law contracts. Unlike the urban North, however, where workers rarely recovered wages from employers when they quit or were dismissed before their contracts expired, southern courts developed a more flexible system. Overseers often confronted planters in court for breach of contract and frequently recovered a portion of their wages. Nonetheless, planters like northern employers were the chief beneficiaries of the law and repeatedly fired overseers before the expiration of their contract with minimal repercussions. Although Schmidt focuses primarily on the agricultural sector, his emphasis on the flexibility of southern labor law helps to explain to some extent the flexibility of slave labor in the tobacco industry.

Focusing on the experiences of blacks in Memphis, Tennessee, between the Civil War and the early Reconstruction years, Dernoral Davis discusses the transformation of slaves to a free wage-earning proletariat. His essay describes the role of military officials and the Freedmen's Bureau in contract negotiations between black workers and white landowners. Although the role of blacks in shaping their own transition to a wage-earning proletariat is less fully developed than federal efforts, this essay complements Schnittman's discussion of black workers in the antebellum era.

Finally, Michael Honey suggests certain continuities and discontinuities in the lives of black workers from the end of Reconstruction through the mid-twentieth century. Drawing upon the extensive oral recollections of blacks in Memphis, Tennessee, Honey places his study within the larger context of southern race relations, emphasizing the debilitating impact on the working class of segregation, disfranchisement, and economic discrimination. His essay also illuminates the emergence of interracial unionism during the Great Depression and World War II, the role of black workers in the rise of the modern civil rights movement, and, most of all, black workers' persistent struggle against inequality in the union, the corporation, and the society around them.

6

SUZANNE SCHNITTMAN

Black Workers in Antebellum Richmond

Shortly after the Civil War the chewing tobacco manufacturers of Richmond reduced the wages and income of black factory workers to one-half their antebellum level. In response, a newly formed society of tobacco hands issued a formal complaint arguing that such meager pay made it "impossible to feed ourselves and family[,] . . . starvation is Cirten unless a change is brought about." When their demand was not satisfied, tobacco factory workers strengthened their benevolent societies, which had long been used to supporting one another, and organized trade unions to work for improved conditions. Early in 1868 one group formed a producers' cooperative under the leadership of freedman Stephen Jones. The American Tobacco Manufacturing Company, though short-lived, demonstrated the determination of some black workers to produce their own tobacco.[1]

Tobacco workers displayed similar commitment in addressing their political needs. When the Republican State Convention opened in Richmond on 1 August 1867, black laborers refused to work in order to attend, forcing manufacturers to close the tobacco factories while their workers advocated "Ultra" Radical Reconstruction plans. In late 1867 and early 1868, when Virginia's Constitutional Convention debated vital issues, huge numbers of black tobacco workers vacated their factories, once again terminating production.[2]

Within a decade after emancipation, tobacco workers were extending their working-class activism to wider arenas. They affiliated with the National Laboring Club, which counted many former tobacco slaves among its members and officers. Their trade unions joined the Tobacco Laborers' Association, which sent delegates to the National Labor Union and Industrial Congress in the early 1870s. Later, black tobacco workers eagerly joined and filled leadership roles in the Knights of Labor when it finally opened membership to them in 1885.[3]

The legacy of slavery that black workers brought to free labor provided a continuity of work experience that bridged emancipation. It promoted a process among slaves similar to the proletarianization of other preindustrial workers. Legal enslavement failed to squelch the participation of slaves in politics or in working-class activism. In many cases slaves sharpened their negotiating skills on masters and overseers. They formed social institutions and networks that helped resist the racial controls of the white community. Slaves realized that white dependency on their labor provided a measure of autonomy.

Recent historiography has confirmed what some have long suspected: slaves in many positions had extensive opportunities to shape working and living conditions. Rural and urban, agricultural and industrial, some working for owners and others for employers, slaves found space to maneuver and made their lives more self-determined. Some created internal economies, hired themselves out as skilled workers, and established customary rights that no master could eliminate. Certain slaves had opportunities greater than those of their fellow slaves that provided leverage and autonomy in some areas of their lives.[4]

Fortunately for all slaves Richmond's tobacco factory slaves succeeded in seizing a significant measure of independence in their lives and work. During slavery these factory slaves provided leadership in factories, neighborhoods, and churches. Once free, a disproportionate number became leaders in black working-class activism and politics throughout the Reconstruction era. What distinguished tobacco slave hands from their plantation counterparts as well as from other urban or industrial slaves was: (1) their numerical majority in urban industry; (2) their frequent status as hired slaves; (3) their independent living arrangements; and (4) their access to cash. While none of these conditions was independently unique to tobacco slaves, in combination they defined a slave group that was more self-determined than most.[5]

The use of slaves in southern cities was common before Richmond's tobacco factories came to rely on them. Although less numerous than those in rural areas, urban slaves had filled vital nonindustrial positions as domestics, skilled workers in petty production, dockworkers, and common laborers since the late eighteenth century. Slaves who performed these jobs were dispersed among many users; in the nineteenth century the average urban household or business rarely held more than ten slaves. Their use in industry, both rural and urban, also had a long history, although again, there were fewer

industrial slaves than nonindustrial. They worked in manufacturing, mining, lumber and shingle production, ironworks, and the construction of
transportation facilities such as railroads and canals. Concentrated in large
numbers, often as many as a few hundred per enterprise, they frequently
dwelled in barracks or makeshift camps near work sites. Because of their
proximity to masters during working and leisure hours, both urban and
industrial slaves were under fairly tight scrutiny.[6]

Slaves had manufactured chewing tobacco since its earliest years as a
plantation "home industry." Expansion of production and location priorities encouraged manufacturers to open factories manned by slaves in
urban Virginia during the 1830s and 1840s. In cities like Richmond, which
would become the largest tobacco manufacturing center in the United
States by 1850, factories were in close proximity to tobacco warehouses and
transportation facilities. Few employers had the space or funds to construct
adjacent barracks for workers, which left hundreds of slaves to find living
quarters in cities ill-equipped to house or control them. Urban industrial
slaves were thus thrust upon communities in unprecedented numbers. By
1860 Richmond's fifty tobacco factories employed 3,400 black males,
mostly slave, a number that represented more than half of the city's male
slave population of 6,636 and approximately one-sixth of its workers. Only
34 women (slaves and free blacks) worked in tobacco factories. An undeter-
mined number of free black males also worked in tobacco, and when the
factories closed for economic reasons, they became a special concern. Nevertheless, the disproportionate size of the tobacco slave population gave
these slaves an advantage: their numbers assured a high visibility and an
opportunity for community formation.[7]

With the tobacco industry requiring 3,400 workers, employers increasingly relied on hired slaves to satisfy their needs. By 1860 as many as 80
percent of tobacco slaves used by manufacturers were hired from masters
who were not their owners. This practice was the second important dis-
tinguishing feature of tobacco slavery. Just as urban and industrial slavery
had been long established in the South, the practice of hiring out slaves was
an old one. Planters, small farmers, widows, or estates with surplus slaves
often eagerly hired them out to friends, relatives, neighbors, or acquaintances, to perform either agricultural work or a variety of skilled crafts and
odd jobs. The contracted hiring time varied from one hour to one year or
more, and payment was made in cash or kind, by the hour, day, month,

quarter, or year. Hired slaves resided with owners and commuted to work, or they lived with employers if necessary. When employment was not close by, rural owners who needed the income rented slaves to urban employers, generally for a year at a time. Slaves hired in southern cities performed the same kinds of jobs for employers as other slaves did for owners, but their large numbers distinguished this industrial group.[8]

By virtue of their multiple relationships with owners, employers, hiring agents, overseers, and the white community, hired slaves had opportunities for manipulation unavailable to many others. Often this maneuvering began during the annual "hiring period," from mid-December to mid-January, when employers contracted with agents or owners to rent slaves for the following year. As in the slave rentals of Richmond's Tredegar Iron Works, contracts frequently required the slaves' consent. William Towles wrote to tobacco manufacturer James Thomas, Jr., that he would rent him Edmund for a second year because the slave liked the arrangements and "informed me he thinks you wish to get him for the ensuing year."[9]

Owner Benjamin Fleet rented his slave Charles to Thomas over at least a ten-year period, always considering the slave's preferences, as demonstrated by Fleet's annual letters to Thomas. Fleet admitted in 1850 that Charles, who "has ever been a mystery to me," was "not willing to come home" from Thomas's factory. He therefore conceded that the slave should continue working for Thomas. After Charles came home to work the plantation a few years later, he feigned illness to convince Fleet he belonged in Richmond. His owner agreed that "working in the hot sun in the country would be worse for him than in the factory." After a later difficult bout with Charles's illness, Fleet wrote, "If Charles is able to work, I would prefer that he remain in the city, as I know he greatly prefers doing so." The preferences of slaves like Charles seemed to have been widespread and did not go unnoticed. During the 1850s the *Richmond Dispatch* complained that manufacturers had been "compelled, in order to secure labor, first to purchase the consent of the negroes to live with them, and then to hire them of their owners." In order to do so, they "have allowed the servants to dictate their own terms as to the amount of board money to be given, the extent of daily labor to be performed, and the price to be paid for such overwork as they may feel disposed to do." Indeed, "in most cases agents and owners allowed servants to select their own homes."[10]

Some slaves wielded nearly total control over employment contracts.

Their owners allowed them to engage in the illegal process of "self-hire," through which slaves procured employers independently, who then paid the owners either directly or through the slave himself. Although public municipal auctions were the official procedures for all hiring, slaves with the privilege to hire themselves understandably preferred to meet employers elsewhere than at the auction block. These "self-hired" slaves, many of whom were skilled tobacco hands, began the custom of gathering publicly in informally designated locations to make contacts with employers, hiring agents, and other slaves with employment advice. Regardless of how the contracts were made, slaves contributed their opinions about employers, bargaining for those with good reputations and rejecting others. This situation afforded some slaves a choice of employers, a key characteristic of free labor. The system altered the master-slave relationship to one that more closely resembled an employer-employee relationship despite the enactment of controls by the state, such as the 1801 Virginia law against self-hire, which was reinforced several times during the antebellum period. The Code of 1860 declared that any person permitting a slave under his control to go at large and trade as a freeman, or hire himself out, should be fined ten to thirty dollars.[11]

Self-hire aggravated a white community already alarmed by the high visibility and mobility of hired tobacco slaves. The *Richmond Dispatch* aimed special venom at self-hiring, which permitted the slave "to exercise a faculty of which he has less than any other quality, to wit, discretion, and under circumstances which leave him no room to give fair play to what little he has." Consequently, the slave "selects a master who he knows will indulge him, will exact little labor, and grant him many privileges and a good deal of time for privilege." The newspaper further warned the community that self-hire led to discord that would be evident as employers "danced attendance upon their black attendants" and scrambled to persuade the best slaves to come work for them. When slaves could choose their own employers, the *Dispatch* continued, those employers often promised them privileges, bribes, or higher wages in order to procure their labor. The paper criticized masters who allowed slaves the leeway to demand attractive working and living conditions, and it argued that slaves who "love to change homes at least once every two years, regardless of how they have been treated," had obtained so much freedom through self-hire that they had become a major annoyance to the city.[12]

The community was further irked by the timing of the hiring period. Each year the fevered activity of slave hiring dominated several city blocks. The sight of slaves swarming the streets raised alarm in Richmond, where the frustration represented by frequent confrontations reinforced the community's beliefs that throngs of black workers did not belong on city streets at all. Christmas was "ruined by the hiring customs . . . making it a day of dismay, discomfort, and destitution," the *Dispatch* reported. The holiday had become "a river of death" that persuaded the public to push for a renewal of the slave trade if that action would remove the burden of the winter hiring period. A few days later the same paper trusted that "the police will have an eye to this nuisance and see that it is abated."[13]

But slaves valued the winter hiring period. It allowed them a chance to relax in Richmond or to travel home to visit family and friends during Christmas, plus adequate free time to return and make hiring arrangements for the next year. All the while, depending on where they resided, their employer or owner supported them. As Virginia's industries required more and more slaves who came from farther and farther away, the statewide hiring period lengthened to three weeks. It was a practice that hired slaves expected regardless of the distance between owner and employer. Just as free Sundays or free Saturday afternoons had become customary rights, so the hiring period became routine and, in effect, nonnegotiable. It dictated the pattern of the urban labor season so that even slaves not hired out enjoyed a break from work while owners supported them. Such sojourns must have been exciting indeed, since slave records indicate that hired tobacco slaves arriving from outlying regions were young men, both single and married. Although they ranged in age from ten to sixty, the median age was nineteen and the average age, twenty-two. The typical owner hired out more than one and less than four slaves to the same employer. At the factory of James Thomas, Jr., for which detailed records exist, the turnover of slave hands was very low, with the same ones working for him as long as a decade. The competition for slaves was often intense; since salt miners in western Virginia hired slaves from the same eastern Virginia farms from which tobacco hands came, travel time required all to share long hiring periods. These occasions also involved celebrations. On Christmas Day in 1858, the *Dispatch* noted that servants were preparing to leave for home, many to "old plantations for holiday breaks, where they were born, to enjoy these rounds of frolic." On 25 December 1860, the *Dispatch* reported that tobacco factories had closed and "negroes, after drawing their winter clothing and extra money, have either gone or are making arrangements to go to country . . . where master cares for them during joyful holidays."[14]

Slaves who worked for their owners in the city may not have had opportunities for holiday trips during the hiring seasons, but they expected a reduced work schedule in the absence of their hired colleagues whose work they were unwilling to assume. When slaves feared the loss of this break, as when Richmond's Common Council tried in 1857 to stagger and shorten hiring periods, they expressed enough resentment over the denial of anticipated furloughs to prevent passage of legislation. The tenacity with which slaves clung to this period forced many firms to halt their operations completely for three weeks during hiring, just as during Reconstruction they would close factories when united worker absence prevented production.[15]

The annual contract signed by the owner and employer or by the owner and agent legitimized the hiring period and all other rental arrangements. Whatever the rental rate, which according to historian Frederick Bancroft "commonly ranged from ten to twenty per cent of market value of the slave" and averaged from one to two hundred dollars a year for tobacco hands, the minimal contractual provisions for all slaves were similar. These included two suits of clothing, one each for the summer and winter, a hat or bonnet, a blanket, and one pair of shoes—all to be charged to the employer, at a cost of about five to ten dollars a year. Medical care, required only in agent-sponsored contracts, often inhered in most others as well. Contracts provided hired slaves with a different foundation for negotiation with masters than existed for other slaves. Hired slaves could bargain with both employers and owners, positing one against the other to insist that the stipulated provisions be supplied. The same contracts limited provisions by their very itemization. Slaves who worked for their owners without contracts had no middle men to manipulate. They received no contractually itemized provisions but could request unlimited noncontractual particulars as needs arose.[16]

If promised a winter suit in a contract, for instance, a hired slave had the right to insist that either the suit or money be supplied, even if he owned one suit already. The records kept by tobacco manufacturer James Thomas, Jr., indicate that contractual agreements for clothing gave slave hands room for leverage. The records also demonstrate that older and more sophisticated slaves might wrangle cash from employers more readily than could younger, less-skilled slaves. One-fifth of Thomas's 80 skilled slaves received an undisclosed amount of money instead of their clothing allotment, while all 100 unskilled slaves received only clothing. About one-tenth of Thomas's slaves managed to procure more than the prescribed one pair of shoes or one suit of clothing per year. The percentage of hired compared to owned slaves in Thomas's crew is unknown, although in 1853 he paid taxes on only 101 slaves. The usual practice was to pay taxes on all slaves held (both owned and hired). It could be inferred that he either failed to pay taxes on some slaves or hired them on a temporary basis. There is also no indication in any earlier records as to which of Thomas's slaves were hired, but the 1860 slave census indicates that 83 percent of all tobacco slaves were hired. Applying this figure to Thomas's list of 180, it can be inferred that in 1853 he hired 149 slaves.[17]

When hired slaves operated under agent-sponsored contracts, great potential existed for maneuvering over guaranteed medical care. Employers had special responsibility for protecting their hired tobacco slaves, but they had options on their degree of involvement in treatment. The care of nonterminal illnesses ranged from personal doctors' visits to diagnosis and medication by the employers or the slaves themselves. Slaves had choices about their medical care depending on how much independence they wished to exercise. Slaves with minor ailments might choose to treat their own sicknesses, request time for self-medication at home, and keep employers distanced from their personal lives. The notorious Henry "Box" Brown, who escaped from Richmond to Philadelphia in a closed packing box, had been a hired tobacco slave when he injured his finger at work. Denied time off for adequate healing, he inflicted more damage with acid, assuring a few sick days and the opportunity to plot his escape. Brown likely would not have welcomed the close scrutiny of a doctor. James Thomas, Jr.'s, accounts, which show little turnover of hired slaves from 1850 to 1860, indicate that medical treatment varied significantly among his tobacco hands. Out of 180 tobacco slaves, approximately 50 slaves were the only ones ever treated by a doctor. A few of these received personal care as often as ten times a year.[18]

Negotiating medical care and clothing allotments, although important, was not peculiar to tobacco slaves, nor was their status as hired workers or their numerical concentration unusual. Rural, urban, and industrial slaves in other enterprises also capitalized upon these characteristics to one degree or another. Of more significance, however, were the third and fourth attributes that distinguished tobacco slaves from many other slaves throughout the South—their independent living arrangement and access to cash.

Because manufacturers could not afford to provide slave hands with adequate room and board in closely supervised urban quarters, they supported slaves by a "board system," unique to the tobacco industry. Developed in the mid-1840s for economic reasons, the board system supplied tobacco slaves with cash payments of seventy-five cents to one dollar a week to procure room and board wherever they could afford it. Sources vary as to the average cost of accommodations in the antebellum South, but most board payment estimates fall within the normal to low range. Employers supplemented board payments with cash "bonuses," common to many industries. Together, the board and bonus systems supplied key reasons why tobacco hands joined the ranks of slaves who took initiatives toward working-class activism. The only other slaves who might have been paid in this manner were those employed in the Dismal Swamp, whom Frederick Law Olmsted argued had very "independent" lives during many months of the year.[19]

The board system gave tobacco workers the choice, though limited, of where to live, a rare opportunity for slaves. The location might be in boarding houses, barracks, dormitories, or their own apartments with family or unrelated acquaintances. Henry "Box" Brown, for example, lived in an apartment he rented for his wife and children for seventy-two dollars a year. Most shelters affordable with board payments were substandard at best, but they provided slaves with the opportunity to live apart from owners and employers, often close to free blacks and other slaves. While many boarded in dwellings similar to plantation quarters or mining-camp barracks, all of which contributed to racial and class solidarity, tobacco slaves enjoyed the additional benefit of mobility. Even those who lived surrounded by whites in the home of a spouse's master, an arrangement codified by an 1857 ordinance, could choose when and where to go independently of their employers.[20]

On plantations, in mines, and at foundries when the sun set, workers could usually return freely to their quarters or barracks. But since they remained within the hailing distance of masters, their leisure time was more encumbered than that of tobacco slaves. This situation was especially true on farms and plantations where work never ended. But factory days, though long, were clearly divided; work commenced and ended with the blowing of citywide whistles. Slaves took midday dinner breaks at work but went home for supper and the evening. Henry "Box" Brown reported that tobacco workers in his factory labored "fourteen hours a day in the summer and sixteen in the winter." According to another report, tobacco factory slaves frequently arrived at work "two or three hours before daylight." This organization of time was something to which slaves and other preindustrial workers were unaccustomed but a situation they eventually internalized. It was an arrangement in which masters controlled only parts of a slave's day, leading him and the community to believe what Frederick Olmsted observed: "slaves were able to take care of themselves."[21]

The one limit to this mobility was the pass or register, which all blacks had to carry to establish their status as free or slave and where appropriate to identify their owner or employer. Most slaves needed separate passes signed for every trip that took them outside the purview of their usual domain, but tobacco slaves received general passes that allowed the necessary leeway to perform daily activities. Since it was convenient to allow slaves to live some distance from factories, employers supplied them with permanent passes that assured the freedom to travel to and from work, church, stores, and neighborhood. Still, by 1859 Richmond's black codes had been solidified into an ordinance that required all slaves to carry passes on the streets after dark. Blacks were also barred from riding in hacks and carriages, from smoking in public and carrying canes on the street, and from frequenting Capitol Square and many parks and other public grounds, including white cemeteries, unless accompanied by whites. They could not loiter on sidewalks or organize black secret societies. Black churchgoers had to disperse within thirty minutes after church services, and no one could sell liquor, guns, or knives to blacks.

This concern with controlling the black population also extended to free blacks. The Richmond Hustings Court Records reflect a significant preoccupation with registering free blacks even after they had established their status with documentation from former owners or from the counties of previous residence. Under such restrictions, forging passes was one of Richmond's most common crimes, and city ordinances fined the forger of a pass up to twenty dollars and punished the offending slave with twenty stripes. Nevertheless, in practice there was at times little to separate tobacco slaves supported by the board system from free blacks. Both were subject to the limitations enumerated by the current Ordinance on Negroes. The unique nature of tobacco slaves' living arrangements allowed them more freedom and mobility than many other slaves could imagine.[22]

The perceived threat of the board system was obvious from the six-year struggle waged against it. The battle began in earnest in January 1852 when the *Richmond Republican* attacked the system as "an injurious practice which has been increasing for years, until it has become almost universal." The *Republican* urged every slave owner and employer to "guard against it" in the new contracts they would be writing that year. The movement to revise the board system continued throughout the decade until 1858, when an ordinance to alter it finally passed. This law allowed employers to continue paying board money, but required closer surveillance, such as reporting slave locations to the mayor on a regular basis. However small the change, many manufacturers ignored the revision and continued to board slaves as they wished. They refused to sacrifice profits and an amenable workforce for the pressures of municipal restrictions.[23]

Board payments and the relative freedom of mobility, when combined with cash bonuses, made a significant difference in the lives of tobacco slaves. Both the slaves and the community experienced a major departure from the system as they had known it. Bonuses had been used as incentives for many years, not only to discipline slaves but to keep production rates high. In Virginia the salt, iron, and coal industries all paid slaves for extra work; according to one historian, since the late eighteenth century about half of all industrial slaves received bonuses usually paid in credit, in kind, or in cash at the end of the year. Tobacco bonuses, sometimes as high as two to five dollars a week, were unique, because they were paid in cash throughout the year to slaves who had the opportunity to spend the money.[24]

Since tobacco manufacturing was organized by the task system, it lent itself to piecework rewarded by bonuses. The actual job of processing tobacco into an attractive and flavorful chewing product involved a variety of skilled and unskilled tasks. Hogsheads of pressed or "prized" tobacco arrived at factories where unskilled "handlers" unpacked, dried, and sorted the choicest leaves, which were then moistened and made pliant. Skilled "stemmers" removed strips of the leaf from the bitter mid-veins or stems to be boiled in a black, syrupy mixture of licorice and sugar by skilled "dippers," then dried and sprinkled with rum, sweet oil, and various spices. "Twisters" and "lumpers" performed the most skilled tasks, shaping tobacco strips into rectangular lumps or long, thin twists. Once formed, these were placed in a large, hand-operated "wing-screw press," in which skilled "prizers" and "pressers" shaped the final product. Slaves or free blacks performed the entire process supervised by white overseers who themselves occasionally acted as dippers.[25]

Once a slave had processed forty-five pounds of tobacco, any "overwork" was rewarded with a cash bonus. Slaves were well enough off, however, so that they could occasionally refuse overwork. When and if workers did so, of course, they lowered the production levels expected by employers, but there would always be an opportunity to earn a bonus on another day, because the nature of tobacco processing made overwork a predictable and constant option. If a hand chose not to work extra hours one week, he knew the work would be available later. The decision to accept or refuse overwork, especially when made in conjunction with fellow workers, was a useful tool for the expression of collectivity and autonomy. Indeed, surviving on board payments alone, without a bonus, did not impose an extreme hardship on the slave.

Certainly, the slaves benefited by keeping the pace of work at a level where they could perform overwork, if they wished, without putting in too many extra hours. Slaves knew the time required for different tasks more intimately than did their inexperienced white overseers. That knowledge plus the unmechanized nature of tobacco manufacturing allowed slaves the option of working slowly in fulfilling the required quota and more quickly for bonuses. The ability to set the tempo gave slave hands a measure of control that would be impossible when tobacco processing became mechanized, as occurred in the 1880s.[26]

One method common to all slaves in setting the work pace was singing. Since the processing of chewing tobacco was a quiet job, songs could be easily heard. Indeed, overseers encouraged singing, "not as an art, but as an economic factor in efficiency." One manager promoted "their singing as much as we can for the boys work better while singing." Slave singing in tobacco factories became a "most celebrated tourist attraction" noted by Richmond travelers and journalists. The singing indicated to management that production was progressing at a regular pace. Some have claimed that singing indicated slave "contentment," but it more probably held workers in solidarity and helped them pass the time. It also signaled resistance, because often they sang spirituals that white management would not understand. Slaves recognized the importance of singing and manipulated management through their choral inconsistency. Aware that manufacturers bragged about their singing and relied upon it to keep production steady, slaves often stopped singing to embarrass owners during public tours or even to cause them financial loss.[27]

The most common reason that slaves stopped singing, slowed the work pace, or refused to perform overwork for bonuses was to protest unjust treatment, including whipping or other physical punishment—practices rural slave overseers had relied on for years but that became less effective in industry. No figures about the extent of physical punishment in tobacco factories exist, but there are a number of recorded incidents in which slaves launched counterattacks against their overseers. Jordan Hatcher, a slave, beat his overseer William Jackson to death with an iron poker. Some slaves provoked managers to criticize them, then attacked before the manager had a chance to deliver the first blow. Occasionally, slaves who harbored resentments about unfair treatment waited until after work hours to attack the overseer.[28]

Some slaves found that setting factories on fire was a safer and more effective way to attack management. In his study of slave criminality in Virginia, Philip Schwarz noted that the "fear of urban fires being set by slaves intensified as Richmond grew larger and larger." Henry "Box" Brown agreed. Richmond "lived in constant fear of slave fires, especially of arson by slaves." Arson generally occurred at night, limiting the loss of life, but extensive property damage sometimes forced the closing of a factory for months. Slaves then received a break in work until the factory could once again operate, but employers had to continue their support or return them to the owners. Convictions for slave arson were numerous, and perpetrators fearing harsh punishment may have found that a threat of arson could be just as effective as the act itself. At least one report exists of an arsonist who claimed responsibility for a fire that had occurred in the past and then openly warned a manufacturer that his factory would be the next to burn if certain demands were not met.[29]

In addition to attacking overseers, setting fires, and engaging in other acts of sabotage common to all slaves, tobacco slaves resisted employers by stealing, an irresistible temptation because tobacco was easy to carry out undetected, and as with other stolen items, it usually could be sold in the underground market. Richmond newspapers printed frequent reports of factory thefts; one even claimed that "tobacco manufacturers were losing more goods to thieves than any other businesses." Because slaves sold the commodity in underground economies, tobacco manufacturers particularly suffered from the "continual traffic between lawless white men and slaves." Blacks learned to deliver what whites would buy; they negotiated to make the theft worthwhile. They persuaded whites to take chances that would make black criminal traffic feasible, manipulating them to their advantage and capitalizing on the fact that blacks could not testify against whites in court. Enough people made money from goods stolen by slaves to sustain the practice regardless of its illegality.[30]

Having ready cash from their bonuses gave tobacco slaves the opportunity to support their own African Baptist and Methodist churches. It also provided entrance into theaters, horse races, cockfights, cookshops, brothels, and gambling houses. A cookshop, for example, was a restaurant that sold food and whiskey to blacks and occasionally to whites; in 1853 those owned by blacks were outlawed because "slaves [were] corrupted in them and even facilitated in escaping to the North." Seven years after passage of the law the problem remained: "Cookshops, kept by Negroes, are forbidden by law, as is the sale of ardent spirits and yet there are scores of the colored continually engaging in these lawless callings." The illegal nature of some activities, coupled with the resistance of slaves inside and outside the workplace, demonstrated the importance of these practices in defining the measure of slave independence. The intense reaction generated in the white community and its frequent condemnation of the bonus system provide strong evidence of the self-determination that tobacco slaves had attained over some aspects of their lives.[31]

As bonuses enhanced leisure time outside the scrutiny of masters the slave community participated in the process of class formation the same as all ethnic workers did. Playing and worshiping together and spending their own money were effective ways for slaves to express self-determination in their personal lives. They carved out lives separate from work that enhanced their solidarity at work. This sense of autonomy in their private lives would carry over to the tobacco factory, as it did for free laborers and for other slaves who took advantage of positions that allowed for negotiation with masters at the workplace.[32]

After emancipation free blacks continued to monopolize the labor force in Richmond's chewing tobacco industry, although they never made inroads in the newly established cigarette- and cigar-manufacturing enterprises. The city maintained its position as the leading producer of chewing tobacco without advancing much beyond the 1860 level of output, and the industry remained unmechanized until the 1880s. Restrictions on tobacco workers and other black laborers became much tighter than during slavery, however, forcing the community of blacks to draw upon the industrial relationship skills they had acquired as slaves. That role as an urban industrial slave force provided the experience needed to consolidate themselves in postwar worker activism.[33]

7

JAMES D. SCHMIDT

Overseers and the Nature of Southern Labor Contracts

"I am suffering under the most intolerable thralldom to which a poor devil was ever subjected, and unless your wisdom can afford me some relief, I must give up in despair," a young Virginia planter complained to the *Southern Planter* in December 1843. "I am afflicted with an overseer who is one of the most faithful, industrious, obstinate, hard-headed and conceited beings that ever walked on two legs." Needing the overseer's knowledge, unable to fire him because of his "hard-fisted honesty," the planter declared himself to be "the veriest slave on the plantation; for I have no will of my own." This Virginian's overblown lament expressed concisely an important type of employer-employee conflict in the Old South: that between planter and overseer. In their response, the editors of the *Planter* voiced the solution most southern agricultural reformers wanted: "discharge your overseer and attend to your business yourself."[1]

For planters, this solution was not as simple as it sounded, for common law contract rules set the terms under which conflicts between overseers and planters could be resolved. In the five decades before the Civil War, these legal constructions of the employment relation underwent a fundamental transformation. Using the terms of English master-servant discourse, antebellum northern jurists fashioned American rules for labor contracts. Agreements made for a specific time and a specific wage were deemed to be "entire," and as such, they required full performance before a worker could collect wages. Labor and legal historians have seen this development as part of the transition to capitalist wage relations. Binding laborers to their contracts through the threat of wage forfeiture offered a valuable form of labor discipline after the removal of traditional restraints on servants.[2] This legal transformation, however, did not affect all workers alike. For agricultural laborers, contract rules aimed to restrict their participation in the labor market at crucial seasons, while contracts for industrial workers attempted to maintain discipline in the workplace. In other words, employers, workers, and jurists designed labor regulations that met the needs of particular modes of production.[3]

Accounts of antebellum labor contract law usually ignore the southern experience.[4] Slavery placed most workers outside the bounds of free labor, but contract relations were not absent from the antebellum South. Hired slaves, free black workers, and urban artisans and laborers constituted a significant sector of the workforce.[5] While these workers' labor arrangements appeared in southern litigations, the dominant experience with free labor contracts and the modern wage relation came from suits involving plantation owners and their overseers.[6] Consequently, southern courts were asked repeatedly to resolve friction between these groups. As South Carolina Justice David Johnson noted in 1834, "Collisions frequently arise out of the relations of overseer and employer, and they are so varied in circumstance as to render it impossible to lay down a rule that will embrace them all."[7]

In constructing doctrines to arbitrate such disputes, southern jurists started with the same English precedents used by their northern counterparts. While most northern courts upheld the sanctity of contract by quashing attempts to apportion wages, southern courts created a much more permissive system of labor contracts. Nevertheless, as with northern doctrines, these rules resulted from the needs of the producers. Owners depended on overseers to make the crop and care for their property in slaves. They required the flexibility to dispose of overseers who threatened the stability of the plantation and endangered agricultural success. Therefore, southern courts created an agricultural contract system that in many ways was the opposite of the northern model, a system in which agricultural stability relied on the ability to violate labor agreements.

Contracts under which overseers worked varied widely. Some employers agreed to give their overseers from one-twentieth to one-fourth of the proceeds of the farm instead of wages. Others paid a cash wage plus provisions for the employee, his family, and his stock. Most offered wages of $150 to $500, payable at the end of the year.[8] North Carolina planter Robert A. Jones's dealings with his overseers illustrate the ways in which wage bargains in the early nineteenth century used all these methods. Jones paid cash wages, but simultaneously provided overseers with supplies for which they settled at year's end. In 1818, he paid P. Skiles a total of $306.50, of which $285 was a cash settlement. The remainder included a cash advance of $15 earlier in the year, $5.25 for a coffin and some geese, and twenty-five cents for "a quart of rum for Molly," presumably Skiles's wife who seems to have lost a child during the year. When Skiles left the next year, Jones employed Micajah Griffith for $250 per year, and by the time Griffith died in October 1823, he had accumulated several small debts with Jones. Jones's agreements with overseers at his two plantations at New Hope and Indian River, North Carolina, in the middle 1820s corresponded with these earlier agreements. These overseers' wages ranged between $150 and $250 per year plus inkind allowances.[9]

Once employed, overseers lived under lengthy sets of rules governing their behavior and that of slaves. Such regulations covered everything from how, when, and what to plant to specific dictates for the discipline of slaves. A Sumter County, Alabama, planter ordered his overseer to "treat the slaves placed under his control with humanity." In nearby Lowndes County, John Murray included a similar clause and added injunctions that William B. Whitely was not to leave the plantation and was "never to drink ardent spirits to intoxication, while in my employ." Other rules were more mundane. In a somewhat ironic reference to the need for fertilizer, a Savannah, Georgia, planter ordered his overseer to "make manure of everything you can."[10]

Improving the management and productivity of the plantation often appeared explicitly in overseers' contracts. Some planters offered productivity bonuses to their managers. In Mississippi, Robert Sale contracted with Harden Hariston for $650 plus a $25 bonus if he could make two hundred bales of cotton weighing five hundred pounds per bale.[11] Planters also reserved the right to discharge their overseers at will. For example, a South Carolina planter stipulated that he could discharge his overseer for good cause and be liable for only the time served rather than for the entire salary. According to an Arkansas overseer, it was "invariably understood" in the state's Red River cotton district that planters could discharge an overseer and pay him for his services and that "the overseers always reserved to themselves the right to quit at any time upon becoming dissatisfied, and to settle and receive their wages in proportion to the time they had served." A contract between overseer Jesse Whatley and planter George Jones provided for payment of $400 for the year or "thirty three dollars and thirty three cents a month if the said George Jones should wish to terminate this agreement before the end of the aforesaid year." When John Ball of South Carolina fired John E. Morton after a month, he considered the overseer's poverty and "allowed him ¼ yrs. wages which was more than he deserved."[12] At inception, overseers' contracts accepted easy dissolution and apportionment of wages.

If at-will clauses were not present and overseers abandoned their arrangements, southern jurists enforced the entirety rule with a zeal worthy of their northern brethren. *Pettigrew v. Bishop*, an 1842 Alabama decision, typified jurists' reactions to abandonment. Pettigrew had contracted with Bishop to manage twelve months for $275 plus twenty bushels of corn. He started on 1 January 1839, but left the job in November. The jury in the lower court awarded him his wages when he sued for recovery, but the state supreme court reversed the ruling. The Louisiana court considered contract abandonment in *Hays v. Marsh* and pointed out directly the threat to the plantation. Hays was an overseer on Marsh's sugar plantation and left before completing the harvest. As a result, Marsh lost forty hogsheads of sugar worth $2,500. The court denied Hays his wages, noting the need for stability. "The agricultural interests of the country are mainly under the control of this description of men [overseers]," the opinion declared, "and if they could abandon their employers in the time of greatest need . . . it is plain that great and remediless mischief would ensue."[13]

The Louisiana court realized that sugar cultivation required constant attention; thus, abandonment near harvest time could not be tolerated. As such, its decision echoed the arguments of northern jurists who enforced entirety of contract harshly against agricultural workers who absconded during harvest. Agricultural production necessitated intensive labor and intensive labor management at certain seasons, and courts in both the North and South were not prepared to allow agricultural workers to influence work arrangements to any great extent.

Most cases involving overseers, however, were not suits for apportionment of wages after abandonment of a work contract. Rather, they were actions in which overseers sought pay after being dismissed. Under such circumstances, both the common law entirety rule and the Civil Code in Louisiana required payment of the entire year's wages. Envisioned as supplying equity in contract arrangements, this side of entirety left southern planters in a predicament. If they fired an incompetent overseer in March, they might be liable to pay for the remainder of the year. Yet if they avoided this unpalatable outcome by keeping him on, they risked mismanagement of their farms and slaves.

Trying to resolve this dilemma, southern courts established a distinctive form of labor law that upheld and even encouraged the violability of contracts between planters and overseers. The leading case and impetus for change was *Byrd v. Boyd*, a decision handed down by the South Carolina court in 1825. In an opinion upholding recovery of wages by an overseer who had been dismissed, Justice Johnson affirmed that overseers could not recover when they abandoned without cause and that masters could not prevent recovery when they discharged without cause. There was, however, "a third class of cases" in which "the employer reaps the full benefit of the services which have been rendered, but some circumstance occurs which renders his discharging the overseer necessary and justified." In these cases, Johnson held, overseers could recover for the time they had served.[14]

By 1860, most other southern states had adopted *Byrd* specifically or had devised a similar rule. Using the South Carolina court's reasoning, Mississippi Justice J. S. B. Thacher noted that "the strict rule of law, governing contracts, has been much relaxed in this country in relation to those made between employer and overseer." The Tennessee Supreme Court also recognized *Byrd* in an 1853 case. William T. Jones had been fired after eight months of service. The court was quick to hold that "abuse and cruelty toward the servants, and of neglect and mismanagement of the farm and stock" constituted sufficient cause for firing him. And while the high court would not allow the lower court jury's $275 award for Jones's yearly wage, it did sanction recovery for the time actually served. "This liberal rule has been adopted in South Carolina, and we think it just and reasonable," the court declared. Courts in Alabama, Arkansas, North Carolina, Texas, and Louisiana took similar courses.[15]

Knowledge of these rules apparently became widespread among overseers. In 1858, Robert P. Ford left Catherine P. Danks's Louisiana plantation, but he was subsequently told by friends that he would be in a better position if he returned and waited to be fired.[16] If overseers possessed information about their legal remedies, the key for planters in avoiding payment of full wages was inducing the court to recognize a sufficient cause for the dismissal. As a result, civil actions for overseers' wages became investigations of the employment relation and its conflicts.

One great source of friction and a common excuse for termination was disputes about supervision and treatment of slaves. Employers such as Plowden C. J. Weston, a South Carolina rice planter, made the duty to care for their chattels unmistakably clear in contracts. "The Proprietor, in the first place," Weston emphasized, "wishes the Overseer MOST DISTINCTLY to understand that his first object is to be, under all circumstances, the care and well being of the negroes." To discover any maltreatment, many masters encouraged slaves to report complaints about overseers. J. W. Fowler of Coahoma County, Mississippi, permitted slaves to bring to him complaints about the overseer and considered genuine reports of cruelty to be "good and sufficient cause for the immediate discharge of the Overseer."[17]

Based on such reports or on firsthand information, planters often fired overseers for mismanagement or mistreatment of their slaves and the courts upheld their actions. One common form of mismanagement was simply being absent from the plantation. In North Carolina, for instance, Gray Armstrong found that his overseer, John Fly, was "very often seen at grog shops, and at a bowling alley at the depot, in the working hours of the day and on sundays, during the three months while he had charge on the farms . . . and was at one time observed playing at cards at about 10 o'clock in the morning, of a week day. Frequently during this time, he was proven to be excited with spirits, but not drunk."[18] Fly claimed that his activities did not cause "any special injury" to Armstrong, but the North Carolina court disagreed. Armstrong, the court ruled, "was not bound to wait until his crops were ruined before he removed the cause of the impending evil."[19]

More common than disregard for the plantation were complaints that overseers accumulated too much control to themselves. Many overseers, as William Scarborough has pointed out, saw themselves as semi-professionals. As such, they wanted more influence in plantation decision-making than planters were willing to concede. Texas overseer Thomas P. Rutledge quit his employers in 1847 because they would not allow him to whip slaves, while Mississippi cotton planter Theophilus Prichard quarreled with Richard Martin in 1851 over which tasks should be assigned to which slaves. A Georgia overseer refused to commence work under his contract unless the planter "would give up to him the plantation, negroes, and stock to his entire and exclusive control and management." Generally, courts refused to countenance such assertions of worker control. "An overseer contracts to do everything according to the means furnished by his employer, which a prudent and economical man would do in attending to his own business," a Mississippi judge intoned in 1854. A North Carolina jurist was even more direct. "It cannot for a moment be admitted," Justice William H. Battle wrote in 1859, "that an overseer has a right to control the slaves under his charge, against the known wishes, much less the positive commands, of the owner." The Louisiana court considered refusal by the overseer to follow the planter's explicit orders on the method of whipping slaves to be "sufficient cause" for discharging him.[20]

The most prevalent justification for discharge was cruelty and injury to slaves. Sometimes such charges were brought in conjunction with allegations of sexual impropriety. South Carolina planter M. D. C. Cane claimed that Samuel E. Dwyer's "conduct with the women of the plantation was grossly and openly immoral."[21] More often owners simply alleged injury to their chattels. While courts did not construe threats of violence to slaves as grounds for discharge, actual harm usually justified an end to the contract. In 1838 Dabney Garth, the overseer on Bird Posey's Missouri farm, beat a slave to death with a handspike. The Missouri Supreme Court held that Posey was justified in firing Garth. "He not only had a right to discharge him," Justice William Scott declared, "but it was his duty to do it." In 1848, the Louisiana Court examined a case in which an overseer's treatment of a slave had been "of a most revolting character," held that the slave codes governing use of violence by masters applied to overseers, and denied recovery of wages. In 1855 the same court considered the gruesome case of a runaway slave named Jim Crack who had been beaten to death with a whip and a handsaw by overseer W. G. Kennedy. Trying to achieve a zero balance in order not to sanction the overseer's action for his earnings, the court allowed the planter's counterclaim for damages to offset his employee's suit for wages.[22]

Mistreatment of slaves and mismanagement of the plantation were the most common reasons for firing an overseer, but numerous dismissals stemmed from a more general conflict between southern planters and their hired managers. Many planters agreed with the Alabamian who wrote that "the great mass of overseers are totally unqualified" to manage slaves. Overseers fought back at these charges. One complained bitterly that he and his fellows were expected to manage plantations and slaves "for wages scarcely if at all in advance of that given to an Irish ditcher." Another suggested sarcastically that "the wise and good show some charity, and instruct and pull us up out of the mire and dirt, rather than getting on our shoulders, and bidding us GOD speed."[23]

With these tensions in the background, disagreements over management of the plantation often became contests about personal honor that ended in violence between employer and employee. These disputes came before the courts when owners or overseers tried to use personal quarrels to excuse breaches of contract. In *Byrd v. Boyd*, the conflict involved southern constructions of class, gender, and honor. The overseer had "managed the crop well, but in July he made use of abusive language to the [planter's] daughter for which he was turned away." In another South Carolina litigation, Henry Suber claimed that he left H. D. Vanlew because a slave woman had complained that he "was too familiar with her" to Vanlew's wife, who had believed the allegation. Suber told the court that "he felt he was above any such thing." A Louisiana overseer added a suit for slander to his claim for wages when his employer accused him of stealing, and a Texas manager claimed $500 damages for "injury to his reputation as an overseer."[24]

Such disputes grew out of a volatile combination of class tension, republican assertions of personal male independence, the honor ethic, and racial ideology that made overseers unwilling to be treated as servants. For example, Richard Martin explained (and the Mississippi court accepted) that while he would be glad to do his duty he "would not worship" his employer. At Darlington, South Carolina, Caleb Boone had a similar reaction to his employer's aristocratic pretensions. Boone believed that John Lyde "wanted him to knuckle to him too much," and when Lyde tried to fire him, the overseer "got into a great rage and got a rail to strike Lyde." Boone's confrontation with Lyde did not produce actual violence, but other conflicts did. Near Macon, Georgia, Benjamin Stiles ambushed his employer, Simeon Henderson, and "brutally beat him with the barrel of his gun." Justice Eugenius A. Nisbet deemed this act a breach of contract and "incompatible with the peaceful exercise of all the rights of dominion over his property on the part of the employed." Nevertheless, the Georgia court and others allowed apportionment of contracts in such situations.[25]

These conflicts centered on a fundamental disagreement about the distribution of power in the employment relation. Planters and agricultural writers believed that contracts established the undisputed dominance of owners. "Subordination to the master is the first of an overseer's duties," the editors of the *Southern Planter* asserted bluntly. An overseer must be unfailingly loyal. "Of his own free will he has sold them [*sic*] to [his employer] for one year, and as an honest man he must stand by his bargain." While the journal's editors framed the terms of power within a mixture of the lexicons of slavery, and capitalist contracts, another contributor placed them in gender discourse. To advance the interests of his employer, the writer noted, an overseer "has one of the requisites of a good wife, 'a keeper of the home.'" Some overseers, at least, recognized such assertions of power and refused to accept them. In regard to planters' unwillingness to contract early for the next year, one overseer noted, "I cannot see what Mr. Farmer wants, unless it is to put the overseer off until the last hour of the day, and then he will have him in his power, and say you may take this, or that, and let it alone."[26]

While most of the events leading to discharging an overseer resulted from the nature of slavery or from the class tensions and code of honor it produced, a few cases resulted more directly from the exigencies of the market. In considering such actions, some justices recognized an additional role for the apportionment of contracts. In 1849, an Arkansas judge held that instead of recovering their whole wages, overseers could recoup only the actual loss or injury they had sustained. If such a rule were not adopted, he believed, "extreme injustice" would befall planters who found themselves unable to retain an employee because of "events that could not have been foreseen and were beyond their control." A Texas jurist also justified recovery for time served by the vagaries of the market. "The planter might, in the course of the year, remove elsewhere, or his plantation might be sold for debts," he noted. "[W]ould there be any justice in an overseer's exacting compensation for the whole year?"[27]

While these two judges focused solely on planters' needs as capitalists, such candid recognitions of market forces were in the minority. Insofar as it pertained to overseers, southern labor contract law was an expression of capitalism only peripherally. Instead of upholding the sanctity of contracts as their northern counterparts did, many southern courts encouraged violability by expanding grounds for discharge and allowing overseers to collect for the time served. Such practices stemmed from the power relationship between planter and overseer, the needs of staple agriculture, and most of all, the peculiarities of slavery. The high level of conflict between owners and managers meant that disputes occurred almost inevitably. Jurists acknowledged these "collisions" and relaxed the entirety rule for discharge to accommodate the prevailing practice of open contracts. Plantation agriculture fostered this course. The planter required an overseer who would produce crops and maintain stability and good health among the owner's valued slave property. If the overseer failed, he must be dismissed immediately, or both crops and slaves might be lost.

By the time of the Civil War, labor contract law had diverged along sectional paths. In the South as in the North, differing methods of agriculture and industry underlay different forms of contract law. For southerners, control of free labor rested ultimately with the planter-merchant elite. To maintain control, they needed the ability to dismiss workers, especially overseers, at will and not face legal consequences. In contrast, northerners had come to see the sanctity of contract as essential to labor discipline, especially in agriculture. As such, contractual relations in labor resulted not from undifferentiated capitalism itself but from the specific needs of its many forms of production.[28]

Hope versus Reality
The Emancipation Era Labor Struggles of Memphis Area Freedmen, 1863–1870

Predictably, emancipation engendered a mosaic of hopes and aspirations among its black beneficiaries with proprietary rights over their own labor being an especially critical expectation of freedmen. Surely freedom meant, blacks confidently assumed, the right to decide how, when, for whom, and at what rate of remuneration they would toil. The unfolding events of the emancipation era, however, would serve compellingly to illustrate how virtually all freedmen's rights continuously were called into question, whether ostensibly guaranteed or merely presumed.

As the site of one of the largest African-American urban communities in postbellum America, Memphis and its surrounding rural environs quickly emerged as a major regional battleground for labor struggles between area blacks and those who would undermine their freedom.[1] In the decade before the Civil War, Memphis, largely because of its strategic location in the Mississippi Valley between St. Louis and New Orleans, seemed the most promising of all southern cities. With the coming of secession those prospects seemingly dimmed, but the city's early fall to advancing Union forces spared it the destruction suffered by other urban areas in the region.[2]

As a federally occupied city, Memphis experienced a deluge of incoming migrants, especially self-emancipated blacks. By early 1863, roughly six months following the fall of Memphis, blacks conservatively numbered more than seven thousand, compared to some four thousand, both slave and free, three years earlier.[3] This escalation in the black population soon spawned a major and recurring concern; namely, would blacks of their own volition endeavor to provide for themselves irrespective of their legal status, which at the time was still murky? That is, would blacks—without being forced—work to feed, clothe, and shelter themselves? The conventional wisdom among whites, northerners as well as southerners, was that blacks needed to be prodded, perhaps even coerced.[4]

The military commanders of Memphis during the war assumed a worse case scenario in addressing this issue. General William T. Sherman, Memphis's first commander, announced in June 1862, almost a month before reaching the city, that slaveowners had nothing to fear from him. He would only consider actions against slavery if its continued existence aided the Confederacy. Sherman wrote a friend that "set[ting] loose negroes too fast" would not enhance the Union cause.[5] In keeping with these sentiments Sherman, upon assuming command on 19 July 1862, moved swiftly to discourage fleeing ex-slaves from entering the city. He initially ordered all able-bodied black males of questionable legal status to work on local fortifications. In exchange for their labor these conscripts were to receive rations, clothes, and one pound of chewing tobacco per month, but no wages. Sherman did indicate that careful records should be kept so that after the war "a fair and equitable settlement" could be made with each laborer.[6]

Sherman eventually expanded his original order to the further detriment of area blacks. Under these amended provisions slaveowners could examine work rosters for runaways. Assuming that prior ownership could be established, the chattel in question would be returned to the planter making the claim. The post quartermaster under the amended order could also recruit as a standing pool of laborers at least one hundred blacks and, when needed, any additional conscripts from the ranks of refugees.[7] Sherman's actions while commander in Memphis were continued by later commanders. To a man, they followed policies that were in keeping with the spirit of the precedents Sherman set.

Brigadier General James Veatch, one of Sherman's successors, took even sterner measures against the influx of refugees. All idlers and vagrants, Veatch ordered in July 1863, had ten days to secure employment or return to the countryside. Violators could expect to be imprisoned or forced to perform hard labor on military fortifications. The order further mandated the creation of a registration system requiring blacks to carry a certificate of identification at all times. Local planters and employers were admonished though not required to make available to the military the names and descriptions of their laborers.[8] Still, even these measures, surely as strict as any implemented previously, proved more symbolic than successful. Indeed, neither these nor subsequent actions effectively stemmed the tide of incoming refugees at Memphis or in other liberated areas of the South where military commanders made use of similar tactics.

Such procedures did reinforce a general perception of blacks as irresponsible and given to idleness. This perception, which was born of paternalism, both colored and informed the operational design of Civil War-era public policy toward freedmen. It was rare, to be sure, when public policies with respect to freedmen did not involve an assumption that blacks could not manage their own affairs, the corollary being that others were more competent to make decisions for them. White reformers, for all their missionary zeal, remained advocates and practitioners of paternalism, believing that the slave experience had caused blacks to descend into the depths of irresponsibility, ignorance, and immorality; and these failings, moreover, could only be ameliorated through the assistance of whites. The struggle blacks had to wage was obvious. They had to demonstrate their capacity for self-directed effort as well as establish property rights over their bodies. But the realization of these goals for the masses of freedmen would prove agonizingly elusive.

During the war, opportunities for area freedmen to prove themselves were infrequent at best. The first genuine and perhaps only real chance came with the arrival in west Tennessee of John Eaton, chaplain of the Twenty-seventh Ohio Infantry Volunteers. In November 1862, General Ulysses S. Grant dispatched Eaton to Grand Junction, Tennessee, with orders to "take charge of the . . . [refugees] that come into camp in the vicinity of Grand Junction, organizing them into suitable companies for working . . . and set[ting] them to work picking, ginning and bailing all cotton now cut and ungathered in the field[s]."[9] The contraband population, the order additionally stipulated, was to be clothed and "in every way provided for, out of their [own] earnings so far as practical." This goal could be achieved, the order suggested, by organizing blacks into working parties either to save cotton or to labor on railroads and steamboats. Using blacks in other capacities was not ruled out. They were not, however, to be coerced "into the service of the government, or be enticed away from their homes except . . . [for] military necessity."[10]

Perhaps realizing the magnitude and gravity of the refugee problem, Grant later expanded that directive. It now provided both the policies and the administrative structure to be used in the supervision of blacks, not only in Grand Junction but in the entire western sector of Tennessee and throughout much of the Mississippi Valley. Not surprisingly, John Eaton assumed the newly created position of general superintendent of contrabands for Tennessee and Arkansas. The appointment of lesser functionaries, assistant superintendents for appropriate districts in particular, became the responsibility of Eaton.[11] For the Memphis district Eaton appointed Chaplain A. S. Fiske of the Fourth Regiment of Minnesota Volunteers.

Eaton believed that in Fiske he had found an administrator who possessed the twin attributes of efficiency and compassion and who would work to relieve suffering and despair in the district.[12] As expected, Fiske was a model of efficiency. Furthermore, he worked effectively with Eaton to produce many creative and innovative proposals for black self-sufficiency. Surely the most ambitious was a project to begin a plantation leasing system. As envisaged by the two, blacks would be granted leases on federally controlled abandoned lands. There would be no direct government supervision of black lessees unless circumstances dictated. In effect, government adopted the role of absentee landowner with the benevolent intent of helping blacks in the transition from slavery to freedom.[13]

When submitted to superiors, Eaton's proposal was quickly and decisively rejected. Rather than encouraging the entrepreneurial and self-help spirit embodied in his proposal, the federal government had decided to mobilize blacks for military service and plantation labor.[14] This decision obviously meant that most blacks would be relegated to work as freed laborers on many of the same plantation lands they had hoped to lease themselves. Obviously, too, the decision was a major setback in the labor struggles of area blacks, because it meant that the government implicitly rejected out-of-hand the proposition that blacks could work independently in their own interests. Further, and ultimately most significantly, the federal government by virtue of its decision set an important public policy precedent regarding freedmen.

A government-sponsored plantation leasing system, however, did emerge. In March 1863, Adjutant General Lorenzo Thomas arrived in Memphis to direct the effort. Moving quickly, he immediately authorized the leasing of most local abandoned lands "to persons of proper character and qualification." It is not known if this provision was exclusionary in intent, since before receiving the government's decision regarding this proposal Eaton had already placed orders for seeds, plows, and other farm implements in anticipation of cultivating with black labor the abandoned plantations next to local refugee camps. Whether intentionally exclusionary or not, it did have the effect of eliminating freedmen. Blacks appeared only rarely among the lease recipients, most of whom were local planters and northern speculators. Lessees were not expected to make any advance payments to the government, perhaps in recognition of the capital investment needed to run a plantation. Under the terms of the lease, the federal government levied a tax in lieu of rent payment on all crops produced. The rates were set at two dollars per four-hundred-pound bale of cotton and five cents per bushel of corn or potatoes—amounts that allowed for a copious margin of profit. The leases further stipulated that leaseholders satisfy their labor needs through contractual arrangements with local blacks seeking employment. These contracts, the first of their kind among area freedmen, lasted for ten months, from March to January. During that time lessees agreed to "feed, clothe and treat humanely" those blacks in their employ.[15]

General Thomas's order also specified a wage structure predicated on the age and sex of the laborers to which lessees must strictly adhere. Under that structure all able-bodied males over the age of 15 were to receive seven dollars a month, women over 15 five dollars, and children between 12 and 15 half these rates. Lessees specifically were forbidden to employ children under age 12 as field hands.[16]

This order created a special supervisory commission as well. The commission consisted of four supervisors, one of whom was John Eaton, who with George Field, Captain A. E. Shickle, and the Reverend D. S. Livermore supervised "leasing [abandoned] plantations and deal[ing] justly with the interests of employer and employed."[17] Besides his appointment as supervisor, Eaton also agreed to serve as Thomas's assistant. Eaton appreciated the dual appointment no doubt because of the expanded responsibilities the positions afforded.

For blacks, however, there could be very little rejoicing or reassurance. They had lost the opportunity to pursue perhaps their most desired objective, that of becoming independent landowners. Instead, they were expected to return to the familiar plantation fields of the mid-South, albeit as wage laborers rather than as slaves. For blacks these developments formed a medley of Civil War-era precedents that directly and adversely affected their life circumstances.

Eaton, for his part, seemed not at all perturbed that Thomas's interest in blacks extended only to their usefulness as plantation and military laborers. The general's apparent lack of concern is subject to speculation, but it may well have been due to a personal conviction that the government's plan of plantation leasing would not succeed. On at least one occasion he called the plan experimental, tentative, and "without doubt faulty in many particulars." Still, he insisted, the aim of the plan was to "benefit the Negroes, and in cases where the lessees proved wise, humane, or even manageable, it fulfilled in practice the hope of its originators." So it is likely, and perhaps very probable, that Eaton viewed the Thomas initiative as only temporarily preempting his own efforts to assist blacks in becoming propertied and self-supporting.[18]

With encouragement and assistance from General Grant, Eaton secured toward his stated objective the purchase of a local tract of land. The site was President's Island, located just beyond the Memphis landing in the Mississippi River. Although many specifics surrounding the transfer of ownership of the island are unknown, clearly the federal government purchased the property from G. W. Seward and George Wells in December 1864 for four thousand dollars.[19] In the year and a half before its purchase, the island served as a refugee camp and was the site of an orphan asylum for black children. At the time the island was sold it supported perhaps as many as three thousand blacks, both adults and children. In addition to the support that island residents provided through their own efforts, the federal government and private philanthropic groups occasionally furnished issues of rations, clothing, and other items of assistance.[20]

In the months immediately following the purchase of President's Island, all arable and unencumbered land was divided into individual family plots or home farms. The specific legal circumstances under which black families held these farms, that is, if by lease or some other arrangement, are unclear. They apparently were expected to engage in subsistence farming and to be principal purveyors of wood for local consumption on the island as well as in Memphis.[21] Even so, the President's Island experiment was short-lived and fraught with unforeseen difficulties. Flooding of large parts of the island had long been a perennial problem, but during the winter of 1864 and spring of 1865 it was worse than usual. Most residents had to vacate their homes and move to higher ground. Those not moving often found themselves waterlogged. The high water, lasting several months, precluded spring planting. The cutting and gathering of wood also languished, and diseases caused widespread suffering, which often led to death. Realizing no doubt that some might misinterpret this unfortunate turn of events, the local Superintendent and Provost Marshal of Freedmen, T. A. Walker, counseled caution and understanding. That original expectations for the island had fallen short, Walker maintained, should "not be attributed to any lack of effort on [the] part [of residents], as we feel that nothing has been neglected[;] . . . all efforts to prevent [failure]" were taken.[22]

As demonstrated by subsequent events, Walker's concern was perhaps well founded. Less than six months after his appeal for understanding, Freedmen's Bureau officials in Tennessee ordered all operations on President's Island stopped. Without more data it is impossible to fathom precisely what considerations led to the decision to close President's Island. Apparently, it was made without consulting local officials, who expressed surprise when ordered to end operations on the island.[23] The failure at President's Island, then, resulted in large part from the government's lack of a sustained commitment to the project. At Davis Bend, Mississippi, by comparison, where the intent was also to create a legion of black landowners, the government had a decidedly stronger commitment. Actually, Davis Bend was to be the fulfillment of Grant's dream of a "Negro Paradise."[24] No comparable commitment, even with Grant's approval, was in evidence at President's Island. Without such support, a project involving black landownership had little chance of success.

Jurisdictional disputes among agencies were often a principal reason for the lack of a more resounding commitment by the federal government to projects intended to benefit freedmen. A case in point is the Yeatman-Mellan initiative of 1864. This plan, which grew from a collaborative effort between James Yeatman, president of the Western Sanitary Commission, and William Mellan, supervising special agent of the Treasury Department, embodied a blueprint for the systematic redress of many of the documented abuses of freedmen in the Mississippi Valley.[25]

This initiative, no matter how well intended, created immediate opposition. Eaton and others in the Freedmen's Department argued that the proposal, however disguised, represented an attempt to usurp part of their agency's authority over the affairs of ex-slaves. As a result, the Freedmen's Department vigorously opposed many provisions in the plan. Three recommendations in the proposal inspired their most vehement objections. These included raising wage rates to between $10 and $25 per month for all agricultural laborers, providing protection to blacks from physical violence at the hands of Confederate guerillas, and supervising more closely the contractual relations between freedmen and planters. After more than a year of wrangling over these proposed measures, Eaton and the Freedmen's

Department succeeded in having wage rates set at between $3.50 and $10 per month plus rations and clothing. The agency also claimed dominion and purview over aspects of freedmen's affairs that Congress had earlier delegated to the Treasury Department. Such interagency bickering continued, and it diverted time and energy from efforts to ameliorate the plight and uniquely vulnerable circumstances of freedmen.[26]

On balance, nevertheless, the war and the developments it wrought had begun to move blacks inexorably away from their prewar condition as chattel and toward a status resembling that of free labor, albeit with its own abuses and degradation. Conspicuously absent from the wartime retreat from involuntary servitude, however, were commitments and transitional structures of opportunities to assist blacks in becoming propertied, which was the key to any real chance they had of achieving genuine emancipation. So while the war dramatized the possibility of change, it provided no assurance as to the inevitability of change. In essence, the war had merely raised the possibility of improvement, leaving events of the postbellum epoch to determine the scope and specifics of more consequential change in the status of freedmen.

Memphis-area freedmen greeted the end of the war with the same enthusiasm and ebullience of others in the emancipated population across the South. They did so despite the myriad of disappointments associated with their experiences as "free laborers" during the war, believing no doubt that what had not been achieved in wartime could be in its aftermath.[27] As liberated men and women they expected to exercise the generally accepted range of freedoms, not the least of which was the right to control their own labor. The depth and resolve of blacks' optimism, however, would certainly not go untested. Indeed, the end of the war and the ensuing postbellum era, especially the years between 1865 and 1870, accelerated efforts to define more sharply and in increasingly narrower terms the status of freedmen. At the center of these efforts was an attempt to have blacks acquiesce to an existence that emphasized structured, if not deferred, freedom; in short, blacks should accept limitations on their freedom in the name of postwar realities and for the good of all concerned.

Such admonitions came from many quarters, most notably from white southerners, planters in particular, and even northerners, many of whom worked as Freedmen's Bureau operatives in the postbellum South. Most blacks expressed little surprise that white southerners tried to convince them that their freedom necessarily had limited implications, but they were surely befuddled when much the same advice came from those they regarded as friends and benefactors. Blacks expected that white northerners as their "liberators," particularly those with government affiliation, would assist them in the realization and validation of every aspect of their emancipation.[28] This abiding belief by many blacks that the white North stood for the cause of freedmen soon gave way to a more sobering recognition.

White northerners, freedmen came to realize, whether philanthropists or bureaucrats, brought with them to the South visions and designs of societal regeneration predicated on the experiences of their own society, which only two generations earlier had abandoned the peculiar institution in favor of free labor and industrialization. Consequently, northerners envisioned a reconstructed South in which free labor was to be the cornerstone of the new economic order. Still, these same northerners willingly conceded that at times coercive supervision of labor was justified.[29]

Freedmen's Bureau labor policies in postwar Memphis and west Tennessee compellingly demonstrated the application and use of state-sanctioned coercion. Davis Tillson, the bureau's first Memphis subdistrict commissioner, left no doubt about his position on the possible use of compulsion. He quickly served notice that force would be used when deemed appropriate in realizing labor-policy objectives. Blacks would be required, Tillson declared, and if necessary forced, to find gainful employment, lest they fall victim to idleness and dependency. Neither circumstance was acceptable, and to minimize the possibility of either, the bureau would compel blacks to sign labor contracts or physically remove them from the city by use of the military.[30]

The rigidity of these policies harked back to the war years when Sherman and other military commanders of the city pursued similar practices in an effort presumably to promote "an industrious and enterprising spirit" among freedmen. Although apparently faring no better than his wartime predecessors, Tillson more than once received praise in the local white media for the bureau's attempts to put blacks to work.[31] But Tillson's efforts merely signaled the beginning of the campaign to carry out the bureau's policy objectives. All three of his successors, two of whom were also brigadier generals, Nathan Dudley and Platt Runkle, and the third a lieutenant colonel, Fred Palmer, followed his example, though generally less zealously.

In opting to continue a system of enforced contracts the federal government pushed ahead with a practice that during the war had proven difficult
to administer. Postwar policymakers, nevertheless, believed in the basic
concept. Better administration and uniformity, they insisted, would surely
guarantee success. Toward this end, the agency added personnel under a
directive from the commissioner of the Freedmen's Bureau, General O. O.
Howard, in the fall of 1865 with an eye toward greater efficiency through
closer scrutiny and oversight. Most of the new bureau employees were to be
local agents assigned to a specific county within each subdistrict. These
men largely came from the ranks of recently retired Union Army officers.
Once appointed they assumed the newly created title of county superintendent, adding yet another layer to the bureau's organizational structure.
They directed all bureau activities at the county level, and their immediate
supervisor was the subdistrict commissioner. Through their appointments,
the bureau hoped to deal more adequately and responsibly with the needs
and problems of constituents at the grass roots, particularly in matters of
labor relations. Indeed, with the additional personnel the bureau fully
anticipated an expanded role in drafting, negotiating, and monitoring labor
contracts between freedmen and planters.[32]

The agency's surviving records indicate that the bureau enjoyed at least a
modicum of early success in realizing this particular policy objective. Ex-
tant "arranged" contracts from the period provide the most compelling
prima facie evidence in this regard. Approximately 1,600 contracts have
survived from the year 1865 for Memphis and Shelby County. More than 15
percent, or 236 contracts, were from February through May 1865. These
contracts, having been arranged through the local office of the superintendent of freedmen, were neither bureau negotiated nor approved. The bureau
negotiated the remaining 85 percent, or 1,339 contracts, between June and
December 1865.[33] As reflected in Table 8.1 the number of arranged contracts
peaked in 1866 when the bureau negotiated nearly 1,700 labor agreements.
In the two years after 1866, the number of such arrangements dropped
sharply, first by over 40 percent and finally by fully two-thirds. There were
several reasons for this trend, the first and most significant being budget
cuts that increasingly undermined the bureau's capacity to negotiate and
oversee labor contracts. Furthermore, the lack of bureau oversight meant
that labor contracts, to the extent that they continued to be arranged at all,
were left to freedmen and planters.

Table 8.1. Contract Laborers by Marital Status and Family Type, 1865–1868

Year	Single		Couples With Children		Couples Without Children	
	male/female		couples/laborers		couples/laborers	
1865	1,374	36	59	375	37	74
1866	1,502	24	66	417	31	62
1867	856	17	43	263	24	48
1868	564	9	34	195	18	36

Year	Single Parent (Male) With Children		Single Parent (Female) With Children		Other Family Variant (i.e., extended)	
	families/laborers		families/laborers		families/laborers	
1865	29	147	19	92	21	113
1866	42	181	24	116	19	78
1867	21	109	16	59	13	46
1868	13	41	7	29	5	19

During the initial phase of bureau activity, more than 2,200 area freedmen entered contract employment arrangements, more than half of whom were single males. Another 800 blacks were bound contractually as members of a variety of family configurations. The most common of the latter were nuclear family units consisting of a father, wife, and children; a husband and wife only; a father and children; or a mother and children. The average age of single men contracting to work was twenty-seven years compared to age twenty-nine for their married counterparts. Unattached fathers with children, by contrast, averaged thirty years of age, and mothers with children, thirty-one years.[34]

A clear majority, some 56 percent, of blacks under contract in 1865 labored on large farms of over one hundred acres where the average number of workers was thirteen. This figure contrasts with the nearly 45 percent of freedmen who toiled on small farms of one hundred acres or less with a workforce that averaged seven laborers. Moreover, whether the venue was a large or small farm, the typical agricultural laborer was a single black male under thirty years of age whose length of contractual service was normally eight to ten months, although occasionally a shorter time period was arranged. Other terms of these labor agreements appeared in a bureau-sanctioned contract form, hereafter referred to as Contract A, which specifically called for the payment of laborers in monetary wages at monthly intervals. Wages were to be predicated on potential productivity or grade, i.e., sex and age of laborers. Under such arrangements single men aged twenty to forty years received the highest wage, usually between $10 and $25 per month. As indicated in Table 8.2, the average monthly wage for males was about $15.

Males contracting in family units received a combined wage for the labor of household members. The exact amount depended on the number, sex, and age of those making up the family unit. The more males present in such families the higher the negotiated wage. Generally, a nuclear family contracting to work in 1865 expected a combined wage of between $18 and $50 per month, or $300 to $360 annually. Family contracts involving a father without spouse, plus children (especially male offspring), commanded as high as $400 per year, or about $33 per month. Black women without husbands, plus children, fared less well, receiving wages of $20 per month, or $100 per year.[35]

Besides wages, Contract A expressly required employers of freedmen to provide "quarters, fuel, substantial and healthy rations, all necessary, medical attendance, [and] supplies in case of sickness." But noticeably absent from Contract A were references both to matters of breach of agreement by either party and to possible penalties. Not even the specific duties to be performed by employed laborers were enumerated.[36] Contract A was almost identical to the contractual document used during the war by the Freedmen's Department and the Memphis office of the Superintendent of Freedmen. Upon superseding these entities, the Memphis subdistrict branch of the Freedmen's Bureau, beginning with the tenure of Tillson, adopted the existing contract form and used it as the primary document of employment arrangement.[37]

During the two and a half years after 1865, there was an inexorable retreat from the rigid application of and adherence to the terms of the bureau-sponsored Contract A. In particular, that period featured a decline in the bureau-preferred mode of labor compensation, that of monthly wages, in

Table 8.2. Average Monthly and Yearly Money-Wages of Black Agricultural Workers by Gender and Family, 1865–1868

Payment Interval	1865			1866			1867			1868			Percentage Difference 1865–1868		
	Men	Women	Family	Men	Women	Family	Men	Women	Family	Men	Women	Family	Men	Women	Family
Monthly Wages	$15	$12	$34	$12	$7.50	$25	$10	$6	$20	$10	$5	$20	−$5	−$7	−$10
Annual Money Wages	$150	$100	$330	$144	$96	$250	$100	$72	$230	$100	$64	$231	−$50	−$36	−$69

favor of a specified shared interest in crops to be grown, which could be either in complete or partial lieu of monetary remuneration. This type of arrangement is hereafter referred to as Contract B, with cotton and corn being the crops of shared interest. Certainly this change was evident, though not dramatically so, during the first half of 1866. By the fall and winter of that year the change had become decidedly more pronounced. Whereas in early 1866 (according to the surviving records), less than half the contracts of the bureau reflected the shared interest clause, by the latter part of the year considerably more than half did so. Over the ensuing year and a half, the percentage of shared interest contracts continued to rise, eventually reaching a threshold of at least two-thirds by 1868.[38]

This drift toward a shared or delayed system of labor remuneration was at the center of a postemancipation process of redefining patterns of agrarian work structures in the South. This process was driven by many of the same forces that collectively orchestrated postbellum southern economic resuscitation. Primary among these forces that would shape postwar southern economic recovery was credit, or more precisely, the relative lack of it.

Uncompensated emancipation, postbellum planters quickly and painfully realized, had not only stripped them of capital in slaves, thereby destroying existing asset structures, but worse still, it had seriously eroded, if not irrevocably compromised, their credit-worthiness. Indeed, without their wealth collateral in human chattel, planters faced the problem of attempting and possibly failing to gain access to what had become highly restricted and expensive forms of agricultural credit.[39] Quite literally, postwar planters confronted a credit crisis of mammoth proportions that threatened their very existence and, consequently, southern economic recovery.

Some measure of the depth of the planters' desperation in attempting to access credit can be gauged from the observations of Whitelaw Reid. Based on his travels throughout west Tennessee and other parts of the cotton belt within the lower Mississippi Valley, Reid found that "scores of planters [are] . . . already announcing their anxiety to borrow money on almost any conceivable terms to carry on operations for the next year [1866]." "From the interior of Mississippi," Reid further observed, "small planters . . . proposed to a heavy capitalist, in considerable numbers to borrow . . . ten to fifteen thousand dollars [and] to mortgage their plantations as security for the loan . . . [by consigning] one-half the crop as interest for the year's use of money."[40] Even J. D. B. DeBow, a southerner and one of the nineteenth century's foremost authorities on the region's antebellum and postbellum economy, worried about the credit difficulties of his postwar planter contemporaries. "Planters find it impossible," he wrote in 1866, "to produce advances to work the estates. Capital is too cautious to seek such adventures. The capital and labor that was to have come from the North or Europe have not yet appeared."[41]

The loss of absolute and unilateral control over labor supply decisions further compounded the dearth of credit available to planters attempting to revive the southern economy. It was a loss that, in turn, had the twin effects of severely undermining their hegemony over the production process while simultaneously raising the real cost of labor services. This dilemma clearly meant that planters would have to reach an accommodation with former slaves, particularly concerning the remuneration for labor. At war's end freedmen knew little of the collapse of the credit system and hardly were predisposed to be sympathetic to the plight of their ex-masters. Instead, they were far more preoccupied with concerns of self-interest, namely, efforts to become landowning agrarians. Blacks reasoned that being landowners would insulate them from having to return to the land as mere laborers, possibly threatening their freedom and future. Thus, battle lines existed for an almost certain clash between freedmen and planters. Such a confrontation would have profound implications for the South as well as planters and freedmen. Planters, for their part, sought to direct the course of developments toward the implementation of several forms of delayed payments and the continuation of the prewar gang-labor work arrangements. Planters maintained that both were required, given their precarious financial circumstances and the need for efficiency in resuming production and economic activity in the South.

Planters absolutely believed, despite many arguments to the contrary, that the most efficient labor group for black workers was the antebellum work gang.[42] Furthermore, the insistence of planters on remunerating laborers through various forms of delayed payments, while certainly informed by economic considerations, was also indicative of a certain mindset about blacks. In advocating post-harvest labor payments, planters hoped to ensure against what they perceived as a tendency by blacks, if remunerated in money wages, weekly or monthly, to abscond every payday and not return to work until their money was spent.[43]

Local planters also worried, with some justification, about the possibility of fraud when dealing with labor brokers. Walter Cartwright, a black labor agent who supplied workers to area planters at five dollars a head in 1865 and early 1866, was accused not only of paying a twenty-five cent kickback to laborers but also of encouraging and assisting them in leaving employers before completing any substantial work. Eventually a La Grange, Tennessee, landowner preferred false pretense charges against Cartwright. Cartwright was arrested and then released after posting a $2000 bond.[44]

The preferences of freedmen regarding the form and frequency of payment as well as work organization differed significantly from those of their planter counterparts. Ideally, blacks wanted to be propertied in their own right and not have to work for others. That failing, blacks were next most partial to renting property from landowners, which afforded them in their minds, at least, the latitude and circumstances to work independently and directly for themselves. If they could not rent land, freedmen then preferred to work as agricultural wage earners with payment in money wages at short and regular intervals.

In general, ex-slaves vehemently opposed working in either a gang labor or a squad system, though less adamantly so in the latter circumstance. They also professed a strong aversion to both long-term and collective contracts. The extreme distaste freedmen held for certain working conditions and their partiality toward others grew from a range of convictions based on experiences and apprehensions. Monetary payments, for instance, when received either daily, weekly, or monthly, could be a hedge against dishonest employers. Freedmen's abhorrence for working in gangs and even squads, unless they were family and kinship based, was owing to the regimentation of such labor force structures and the similarities to slavery.[45]

Freedmen similarly loathed long-term contracts because they represented a threat to freedom of mobility and precluded freedmen from taking advantage of other work opportunities that might arise. Collective contracts, those involving large numbers of workers bound together contractually for purposes of completing a common task, were likewise disliked because such a labor regimen undermined individual initiative and enterprise, with landowners as the exclusive beneficiaries.[46]

Given the enormous disparity between the preferences of planters and freedmen, an obvious question arises regarding how an accord ever evolved between the two. As the pattern of historical developments suggests, planters during much of the first year after the war gave in to the pressures of the moment and agreed to pay, with some difficulty no doubt, money wages under contracts averaging less than a year in duration. Many of these contracts, as noted earlier, involved groups of single, and presumably unattached, black males who agreed in collective written agreements to work in either a gang or squad labor force arrangement.

Southern agriculture, however, was undergoing a process of reorganization, as events and developments of the immediate postwar era clearly suggest. Frequently and significantly, practices approximating coercion and intimidation were used against black laborers in west Tennessee and throughout the South, generally to effect desired reorganization. Maltreatment of blacks, which took many forms, often resulted in loss of personal property, physical injury, and even death. Planters apparently sanctioned, and possibly even inspired, such truculence.[47] At the heart of this evolving historical saga was the fragmentation and decentralization of the postbellum plantation. By 1868 the gang system of labor organization was in rapid decline, if not already an agricultural relic. It was supplanted by the collective contract with laborers, mostly men, working for crops over a short term.[48]

Among black agricultural laborers of postwar Memphis and Shelby County who contracted as agricultural laborers, women comprised a mere 30 percent of blacks under contract between June and December 1865. In succeeding years their numbers among agrarian laborers declined still further to just one in four in 1866 and to only one in five by 1868. When black women did contract they were usually part of an arrangement that included a spouse or children or both. The family contract, that is, one encompassing husband, wife, and children, was the most common type involving women. Between 1865 and 1868 this type of arrangement comprised at least a third of the agreements that included women. Contracts by married couples were a distant second followed by labor arrangements with single parents, either fathers or mothers, plus children.

Black women rarely contracted to work singly as laborers. When and if they did, it was usually as house servants. These women were invariably young, almost never older than twenty years of age. Single, widowed, or otherwise unattached middle-aged women were rarest of all. Between 1865 and 1868, only 86 instances of such black women were found among the nearly 2,200 female laborers entering contracts.[49] Table 8.3 evidences this emerging pattern, which is consistent with the findings of other scholars

Table 8.3. Black Agricultural Labor Force Participation Rates by Gender in Memphis and Shelby County, 1865–1868[a]

Year	No. Males		No. Females	
1865	1,698		727	
1866	1,983	Increase difference for males, 1865–1866 +17 percent	673	Decrease difference for females, 1865–1866 −7 percent
1867	1,554	Decrease difference for males, 1866–1867 −22 percent	516	Decrease difference for females, 1866–1867 −23 percent
1868	982	Decrease difference for males, 1867–1868 −22 percent	245	Decrease difference for females, 1867–1868 −53 percent

[a]Based on surviving bureau-approved contracts only.

whose research likewise reflects a paucity of black female laborers in early postbellum southern agriculture. Very probably this development was occasioned by a conscious attempt on the part of black couples and families to remove wives, mothers, sisters, aunts, and daughters from the exacting labor of the plantation fields.[50]

The scarcity of black women in southern postwar agriculture was probably also attributable to a general reluctance by planters to contract with females, especially older ones, as agrarian laborers.[51] The withdrawal, however, of substantial numbers of black women from the agricultural labor force in the early postwar era would prove ephemeral. By the mid-1870s the incidence of family sharecropping had become more frequent, effectively returning thousands of black women to the rural workforce of the region. The impact of the reentry of large numbers of black females into southern agriculture was twofold. It at once eased an acute postbellum labor shortage and paved the way for the eventual emergence of family-based sharecropping as the dominant type of agricultural work arrangement in the latter nineteenth and early twentieth centuries. Increasingly, too, as Tables 8.4 and 8.5 clearly illustrate, remunerating laborers in shares soon became more common than payment in money wages. And this method was used on both large and small farms.

Monetary remuneration for agricultural labor did continue, albeit less frequently, despite the prevailing trend toward collective squad contracts and, eventually, family sharecropping. In those instances in which contracts called for the payment of monthly wages, the amount of compensation was declining from an early postwar average of $15 to $25 to an 1868 low of about $10. In annual monetary payments, there were corresponding income retreats from as much as $150 to as little as $100 by 1868.[52]

The Freedmen's Bureau, even given its mandate to influence agrarian reorganization, ultimately played a decidedly inconsequential role in postwar labor developments in the South. Actually, very few if any of the changes that pervaded the postbellum southern agricultural landscape reflected the efforts of socioeconomic engineering by the bureau. In being charged with revolutionizing southern agrarian society, the bureau took on a responsibility that was at the least exceedingly difficult even under optimal conditions, but given postwar circumstances, it was clearly herculean. Even so, it is unclear whether bureau policymakers fully understood the magnitude of their task, though Commissioner O. O. Howard appeared

Table 8.4. Frequency of Share Payments Versus Monetary
Payments of Large Farms, 1865–1868

Year	No. Large Farms	No. Laborers	Ave. No. Laborers Per Plantation	% Laborers Paid by Shares	% Laborers Paid by Money-Wages
1865	102	1,367	13.4	46	54
1866	128	1,636	12.8	58	42
1867	72	985	13.6	61	39
1868	56	749	13.3	66	34

to understand somewhat the great challenge of the mission before him and his subordinates.[53]

Success required that the bureau at the very least convince the two principals, freedmen and planters, of the need to work in concert to revive the southern economy, which putatively would be mutually beneficial. The agency, however, failed miserably in promoting harmonious labor relations. To be sure, numerous and unmistakable indications existed early that neither planters nor blacks had embraced the bureau's vision of a reconstructed South. By 1866 the evidence was irrefutable that federal reconstruction labor policies were not working. In the summer of that year, Memphis area freedmen with other blacks across large parts of the South demanded that planters rent them land. Otherwise, they vowed not to renew their contracts. Planters held firm in their refusal to enter rental agreements with black laborers, and with bureau approval and assistance, they physically removed protesting freedmen from their land, deeming them squatters.[54] Further, as noted earlier, contract arrangements were shifting decidedly away from money wages, a preference of the bureau, and toward some variant of the share payment system.

These developments, coupled with the chronic inability of the bureau to protect blacks either physically or in their economic relations with landowners, precluded any real possibility of an agrarian revolution. Surviving bureau records clearly reveal a pattern of abuses, physical as well as financial, perpetrated against freedmen. Fully two-thirds of the 341 cases filed with the Memphis Freedmen's Court between 7 November 1865 and 20 March 1866, for instance, involved allegations of whites financially mulcting blacks. Another fifth of the court docket during the same period concerned accusations of physical violence and maltreatment brought by black plaintiffs against white defendants.[55]

The reports of Memphis subdistrict commissioners confirm the frequent and widespread nature of such occurrences. In an April 1868 report, for example, subdistrict chief Fred Palmer recounted to the district's assistant commissioner in Nashville a recent incident of the mistreatment of blacks at the hands of whites. On or about 3 April 1868, Palmer reported, James Glenn, Robert Weaver, and seven other white men went to the homes of Turner Popugh and several of his neighbors, all farmers. After forcing them from their homes, located about five miles outside Memphis, the white perpetrators robbed the freedmen of a watch, shotgun, and five dollars. The whites also demanded that these same blacks leave their crops and homes within twenty-four hours. In this instance, which represents a clear case of whitecapping, the bureau secured the arrest of several of the accused, who had to post bonds of three thousand dollars while awaiting grand jury action.[56]

The failure of the bureau to effect desired changes in the postwar South and, in particular, to protect freedmen resulted in part from a lack of sufficient resources to fulfill its mandate. From its inception the bureau had been given neither adequate funding nor the authority to carry out its charter. Under the legislation that created the bureau, the agency was to exist for only a year, the rationale being that while there was a need for a

Table 8.5. Frequency of Share Payments Versus Monetary Payments of Small Farms, 1865–1868

Year	No. Small Farms	No. Laborers	Ave. No. Laborers Per Farm	% Laborers Paid by Shares	% Laborers Paid by Money-Wages
1865	156	1,053	6.7	42	58
1866	144	983	6.8	55	45
1867	136	890	6.5	65	35
1868	106	738	6.9	69	31

federal agency, given the extraordinary problems created by wartime emancipation, that entity should be short-lived. Even the statute establishing the bureau was vague in terms of the authority it afforded the agency. The law clearly gave the bureau control over southern property seized by the federal government under the Confiscation Acts of 1862 and 1863 and authorized it to rent such properties to private individuals to generate income to help defray the cost of operation. The agency also could use at least some abandoned property to create forty-acre tracts to be initially leased and eventually sold to both black and white refugees.[57]

Additionally, the bureau with assistance from the military could provide indigent and destitute refugees issues of provisions, including clothing, fuel, and temporary shelter, as it deemed necessary, but it could not give medical care, establish schools, supervise labor relations, or furnish legal protection for refugees. Nor did funds exist for the salaries of agents. Instead, the army was to make available officers to be used as bureau personnel.[58]

Many in the bureau repeatedly complained about personnel shortages, underfunding, and the lack of authority, but to no avail. The Republican-controlled Congress, with growing opposition from northern Democrats, refused to vote increased appropriations and powers of enforcement to the bureau. In each successive vote on the agency, Congress trimmed its budget and curtailed its activities. Then in July 1868 Congress killed the bureau by voting it out of existence as of January 1869. This final act, along with the failure to provide the agency the means to fulfill its mandate, constituted an opportunity lost.

Ultimately, perhaps, its insistence on not retreating from original policy objectives proved more damaging to the agency's efforts in the South than any of the constraints already cited. Not even in the wake of an obvious need to adjust its thinking and policies did the bureau do so. Commissioner Howard adamantly kept the bureau committed to a contract labor policy. He believed that to rescind this policy would serve only to heighten enmity between freedmen and planters and possibly even compromise social order and stability in the region.[59]

But what reasonable or viable alternatives existed to the contract labor system? Or, how might the bureau have responded differently to improve the position of freedmen while not penalizing planters? If the bureau after 1865, in the face of mounting evidence of failure, had suspended use of the contract system freedmen could have taken advantage of the prevailing labor shortage to press planters for more favorable employment terms. The bureau also might have vigorously supported the demands of freedmen for rental agreements from planters. The bureau's refusal to encourage or exert pressure on landowners to accede to black demands was surely a major blunder, as was the agency's stand against collective action by freedmen. The bureau maintained that despite the inherent advantages planters enjoyed, which allowed them to depress wages and defraud freedmen as well resist renting to them, it was far better not to encourage any "unnatural advantage" through black concerted action. Such action, the bureau feared, would jeopardize market forces and free labor in the region. But the agency's most crucial shortcoming was its failure to push aggressively enough to help freedmen become propertied.

As already noted, the bureau in its original mandate could create opportunities for blacks to own land. Admittedly, Howard did lobby Congress both to confirm title to land in South Carolina and Georgia given to blacks during the war and to pass a Southern Homestead Act, providing freedmen with property. The Southern Homestead Act passed in June 1866 reserved all public lands in Virginia, Florida, Arkansas, Mississippi, and Louisiana exclusively for the use of blacks and loyal white refugees until 1 January 1867. Yet, the legislation failed to increase even marginally the number of landowning freedmen in Shelby County and west Tennessee. Regionwide, while approximately 6,500 blacks, mostly in Florida and Virginia, attempted homesteads, only 1,000 eventually received certificates of land title. The inordinately small percentage of freedmen who applied for homesteads doubtless resulted in part because many of their labor contracts did not expire until 1 January 1867, when the exclusionary proviso of the legislation expired. Neither the bureau nor Congress, upon realizing this fact, moved to redress the problem by extending the exclusive entry date to at least a full year. Nor did the bureau in the face of the Southern Homestead debacle revise its labor policy to emphasize rental agreements over wage contracts. The lack of recourse to this and other, earlier delineated options seriously undercut black efforts at self-reliance and independence while creating credibility problems for the bureau among postwar freedmen.[60]

The consequences to freedmen of these official paths not taken became critically significant. Most obvious, blacks remained highly vulnerable. In neither their physical security nor economic lot were freedmen arguably better off during the stint of the bureau. If the experiences of postwar black Memphians and Shelby countians mirror the region as a whole, postbellum freedmen, despite the best efforts of the bureau, were still often and variously victimized. White west Tennesseans exhibited no reluctance to perpetrate violence against area freedmen. Blacks in Memphis and Shelby County lived an economic existence that fluctuated between the precarious and the dire.

Even the supposedly more hospitable urban environs of Memphis offered no real promise of improved material circumstances for area freedmen. Available indices for the period leave little doubt that blacks in Memphis struggled against incredible odds.[61] Not unlike rural Shelby County freedmen, black Memphians faced a myriad of obstacles in efforts to take best advantage of their emancipation. Whether rural or urban, area freedmen during the postbellum epoch experienced few of the much anticipated fruits of freedom. Instead, most found themselves sinking ever deeper into economic chaos and into life-styles that were hauntingly reminiscent of an earlier era. Such stark postwar realities easily clashed with the hopes and expectations of the freedmen, but they furnished compelling confirmation that real emancipation would entail a protracted and committed struggle.

The magnitude and significance of this struggle cannot be overemphasized. It had implications for several generations beyond those living in the immediate postemancipation period. At its core, emancipation was a struggle over the meaning of freedom and the political economy of emancipation. It also was about autonomy—more specifically, about establishing meaningful measures of economic independence through landownership while resisting planter efforts to create a southern agricultural proletariat.

The conflict over land possession was pivotal, an irreconcilable imperative that divided freedmen and planters. Moreover, the new socioeconomic and political order that blacks hoped would emerge and endure at war's end soon evaporated. Thwarted aspirations aside, Memphis area freedmen and other black southerners of the period held steadfast in their determination to realize the true meaning of emancipation; indeed, their resolve was a critical part of the larger dynamics of the emancipation experience. The totality of that experience, including the specific failures and tragic legacy for blacks in west Tennessee, became a fundamental chapter in the African-American historical saga.

9

Black Workers Remember
Industrial Unionism in the
Era of Jim Crow

Segregation, from roughly the late 1800s to the mid-1960s, divided black and white southerners into separate and unequal worlds. While based on skin color, the segregation system had an economic as well as a racial purpose. Serving as a replacement for slavery, the laws and practices of the segregation era ensured that most black workers could not rise above minimal levels in wages, skills, or status; by holding down blacks the racial system depressed the labor market for unskilled white workers and drove down their wages as well. In addition, the disfranchisement of poor whites and blacks through poll taxes and undemocratic election laws virtually destroyed the possibility of interracial, class-based political and economic alliances among working people. The system thus ensured the political and economic dominance of white landowners, bankers, real estate investors, and manufacturers. Under this system, like the slave masters before them, the indigenous upper classes in cooperation with northern investors ran the South with little interference from working people for much of the twentieth century.[1]

Although this system certainly played a major role in keeping white workers powerless and poor, most had difficulty identifying it as their enemy. Instead, they accepted the belief that keeping all African Americans down elevated whites, even if ever so slightly. Racial distinctions did lift white workers above blacks socially and to some extent materially, although most white industrial workers could expect to live just as poorly and expend their life's work with as little reward as did most southern blacks. Everyone believed that in the zero sum game of capitalism someone had to be a loser in order for someone else to be a winner. Hence, many southern poor and working-class whites viewed attempts to unite them with black workers as threats to their already marginal economic conditions, instead of seeing interracial unionization as a means to improve the lot of both groups.[2]

For black workers, the relationship of their poverty and powerlessness to the racial system remained quite apparent. The realities of segregation meant that employers could keep them at the bottom of the wage scale, without access to bank loans to buy a decent house or car and without the power to challenge oppressive economic conditions at the ballot box or in a court of law. Segregation also divided African Americans from natural allies in the factories where they worked, setting white production workers against them and making unionization difficult. Hence, most black workers recognized the need to join white workers at some level to change power relations between themselves and employers and to find allies who would help them eliminate racial barriers within the factories, at the voting booth, and in the streets, public places, and schools.

It is not surprising, then, that blacks in southern towns such as Memphis became the strongest supporters of the movement for industrial unions. Virtually every observer of the local labor scene pointed out that in the 1930s and 1940s African Americans, who made up 80 percent of the unskilled factory labor force, provided the backbone for the Congress of Industrial Organizations (CIO). The CIO sought to organize all workers in any given industry into one unit, based on a stated policy of equal rights for all. This policy offered a contrast to the craft unions of the American Federation of Labor (AFL), which excluded blacks altogether or organized them into separate "federal" units. AFL unions mostly failed to organize industrial workers, but even when successful they usually offered little to African Americans. By contrast, the inclusiveness of CIO industrial unions proved extremely attractive to black workers. Their support not only provided the key to CIO growth in the 1930s and 1940s, but to the organization of black sanitation and other public workers as well as hospital workers and furniture workers in the 1960s and 1970s.[3]

Black support for unionization raises questions with the findings of Robert J. Norrell, Herbert Hill, and others who suggest that unions may have been as great an obstacle to black progress as any other factor. While CIO unions adhered to equal rights in principle, in the early years especially most CIO unions did little to resist the segregated structures of employment rampant in American industry. Indeed, Norrell found that Birmingham's industrial unions functioned much as those of South Africa, excluding blacks from adequate-paying work and ratifying occupational segregation through union contracts. According to Hill, the entire history of unionization, in the industries as well as the crafts, reveals efforts to use unions as a means to keep blacks at a lower economic and social level than white workers. Both authors find little positive to say about unions as instruments for breaking down the Jim Crow system.[4]

Institutionalized discrimination through contracts negotiated and enforced by white union members clearly existed in the CIO in Memphis as elsewhere. How, then, can the unremitting black support for industrial unionization in such places as Memphis be explained? Oral history as told by black workers themselves offers important insights into the complexity of their conflicts and alliances with union leaders as well as with the white working class. Many African Americans engaged in the union struggle, but their story seldom was reported in the mass media and rarely appears in history books. Even accounts of the civil rights movement, whose foot soldiers included tens of thousands of working-class blacks, reveal little about the role of black workers in social change. Although Martin Luther King, Jr., gave his life in Memphis in a battle for the dignity and rights of black poor and working people, little is known about these workers. Fortunately, the testimonies of even a few individuals in Memphis illuminate the meaning of the black working-class struggle.

As the result of depression and then mechanization in the Delta cotton country, tens of thousands of black agricultural workers went to the cities looking for work. In Memphis, as elsewhere, many joined the urban unemployed. Among those who found employment, most females worked in white households doing domestic tasks, the largest employment category in the black community during the 1930s. Male workers, too, performed personal services for whites, as chauffeurs, waiters, and household attendants. Their largest share of jobs, however, came in positions as unskilled laborers in the manufacturing, transportation, and public service sectors. Blacks, numerically speaking, dominated the workforce with the exception of a handful of supervisory and machine operative positions held by whites in the lumber, furniture, cotton processing, and other agricultural and resource extractive industries. African Americans made up a significant portion of the workforce in Memphis's few mass production industries as well, and they continue to play a significant role in the manufacturing and service economies in the 1990s.[5]

From the 1930s onward, black workers in Memphis struggled not only with employers, the city's political machine, and the police, but also within the industrial unions. They fought first for survival, then to improve their conditions, and eventually to overthrow altogether the systematic discrimination and oppression they experienced. Hilley and Laura Pride were among the immigrants in the 1930s who left cotton picking in the fields for factory work in the city. At first, Laura shuttled between Memphis and Arkansas, supplementing Hilley's meager ten to fifteen cents hourly wages at the Fisher Body factory. Laura earned even less hoeing, chopping, and picking cotton. Planter, police, and vigilante violence crushed efforts by the Southern Tenant Farmers Union in the mid-1930s to organize agricultural workers such as the Prides across the river from Memphis.[6]

At the time Hilley began working at Fisher, unions existed, if at all, only among a few white skilled workers. "You didn't have no union, no help, no nothing," Pride recalled, but he appreciated even the low wages, since others during the depression had nothing at all. Nevertheless, he resented his twenty-minute lunch break, the hazardous and heavy labor, and his treatment by the supervisors. He labored long hours in suffocating heat, and over the course of his life working at Fisher and then Firestone Tire, he suffered the loss of hearing and sight caused by the harsh, unregulated factory environments. These working conditions only gradually and partially improved, leaving many other workers debilitated in their later years. Pride was not confused about the need for a union, one which united all of the workers in the plant. "Nobody said nothing for you at all, until the union got there," he recalled. "You were just like mules and hogs."[7]

Matthew Davis also remembered the difficult conditions. At the Firestone factory he hauled blocks of raw rubber, each weighing hundreds of pounds, ran them through splitting and compressing machines, washed the heavy material, and hung it out to dry. He worked in water in the midst of winter with cold air blowing in from the loading dock. Other blacks handled a tire pigment called lamp black, which washed out of Eddy Harrel's and Hilley Pride's skins onto towels and into bath water years after their retirement. Numerous black Firestone workers, who monopolized the dirtiest jobs in the plant, died of carcinogenic illnesses. Not surprisingly, blacks working in these conditions became the CIO Rubber Worker Union's strongest supporters.[8]

Unskilled white workers, who in the 1930s earned little better wages than blacks, had similar complaints about job conditions, overwork, and lack of respect from supervisors. But blacks suffered additional indignities, for the mores of segregation forced them to occupy a lower status than whites. The management, when opening the plant in 1937, instituted an "A,B,C" system of wages. Adult white males received thirty-two cents an hour; boys between eighteen and twenty-one years of age and the "colored" made twenty-eight cents an hour. Jobs were assigned on a racial basis, the worst going to blacks. Where the races worked together, management assigned blacks as "helpers" at lower rates of pay, even when a black ran the job. Whites not only received higher wages for the same work, but also had access to a promotional ladder denied to blacks. As Matthew Davis recalled, "all you had to do was come in there and your face be white, brother, and you'd move up." Experienced blacks, such as Matthew Davis, trained whites to be supervisors over them. Other whites received similar positions after being sent to training schools. Often, these new white workers, due to lack of experience, ruined tons of rubber. "My point," Davis stated, "is the fellas what were working there, they knew better, but see the supervisor be tellin' them to do it wrong. They go on and do it because the supervisor said to do it this way, but it just messed up a lot of stuff." The refusal of factory owners to respect the knowledge of "unskilled" black workers provided one of the reasons for the factory's eventual failure, Davis believed, although others contend that the plant closed because it became obsolete.[9]

Firestone's Jim Crow practices of paying uniformly lower wages to blacks, designating jobs by race, and classifying knowledgeable black workers as "helpers" to less skilled whites, prevailed throughout most industries. While such discrimination activated a growing demand for unionization among blacks, most white workers supported the racial system and rejected biracial unionization drives by the CIO. Union campaigns took place in an atmosphere that terrorized blacks and made it difficult if not impossible for most whites to view them as fellow workers. Segregation proved to be a mighty obstacle to organization.

George Holloway, a native of Memphis, grandson of a slave, son of a Pullman porter who was vice-president of his union, saw as a teenager the demeaning and degrading sins of segregation and racism: the denial to blacks of access to educational facilities, swimming pools, sports, and parks; beatings of black teenagers for having fun in the balcony of a segregated movie theater; arrests for walking through white neighborhoods; the vacating of seats on streetcars when whites demanded them; random police brutality; the terrors of being sent to the county penal farm; the daily insults to blacks in the newspapers. In addition, the poll tax put a price on the right to vote, disfranchising the poor and creating a basis for the political machine of E. H. Crump, who paid people's poll taxes and told them how to vote. These memories remained with Holloway for the rest of his life. "We knew all of this was wrong as youngsters, and we didn't enjoy it, but there was nothing we could do about it," he recalled.[10]

The National Association for the Advancement of Colored People barely existed, driven underground by Memphis's repressive atmosphere, and no other organizations emerged to fight segregation except the union. "I joined the union to help change these things," Holloway recalled. He viewed unionism as virtually synonymous with his struggle as a black man for civil rights, although he was quite aware of the racism of white workers. The AFL unions, for example, had segregated or excluded blacks, and they forced the few black unions that did exist to meet in the old servant's quarters behind the AFL hall. Holloway knew that the black union leader, A. Philip Randolph, had been forced to leave Memphis when he came to speak in the 1920s and that it could be dangerous for blacks to organize. William Glover, a black Pullman porter and organizer, was arrested, beaten, and run out of town by the police in 1938 on the trumped-up charge that he had propositioned a white woman. The police, in 1939, tried to murder black longshore leader Thomas Watkins for leading a strike of black and white river workers. But Holloway, through his father's experience, understood why the authorities were so opposed to unionization: it worked. The Pullman porters, for example, once organized, made some of the best wages in black Memphis. His father's job on the railroad enabled him to buy a car and send his son for two years to Tuskegee Institute.[11]

After Tuskegee, Holloway got a job at the Firestone Tire factory and became plant chairman for the Rubber Workers Union when organizer George Bass came to Memphis in 1940. Although Bass was a native southern white from rural Tennessee, he set up the union on the stated principle of equal participation by blacks and whites. He gained allies among a few whites, but drew his strongest support from blacks, who made up one-third of the nearly two thousand workers at Firestone. In response, the company repeatedly stirred up fears of "nigger unionism" among white workers and paid supervisors to organize a mob that beat Bass nearly to death in front of the factory. Bass then brought in his husky farm-hand relatives as bodyguards, and Holloway one morning led a march of black union supporters through the plant, defeating the company's campaign of fear. Nevertheless, Firestone's racial ploy succeeded. In the first National Labor Relations Board election held in December, 1,008 workers, almost the entire white work force, voted for the AFL, while another 805 workers, almost all of them black, supported the CIO.[12] Holloway quit his job before the company could fire him and went to work as a Pullman porter. Meanwhile, the AFL virtually excluded blacks from any meaningful participation in the new union; blacks retaliated by slowing production, which undercut the piece rates paid to whites in some of the skilled occupations. For the next twenty years, black and white workers at Firestone struggled over the racial terms of unionization.[13]

Clarence Coe became one of the stalwarts in that fight. He came to the city in the 1930s to avoid the racism in the countryside of west Tennessee. His slave grandparents had bought land after emancipation, and his parents became self-sufficient farmers. Coe, unlike the children of most sharecroppers, finished high school, and through the Farm Home Administration start-up funds, he could have purchased a farm of his own. But Coe could not adapt to the relationships expected by the paternalistic system in the rural areas. "[N]ot having grown up around them on a plantation," Coe recalled, "I just couldn't handle" the deference that whites expected from him. After Coe saw the body of a lynched black man, he left for the city in 1936. "I wanted to get away from this environment," Coe remembered. Instead, he found that "you run into the same damn things" in the city. But his world expanded. He had heard of the Scottsboro Boys, read the black press, and even wrote for it at times. Coe started work by pressing clothes, then took a factory job. He lost it and received a beating for union organizing. He also gravitated toward the NAACP, even though the organization barely existed in Memphis, and worked for the postal service.[14]

In 1941, Coe got a job at the Firestone factory, and his life became intertwined with the struggle for union rights and civil rights. He saw whites as well as blacks beaten for holding union meetings, and he realized the value of having white allies. At the same time, whites in the plant discovered their mistake in voting for an AFL union that offered no benefits for semi-skilled factory workers. White employee Richard Routon recalled that "we soon found out that we'd been duped into joining a[n AFL] union simply to keep [out] a bona fide industrial union that knew something about representing mass production workers." With the onset of World War II,

Routon, who had initially supported the AFL because of its racial exclusiveness, helped lead whites into the CIO. During a walkout over a racial conflict, he addressed fellow workers in the parking lot and warned that an effective union could never exist until blacks and whites joined efforts. "By that time," Routon recalled, "those of us in production didn't give a damn if they were polka-dot. We were tired of the sweatshop conditions, and we were ready to join together and try to do something about it." They all went back inside and soon voted in the CIO Rubber Workers Union, electing Routon as its first president.[15]

Clarence Coe relished working with the new union, but he quickly discovered that unionization alone would not end the multitude of degrading Jim Crow practices in the factory. Among his grievances, Coe found the treatment of blacks by individual whites to be the most aggravating. An African American could not question anything a white supervisor or a white worker said without experiencing physical intimidation or dismissal. "Whatever a white person said, that was it," Coe recalled. Unwritten laws at Firestone also prohibited blacks from taking any job that appeared to place them on a level of equality with whites and forced blacks to use separate cafeterias, drinking fountains, bathrooms, locker rooms, time clocks, and parking lots. Although white leaders such as Routon stood up for blacks in individual cases and developed strong sympathies with the black struggle to abolish Jim Crow, no white unionist at Firestone came out openly against segregation. Whites accepted blacks into the union but not on the basis of full equality.[16]

The American fight for "freedom" during the war proved especially trying to Coe and other black workers. The plant became a racial powder keg, with whites on numerous occasions walking out when they thought blacks might be taking "white" jobs. Blacks retaliated in kind. One of the major black wildcat strikes protested an incident in which a white guard hit a black woman in the mouth. The woman had refused to yield her seat to whites on a crowded city bus and wait in front of the plant until the next vehicle arrived. Her treatment reminded Coe of other incidents across the South in which whites pulled black soldiers from troop trains and beat them for not "staying in their place." In contrast to this treatment of blacks, George Holloway recalled that military authorities had allowed German prisoners of war to eat from crystal in a fancy dining hall during a train stop in Little Rock, while he and other Pullman porters were forced to eat in the kitchen. This incident and many others highlighted for him the failure of the United States to practice at home the freedom it claimed to be fighting for abroad.[17]

Coe observed the inflamed racism of the war years and decided that "I want no damn part of this." He used his asthma to avoid military service, but he paid a price, nonetheless. At the Firestone plant he worked seven days a week, and a whole year passed in which he never saw the sun set because he was working. As a few black women gained entrance to the industrial workforce, they too faced intense exploitation. Most of them at Firestone did menial tasks. Evelyn Bates, who aspired to be a beautician, worked outside, lifting heavy tires, suffering from mosquito bites and encounters with snakes that nested in the tires. Reacting to such conditions, hundreds of blacks at the Firestone plant joined the Memphis NAACP, for the first time making it a mass organization. At war's end, Coe witnessed yet another resurgence of racism, as whites abused black veterans in the streets and in the plant so that they would remember "their place." "When it came time to serve, you had to go in; suffer and die, too, for freedom that you'd better not even act like you wanted when you got out," said Coe.[18]

The bitter war experiences as well as conditions in the factory transformed Coe and others into racial militants. Holloway recalled that "a lot of blacks thought it was time to get some justice." In 1946, Holloway left his job as a porter and became one of the first people hired at a new International Harvester plant in Memphis where he became the leading black union activist. By this time, white workers had progressed to the point of nonresistance to the CIO, which had become the largest organization in the city, and the United Auto Workers union came into the Harvester plant by acclamation. But few white workers accepted the right of blacks to have equal access to jobs, and many of them insisted on segregating workers within the new union. Typical of whites throughout Memphis industries, they no longer tried to exclude blacks from the union, but resisted equality at the workplace and in the union hall. Black unionists, who made up one-third of the new UAW local, at International Harvester and other factories increasingly struggled not over the right to be included but the terms of the inclusion. In doing so they challenged white workers and the segregation system itself.[19]

Black Harvester workers elected Holloway as committeeman and a trustee of the union, and in 1948 he joined the first union negotiating committee. One hotel refused conference rooms to the company, the union, and the National Labor Relations Board because a black man would be meeting on a basis of equality with whites. A second hotel rented the facilities but forced Holloway to enter through a service elevator where garbage and cleaning disinfectant splashed on him every morning. One company negotiator insisted on referring to Holloway as "the nigger," a slur that none of his white union colleagues protested. As a committeeman in the plant, Holloway had a hundred stewards working under him, black and white, and yet white union leaders refused even to give him a ride to work. As a result, he had to hitchhike or walk miles to his job. In 1949, when Holloway became the first black at the Harvester plant to operate a machine, white workers tampered with it while he was on break. Had he not checked the machine before restarting it he could have been injured or killed.[20]

For the next ten years, Holloway struggled with racist local UAW whites who misused union dues to purchase a union hall in their own names and then segregated its use. At Holloway's insistence Walter Reuther and Pat Greathouse of the national UAW intervened and put the local in receivership. For two years, no union meetings were held. White union leaders, some of them affiliated with a budding White Citizens' Council, carried guns and intimidated whites sympathetic to integration. Vigilantes, perhaps at the behest of the city's political machine, broke all of the windows in Holloway's home, and for two years he and his wife, Hattie, regularly received threatening phone calls in the middle of the night. During one entire summer, Clarence Coe's brother, Lint, guarded the Holloway home at night with a shotgun after finishing work at the Firestone plant. Fortunately, Reuther and other top UAW officials came to Holloway's aid, as did Carl Moore, who was sent to Memphis as the organization's regional director. With their help, Holloway and other blacks integrated the union hall as well as the plant's facilities, and they opened jobs to blacks in higher skilled occupations. During these struggles, whites fired into the home of Moore, and several union meetings nearly turned into race riots.[21]

The racial strife at International Harvester had parallels at the Firestone plant. There, Clarence Coe and other blacks fought to end departmental seniority that discouraged blacks from bidding for better-paying jobs. They sought to abolish segregation in the plant and union hall, and they tried to elect blacks to high offices as representatives of both races in the plant.

Whites twice tried to maim or kill Coe when he moved into a "white" job. By the 1960s, as he later recalled, he kept a gun in every room of his house and in his car. When his income increased, enabling him to buy a new car, plant security guards slashed the tires. Coe, like Holloway, sought respect as a committeeman and union leader and constantly contended with white workers and factory supervisors over their use of the term "nigger." In some of these battles, the union helped, and white union president Rip Clark surreptitiously aided black efforts legally to desegregate the plant. But the initiative came from the blacks themselves, as Coe and others secretly collected money at the plant and hired a private attorney who sued both the company and the union to end segregation at the Firestone facilities. They did not completely attain this goal until the early 1970s.[22]

African Americans in other Memphis industries fought similar battles. In fact, Local 19 of the Food, Tobacco and Agricultural Workers Union (FTA), active since the 1930s, had the first integrated picket lines and union meetings and elected a black president, although about one-third of the membership was white. During World War II, at black worker George Isabell's initiative, Local 19 broke down segregated job designations inside the Buckeye plant, and shortly after the war the union ended departmental seniority at the factory. In the postwar civil rights battles, Local 19 led the unions in promoting voter registration and in 1948 helped elect the white liberal, Estes Kefauver, to the U.S. Senate. In 1950, Leroy Boyd and seventeen other black members of Local 19 traveled to Mississippi to protest the execution of Willie McGee, a black man falsely charged with the rape of a white woman. Arrested by authorities, they barely escaped Mississippi without being lynched.[23]

Local 19 proved exceptional, for not only did blacks take the lead in the civil rights protest, but they did so with strong white support. Its original organizer was a white Christian Socialist and former YMCA official named Harry Koger. After the war, business agents Karl Korstad and Ed McCrea, both dedicated anti-racist whites, also became involved. Other white allies of the black civil rights movement in the Memphis CIO included W. E. "Red" Davis, Morton Davis, and Lawrence McGurty, all members of the National Maritime Union (NMU). These and other white NMU members helped build Local 19 and other Memphis unions with large black memberships, particularly the Woodworkers and Furniture Workers unions. Radical whites promoted explicitly integrationist activities within the local

CIO. In 1947, McCrea and Red Davis tried to get the CIO's Industrial Union Council to remove "white" and "colored" signs over the bathrooms in the CIO hall. For their efforts the Council banned them from further meetings. Davis, McGurty, McCrea, and a number of white union militants continued their efforts. In 1948 they came to the aid of 450 unskilled black workers at the Nickey Brothers lumber company, saving a strike that appeared to be lost because of scabbing by whites. The next year, Davis led another campaign in support of striking black workers, most of them women, at the Memphis Furniture company. This strike failed. In Jackson, Mississippi, Davis was arrested along with Local 19 workers protesting the Willie McGee execution. Meanwhile, his wife, Carmen, played an important role in the national Civil Rights Congress campaign to save McGee.[24]

In these and other efforts, a small group of white CIO leftists during the 1940s initiated significant activities in support of black workers and against the segregation system. But most integrationist whites belonged to the Communist Party, and by the time the civil rights movement heated up in the 1950s the Memphis CIO Council had banned all of them. Meanwhile, the national CIO in late 1949 and early 1950 expelled the FTA and ten other Communist-led unions with nearly a million members. The Memphis CIO Council provided star witnesses against Local 19 leaders when Mississippi Senator James Eastland's Senate Internal Security Subcommittee (SISS) investigated "communism" in the Memphis labor movement. The hearings led to the virtual destruction of one of the city's oldest, most effective, and certainly most racially egalitarian CIO unions. During the hysteria over "communism," the CIO lost the only clearly black-led industrial union in Memphis, along with its strongest white supporters of black civil rights. Black labor activist Earl Fisher managed to revive Local 19 but was forced to abandon his civil rights activity. The CIO attacks on leftists also destroyed black-led unions in other parts of the South as well.[25]

The anti-Communist hysteria of the Cold War years did not end black agitation for civil rights, as the stories of Coe, Holloway, and numerous other black CIO union members reveal. Rather, black workers became increasingly sensitive to discrimination in the industrial unions that, at best, had a very mixed record on civil rights. Josh Tools, a black union stalwart at Firestone, complained bitterly because neither the international nor the local would take action to implement forthrightly the union constitution that mandated equal rights for all. The reluctance of white union leaders to support equality also disgusted Coe and other black workers. As a result, they lived with Jim Crow for years, in part because most white unionists would not take a firm, public stand against such practices. The result of this white reluctance was evident years later in the vast disparity in wages between whites who received the better-paying jobs from the beginning and blacks whose wages increased only later.[26]

Without white support, it took years for black workers to end Jim Crow conditions in the organized shops of the CIO. A white worker "just wasn't going to support you in job equality or equal pay," Tools recalled. Clarence Coe also vented his frustration at the slow pace of change. "Hell, [it took] thirty-five years of my work out there" to gain equal rights. "I have seen the time when a young white boy came in and maybe I had been working at the plant longer than he had been living, but if he was white I had to tell him 'yes sir' or 'no sir.' That was degrading as hell [but] I had to live with it." Coe believed that white union leaders could have helped to make the changes sooner and resented that "it took all of my time. And it's just not fair for an individual to have to waste a life," said Coe; you "had to fight for every inch. . . . Nobody gave you nothing. Nothing!"[27]

It would be a mistake, however, to conclude that the CIO unions merely became yet another instrument for white control over blacks. In fact, black unionists in Memphis said quite the contrary: it was the union that helped them remove the barriers of Jim Crow, that made it possible to rise out of the semi-slave conditions of the 1930s and that provided the basis for civil rights protest. But the union represented black self-activity, not rights handed down from the international or local white union leaders, the National Labor Relations Board, or other government agencies. The union exacted years of sacrifice from people like Coe, Holloway, and many others. These men and other blacks used the union as an instrument to break down segregation and to gain a degree of black power. Both Coe and Holloway became so well versed in the union contract and the rights embodied therein that they could settle disputes in the plant without consulting it. They won many grievances for whites as well as blacks, thus gaining the grudging respect even of racist whites. In so doing, they helped to raise the wage rates and improve the working conditions of the Memphis working class. At the same time, they struggled for black civil rights inside and outside the factories.[28]

Firestone workers were many of the members of a revived NAACP.

Matthew Davis, Josh Tools, and others in the Firestone local actively participated in voter registration drives and community mobilization. In the 1960s, Furniture Worker leader Leroy Clark led the NAACP in street demonstrations and school boycotts after the assassination of Dr. King. His wife Alzeda's voter registration activities in the 1960s paved the way for black political victories and the eventual election of black Congressman Harold Ford. It was of even more importance that the children of thousands of black workers could go to college as the result of their parents' rising incomes and status because of unionization. Children of unionized workers helped break the barriers of segregation at Memphis State University, the public library, and other institutions. Some of these children, with Ph.D. and medical degrees, became leading citizens in Memphis and other areas of the United States.[29]

How, then, should this era be remembered? Participants in the industrial union movement recalled the history in different ways. White racial moderates among the Rubber Workers remembered their role in breaking down segregation and in prodding the CIO to progress in race relations. Radical whites from Local 19 and the NMU remembered their strong support for civil rights, but deplored the CIO's unwillingness to move more promptly on racial questions as symptomatic of its compromise with the established order during the Cold War years. Both moderates and radicals thought that most white industrial workers came to accept blacks as union members but still wanted blacks to participate in the CIO as second-class citizens. Indeed, most CIO unions continued segregated seating, eating, and work arrangements well into the 1960s.[30]

Black workers, for their part, acknowledged and appreciated a degree of white support within the CIO for civil rights, but they also remembered how white resistance had long delayed their demands for change. They spoke with some bitterness because their unions were reluctant to tackle Jim Crow, and they could not forget the years of hurt inflicted upon them by white workers who refused to relinquish the old ways. But they all felt pride in what they had achieved. "I'm a living example of UAW justice," Holloway recalled. He became the first black UAW staff member in the South, negotiating local contracts from Miami, Florida, to Tennessee, and to Delaware. During his eighteen years of staff work, he met Martin Luther King, Jr., and other civil rights leaders, worked closely with Walter Reuther, helped build the Memphis NAACP, sent his son to the University of Michigan, and provided a good life for his family. "I learned about kindness and fairness in the labor movement," said Holloway. When he died in 1990, he had spent nearly his entire adult life in the union movement serving others.[31]

Irene Branch, who took care of white children (and her own) during the day and who worked at Firestone at night, like many black women raising families, had no time to attend union meetings. Indeed, women remained almost completely absent from the ranks of official leadership in the CIO unions. Nonetheless, Branch appreciated what the union had done. "If it wasn't for that union I wouldn't have stayed in there," she recalled. "That's what kept me in there. Cause they curse you and call you 'nigger' and everything else, and spit on you. Do anything to you. Blacks were really treated bad. And they'd fire you in a minute." Although white workers could act as viciously as the supervisors, the existence of a union ultimately made it possible for blacks to challenge racism on the job. "Nothing didn't go right, we didn't see freedom until we got that union. . . . We had protection then. They didn't mistreat you then. If they curse you, you'd go to the union and they'd get on the supervisors . . . and they were really nice after they got that union," said Branch.[32]

Black workers could easily point out the changes that occurred between the 1930s when they lived without unions and later years after their conditions improved. People such as Hilley Pride, who started out making ten and fifteen cents an hour, ended up with ten and fifteen dollars an hour, a thousand percent increase in wages. Yet, skilled whites continued to earn more, and blacks paid a high price to achieve even the smallest improvements in their conditions. Nevertheless, in retirement blacks had full health coverage, pensions, and a respected place in their communities. Irene Branch, whose husband died in 1947, decided that "I don't need no husband, no how. Firestone takes care of me." And by the time Hilley Pride retired, he looked back with satisfaction to the fact that blacks and whites had equal access to jobs. Separate drinking fountains, cafeterias, time clocks, and all other vestiges of segregation had been eliminated at the plant and in the union hall. "The union was a real good thing," he said, "cause it broke up that mess."[33]

Momentous changes had occurred in the lifetimes of these black industrial workers. But Pride also pointed out that the victories he had gained were later largely lost to the younger generation of blacks. "Poverty and people's situations are worse now than they were in the depression" for many black youngsters, he said in 1989. "A lot of people can't see it, but I've been here long enough to know what I'm talking about. Things are worse now than they've ever been. . . . So many people suffering, don't know what's happening. No job, no nothing." Although Pride had his pension and benefits, the destruction caused by unemployed or drug-addicted young people in his community made it difficult to walk down the street or even to be secure in his home, and he decried a system that allowed fantastic wealth and absolute poverty to exist side by side. "We have to go back and make some change in this country. This nation has got to start doing something for the people that aren't working to get them some work. Who's going to help you? We're really being ripped apart by the moral structure of this country."[34]

Looking back on his lifetime of commitment, Clarence Coe remembered that the struggle against racism had been a continuous one in which the CIO unions played only a partial role. "I tell you when both of us get in a ditch together and stay there long enough we'll find the means to get out together, and the CIO was that." But the CIO lacked the moral imperatives concerning race that the civil rights movement brought to bear and that finally brought an end to Jim Crow. In Memphis, the triumphs of the civil rights years were blighted by the tragedy of King's death. Changes in national economic and political priorities left the black community bereft of meaningful jobs, especially for its young people. Coe thought that many whites still believed, mistakenly, that "they can make it without us."[35]

As unionized black workers remembered the era of Jim Crow, however, they were also mindful of the changes that occurred through organizing. Despite the disappointment that more was not accomplished sooner, they viewed their accomplishments as a giant step toward social change for the African-American community and the society as a whole. Clarence Coe believed that the time for a mass movement would come again. In the formative era of the CIO, he recalled, whites did not want to make alliances with blacks, but "we were pushed into it, we just had to do something." Today, "the powers that be . . . keep you thinking you're going to make it and they're constantly drowning you." If whites in the postindustrial era had not quite reached a point of rebellion, he believed they soon would. And when they did, he also believed that they would have little choice but to join with African Americans and other people of color in a labor-based movement for change. "As it has always been," mused Coe, "I think when people are badly enough oppressed, they'll find a way and do it. And organizing labor is the only way; it's the only way you can do it."[36]

Part III.

Labor and Politics in the New South Era

CLIFFORD M. KUHN

Introduction

Over the past two decades, the field of southern labor history has undergone vast changes. Drawing from a variety of sources and intellectual wellsprings, a new generation of historians has tested and successfully challenged traditional notions about labor in the region. Whether providing multifaceted descriptions of life in mill villages, mining camps, or African-American urban communities, these scholars have enhanced our knowledge about the contours of regional industrialization and the nature and extent of southern exceptionalism.

Much of this scholarship has focused on the social and cultural dimensions of the working class, often to the relative exclusion of politics, however broadly or narrowly defined. This emphasis has occurred for various reasons. The new historians of the working class, in their admirable attempts to contest two-dimensional images of the region's downtrodden or docile workers, have traced family, work, and community life in considerable detail. By emphasizing the importance of semiautonomous, if not counter-hegemonic, cultures, however, they, like many of their counterparts in other fields, have paid comparatively little attention to such issues as the inequities of power, the nature of political discourse, and the role of the state.

In addition, the particular course of southern history since 1865 has contributed to this comparative de-emphasis on the politics of labor. The power and persistence of "Herrenvolk democracy" among whites, the New South industrial crusade, and the advent of one-party politics helped to mute organized class-based political expressions. The character of southern electoral politics, often rural-dominated, driven by personalities, and marked by fraud, intimidation, and violence, further tempered working-class political activity. Disfranchisement measures designed to eliminate blacks from the ballot box had also the effect of removing large numbers of working-class whites as well.

For these and other reasons, organized working-class political activity has been limited for much of the twentieth century, particularly for black workers whose experience under segregation bore little resemblance to life in a liberal democracy. Robin D. G. Kelley recently noted that the realities of a Jim Crow world meant that much if not most black working-class political activity took place outside of formal organizations; instead, it occurred during daily conflicts and power negotiations. Building upon the work of political scientist James C. Scott, Kelley argues that an understanding of black working-class political activity in the twentieth-century South hinges upon exploring black community "infrapolitics," the political discourse hidden from (white) public view.[1]

Such an approach, however, obviously poses formidable conceptual and methodological challenges, as the limited historical literature on the infrapolitics of the working-class South, white or black, indicates. In contrast, other historians have emphasized organized working-class political activity and the impact of the state upon southern workers. For instance, an older historical literature detailed trade unionist involvement in Progressive Era coalitions, especially at the municipal level, to promote such issues as child and convict labor reform.[2]

More recently, the largest body of works on southern labor politics focuses on the development and impact of public policy. It is not surprising that most of the studies that explicitly deal with labor involve federal initiatives, particularly of the New Deal. They include works by Donald Grubbs, James Hodges, and Wayne Flynt.[3] Other writings on various aspects of the New Deal, while not primarily concerned with labor per se, also have provided a great deal of information and insight about the impact of public policy on the region's workers. Included in this body of scholarship are Douglas Smith's book on the New Deal and the urban South and recent accounts of the TVA.[4] State and municipal studies on the New Deal in Georgia, Tennessee, North Carolina, Kentucky, Atlanta, and Memphis have similarly addressed aspects of the politics of southern labor.[5]

A resurgence in political biography has shed light on the role of workers in the region's electoral politics. Recent profiles of James "Big Jim" Folsom, Lister Hill, and Carl Elliott, three politicians from Alabama, the Deep South state where organized labor made the greatest inroads, trace labor politics in some detail. Similarly, Julian Pleasants's and Augustus Burns III's study of Frank Porter Graham's 1950 campaign for the U.S. Senate documents the involvement of the CIO's Political Action Committee (CIO-PAC). Also, Nell Painter's biography of black radical Hosea Hudson describes early efforts of African-American workers to obtain the vote.[6]

Yet for all their attributes, both the New Deal studies and southern political biographies tend to place workers in the background as secondary players whose fortunes were essentially decided by policymakers and politicians. In contrast, other historians have begun to focus directly on the activities of workers and their organizations in the realm of electoral politics, especially since the depression. These newer studies include articles by Wayne Flynt, Robert Norrell, and Bryant Simon detailing labor politics in Mississippi, Alabama, and South Carolina. (Additional work by Simon on South Carolina textile-worker politics is featured in another section of this volume.) In addition, Daniel Powell, a former regional director of the Committee on Political Education (COPE), the AFL-CIO's political arm, has provided an overview of organized labor in southern politics from the establishment of the CIO Political Action Committee in 1943.[7]

The four essays included herein ably build upon this existing literature. From quite different perspectives, they suggest new directions in the historical treatment of the politics of southern labor. Alex Lichtenstein's examination of the development of the task system in Georgia's mines and the tensions surrounding convict labor joins an exciting new body of work on that subject. Collectively, these studies explore such diverse topics as the system's place in the region's political economy; the formation of a black industrial proletariat; the evolution of convict labor law; and the origins, nature, and impact of penal reform.[8]

Lichtenstein describes the particular features of Georgia's postbellum mining industry; the attitudes about race, labor, and criminals that informed convict mining practices; and the complex, evolving interaction that involved the state, Georgia capitalists, and the laborers themselves. He demonstrates the inherent contradictions within the task system, and the conflicting dual role of the state as the final enforcer of discipline while also serving as the ultimate protector of the convicts' welfare. Lichtenstein clearly points out the uniqueness of the system; yet, in many ways his methodology can be applied to other situations as well. Certainly, his exposition of the periodic tensions between state officials and the "employers" of labor casts some doubt on the presumption that state governments existed simply as handmaidens to industry. Indeed, a more complicated relationship developed, one needing exploration in greater detail.

Arguably the most ambitious and provocative of the four essays included here is Michael Goldfield's essay, designed really as a think piece at the outset of a major research project. Building upon the concluding chapter in his 1989 book on organized labor's decline in the United States, Goldfield posits that the failure of the CIO's Operation Dixie after World War II marked an important turning point in American political history.[9] Goldfield speculates that the failure of Operation Dixie not only contributed to a steady decline in unionism and the marginalization of the labor movement in national politics, but also left the system of white supremacy intact and Dixiecrats in control of the South. Had Operation Dixie succeeded, however, it would have ensured a strong reservoir of southern white working-class support for civil rights. Instead, its collapse eventually led to the Republican party's "southern strategy" in the late 1960s and afterward. In arriving at these conclusions, Goldfield joins a number of historians who have recently suggested that there existed in the post-World War II South a slim opportunity for progressive change in the region.[10]

The second half of Goldfield's essay examines the failure of Operation Dixie. He reviews various traditional explanations for the comparative lack of unions in the South, ranging from the characteristics of its economy to aspects of the regional culture. He concludes, these arguments aside, that the failure of Operation Dixie was not predetermined but rather occurred because of deficiencies on the part of the campaign's leadership.

While Goldfield's important hypotheses demand close scrutiny and testing at the local and state levels, the next two essays strongly imply that even had Operation Dixie succeeded, both the internal and external obstacles facing a progressive, class-based politics in the region would still have been formidable indeed. In a pioneering study of southern labor in the postwar period, Douglas Flamming documents how the union movement in Dalton, Georgia, one of organized labor's foremost strongholds in that state, was shattered during the mid-1950s.[11] Rejecting exceptionalism as the reason for labor's collapse, Flamming points to a more generically American anti-Communism that placed union organizers and the labor movement in a nearly untenable position. In describing the pro-labor activities of Dalton's Church of God and Union Assembly and its leader, Reverend Charlie T.

Pratt, Flamming also provides a welcome reminder that the multifaceted and dynamic relationship between religion and the labor movement in the South is certainly worthy of further scholarly pursuit.

In the final essay, Alan Draper describes the decimation of the Alabama labor movement over issues of race and white supremacy. After the 1954 *Brown v. Board of Education* decision, the state labor federations were caught between a national labor leadership increasingly active on matters of civil rights and a white rank and file often adamantly opposed to integration. As civil rights dwarfed other issues and as Governor George Wallace emerged as the South's foremost segregationist, tensions increased, particularly when the Alabama AFL-CIO refused to support Wallace in his 1964 presidential bid. Because of this stand, many local unions withdrew from the state federation, and overall union membership declined precipitously. In addition, the state council's political influence severely declined. As Draper relates, it took a decade for the AFL-CIO's principled position to bear political fruit in the emergence of a black-labor coalition that, although admittedly weaker, still sustains the state's Democratic Party today.

While demonstrating how race overwhelmed Alabama's class-based politics during the charged climate of the post-*Brown* era, Draper's study also reveals several avenues for further scholarly inquiry. While some Alabama workers and their unions opposed the *Brown* decision, embraced Wallace, and broke from the state AFL-CIO, it would be interesting to know why others did not. A comparative study of the various state labor councils during the civil rights movement would also be illuminating. Finally, one wonders how the complicated relationship between organized labor and civil rights in the region affected developments in national as well as regional politics. Draper and the other authors featured in this section deserve praise for raising these and other important questions in addition to producing essays that add historical perspective to the politics of southern labor.

Twice the Work of Free Labor?
Labor, Punishment, and the Task System in Georgia's Convict Mines

In Atlanta in mid-July 1886, the talk of the black community was the mutiny of the convicts who worked at Joe Brown's Dade Coal Company near the Tennessee line. On 12 July, 109 prisoners refused to go to work and barricaded themselves inside their quarters. The convicts insisted that they would not return to work until the "squad boss" who supervised their labor and meted out punishment was dismissed, the quality of their food was improved, and corporal punishment was abolished at the camp. The principal keeper of the penitentiary, John Towers, quickly traveled from Atlanta to isolated Dade County and was informed by the strike leaders that their demands had to be met or they "would have to be brought out dead." Towers reportedly replied to the rebellious convicts, "then you will be brought out dead." Although the convicts had saved rations so that they could maintain their premeditated strike, by the morning of the third day Towers believed that half of the hungry convicts were willing to capitulate and leave the stockade. By late afternoon on 14 July, he was able to telegram to Atlanta that the "mutiny [is] over [we] are taking them out as fast as irons can be put on . . . glad we did not have to kill any."[1]

Later, in his report for 1886, Towers suggested that the "mutiny" was "under the control of a few leaders" who threatened to kill any convicts who returned to work. He did note, however, that the rebels referred to their action as a strike and "alleged several causes in justification of it." The legislative committee that visited the Dade County convict camps in December 1886 found that the convicts did have several justified complaints about the vicious and arbitrary behavior of their "Whipping Boss," one Killpatrick. The committee recommended to the governor that he replace Killpatrick—the principal demand of the striking prisoners six months earlier.[2]

In many ways this incident differed little from most industrial conflicts of the late nineteenth century in the defiant nature of the workforce, the potential for violence, and the intervention of the state on the side of capital. But the revolt of these convicts also illustrates some of the more significant features of the industrial convict labor system of the New South. On the one hand, it appears that the company had great latitude in coercing its bound labor force. There was a legal basis for punishing those workers who did not meet the pace of work, a pace set by the imperatives of the lessee. On the other hand, extraction of labor from the prisoners had limits imposed by the convicts themselves and even by the state, which played the contradictory role of final enforcer of discipline and yet ultimate protector of the convicts' welfare.

These tensions became evident on such rare occasions of concerted convict resistance to the lease system. Indeed, four convict "revolts" occurred in Georgia between 1886 and 1892, though the one in 1886 most resembles a strike. There were rumors of a strike and then an actual mutiny in December 1886–January 1887 at the Rising Fawn furnace in Dade County, a mass escape attempt at the Dade Coal mines in June 1891, and a revolt of convicts at the Walker County coal mines in April 1892.[3] But an examination of the daily work experience of convicts in Georgia's coal and iron complex reveals that conflict over the level of exploitation of prison labor was constant, inherent in the structure of the work and the penal system. At the "point of production," this conflict was embedded in the task system of labor that prevailed in the convict mines; and in the penal system itself, at issue was who defined the pace of work, the state or the lessee.

Georgia's coal and iron producers initially turned to forced labor because of the "unreliability" of free labor in an already tenuous southern industry. "The [Dade Coal] company has had to get more convicts on account of the scarcity of free labor," noted a local paper in 1891. The coal companies themselves suggested that "the convicts are employed in the operation of the iron furnace in Dade County, and of its iron mines in Bartow County, [because] the procurement of free labor is practically impossible. . . . Free labor is exceedingly scarce and difficult to get" even with the help of four labor agents, complained the convict lessees.[4] When labor was obtained in this rural, isolated, and mountainous area with a long tradition of self-sufficiency and independence, it could not be held. "A miner is like a bird. He goes and comes. Here today and somewhere else tomorrow," the doctor at the Durham mines claimed.[5]

Thus, rather than rely on in-migration to a remote corner of the Georgia mountains or the begrudging labor of dispossessed tenant farmers, the area's two coal companies used the state's penal system to recruit and retain the essential component of their mine labor force. The convict-lease, which concentrated prisoners in the coal industry, was touted as the best penal system available because it was "adapted" to the prison population in Georgia, "ninety per cent of them being common negro laborers."[6] "The best adapted" prisoners for the mines and coke ovens were also, apparently, those with the longest sentences. If one of the problems with free labor was, in the words of the principal keeper, that it was "constantly changing employment and becomes skilled in none," it would be foolish to reproduce this turnover problem by working short-term convicts in the mines. Long-term convicts were especially prized by the lessees with heavy permanent capital investments, such as coal and iron mines; indeed, by law, in the lease authorized in 1876, all convicts sentenced to over five years were automatically destined for the Dade Coal Company.[7]

The result was an ever-increasing number of long-term or life-sentence prisoners in the mines, since each year these convicts were sentenced but rarely discharged. Thus by 1882, 56 of the 315 convicts held by the Dade Coal Company were sentenced for life, and an additional 186 were condemned to work for the company for ten years or more. Of the lifetime labor force, all but 6 of the 56 were black; 28 were convicted of murder, 11 of arson, 3 of burglary or robbery, and 3 of bestiality. Another 11, all black, were sent to the mines for life for rioting in Dodge County. It is interesting that 38 of these convicts sent to labor in the mountains were from plantation belt counties where they had most likely been agricultural workers. Yet not all convicts at the mines were violent offenders; of the 186 long-term (ten or more years) convicts in 1882, 86 were guilty of burglary, and 20 had been convicted of other property crimes, such as larceny, horse stealing, or forgery. Of these, 34 were from the plantation belt (33 of them black), and 35 (all of them black) came from urban counties such as Fulton (Atlanta), Richmond (Augusta), and Chatham (Savannah). This group of blacks, sentenced in the growing cities or tightly controlled plantation belt for committing property crimes and sent to work in the mines, exemplified the lease's simultaneous function as a mechanism of labor recruitment and social control.[8]

By 1894, the Dade Coal Company and the Durham Coal & Coke Company together controlled 970 of the state's convicts, with 840 working the mines and 130 others in subsidiary iron-ore and pig-iron production. This number was 45 percent of the 2,000 convicts leased by the state, and the 550 convicts in the Dade coal mines were by far the largest concentration of bound laborers in Georgia.[9] Black convicts continued to outnumber whites in the coal mines as they did in Georgia's entire penal system. In 1880, for instance, of the 371 convicts at the Dade mines, 340 were black. A decade later, the proportion remained the same, and by 1902, when all of the state's miners were convicts, 88 percent of state convicts were black.[10]

The ability to command a large stable force at a price negotiated with the state gave capitalists a powerful incentive to lease convicts. Under the Penitentiary Act of 1876, the Dade Coal Company obtained the right to acquire a proportion of all state convicts for twenty years (1879–1899) for a fixed annual cost of $25,000.[11] The combination of this fixed cost, negotiated only once but covering the last two decades of the century, and a long-term guarantee of labor that could become more efficient as it gained experience was particularly advantageous in the production of coal and coke that undergirded Georgia's postbellum iron industry. The coal deposits in northwest Georgia were defined by two characteristics: thin and irregular seams, which made mining expensive and unpredictable, and a high carbon content, which made the coal ideal for coking, the key step in the integration of coal mining with efficient pig-iron production.[12] Thus, if the coal could be dug cheaply and consistently by convicts and if labor were eliminated as a variable cost of production, the product could then be used to produce coke and pig iron. As a result, Georgia's pig-iron industry became extremely dependent upon the convict coal mines as a means of sustaining production. Moreover, the labor process had to be constant, so that there would always be enough coal to feed the coke ovens, which would go cold if production were halted or slowed. "It requires the working of a certain system to get the coal there and have it there," claimed one manager, and forced labor assured the company of a constant supply. Since the company's iron was sold by contract in advance, the production of coal and coke by the convicts was essential to the ability to meet these contracts. Thus, Senator Joseph E. Brown's Dade Coal Company insisted that "the labor of the convicts has been secured for the operation of its coal and iron properties which . . . are so situated that they can be worked with greater advantages by convict than free labor."[13]

Given the organization of labor in the "hand-loading era" of coal mining, the difficulties of recruiting a consistent, well-trained labor force were compounded by management's inability to exercise control over the labor process itself. Mine labor at the coal "face" took place far from the eyes of management, in underground "rooms" connected to a central mine shaft that ran into the hillside. The free coal miner was essentially an independent artisan who worked his room by blasting coal loose and loading it into a coal car. By attaching a numbered identification tag to his cars a miner's tonnage could be counted, and he was paid for the number of one-ton cars he sent out of the mine. In addition, a miner was responsible for "dead work"—clearing debris, timbering the rooms to prevent cave-ins, and laying the track that took the loaded cars from face to mine-head. Because the prevailing form of wage payment in the coal industry was based on unsupervised piecework, the notorious "miner's freedom" hewed from this system severely constrained management in the struggle for control over the pace and conditions of labor. "The principal characteristic of the hand-loading era," contends one of its most astute scholars, "is that management did not directly control the pace of production." The miner's retention of customary rights was thus increasingly "incompatible with the managerial need to plan, to coordinate, and to control the labor process for maximum profits."[14]

Georgia's mine operators, however, found a novel way not only to subvert the miner's customary rights and control embedded in the tonnage system, but to turn it to their advantage. With free labor a piece-price system allowed workers to contend for control over production, but convict labor transformed the work into a task system that could apparently push labor extraction to its utmost limits, precipitating a different kind of struggle. The fixed nature of a convict labor force allowed the lessee to bypass the obstacles of labor recruitment, retention, and negotiation; but this situation was a double-edged sword. Without the incentive of wages or the threat of dismissal, convicts had no reason to work at all, and their main object was to avoid labor as much as possible.[15] In the absence of a free market in labor, a wage relation, or even a patina of paternalism, the extraction of industrial forced labor in the postbellum period took on a special character, mediated by the task system. Convicts were commanded to produce a predetermined quantity of coal each day or suffer corporal punishment. Antebellum task work in agriculture and industry may have permitted some slaves to carve out a uniquely autonomous sphere for themselves allowing them to define the pace of work and the allocation of tasks, to profit from paid overwork, and even to obtain property. But in a postemancipation society supposedly committed to the sanctity of free labor relations, the task system when wedded to the convict-lease could be nothing other than the ultimate form of labor extraction that capitalists sought and failed to obtain from free workers.[16]

Ironically, the task system initially developed as a concession to the convicts working in Joseph Brown's mines. After they complained in 1874 about the rigor of the labor, tasks were instituted and rewards were tendered for work done beyond the set task.[17] This opportunity for the convict to cross, from one hour to the next, the threshold from uncompensated slave to wage worker could be regarded as one of the few benefits prisoners might reap from the system. One convict in the Alabama mines, for instance, claimed that he could finish his five-ton task by nine in the morning and then "cut five or six tons for myself at 40 cents a ton."[18] Even at such an unlikely Stakhonovite pace, however, this convict would receive only two dollars while producing ten tons of coal for the company; the pay for free labor for the same output, at sixty cents a ton, would be six dollars. Moreover, in Georgia's mines convicts were paid in scrip redeemable only at the prison commissary.[19] Finally, what the company could provide it could take away. Frustrated with the low productivity of the convicts at the Dade mines in 1893, the president of the Dade Coal Company, Joseph Brown's son, Julius, reported to the stockholders that "I have not been able to get as satisfactory work out of this division of the property as I had hoped. . . . I have ordered payments of extra compensation for convicts entirely shut off. . . . [W]e [are] not running a summer resort hotel for criminals."[20]

Task work for convicts in coal mining was defined by two factors unique to that industry. First, the ability of a convict to meet his task was dependent on a host of contingencies, over none of which he or the company had much control. "The reasonableness of these tasks depends largely on the size of the vein [of coal], the conditions under which mining is carried on, on the expertness of the particular operator, [and] on the amount of 'propping' to be done [to prevent accidents]," claimed one observer, not to mention the amount of slate in the coal, the distance a miner's room might be from the main shaft, and the availability of cars to fill. This habitual uncertainty of the industry was one of the reasons mine operators turned to coerced labor in the first place. But the notorious variability of mine work made fair tasking incompatible with a system of labor based on punishment; the "idea of an arbitrary task is preposterous," testified E. D. Brock, warden at the Dade mines.[21]

Yet, the second factor of mine work, the impossibility of direct super-vision of recalcitrant convicts spread out for miles underground, made task work an absolute necessity. "We were absolutely taken away from the guards when we entered the mines," testified one convict.[22] Thus, the task itself was not merely an instrument of labor extraction but also the primary means to enforce the prescribed punishment of hard labor, since not meet-ing the task would result in a whipping and to meet the task required steady work throughout the day.[23] "No punishment shall be administered to a convict," proclaimed the Georgia Prison Commission, "except in cases where it is reasonably necessary to enforce discipline or *compel work or labor by the convicts*."[24] What gave convict-leasing its unique character as a particularly brutal penal system was the subordination of all penal functions to the single goal of labor extraction. Consequently, the determination of the task and whether it could be "reasonably" obtained was the main arena of conflict in the mines. Shaped by this question were the conditions of labor and safety, the convicts' attempts to resist forced labor and avoid punish-ment, and the issue of who wielded ultimate control over the convicts and their labor, the lessee or the state.

When convicts arrived at the Dade coal mines they were greeted by the "boss" who would introduce them to their work with these words: "Now boys, I don't want to have to punish you. I want you to get your task done. If you get your task done everything will be all right. I want to get along all right and I want to treat you boys right, and if you get your task done, we will never have any trouble."[25] The ease or difficulty with which the work could be accomplished was a common point of scrutiny in the routine grand jury and legislative investigations of the convict camps that passed for oversight of the lease system.[26]

Joseph Brown, not surprisingly, insisted that only "moderate work" was required of the convicts in his mines. The Dade County grand jury in 1898 remarked that "some [convicts] complained that their tasks were too heavy, while others said they could complete their tasks in the allotted time." "We think the men are overtasked, owing to the small vein of coal where they work," concluded the grand jury convened in 1901.[27] The legislature as well found fault with task work. In 1890 the House Penitentiary Committee visited the Dade mines and had harsh criticisms of the conditions, perhaps because the committee members took the unusual step of actually going underground "to see the kind of work and the amount required of each man, . . . an experience never to be forgotten." In order to obtain the set task "the men [were] working in such places as rendered it necessary for them to lie on their stomachs while at work, often in the mud and water, in bad ventilation," the committee found. "We condemn in the strongest terms the rule that requires each man to mine a given quantity of coal daily or receive . . . punishment," they concluded.[28]

Such condemnation went unheeded. Eighteen years later, in the 1908 legislative investigation that culminated in the abolition of the lease and convict mining in Georgia, the task system was regarded as one of the prime instruments of cruelty under the existing penal system; "the possibilities of the cruel treatment of the convicts in regard [to the task] are limitless" was the overwhelming conclusion of the investigators.[29] The committee remarked that at the mines there were "an unusually large number of whippings . . . for 'shortage on tasks' and 'slate in coal.'" The convicts at the Durham mines "were given very heavy tasks and were punished severely if they failed to get through with the tasks," an ex-convict testified. Noting that a squad of fifty convicts had been transferred from a brickyard, where they had worked quite satisfactorily, to the mines, where they suddenly received frequent whippings for "idleness" and "failure to get tasks," the committee resolved that the labor expected of convict miners must be unreasonable. "Men, even convicts, are not going to 'idle' or fail to get their tasks, week after week, when they know a whipping is certain, if the tasks are fair, reasonable and within their ability," the committee concluded.[30] Even the whipping boss, who was authorized to punish the convicts, admitted that "there is a great deal of difference in digging coal than in making brick."[31]

How much coal were prisoners actually expected to produce? As did free miners, convicts worked in rooms off a main shaft down which ran a track for the coal cars loaded by the prisoners at the coal face. The convict would dig about ten feet under the coal face and blast the coal loose with shot powder.[32] He would then load a car with the loose coal, being careful to pick out the worthless slate, and push it back to the main shaft. This work entailed digging coal lying down or on one's knees, due to the thinness of the coal seams (sometimes as narrow as eighteen inches and rarely thicker than four feet) often in water in a tunnel six to eight feet wide illuminated only by the miner's head lamp, which frequently dripped oil in his eyes and overcame him with fumes.[33] According to the coal operators, several criteria were taken into account in determining a man's allotted task under these conditions, including the width of the seam in his room. Tasks were even "purposely placed lower than they would otherwise have been" to create an incentive for paid overwork.[34] Free miners in southern Appalachia during the hand-loading era might produce between four and six tons daily, although there is evidence of deliberate attempts to restrict output in order to keep piece rates high. In practice, most of the evidence points to a relatively inflexible similar task of four or five tons for convicts, which many prisoners struggled to meet.[35]

After about twelve beatings for the crime of "shortage" a convict's task might be reduced; even so, one ex-prisoner testified, 40 percent of the convicts in one mine were unable to finish their tasks by nightfall.[36] Yet, "if they found a man could dig a task and get through with it by three or four o'clock in the evening they would increase it, and fix it so that he couldn't get out at that time," one ex-convict testified.[37] Convicts complained that many miners could not even take the time to eat for fear they would fall behind and not make the task. Cleanliness suffered as well since keeping their beds and clothing clean required the convicts' time, and time was money.[38] As the investigating committee in 1908 pointed out, punishment was inflicted often, without much regard for the ability of the convicts to meet the task; indeed, recent arrivals at the Lookout mines were whipped simply to "break them in."[39] "Did they whip them much for not working?" one convict was asked during an investigation. "Not much," he replied sardonically. "They did not whip them much for not working, they whipped them for not working as much as they wanted them to."[40] Confronted with evidence of such treatment, one state prison official responded that "a negro can't get along without it." Significantly, the leather strap used to punish convicts for failure to work at the pace set by the company was colloquially known as a "negro regulator."[41]

Safety was a frequent casualty of the enforced pace of work. Again, as with free miners, convicts in addition to their task had to perform the mine's dead work, most significantly the timbering of their tunnels and rooms to prevent falls of slate. Accidents in the convict mines were frequent, and the labor was in places "where they are liable to be crushed to death at any moment." Convicts were killed or badly hurt by the coal cars, by explosions, by pick wounds, and most frequently, "mashed by slate," "injured by slate," or "killed by slate fall." In the years 1888 to 1894 there were over 100 injuries, 15 of them fatal, in the Dade mines where at the time about 500 prisoners worked. This fatality rate of approximately one death per 100,000 tons of coal mined far exceeded the 1896 West Virginia rate of 200,000 tons in bituminous mining, and it compared unfavorably to what the U.S. Geological Survey later called the "year [1907] in which the darkest record was made in the history of the industry," when only 145,000 tons were mined for every worker who lost his life.[42]

In the convict mines, a large proportion of the recorded casualties were attributable to cave-ins. Naturally, the tendency was to blame the convicts for accidents. The mines were "as safe as well can be," reported the Dade County grand jury in 1897. "We find that the accidents that have occurred was [sic] by the carelessness of the convicts themselves." One guard at the mines estimated that there was at least one casualty from falling slate each month, but he likewise attributed such incidents to convict negligence or incompetent timbering. A member of the Prison Commission, an ex-slaveowner who admitted he had never entered the mines and had no idea what a reasonable task might be, blamed the mines' poor safety record on the carelessness of black convicts. He claimed, falsely, that "you never see a white man mashed up" from a slate fall. In truth, however, the relatively few injuries sustained by whites clearly resulted from their paucity and their assignment to less dangerous work outside the mines.[43]

According to the convicts themselves, any "carelessness" was dictated by the requirements of labor rather than their alleged racial characteristics. Since a convict had a certain number of tons to produce on the pain of punishment, "he would not take the time to brace the slate and it fell on him," testified one prisoner. If the men did "timber [the mine roof] properly . . . they would not finish their task," another concurred. As a result "men were continually getting their legs [and] arms broken or their body bruised up in some way."[44] The 1908 investigative committee noted that at the Durham mines pressure to make the task was responsible for the "large percentage of cases in the hospital resulting from accidents in the mines, from falling slate."[45]

The convicts were not helpless in the face of this mechanism of labor extraction. Evidence exists of sporadic "mutinies" that might on occasion revolve around the prisoners' treatment at the hands of the whipping boss.

Convicts in the Durham mines advocated a strike to protest ventilation and gas problems that were so bad, according to the warden, that "if [the] mine was situated in any of the states where mining laws were enforced it would be immediately closed."[46] Convicts would also purposely knock out timbers in order to cause a cave-in, so that a day could be taken out from the task to clear a room of debris.[47]

But less drastic measures of "day-to-day resistance" could be taken. One common method of cheating the whipping boss was to load slate at the bottom of a car in order to make the task more quickly. This practice was particularly irksome to the company officials, since they had trouble selling coal mixed with too much slate. "It injures the class of coal in every respect," lamented one whipping boss.[48] In addition to frequent punishment for "shortage," "idleness," "slate," and other designations referring to resistance to the task, the "whipping reports" also show beatings for "feigning illness." This practice, also known as "betting the doctor," was a popular means of avoiding work altogether and "beating the company out of a day's work."[49] Discipline was meted out for these various methods of circumventing the task, as the records kept by the whipping bosses show. At the Dade mines, for instance, between 1901 and 1904 fully 58 percent of the nearly one thousand whippings administered were for such labor-related infractions. The rest were for fighting, gambling, or general "disobedience." Frequently these violations involved more than one prisoner, suggesting the possibility of collusion at least on a small scale (see Table 10.1).[50]

The task system was open to manipulation in other ways as well. One convict pointed out that while he was able to make his task "in a good reasonable place," others fell behind, not least because "a heap of times the men would get behind by loading [coal] for other fellows." This method aided convicts less able to keep up with the work, either because of their physical condition or because, as one convict complained, "the boss man . . . put me in a place that I couldn't hardly get my task." "If they have [a task] of five cars [i.e., five tons] maybe they might load two or three cars, and some other fellow would load two, and that would make his task," a convict testified. If tasks were set weekly, as they sometimes were, this sort of mutuality was extended to convicts who had eight to ten cars left to load at the end of the week; but it also appears to have been provided to the mines' "gal boys," or known homosexuals.[51]

In other cases, "some of the men that cannot get the amount of coal required of them are paying other men that get their [own] task [done] to

Table 10.1. Labor-Related Punishment, Cole City Convict Mines, 1901–1904

Month	# Punished	Labor-Related[a] (on same day)
October 1901	27	14 (5, 4, 4)
November 1901	52	44 (8, 7, 5)
December 1901	35	28 (7, 7, 4)
January 1902	30	13 (6)
February 1902	26	15 (7, 6)
March 1902	31	15 (7, 6)
April 1902	10	4 (3)
May 1902	26	9 (4, 3, 2)
June 1902	25	15 (5, 3, 3)
July 1902	17	10 (5, 2, 2)
August 1902	16	13 (6, 5)
September 1902	17	8 (4, 3)
October 1902	30	19 (6, 5, 4)
December 1902	39	15 (4, 4)
January 1903	31	12 (4)
February 1903	32	7
March 1903	36	15 (8)
April 1903	56	36 (5, 5, 3, 3)
May 1903	51	41 (9, 8, 4, 3, 3, 3)
June 1903	53	34 (9, 7, 4, 4)
July 1903	54	39 (15, 9, 6)
August 1903	23	14 (5, 4)
September 1903	43	35 (8, 5, 3)
October 1903	31	21 (5)
November 1903	53	27 (5, 4)
December 1903	28	15 (3)
January 1904	39	18 (6, 4, 3)
February 1904	14	3
March 1904	19	12
TOTAL:	944	551 = 58%

[a]Includes "Idleness," "Short on Task," "Slate" (i.e., loading too much slate with coal), and "Doctor" (i.e., feigning sickness). There were between 100 and 150 convicts at Cole City in this period. See Prison Commission, *Reports.*

Source: Monthly Reports of Convicts Punished ("Whipping Reports"), vol. 1, Cole City Camp, 1901–1904, Records of the Prison Commission, Records of the Board of Corrections, Georgia Department of Archives and History.

help them," the grand jury noted. Aid might even be extended to convicts weakened by punishment. But if the mine boss discovered such collusion, the helper's own task would be increased to fill his available time. Another trick the convicts discovered was to switch numbers or car tags in order to get credit for cars filled by other miners, though it is not clear that this practice was always by mutual agreement. Certainly, desperation to make the task and avoid punishment led to less admirable behavior at times. For instance, when the distance between the coal face and the main shaft was extensive, convicts would pilfer coal from another's car as it rolled past in order to help make their own task.[52]

The struggle between convicts and their masters over the extraction of labor was overlaid with another conflict, that between the lessees and the state. From the point of view of the state, the lessees bought only the *labor* of the convicts and in exchange incurred the responsibility of caring for their bodies. Even criminals "are certainly entitled to something like humane treatment," the House Committee on the Penitentiary proclaimed, "and it is the duty of the State to see that they receive it." Four decades of convict leasing in Georgia were punctuated by repeatedly futile attempts by the governor, the principal keeper, the penitentiary physician, the legislature, and various investigating committees to press the lessees to meet their obligation to maintain humane conditions "so far as it might be consistent with the working of convicts."[53]

In order to do so, after a legislative investigation in 1881 turned up numerous "existing evils in the penitentiary system," the investigative committee concluded that "humanity and justice require that the state appoint an officer at each camp to stand between the convict and lessee."[54] But until 1897 the lessees retained what they justifiably regarded as their most significant privilege: "being charged with the management of these convicts we must insist upon the right of naming the men who shall control them."[55] This facet of lessee control was crucial for the maximum extraction of labor, because it allowed the company leasing the convicts to define the pace of work—the task—and mete out punishment for the failure to meet it.

The authority of the company to compel labor resided in the person of the whipping boss. In response to the legislative recommendation in 1881 the state ostensibly controlled punishment by approving the appointment of the men authorized to administer whippings at each camp.[56] In practice, however, this whipping boss was nothing more than a loyal employee chosen by the lessee and might even be the same person responsible for the overall direction of the enterprise that utilized forced labor. "Whipping Bosses are not the Agents of the State," Governor John B. Gordon, himself a former lessee, acknowledged in 1887 after discovering "excessive whipping and in some cases . . . unreasonable and excessive labor" at the convict camps.[57]

The lessees vigorously defended the prerogative of designating the whipping boss as a necessary component of maintaining "discipline" at their camps. The "superintendent of labor and convicts" at the Dade coal complex in 1889, for instance, wrote to his employer, Joseph Brown, that the appointment of an additional whipping boss was needed because of an increase in the number of convicts under the company's control. "I believe under the law these appointments are made by the company or lessee and endorsed by the Penitentiary officials and the Governor," he informed Brown, who sent the note on to Governor Gordon. "The uniform practice in the Executive Office since the lease has been . . . that the individual lessee having control of the convicts should name the Whipping Boss," Brown protested to Governor W. Y. Atkinson in 1896 when his desired appointments were delayed. "Serious trouble is apprehended at the Mines, unless some one has authority to impose punishment," he added ominously.[58]

Indeed, it was the very power of appointment of the whipping boss that the state claimed upon reorganization of the penal system and the lease in 1897, as the twenty-year lease drew to a close. Under the "Act to create a prison commission" of that year the whipping bosses were transformed into deputy wardens, and the power to punish prisoners was placed in the hands of these men, now supposedly wholly employed by the state rather than by the lessee of convict labor. By this law the principal keeper was replaced by a three-person prison commission that was granted "complete management and control of the state convicts," including the right to "regulate the hours of their labor [and] the manner and extent of their punishment" through direct appointment of the supervisory personnel at the convict camps.[59]

Although this same law also authorized a new five-year lease of the convicts to begin on 1 April 1899, the new prison officials disingenuously insisted that this reorganization eliminated state leasing of prisoners in Georgia since the convicts were never alienated from the state's control. Under the "lease system" of the past two decades, the prison commis-

sioners proclaimed in 1900, "the state not only sold the labor of the convicts, but parted with their custody and control" as well. Since the wardens,
or whipping bosses, were "dependent for their positions and wages upon the
lessees, the State's interest and the welfare of the convicts were made
subservient to the interest of their employers, profitable results from the
convict labor." This statement was an admirably accurate critique of Georgia's penal system, but the subsequent assertion that "the new system is [in]
no respects a lease system" because "the state through its own officers and
employees [is] controlling and working [the convicts]" was a less penetrating observation. Indeed, in its report the previous year, the commission had
listed as one of the warden's or deputy warden's primary duties that he
"require the performance of good and faithful labor by the convicts for the
employer."[60]

This reform was unable to overcome the basic contradiction of penal
labor in Georgia; the enforcement of discipline was congruent with the
extraction of labor and thus in the lessee's interest not the state's. There
continued to be considerable ambiguity in the warden's ultimate allegiance
in a convict mine, an ambiguity that the lessees did their best to exacerbate.
If the prisoners "fail[ed] to secure these tasks or have too much slate in the
coal, on the complaint of the mining bosses they [were] whipped by the
State's Officers," a legislative investigation noted. But the "mining boss or
foreman, an employee of the lessee, fixes the task and decides if it has been
obtained or if there is too much slate in it."[61] The warden "generally took
the word" of the boss in this matter, and they had "no trouble" with each
other—especially if warden and boss were the same man.[62] This dual
identity occurred when a lessee would propose that the state name his own
camp superintendent as warden, who could then continue to direct the
labor in his capacity as a company man but punish the convicts for failing to
meet the task in performance of his duties as a state officer.[63] Alternatively,
lessees paid wardens and guards a salary in addition to what these employees received from the state in their official capacities, sometimes as much
as 150 percent more. This extra money was "simply paid to keep these
wardens from becoming cross wise with the Company."[64]

The lessees and wardens, with feigned innocence, protested that this
"customary" compensation was for "rendering them services." "They
doubtless were," scoffed the 1908 investigating committee. The convicts
had no problem with such fine points: "the [lessee] paid large sums of

money to the deputy warden of the state who was located at the works and thus . . . made [him] its agent and employee and not the employee of the state," claimed a prisoner in a lawsuit against his former custodian. Regarding the work of mining coal below the surface, testified another convict, "the state had no jurisdiction over us." With disarming candor, Joel Hurt, who after 1900 operated the coal mines that had previously belonged to the Browns, was quite blunt about the reason for the extra compensation and the dual appointments. It enabled him to get more work out of the convicts.[65]

Such subterfuge did not always suffice, however, for despite these ruses the question of labor and punishment led to occasional friction between lessees and state officials. James English, lessee of convicts at the Chattahoochee brickyard and the Durham coal mines, firmly believed that the warden or deputy warden should work the convicts to the advantage of the contractor who, after all, had paid for the labor. "The State's representative [is there] simply to see the negroes give [the lessee] reasonable labor," he claimed. But the legislative committee investigating the lease in 1908 suggested that the warden "ought to be taking care of convicts, instead of bossing them."[66] Joel Hurt was particularly disgruntled because the warden at one of his convict camps would not always whip prisoners for "the lack of work." Hurt complained that at the end of the day his convicts broke into song, singing "Promiseland," and insisted that "men ought to be worked so hard they couldn't sing." He demanded that the state officials at his mine use discipline to get more work out of his bound labor force. The chair of the prison commission, Joseph S. Turner, countered that "the contractors only buy the labor," which the state had a right to limit in the interest of humane treatment. Yet Turner also admitted his belief that "when convicts work, I think they necessarily have to do the same work free men would do"; in fact, the prison commission determined if the contractor was provided with "reasonable labor" in the mines by comparing the output to free labor.[67]

Indeed, the issue of productivity was the crux of the matter. Despite the fact that the most ardent defenders of convict leasing claimed that prisoners could do twice the work of free labor, the relative efficiency of convict miners is open to dispute. The prevailing attitude about race, labor, and penal discipline among prison officials and lessees in the South was "that more work is done by a colored convict than by the average colored free laborer."[68] But coal mining was a fairly skilled occupation in which forced labor with no commitment to the work might have limited productive capability, whatever its "reliability." Despite the faith in forced labor shown by the lessees who claimed that they could not recruit and retain free workers, despite the control they exercised over convict labor with the task and punishment system, and despite the fact that long sentences offered "an unusual opportunity for training the convicts for skilled labor,"[69] raw data indicate that the daily tons of coal raised per man in Georgia, where nearly all miners were bound workers, was consistently well below the national average. Over time, Georgia's convicts produced only one-half the amount of coal dug per man in states where free labor predominated (see Table 10.2).[70]

This low mining productivity and its relationship to convict labor can be understood two ways. Although Georgia's mines almost always recorded more days worked annually than any other state in the nation, convict labor may have been woefully inefficient because of the lack of skill and training as well as resistance to an enforced task.[71] At times the lessees expressed their mounting frustration, particularly as productivity steadily increased in other coal fields. In the 1896 investigation of Georgia's convict coal mines, the Dade Coal Company's general manager admitted that the "amount of coal for [the] number of men employed . . . was not coal enough. It was nothing in proportion to the amount of coal gotten out in other mines with the same number of men." Remarking on a decrease of 40 percent in coal production in Georgia during the 1890s, the U.S. Geological Survey also noted that the number of miners and days worked had not decreased proportionately. The USGS directly attributed the dismal output to the employment of convicts in the mines. After the turn of the century the Geological Survey continued to suggest that "the apparently low average of efficiency [in Georgia's coal mines] is explained by the fact that state convicts are employed to a considerable extent, . . . and these in the large majority of cases have for experience as coal miners only the periods of their incarceration."[72]

Alternatively, low productivity can be understood as the reason for reliance on forced labor in the first place. That is, the geological, topographical, and economic constraints on the area's coal production—thin and uneven seams that were relatively inaccessible and weak markets—made mining with free labor an unprofitable proposition in Georgia for capital and labor alike.[73] It is interesting that the marked increase in U.S. mining

Table 10.2. Productivity in Coal Mining, 1880–1910: Tons
(Bituminous) Raised Per Miner/Per Day Worked

	U.S.	Georgia	Alabama	Tennessee	West Virginia
1880	1.90	1.17	0.71	1.78	1.97
1890	2.56	1.72	1.77	1.62	2.66
1891	2.57	0.64			
1892	2.72	1.67			
1893	2.73	1.48			
1894	2.84	1.60			
1895	2.90	0.99	2.25	2.21	3.05
1896	2.94	1.10			
1897	3.04	1.37			
1898	3.09	1.63			
1899	3.05	1.36			
1900	2.98	1.90	2.34	1.90	3.36
1901	2.94	1.54			
1902	3.06	1.76			
1903	3.02	2.05			
1904	3.15	1.96			
1905	3.24	1.63	2.69	2.20	3.74
1906	3.36	1.62			
1907	3.29	1.71			
1908	3.34	1.51			
1910	3.46	1.73	2.91	2.65	3.94
MEAN	2.96	1.53			

Source: United States Geological Survey, *Mineral Resources of the United States,* 1883–1910.
Statistics necessary to calculate productivity are unavailable for 1881–1889 and 1909.

productivity at the century's end attributable to technological developments such as mechanized coal picks was not duplicated in Georgia's
mines, but this fact is similarly ambiguous. By 1900, 25 percent of the
nation's bituminous coal was mined by machine, and a decade later the
figure was 41 percent. But mining machines were not used in Georgia; this
lack was directly attributed to reliance on cheap black forced labor, which
inhibited the incentive to modernize. "As a large part of the work in

[Georgia's] mines is done by convicts," the U.S. Geological Survey reported in 1905; "mining machines have not been introduced."[74] In convict mines the labor force itself was already capitalized; indeed, the convicts were regarded as "machines for whose rental a certain price is paid," so the tendency to replace this labor with what Marx referred to as "dead labor" was restrained.[75] But whether the continued lag and widening gap in productivity caused a constraint on profits in a highly competitive industry or whether these mines could be profitable at all without forced labor remains an open question.[76]

After 1897 the problem of low productivity was coupled with a new constraint as the price for leasing convict labor increased dramatically and approached the cost of free labor. Before that date lessees paid a fixed price to the state; as the number of convicts increased, the actual cost for each one was reduced by the 1890s to approximately $10 per annum. But when the lease was renewed after 1897, over fifty companies bid for convicts per capita at an average price of $100 per annum for *each* convict. After 1900 prices for coal, iron, lumber, brick, and naval stores—all produced by convicts—began to rise, and in an increasingly competitive labor market convict lessees continued to bid up the price of acquiring forced labor. By 1904 the coal companies were paying between $225 and $250 a year for each prisoner they brought to the mines. In 1902 the prison commission claimed that "no [financial] advantage accrues to the contractor employing [convict] labor, except that his supply is more constant."[77] As a result of this increased capital cost, the lessees likely sought to increase the recalcitrant prisoners' output in order to maintain high profitability. But the result was exacerbation of the central contradiction of the convict-lease and task system, that between penal function and labor exploitation, between state protection of the convicts' welfare and their status as state-created slaves. This cost increase may explain some of the increasing tension over the control of the pace of work, which helped lead in 1908 to the abolition of the lease in Georgia.[78]

Ultimately, the viability of convict labor rested on the degree to which productive forced labor could be made compatible with the penal rationales of custody and punishment. The brutality of convict leasing derived from the prisoners' dual identity as objects of correction and of production; its limits were defined by the convicts' resistance to complete enslavement and the state's resulting willingness to enforce the notion that "there is or should be a difference in the life of a prisoner and that of a slave."[79] For the state, the lessee, and the prisoner, these conflicts shaped daily life in Georgia's convict mines and on occasion broke out in full confrontation. The meaning of the task system that lay at the heart of these conflicts is perhaps best expressed by the oral tradition of the men who struggled against it, as in this convict work song:

> The captain holler hurry,
> Goin' to take my time. Say captain holler hurry,
> Goin' to take my time.
> Say he makin' money,
> And I'm trying to make time.
> Say he can lose his job,
> But I can't lose mine.[80]

The Failure of Operation Dixie
A Critical Turning Point in American Political Development?

Operation Dixie

In early February of 1946, the Congress of Industrial Organizations' (CIO) executive board launched Operation Dixie, an attempt to unionize all industry in the South. Philip Murray, the CIO president, told the board that the southern organizing effort was "the most important drive of its kind ever undertaken by any labor union in the history of this country." Such sentiments, along with reports of initial successes, were echoed in virtually every issue of the weekly *CIO News* beginning in early March 1946 and continuing for at least a year. The American Federation of Labor (AFL), the former parent and later rival of the CIO, began its own campaign to organize the South at its Southern Labor Conference held in Asheville, North Carolina, 11 and 12 May 1946. The AFL paper, *The American Federationist*, described the AFL effort as "the most intensive Southern organizing drive ever undertaken by the trade union movement."[1]

The idea of organizing the South and its critical importance both for the national strength of unions and for their long-term survival in other parts of the country was not a new one. Major statements and resolutions appear in *The American Federationist* as well as in AFL convention proceedings for decades prior to 1946. The AFL explicitly underscored the importance of the South by holding its 1928 annual national convention in New Orleans. The 1929 convention mandated a conference of all unions to begin a massive southern organizing drive. The drive was begun and regularly trumpeted by AFL President William Green and others in the pages of the 1929 and 1930 issues of the *Federationist*. The CIO likewise emphasized the importance of organizing the South. Its first convention in 1938, as an organization officially independent of the AFL, resolved to begin a southern organizing campaign. In 1939 top CIO officials met with CIO President John L. Lewis to map plans and allocate resources.[2]

The year 1946, however, seemed to many union leaders to be an especially propitious one to launch a new, successful southern organizing campaign. Unions appeared to have good reasons to be optimistic. Trade union membership had increased from less than three million members in 1933 to more than fourteen million in 1945. Thus, the commitment of enormous attention, energies, and resources to organizing the South by both labor federations seemingly promised grand results. During World War II there had been significant union growth across the South. Industrial centers including Gadsden and Birmingham, Alabama; Laurel, Mississippi; Savannah and Atlanta, Georgia; Baton Rouge, Bogalusa, and New Orleans, Louisiana; Galveston, Texas; Memphis, Tennessee; and Tampa, Florida, had all become heavily unionized. Union organizing successes ranged across the main southern industries, including coal, metal mining, oil refining, mass transit, tobacco, pulpwood and paper, and even major textile mills in the Piedmont region. In its November 1946 issue, *Fortune Magazine,* no friend of unions, saw resistance to unions as weak and complete unionization of the South as inevitable.[3]

Significance of the Failure. Despite the devotion of substantial resources by unions and optimistic prognoses from many quarters, Operation Dixie failed abysmally.[4] Not only did unions gain few new members and locals, but most of the gains made during World War II were subsequently lost. The significance of this defeat may be viewed on several levels: first, it marked the end of the dramatic union growth that started in 1933 and the beginning of the steady decline in union density that continues through the early 1990s.[5] The 1945 high of 35 percent of the nonagricultural labor force organized into unions, although approached in 1953, has never been exceeded. In 1992, the figure stands at 15 to 16 percent; subtracting the more recently organized governmental employees, the figure for private sector workers is 10 to 11 percent, at or below the pre-depression level.

Second, the failure to organize the South marginalized the labor movement in national politics. Despite their important regional political influence in the Northeast, the upper Midwest, and to a lesser extent in California and the Northwest, unions never effectively mobilized majorities in Congress that would have overcome the combination of the Solid South and traditional Republican and business support in other areas of the country. Nowhere was this inadequacy more sharply illustrated than in the unions' inability to stop the passage of the anti-labor Taft-Hartley Act in 1947. Characterizing it as the "slave labor act," both union federations made all-out efforts to defeat it. Southern Democrats provided the margin necessary to override President Truman's veto of the act. With labor's weak legislative leverage apparent for all to see, union influence within the Democratic Party declined further; union political demands became more modest.[6]

Third, rather than being just another episode in the changing fortunes of organized labor, the inability of unions to organize the South has had even wider social and political ramifications. The failure of Operation Dixie left southern Dixiecrats and the system of white supremacy with complete social, political, and economic hegemony intact in much of the South. Successful unionization was by necessity interracial and to varying degrees anti-racist. Independent organization in the South by CIO unions—the Mine, Mill, and Smelter Workers, the United Mine Workers, the tobacco workers, the longshoremen, the maritime workers, and the packinghouse workers—often formed islands of opposition to racial discrimination and resources in the fight for equality, including, for example, campaigns against the poll tax and lynching. Successful unionization of the South would have most likely hastened the civil rights movement by many years.[7] It also would have ensured not only more extensive involvement and aid from northern unions, but also a strong reservoir of southern white working-class support, largely absent from the southern struggles of African Americans in the 1950s, 1960s, and 1970s. The unionization of the South had the potential to minimize the mobilization of white backlash, a central feature of post-World War II politics.

Southern racist Dixiecrat hegemony made possible South Carolinian Strom Thurmond's 1948 Dixiecrat Party presidential campaign, a movement that drew its strongest support from whites in the most heavily African-American section of the South, notably in South Carolina and Mississippi. It also made possible George Wallace's 1968 presidential campaign, based on racist-populist appeals to white backlash.[8]

These originally regional appeals, however, paved the way for the Republican Party's "southern strategy," a successful attempt to win the support of southern and other whites, many of whom were traditional Democratic voters. And, it is the failure of Operation Dixie that has allowed the Republican southern strategy, from Presidents Nixon to Bush, to be successful in shaping the more recent decades of American politics.

Critical Turning Points. Thus, the failure of Operation Dixie represents a critical turning point in American politics and a key to understanding the present political conjuncture. The question remains open as to what a critical turning point is and to what extent Operation Dixie actually represented one.

Most students of American political development and historical sociology recognize a number of critical turning points that have shaped American politics. Virtually everyone accepts that the Revolution-constitutional period had both an immediate and lasting impact on American politics. The same can be said for the Civil War. Though less agreement exists on most other periods, there are those who have argued for the colonial period (e.g., Morgan), Jackson's presidency (e.g., Schlesinger), Reconstruction (e.g., Du Bois), the Populist era of the 1890s (e.g., Goodwyn), the Progressive era (e.g., Skowronek), the 1960s-1970s civil rights era, and even the more recent Reagan ascendancy.[9] Many of the arguments about the importance of these periods are convincing, particularly those on the founding of the Republic and the Civil War. The current working hypothesis of this essay, however, is that the shape and structure of U.S. politics in the entire post-World War II period have been largely determined by events that happened in the 1930s and 1940s, the Great Depression-New Deal period. Thus, to understand politics and society in the United States in the 1990s, one must understand both this critical turning point and what emerged after it.

As a first cut, such a working hypothesis is not unusual. There is a common argument that traces many aspects of postwar public policy and state structure to the Roosevelt era. This argument notes the electoral realignment and the current bases of electoral support for the two major parties that can be traced to the 1930s (e.g., Sundquist). The development of social welfare policies and a "social democratic tinge" begins in this period (e.g., Hofstadter). Special importance is also attributed to the emergence of a strong centralized executive branch under President Franklin Roosevelt (e.g., Neustadt). While these factors were important, they are only part of the picture. At least as important were the channeling and dissipation of the radical politics, social movements, and labor activism of the period.[10]

The 1930s and early 1940s in the United States were a time of unusual social and political upheaval. During the 1930s, millions protested, engaging in marches, demonstrations, and more disruptive forms of activity, more often than not under left-wing leadership. The unemployed, farmers, African Americans, students, intellectuals, retirees, and others were broadly mobilized. Workers seized their workplaces and engaged in high levels of strike activity, while union membership grew at unprecedented rates. Third-party activity, to the left of President Franklin Roosevelt, ranged from well-entrenched state parties, most notably the Minnesota Farmer-Labor Party and the Wisconsin Progressive Party, and hundreds of local ones, to the charismatic Huey Long's Share-the-Wealth movement with its millions of supporters. Radicals, predominantly Communists, were not only the leaders of many insurgent organizations, but had become an important ingredient in mainstream political considerations.[11] Although this activity played a major role in the passage of social welfare legislation and in the formation of public policy and was an important ingredient in the rising fortunes of the new Democratic Party electoral majority, what is most surprising is how little impact the 1930s radicalism and labor activism left on subsequent politics after World War II.

Various questions therefore emerge: What was the status of the labor activism and radicalism of the 1930s and early 1940s? Was it merely the more boisterous fringe of a generally liberal reforming movement, as many previous scholars have contended? Or, from the standpoint of the 1990s, were these movements, along with the liberal Democratic realignment, perhaps merely a blip on the historical screen, caused by the country's worst depression, outliers in an otherwise conservative, individualistic politics that is the true American norm? Or, alternatively, were there more radical suppressed historical possibilities presented by this period that might have emerged had circumstances been slightly different? Was a stronger, much more influential labor movement or even the formation of an electorally significant labor party possible during the 1930s and 1940s? Some think such counterfactual questions are inappropriate in historical analysis. Nevertheless, it is impossible to understand what did happen, why certain broad historical outcomes did take place, without understanding the alternatives that did not. The analysis of Max Weber in *Methodology of the Social Sciences* and the more recent work on counterfactual analysis by Jon Elster and David Lewis strongly support such an analytical research perspective.[12]

Now the failure of Operation Dixie represents one of the most important setbacks dealt labor, liberal, and radical forces in the 1930s and 1940s. Thus, an attempt to understand it is both a good starting point for examining the more general questions and a prism for looking at the political outcomes of the 1930s and 1940s.

Could Operation Dixie Have Succeeded? Even if the failure of Operation Dixie was virtually inevitable, an understanding of the circumstances would still help us comprehend post-World War II American society and politics. If it is plausible, however, to presume that the failure to organize the South during the 1930s and 1940s was not predetermined, then a careful examination of this conjecture might lead an open-minded investigator to very different conclusions about American reality.

There is a standard, commonly accepted argument that the South could not have been organized during the 1930s and 1940s. This argument stresses the concentration of industry (particularly textiles, the South's largest) in company towns dominated by an interlocking structure of factory owners, church officials, politicians, law enforcement officers, newspaper editors, and others with little concern for the democratic and constitutional rights of their opponents, particularly union organizers. In addition, commitment to the status quo and opposition to unionism, often by necessity interracial, were reinforced by a powerful system of white supremacy that dominated all other aspects of political and social life in the South.[13] Opposition to unions was strengthened by an ideological hegemony rooted in southern traditionalism. Workers themselves were imbued with conservatism, generally supporting the status quo. The predominantly agrarian background of most workers helped reinforce both submissive and highly individualistic traits, judged to be intrinsic to southern character and antithetical to union membership. Though some of these features existed in the North, there was no general parallel, so the argument goes, in other parts of the country. This explanation for the failure of unions to organize the South is put forward by, among others, Liston Pope and more recently by Barbara Griffith.[14] While this explanation has its prima facie compelling features, it is not unproblematic. Many southern industries were successfully organized during the 1930s and 1940s. These included coal mining, metal mining, oil refining, longshore and maritime, tobacco, and transportation. The question thus arises of the degree to which these industries shared the characteristics attributed to those industries where union organizing failed. If the successful arenas of organizing were typical, then other variables must be located. Perhaps the strategies of unions and organizers were different. The main problematic is as follows: Why did the attempt to organize the South fail? Was it owing to objective circumstances, fortuitous conjunctural factors, or possibly faulty strategic plans and decisions by unions themselves? Answers to these questions are the cornerstone to understanding why U.S. politics in the post-World War II period developed as it did.

Some Working Hypotheses

One way to begin answering our questions is to examine carefully some of the hypotheses about why unions generally have had so much trouble in the South and more specifically about why Operation Dixie failed. Although many of the arguments that follow are intertwined, they have been kept distinct, at least initially, for analytic purposes.

The Southern Economy. One important and compelling set of hypotheses targets special features of the southern economy as the reasons for the difficulties of union organizing in the South. Ray Marshall, for example, argues: "There is evidence that of all the influences on union growth in the South, the most significant are economic. Legal and social forces seem to have only marginal effects." Or, in Frederic Meyers's words, "It is the usual view [to which Meyers subscribes] that the development of a stable labor movement is dependent on the development of an industrial economy." Meyers argues that southern unions remained weak because "the South [has] . . . been preindustrial."[15]

The economy of a country or region is quite clearly the place to start if one wants to understand the level of union organization there. It is incontrovertible that organization of workers requires a minimal level of industrial development and concentration of workers in large workplaces. Collective action and collective organization quite naturally require a collectivity. What level and what size are necessary, however, is not always clear. Meyers argues that Texas, because of its then recent, rapid industrial development compared to the rest of the country, was in the process of catching up in unionization rates as well.[16] There is much evidence to support this argument. Concentrated workers have more social weight and more social contact; thus, they are more likely to be organized. Workers in industrial cities, even in the

South, tend to be more highly unionized than those in isolated areas. Workers in Louisville, Richmond, Memphis, and Norfolk-Portsmouth, for example, are not only more organized than southern workers in other locales, but they are as organized as their counterparts in many cities in the North. Studies have shown that southern textile workers, a traditionally low organized group, are more likely to be in unions if they are close to a unionized coal mine. Data consistently show that larger workplaces are more likely to be unionized than smaller ones. The South with its many small workplaces, especially in textile, mining, and lumber, its fewer industrial cities, and its lower level of industrial development would be expected to have a lower rate of unionization.[17]

A special problem faced by unions in the South was directly related to the large size and low standard of living of the agricultural population in the 1930s and 1940s. As Marjorie Potwin explained, early twentieth-century textile workers came from "three streams": tenant farmers, mountaineers, and those who already lived around the mills. A tenant family might earn on average $375 per year in 1909 and a mountain family still less. Even at meager wages paid in southern textile mills, a family of three workers could expect to receive "on the lowest earning basis, $900 per year." Thus, as Marshall concludes, "the southern farmer or mountaineer found that his lot improved considerably when he moved into a mill village." While southern workers lived poorly, worked longer hours, and were paid considerably less than their northern counterparts, they were supposedly more satisfied and less likely to want a union to represent them, since they were doing quite well by the rural, agrarian standards with which they were familiar. The poor, agrarian economy that was the experience of most workers in the South made southern workers less attracted to unions.[18]

Conversely, the declining, overpopulated southern agricultural sector made for a high level of competition among workers for those industrial jobs that were available. The existence of a surplus agricultural population meant that there was almost never a tight labor market that would force southern employers to pay higher wages. It also meant that there were greater risks at trying to organize a union. Workers identified as trouble-makers could easily be replaced. When they went on strike there was always an abundant supply of strikebreakers from rural areas without the work-place experience that might have led them to join the strikers. The agrarian economy thus made it more difficult for workers to gain the leverage that they needed to organize, even if they had so desired. These problems were especially accentuated in industries such as textiles where skill levels for most of the work were low. In certain industries, where the skill level was high, as on railroads and in construction, workers could organize more easily since the barriers to entry from unskilled agricultural labor provided protection from competitors and most strikebreakers.[19]

The South, as a less developed region of the country, also suffered because of the type of industries that existed there. Marshall, among others, argues that the composition of southern industry is one of the reasons for the low level of unionization: "It is therefore clear that one of the reasons for the South's low proportion of unionization is the concentration of that region's employment in industries which are not well organized." Oligopolistic, capital-intensive firms, according to this argument, can afford to allow their employees to unionize. Southern industries were disproportionately extractive, labor intensive, and organized in large numbers of highly competitive firms. With low skill levels and often low start-up costs, union recognition and the increased costs of better conditions and wages for employees might easily drive a company out of business.[20]

An additional proof of the importance of the economy for southern union organizing may be seen in looking at the effects of the business cycle. For much of the twentieth century, many southern industries have been in a state of crisis, in part caused by international competition, but also by the domestic overproduction that often results from highly competitive industries with low barriers to entry. During periods of high economic activity, however, much successful organizing took place in the South. During the World War I boom, for example, extensive union growth occurred in key southern industries, such as tobacco, coal and iron ore mining, steel production, timber, and especially cotton textile. In the last industry, workers in major North Carolina textile centers, including Charlotte, Rock Hill, Huntersville, Concord, and Kannapolis (all places where CIO organizers failed during Operation Dixie) were highly organized in militant unions. As H. M. Douty concludes, "Clearly, a fairly extensive labor movement existed in the South during the World War I period." Much of this union organization collapsed in the early twenties with the onset of the post-World War I recession, as it did in other parts of the country as well. Douty implies, however, that some of the destruction of union organization took place because of poor tactical leadership, including the calling of ill-advised strikes, where workers had almost no leverage over their employers, who could not sell their current finished products in saturated, depressed markets. Frank deVyver argues that a similar upsurge in union membership took place from 1938 to 1948: "The upswing of the business cycle and the wartime economy have made gains in union membership almost inevitable, for during such periods workers feel the need for help to meet higher prices, and employers are able to grant wage increases and fringe demands more readily than at other times in the economic cycle. Thus unions are able to get something for the workers and the membership increases." During World War II, the labor market was especially tight, even in the South. Millions of potential employees were in the armed forces, while industrial production reached unprecedented levels. Not only did many southerners leave their farms, but southern workers also quit their jobs. Both groups sought, not primarily better jobs in southern industry, but the higher paying industrial jobs of the North. Southern industry had to compete for workers, no longer having the ready surplus labor force to which it was accustomed. Industries were also under pressure from the federal government to settle labor disputes quickly so as not to interrupt war production.[21]

It is clear that economic factors play a critical role in determining the level and possibilities of union organization. In certain circumstances they can prove more decisive than extreme government and employer opposition. Recent unionization in South Korea and among African workers in South Africa may plausibly be attributed to rapid industrial expansion during the 1970s and 1980s. Unions, however, have formed in many places, at very early stages of industrial development. They have also lost members or been inhibited at high levels of industrial development as in the United States today. Thus, despite the central importance of economic development, other factors may also play a determining role.

Union-Resistant Attitudes of Southern Workers and Southern Culture. Perhaps the most popular hypothesis for the difficulties of unions in the South points to aspects of southern culture and the character of southern workers. While there are clearly many Souths and many large variations in southern culture, from New Orleans to Birmingham and from the Delta to the hill country of Tennessee and North Carolina, it is also clear that there exist certain distinctive features of the South as a whole.

Patterns of speech, food, and music (from blues and spirituals to bluegrass), strains of Protestant religious fundamentalism, and a warmer climate are easily recognizable as southern. Their political import, however, is less clear. Other factors, including the relative ethnic homogeneity of the white population, the large historic percentage of African Americans, the heritage of black slavery and the plantation economy, the intensity and pervasiveness of the long-standing system of white supremacy, the violence and assertiveness of many southerners, and the defeat by the North in the Civil War, have political ramifications. The question, however, is not whether the South is different, but the degree to which its distinctive culture has held back the development of union organization.

Most commentators have answered that southern culture has been a major impediment to union organization in the South. They focus in particular on many traits that they ascribe to white southerners as a group; sometimes they include African-American southerners in these characterizations. There are many characteristics that are supposedly identifiable as central to southern character, all of which make union organization difficult, unlikely, or impossible. First, the heritage of the plantation system, with a large percentage of the population having roots as sharecroppers and tenant farmers, has supposedly left an ingrained psychological stance of docility, submissiveness, and acceptance of paternalistic relations.[22]

As Liston Pope argues in his classic case study of the 1929 Gastonia, North Carolina, textile strike, "The labor supply was also notable for its docility. This trait has been overemphasized by chambers of commerce and power companies seeking to attract Northern capital to Southern communities. . . . The first generation of workers appears to have been . . . patient and long-suffering in spirit. . . . They had been accustomed to working from sunrise to sunset without murmuring, and to expect little in return. They took it for granted that all members of the family would work as early as possible, and offered practically no opposition to child labor in the cotton mills."[23]

Joseph McDonald and Donald Clelland, in an analysis of attitudinal data among contemporary southern textile workers, write: "The analysis suggests that these textile workers remain affected by the paternalistic ideology, even if paternalistic practices themselves have changed ([Jeffery] Leiter, [Richard] Simpson], and that the deference felt toward management authority does reduce support for unions. We believe that the peripherality of both the southern region and the textile industry is the starting point for understanding these findings."[24]

Robert Blauner, writing in a different academic language, talks of the submissiveness and complacency of southern textile workers: "Workers with traditional orientations do not value control and self-expression as much as do modern industrial workers." And, in a stereotypic male chauvinist analysis: "The submissiveness required of male textile workers must be damaging to the maintenance of a sure sense of masculinity," a submissiveness, Blauner finds, that comes more naturally to female textile workers. Second, there is supposedly an attitude of extreme individualism and explosive violence, usually directed at other poor people—whites against other whites, blacks against blacks, oftentimes white violence directed against blacks. This individualism allegedly makes it difficult or unlikely that southern workers will organize collectively, except for the shortest outbursts of angry protest. Sustained cooperative behavior is supposedly alien.[25]

Liston Pope writes: "The workers brought with them to the mill villages an individualism nurtured by solitary life on small farms and sparsely populated mountainsides; this individualism resulted, in the sphere of industrial relations, in personal dealings as individuals with the employer, with collective labor action appearing only sporadically and always being short-lived. The early manufacturers, lacking capital and depending heavily on uninterrupted production in order to remain solvent, had available a labor supply largely unamenable to outside influences interested in the organization of labor."[26]

Writing in the November 1928 issue of *American Federationist,* George Googe, the top AFL official in the South argued, "The native Southerners of the small towns and country communities are traditionally independent in their own estimation, believing themselves sufficiently capable individually to take care of their own interests, and feeling that it is an admission of weakness to call upon their fellow workers for assistance or concerted action." Further, "The problem confronting the organizing of workers in the South is vastly different from that of any other section. The type of the native worker, his environment, mental attitude and traditions tend to create extreme lethargy towards his own betterment, particularly relative to activity in the labor movement."[27]

Or in the words of Irving Bernstein, the noted historian of labor in the

1920s and 1930s, "His rural tradition, his ingrained individualism, his igno-rance, his isolation, his restless mobility, his apathy, his poverty, his suspi-cions of northerners joined to impede his capacity to act collectively" and helped to defeat the textile strikes of 1929.[28]

Third, an ingrained social conservatism is supposedly endemic, stem-ming from an intense patriotism—involving both the nation as a whole and the South in particular—and deep religiosity. This conservatism is tied to the ever-present duty to accept and defend the prevailing system of white supremacy and the previously discussed acceptance of hierarchical and paternalistic social, political, and economic relations.

With regard to the textile revolt in 1929, the renowned historian of the South, George Brown Tindall, states, "The rebellion of 1929 revealed new elements in the southern industrial pattern, but highlighted the prevalence of the old. If southern workers had grown mutinous at class subordination, poverty, and the stretch-out amid prosperity hoopla, they remained close to their native culture. 'At the core of the Southern mill workers' outlook on life,' Paul Blanshard found, 'are the Sunday School, the Star Spangled Ban-ner, and personal friendship for the boss.' . . . He seized upon the union as an instrument of immediate protest rather than as an agency for long-range collective bargaining."[29]

And in a more general discussion of southern working-class values, Ray Marshall ties them to the predominant agrarian economy: "The abundance of low-income agricultural workers in the South has been a great obstacle to union growth. Not only have the workers frequently been willing to break strikes in order to escape their poor conditions, but they were also likely to be satisfied with their manufacturing jobs, removing the element of discon-tent which is usually a prerequisite to union organization. In addition, they generally have the values of rural people which precludes interest in or sympathy for unions."[30]

All the above aspects of the argument on southern values and culture are expressed in W. J. Cash's influential work, *The Mind of the South*. This book was often recommended reading by CIO southern leaders, particularly for their northern colleagues attempting to organize unions in the South. Cash stresses all the themes that we have so far mentioned. He has an impres-sionistic style, often insightful, sometimes woefully wrong and ignorant. On the latter, he asserts, for example, that the 1929 strikes were "the first serious labor revolt the South had ever known," thus displaying his ignorance not only of the extensive activity of the Knights of Labor organizing in the late nineteenth century and the mine workers of the late nineteenth and early twentieth centuries, but also of the high degree of organizing in the textile industry in the 1915–1921 period—a fact of which George Googe, for example, is pointedly aware. Cash, throughout his book, describes the intense individualism of southern workers, often with great insight. He explains the 1929 strikes, however, as follows: "And in fact most of the strikes were inspired by such grievances and had the character of unstudied mass action rather than of unionism. In most cases the union not only collapsed once the strike was lost but numbered no more than a negligible fraction of workers in the mill until the strike had actually begun." Cash viewed southern workers as incapable of preparing for a strike or even of paying regular union dues. "And as for winning a strike—they hadn't a chance. So much follows from what I have said, from the lack of coherent organization and the absence of a war chest. It followed, too, from the very carelessness of their psychology—from their willingness, once they had discharged their irritations, had their lark, and begun to get hungry, to drift cheerfully back to work, regardless of the fact that even their immediate aim had not been accomplished."[31]

Finally, in a point that will be discussed in more detail later, there is the whole system of white supremacy fostering white chauvinist attitudes among white workers. These attitudes become easily directed against unions, which represent at least in principle an integrationist egalitarianism of all workers, sometimes portrayed as originating in the North in order to undermine the values of the South—God, family, flag, and ethnic purity.

Unified Opposition to Unions. Other writers have stressed, in contrast to or in addition to the above causes, the high degree of integrated control over workers by those opposed to unions. This unified opposition had a number of dimensions, few of which supposedly existed in the North, at least to the same degree. Anti-union hegemony begins with the textile villages, where the company owned the streets, the houses where workers lived, and the stores where they shopped. Troublemakers and union sympathizers, thus, were not merely fired, but evicted from their houses and even occasionally arrested for trespassing in the company town.

There was also an extremely close integration of economic, political, social, and cultural power in parts of the South. Many sheriffs and law enforcement personnel were without even the nominal show of independence from local capitalists, in part a heritage from the plantation era. In some places no pretense was made of respecting the civil liberties of union organizers or pro-union workers, who often received violent punishment for their defiance, including tarring and feathering, lynching, and murder, sometimes with the open complicity of law enforcement officials. The judicial system generally served to exonerate perpetrators of crimes committed against union supporters, while often charging and sometimes even convicting the victims themselves of crimes that were in many cases preposterous. Not merely law enforcement but other aspects of southern life were either under the close control of or acted to serve southern capitalists. There was a close integration of ministers, the press, and all other aspects of life. This intense opposition to unions was fed by the insecurity that mill owners sometimes felt in trying to make profits in a highly competitive, labor intensive industry.[32]

Weakness of Union Leadership. Despite all of these problems, some industries and unions organized successfully. Coal miners living in company towns, working for small, decentralized, highly competitive companies, often faced opposition as intense as those in textile mill towns; metal miners, predominantly white oil workers, integrated maritime and dock workers, and others formed unions successfully during the 1930s and 1940s. Thus, some commentators have concluded that it was not the external conditions that hindered the unionization of southern workers but the leaders and organizations themselves.

The various textile workers unions have most often been the object of criticism. Barbara Griffith quotes Jim Pierce, a southern-born, nonradical official of the Communication Workers of America, who voiced a sharp indictment of the CIO Textile Workers Union: "The Textile Workers could never decide to do anything, or how to do it, and still can't. Back and forth, back and forth. They get militant for a few days; then somebody hits them and they slump back. That has its effect on people. Union representatives can only be really good if they've got good strong unions to back them up. And they didn't have it in textiles." Dennis Nolan and Donald Jonas argue that a consistent pattern of incompetence existed among textile unions from 1901 to 1932. They accuse the AFL United Textile Workers Union of "an almost unbelievable tactical ineptness." They see a history of intense, disruptive factionalism, conservatism, and lack of militancy by northern business union leaders, failures to understand the intensity of the opposition to unions by southern textile mill owners, and a general unwillingness to give concrete support, particularly money and organizers, to even the most promising southern efforts: "It is hard to avoid the conclusion that whatever the strength of outside forces, the workers and their organizers were often their own worst enemies. Time and again, burgeoning union movements were crushed by poor preparation, lack of strategy, internal divisions, inept leadership, and refusal of those with a stake in the dispute (especially northern textile unions and the AFL) to support the striking workers."[33]

The most incisive and far-ranging argument that focuses on the character of unions is that of William Regensburger, who argues that the only successful industrial unions were those either led by Communists and other left-wingers or those with a strong left-wing faction that contributed disproportionately to union organizing. According to Regensburger the unions that succeeded in the South had a number of characteristics that distinguished them from those that failed. First, the radical organizers emphasized broad class issues and instilled a long-term perspective on the struggle of workers against their employers. Thus, when major strikes failed, as they did at one time or another in all the successfully unionized industries in the South, organizers and radical workers did not fold up shop. They kept workers actively organized, engaging them in in-plant job actions, telling them that defeats were normal in a long struggle. More conservative unions generally disappeared once they were defeated in a major strike. Second, radical organizers, particularly the Communists, pushed hard on the question of racial equality in their work among whites. Conservatives, whether the right-wingers in the AFL or the centrist figures in the CIO, like those in charge of Operation Dixie, tended to downplay questions of racial egalitarianism. Such activities gained them little since the southern press and the companies accused even conservative unionists of integrationist and communist sympathies. Third, radical organizers were usually not afraid to make direct appeals to African-American workers and openly defend their demands for equal rights. They did not hesitate to organize the majority of black workers first, whereas most conservative and liberal unionists often believed that it was necessary initially to go after the white workers first if one was to have a viable union, thus often failing to gain as strong support from the initially more pro-union African-American workers. Regensburger argues that these approaches were the main determinants of success or failure in southern organizing.[34]

An issue raised by Regensburger's argument and much disputed in the literature is whether radical organizers were a liability in the conservative South or a boon. This question must figure prominently in the evaluation of the hypothesis about the degree of responsibility of union leaders for the failure of Operation Dixie.[35]

Tentative Conclusions and Open Questions

In the endeavor to answer these questions and evaluate the foregoing hypotheses the following strategy will be applied: First, it is impossible to look at one industry by itself during one period and begin to understand the reasons why a union might have been successful or unsuccessful there. As most social scientists well know at least in the abstract, a one-shot case study rarely leads to convincing generalizations. Thus, those situations in which unions failed will be compared with others where they succeeded. This comparison is done across industries during the 1930s and 1940s in the North as well as in the South, and historically across the South; particular attention is focused on those examples of relatively successful organizing. The objective is to evaluate to what degree the failures in the 1930s and 1940s, especially those during the Operation Dixie campaign, resulted from some or all of the four reasons discussed above. The evaluation is based generally on a wide reading of the secondary literature on southern labor organizing. In addition, it is based on archival research on Operation Dixie and other union activities in the South during the 1930s and 1940s. Also brought to bear are various statistical measures, including detailed strike and economic data for the South. The goal is to understand what happened and what was the range of political possibilities generally in the 1930s and 1940s, particularly if the South could have been organized. Specifically, an effort will be made to pinpoint what factors would have had to have been different to have allowed this organization to occur. Offered here are merely some preliminary conclusions and questions:

1. While one should not underestimate the competitive economic pressures on textile mill owners nor the degree of repression against unions in textile mill towns, the situation was not in principle different from that

faced by southern and Appalachian coal miners. While there are crucial variations, the parallels among the numerous failed southern strikes, the violence and brutality, which were if anything worse for coal miners, and the long-standing successful organization of the northern wings of both industries (Illinois and Pennsylvania in coal) are instructive. Although textile workers have not traditionally been the first organized or necessarily the most militant, in South Korea, czarist Russia, and in a wide variety of circumstances worldwide throughout modern history, they have not proved to be unorganizable. While the circumstances of southern textile workers in the 1930s and the 1940s presented difficult obstacles to overcome, there seems to be no reason to assume that the repression or the economics of the industry were such as to preclude their unionization. An even more puzzling industry, timber and lumber, had an integrated workforce with little hierarchical division of labor and job categorization, in contrast, for example, to the racially based job hierarchies in tobacco. The "objective situation" made the timber and lumber industry seem ripe for organization, yet no major attempts were made as in textiles; workers themselves seemed to give little indication that they were ready for unions. But the same industry in the Northwest was militant and well-organized during the 1930s and 1940s. Many southern timber workers had been organized from 1910 to 1913 under the radical leadership of the Industrial Workers of the World. Textiles similarly had seemed organizable during the economic booms surrounding the two world wars. Understanding these two industries, the two largest in terms of employment in the South during the 1930s and 1940s, is critical. In contrast, certain unions had completely organized their southern jurisdictions during this period: the United Mine Workers (1934), the Mine, Mill and Smelter Workers (1938), the United Steel Workers (1939), the National Maritime Union (1940), and the Oil Workers International Union (1941). Also noteworthy are the strong inroads made in the tobacco industry by the Food, Tobacco, Agricultural and Allied Workers, and in southern meatpacking by the United Packinghouse Workers—two unions characterized by strong anti-discrimination policies. Were these successes aberrations or possibilities that others might have emulated?

2. Although it is clear that questions of culture, group and ethnic identity, group history particularly in struggle, and regional character are significant and cannot be ignored, it is important to register skepticism about whether these factors are usually able to determine that a group will not be

unionized once it becomes employed in large-scale modern industry. There is a long history of pronouncing certain types of workers as unorganizable during times when they were, in fact, not organized. A long tradition in this country, now recognizable as white chauvinist, pronounced African Americans as submissive, too tied to the bosses, unable or unwilling to express solidarity, and more likely candidates to be strikebreakers rather than reliable union members. Today, as in the 1930s and 1940s, African-American workers have tended to be more solidaristic and union conscious than similarly placed white workers by a wide variety of indicators. A more penetrating analysis of earlier periods would show that the more traditional interpretation was unattuned to the degree of discrimination and exclusion faced by African Americans both within industry and from unions.[36]

Additional perspective may be gained by studying the tobacco industry. Prior to the 1930s, its workers seemed more impervious to unions than those in textile. As Herbert Northrup notes, "In few industries have conditions been so unfavorable to organized labor as in the tobacco industry." Northrup cites the rapid automation that displaced most of the skilled workers and the concentration of the industry in a few concerns, most of which were strongly anti-union and located in the South. He also argues, "But more important has been the racial division in the ranks of labor. The jobs are divided almost evenly between whites and Negroes, who are, however, sharply segregated on the basis of a racial occupational division. In addition, more than one-half of the workers of each race are women, a fact which, when coupled with the racial division and southern mores, makes the task of labor organizations most difficult." The final hindrance was the "timid and inept leaders" of the AFL Tobacco Workers International Union. Beginning in 1933, insurgents within the union began to organize workers in the industry, eventually removing the old leadership of the union in a bitter, lengthy struggle. By 1941, tobacco workers were no longer thought to be unorganizable.[37]

Moving northward, Morris Hillquit describes the perception of Jewish cloak workers by Socialist and union organizers in 1910:

> Practically all were recent immigrants, prevalently Jews from Russia, Austria, and Romania with a sprinkling of Italians and other nationalities. Their

pay was miserable, their work hours were long, and their general conditions of work and life were almost intolerable.

Like most Jewish workers they were long-suffering, meek, and submissive. But every once in a while they would flare up in an outburst of despair and revolt, and go on strike. The strikes were spontaneous and without preparation or organization. . . .

The cloak workers were long the despair of professional and union organizers, including my own circle of young Social propagandists. They seemed hopelessly unorganizable on a permanent basis.

The change came in 1910.[38]

The Jewish cloak workers eventually became the most staunch and disciplined of union supporters and a bastion of support for Socialist and Communist politics. The descriptions of their docility and resistance to unionization, however, are not unlike those of southern mill workers. Jews were not the only immigrants thought to be unorganizable. Similar claims were later made about eastern European immigrants during the Great Steel Strike of 1919, although these workers acquitted themselves more admirably than most at the time.

Casting the net a bit wider, it may be instructive to look at the convincing, sometimes eloquent, arguments given by scholars before 1960 as to why governmental employees could not be organized into unions. They were white collar, too professionally minded; their strikes were illegal and harshly punished; they had job security unavailable to private sector workers; strikes against the government had no public sympathy; and so on.[39] Government employees are today among the most militant, highly organized of U.S. workers, approximately 40 percent unionized. Thus, it should be clear that explanations about why a group is unlikely to form unions, based largely on the fact that they are not at the time organized, as government employees were not prior to 1960, should be treated with some degree of care. Similarly, before the 1960s, many scholars believed that women were less likely to join unions. A typical remark from the industrial relations literature is that of Jack Barbash who writes, "Women workers, with notable exceptions, are not the material out of which strong unions are typically built." In retrospect it is easy to see that such assessments were based on stereotypes and prejudice, as events such as the militant struggles of women schoolteachers and of female factory workers including those at the Watsonville Cannery (California) in the 1980s have shown.[40]

Finally, a reading of oral history interviews of southern union activists and radicals suggests that many of the traits that are sometimes described as too individualist to foster collective behavior were oftentimes seen by the workers themselves as the basis for their decision to become union activists or even Communists. Regensburger convincingly argues that "southern values of individualism, family, home, personal honor, independence, and violence were blended into an explosive mixture of working class militancy." One interview quotes a former southern left-wing organizer, "See, you gotta understand, southern workers aren't harder to organize. When we start a rumpus, it's a real rumpus! When we say somethin', we mean what we say." Another of Regensburger's interviewees tells him, "A man who won't fight for his rights is no good. He's no good to his family. He's no good to his children."[41]

3. Anyone examining the role of different types of union leaderships and organizers must take seriously the argument presented by William Regensburger. He describes the successful strategies and the audaciousness of radical organizers. An interesting case is that of the Oil Workers, who initially had little success in their southern organizing during the 1930s. Then they were incorporated by the CIO into a broader Oil Workers Organizing Committee (OWOC). Left-winger Edwin Smith, former chair of the National Labor Relations Board, was placed in charge of OWOC by the CIO. Smith appointed a number of experienced Communists and other leftists as organizers and mid-level staff. Through a series of dynamic campaigns with broad support from a number of other unions, including the left-wing National Maritime Union, OWOC began to organize the bulk of the southern oil industry.[42]

The history of southern organizing, not only of the early AFL unions, but also of the tactics of much of Operation Dixie, often seems a long list of missed opportunities and excuses. One is struck in reading through the Operation Dixie Collection by the narrowness and lack of dynamism of many of the Operation Dixie leaders, certainly those at the top, Van Bittner, George Baldanzi, and John Riffe. Griffith describes Bittner as "something more of a trade union functionary than a labor activist," but this assessment is far too charitable. Even the harsher descriptions she reports by others seem not to do Bittner justice.[43] He was an old-fashioned time-server from John L. Lewis's mine workers. His only talent seemed to be his terrible vindictiveness not only toward Communists, but toward anyone who was extremely militant, particularly those who had defied the Lewis leadership. Van Bittner played an important role, for example, in 1931 in red-baiting and attempting to smear Frank Keeney, a rank-and-file leader of UMW District 17 in West Virginia. All the while in Bittner's correspondence, in which he often complains vociferously about those to his left, he tells his friends and subordinates that he has a long reputation opposing red-baiting. Bittner not only attempts to keep all left-wing organizers off the Operation Dixie staff, supposedly to keep the campaign from being red-baited, which happened anyway, but he insists that staff members break ties with all "outside" organizations, including the CIO Political Action Committee (PAC). Rather than enlisting broad support for Operation Dixie, on 18 April 1946, Bittner publicly denounces a rally in support of the drive, called in New York by left-wing groups to raise money and other aid.

Bittner's correspondence is filled with moralisms about organizing local unions, how Operation Dixie does not discriminate by color or any other criterion, and the importance of working hard, among others. He seems at his most vigorous, however, in demanding that there be no exceptions during organizing campaigns to collecting the one dollar initiation fee from prospective members. He spends much energy castigating state directors who ask for permission to overlook the rule in exceptional cases. Waiving of initiation fees, of course, was common in successful campaigns, particularly where there had been previous unsuccessful organizing and workers remained skeptical. One cannot help but feel that placing Bittner in charge of earlier major CIO drives, North or South, would have ensured their failure as well.[44]

Bittner and his subordinates presided over the assembling of a largely southern, inexperienced, unpolitical staff. Although it is difficult to evaluate degree of commitment and amount of work (and it appears from correspondence and organizers' reports that most staff tried hard and meant well), one is struck by complaints even from Bittner about organizers not wanting to work weekends or to put in the extra efforts so often required in critical organizing drives.[45]

The major textile campaigns of Operation Dixie seem to be stamped with a lack of audacity compared to successful campaigns in the past, North or South. Most significant, and a point worth exploring at length in the future, are the hesitancies on the race question, compared to the more successful southern drives. Operation Dixie in many ways seems to follow the lead of the early AFL rather than the newer tactics used so fruitfully by the CIO. Like AFL President William Green's 1929–1930 tour of the South and many speeches to chambers of commerce, Bittner and his associates seem to rely too heavily on creating goodwill with southern elites. Thus, it is hard not to be hesitant in sharing Barbara Griffith's conclusion: "Had the South been organizable through sheer will and effort, the CIO staff of 1946 possessed enough of these qualities to have succeeded. One comes away from a prolonged study of the people and events that formed the day-to-day life of Operation Dixie with the settled feeling that the men and women of the CIO cared enough, and tried hard enough. But more than will was required."[46]

4. The Communists were not without blame in the failures of the 1930s and 1940s, but their problems were not in general those ascribed to them. They probably were, for example, no more manipulative than other organizers in the labor movement and a good deal less so than some, including a number to their right. The unions that they led were often, perhaps by necessity, more democratic than some of the right-wing unions.[47]

5. Another question to be examined is the impact of the peculiar nature of the New Deal-Democratic Party coalition on southern organizing. The Democratic Party included left-wing CIO unions and southern conservatives as well as advocates of lynching and the potential lynchees. The southern Democratic congressional contingent had grown more conservative by the end of World War II.[48] Roosevelt had unsuccessfully tried to defeat a number of conservative southern Democrats in the 1938 election. After his failure, political expediency demanded that he mend his fences. Did the subordination of all wings of the CIO, including the Communists, to the Democratic Party hamper it from fully confronting Dixiecrat opposition to unions in the South?[49] In 1936, a number of strong state-level parties existed, including the Wisconsin Progressive Party and the Minnesota Farmer-Labor Party, which controlled the governorship and a majority of the congressional delegation. There were also perhaps hundreds of local labor parties of major importance. Why did the CIO abandon these efforts in favor of the Democrats? Was it necessary to subordinate themselves totally to the New Deal coalition?

6. Finally, to what extent was the "civil war" between the AFL and the

CIO responsible for the failure of Operation Dixie? What role did the conflict between conservative and moderate CIO leaders and Communists play in the defeat of southern industrial organizing?

It is along these lines that some of the hidden structure of contemporary American politics will be discovered.

12 DOUGLAS FLAMMING

Christian Radicalism, McCarthyism, and the Dilemma of Organized Labor in Dixie

The story of organized labor in the post-World War II South is a tale of woe, especially for the textile workers, who remained largely unorganized. There are two standard explanations for this situation. One view is that southern millhands maintained a distinctive rural-bred culture. They were localistic, fatalistic, uneducated, clannish, anti-union, Protestant fundamentalists. They were not the union type. A second view is that southern millhands had seen too many union failures to place their faith in organized labor. Although disposed toward unionization, textile families in the postwar era recalled past defeats, especially the General Textile Strike of 1934, and decided to remain aloof and anti-union during postwar organization drives.[1]

The unionization campaign in Dalton, Georgia, during 1955 makes it difficult to accept either of these explanations. The campaign was a disaster for the Textile Workers Union of America (TWUA), but neither of the dominant interpretations helps explain why. Dalton's cotton mill workers had established unions in the early 1930s, and by the end of World War II organized labor in the north Georgia city was a force to be reckoned with in local and state politics. Simultaneously, a new industry—broadloom carpet manufacturing—was rapidly developing in Dalton and was doing so with nonunion workers. Given the town's strong labor tradition, carpets should have been easy pickings for the TWUA. As it happened, the TWUA not only failed to organize the carpet plants, but the campaign itself mortally wounded Dalton's existing unions and all but guaranteed that the town would have a nonunion future. That the effort occurred at all had something to do with a brand of working-class Protestantism that stood in opposition to the status quo. That it collapsed had something to do with the political culture of the 1950s. The Dalton campaign of 1955 was yet another disaster for organized labor in the South, but the reasons for that failure were less regional than national, due more to McCarthyism and the CIO's own anti-Communism than to any peculiarity in southern textiles.

From the 1880s through the 1920s, Dalton was a typical southern textile town, with several major cotton mills dominating the economy and a substantial population of white mill workers living in the company-owned villages. But in the 1930s Dalton's economic history diverged from regional norms in two important ways, both of which led to the 1955 campaign. First, millhands in Dalton enjoyed unusual success in forming and maintaining unions. All of the major mills organized in the early 1930s later became solid TWUA locals, active and influential in community affairs. The two dominant unions were TWUA Local 185 of the Crown Cotton Mill, which had witnessed a dramatic increase in membership during the early 1950s, and TWUA Local 134 of the American Thread Mill. Both were strong organizations, but by the 1950s they found themselves in a most peculiar situation because of the town's second economic peculiarity. An entirely new industry had emerged in Dalton during the late 1930s when the production of tufted, or chenille, bedspreads (an Appalachian cabin-craft art) became mechanized. Bedspread manufacturing gradually evolved into the modern carpet industry, which by the 1950s was turning Dalton into the nation's "Carpet Capital." The power behind the carpet boom was Dalton's Tufted Textile Manufacturers Association (TTMA), an organization determined to keep carpet plants union free. So, by the mid-1950s, the influence of Dalton's traditional TWUA unions was being undermined by the TTMA and its nonunion chenille workforce. An obvious solution for the TWUA locals was to help organize the carpet plants and thereby broaden the foundations of labor power in Dalton.[2]

Unfortunately for Dalton's organized faithful, the obstacles to southern unionization drives in the early 1950s were numerous indeed. Operation Dixie, the extensive postwar effort to organize southern workers, floundered from the start and had ground to a halt. The National Labor Relations Board was no longer organized labor's aggressive supporter. Georgia's "right to work" law hampered the TWUA's efforts to bring more textile workers into the union fold. Such legislation found sanction in the anti-labor Taft-Hartley Act, which pro-union forces had been unable to overturn. As their sympathetic congressman, Henderson Lanham, reported to north Georgia's labor unions, the national labor law was not likely to improve any time soon, and unions were going to have to learn to live with it. Instead, more frequently they died with it. The problems of the TWUA in Dixie were further aggravated in 1952 by a schism in the regional organization, as southern director George Baldanzi bolted for the AFL after a conflict with TWUA president Emil Rieve. Baldanzi's departure took about twenty thousand southerners out of the TWUA at a time when its membership in the South was already quite sparse. Dalton's unions remained with the TWUA, although Crown's Local 185 began to distance itself from the state TWUA office in Atlanta.[3]

Even so, many chenille workers in Dalton were already thinking union, especially those who were members of the Church of God of the Union Assembly. The Union Assembly was headed by Dalton's own Reverend Charlie T. Pratt, who had been active in labor affairs and progressive politics since the early 1930s. Pratt's Holiness church in Dalton had over five hundred members and over ten thousand more scattered in congregations across the South in Georgia, Alabama, Tennessee, Kentucky, West Virginia, Texas, and Arkansas, as well as at midwestern manufacturing centers in urban areas in Ohio, Indiana, and Michigan, where poor southern whites were migrating for work. Pratt's son, the Reverend Jesse F. Pratt, led a church in Detroit. But the Union Assembly headquarters was in Dalton, where Charlie Pratt served as the church's "national moderator." Pratt's Dalton congregation consisted primarily of chenille plant workers, along with some cotton millers and a smattering of poor farmers. The Union Assembly, largely a communal organization, had many church-owned businesses. By 1955 Pratt's congregation owned and operated a flour mill (the Whitfield Milling Company) and the Union Supermarket, which one observer called a "large modern and first-class food store." The church also ran a cannery that preserved vegetables raised on Church of God farms, a modernly equipped dairy that distributed free milk to poor families, the Union Slaughterhouse, and the Dalton Tourist Court and Restaurant. Pratt, who had led several volatile labor campaigns in Dalton during the 1940s, was widely distrusted by the business community.[4]

With the carpet industry running strong in 1955, Pratt pushed his pro-labor program a step further by recruiting a fellow radical minister, Don West, to publish a newspaper on behalf of the Union Assembly and the working people of the South. The result was *The Southerner: A Voice of the*

People, published monthly in Dalton. West was a long-time southern radical, a native of the north Georgia countryside, and a deeply religious man. He had spent his late teens doing church work in Appalachian mountain communities and working his way through college, earning in 1932 a bachelor of divinity degree from Vanderbilt University, where he had studied under Alva W. Taylor, a southern theologian committed to social change. One year out of college West joined with fellow southern radical Myles Horton to establish the Highlander Folk School, which became a leading center of southern dissent. West soon left the school, but he spent the remainder of the depression decade championing liberal and radical causes throughout the South. During the 1940s, West held pastorates in Congregational churches in Georgia and served as superintendent of public schools in the town of Lula, Georgia. He also continued his education and by war's end had completed his doctoral degree, after which he secured a position in the English department at Oglethorpe University in Atlanta. He then took up Henry Wallace's cause in the presidential campaign in 1948, and that move led to trouble. Support for Wallace's Progressive Party made West an easy target for Cold War anti-Communists, and it spurred opponents to look into his radical past. Under pressure from the *Atlanta Constitution*, Oglethorpe fired West from the faculty. The campaign of 1948, nonetheless, created new opportunities for West, since C. T. Pratt of Dalton was co-chair of the Progressive party in Georgia. The two became friends during the campaign, and West later became an ordained Church of God minister.

Whether or not West had become a Communist Party member during the early 1930s, and if so for how long, is not easily determined. In Dalton, in 1955, under fire for his radicalism, West claimed he was not a Communist, without commenting on the possibility of past affiliations. In any case, he had supported all manner of "Popular Front" campaigns during the 1930s and worked closely with Communist Party members, activities that cost him his job at Oglethorpe. By the time he accepted Pratt's invitation to establish a radical labor press in Dalton, he knew all too well the dangers associated with postwar anti-Communism. But West was not the sort to capitulate easily.[5]

When Don West's first issue of *The Southerner* hit the newsstands in March 1955, the paper's ardently pro-labor stance was obvious. West took every opportunity to boost unionization, and he enlivened the pages with stinging political cartoons aimed at anti-labor groups and also at racism.

Judging from letters to the editor from across the nation, *The Southerner* enjoyed a wide, though numerically limited, circulation. Affluent whites in Dalton must have viewed *The Southerner* as Protestantism gone afoul.[6]

Pratt and West, however, saw it as Protestantism redeemed. They perceived the world in terms of a struggle between the rich and the poor, with God on the side of the oppressed. Their religion was one of deliverance in the here and now (as well as in the by-and-by). Their message was that Christ sides with poor laborers; that unions offer poor workers a better life; and that Christ, therefore, favors unionization as a form of Godly retribution. One minister voiced a common theme when he stated that "God was going to bring the proud and mighty low and lift up the weak and lowly." Often, too, the Union Assembly blended its pro-labor message with the message of American liberty, as in one editorial that concluded: "we believe in the principles of organized labor because we believe in the life and teaching of Jesus Christ; because we believe in the principles of our founding fathers; because we believe in genuine Americanism." In practice, these beliefs meant avid union support, or, as one minister wrote, "You can't be a Christian and a scab. The two just don't go together."[7]

Union Assembly leaders knew they would be branded as Communists. As Charlie Pratt wrote, "Anybody who ever stood up for the poor people has been called a communist. I've been called a communist. I'm not a communist, but I've always stood up for the laboring people." A minister from Tennessee put it more strongly, "If you are afraid of being called a communist, don't preach God's Bible," and, he added, "If you don't want to be called a communist join up with the McCarthy gang and the Roman Catholic Hierarchy." This final barb was no passing addendum. The Union Assembly folks were strongly anti-Catholic, in part because they associated Catholicism with McCarthyism. Hence, at a Union Assembly Labor Day rally in 1955 Jesse Pratt stated he would rather be "called a communist than a Catholic." Don West even suggested a parallel between Catholic McCarthyites and Judas, both being "children of the devil" who accused the righteous. This sort of rhetoric was hardly likely to win support from the TWUA international office.[8]

Dalton's unions nonetheless applauded *The Southerner* and immediately aligned themselves with West and the paper. TWUA Local 185 was particularly supportive, taking out a full-page advertisement in an early issue and contributing its own "As We See It" column written by Jack Gregg and

John R. Bunch, the local's president and secretary. Their column stressed the democratic system of union government and the community-mindedness of Dalton's locals. It also condemned the "shameful low wage level" in Dalton's chenille plants and recommended unionization as a solution. The town's newest union, TWUA Local 1376 of the Dalton Textile Corporation, also published a strong pro-union letter in the paper, adding that "if we all stick together I believe some day we will have all the plants organized in Dalton."9

While such optimism pervaded union circles in Dalton, opposition to *The Southerner* and its aims quietly coalesced around Marc Pace, editor of Dalton's two mainstream weeklies. Like Don West, Pace was young, dynamic, and a relative newcomer to the city. Unlike West, Pace operated squarely within the circle of Dalton's business leaders. Part of a new postwar breed of southern journalists, Pace offered a format more professional than previous weeklies and sought an appropriate balance among local, national, and international news items. Pace was a moderate (some white southerners might have said liberal) on the two most explosive regional issues of the era, organized labor and race. He derided the postwar Klan and published pictures and stories applauding the accomplishments of local blacks, something Dalton papers had never done before. Pace also accorded local unions and working people in general a modicum of respect, but there were limits to his restraint. He opposed racial integration and scorned the CIO's national leaders. And when it came to Communism, Pace left moderation at the editorial door.

When Don West first arrived in town in late 1954, he stopped by Pace's office to talk about setting up *The Southerner.* Pace recognized West from the Wallace campaign in 1948, recalled the minister's reputation as a radical, and confronted West on his alleged "Communistic background." As later reported by Pace himself, West took offense and denied any links to Communism. Thus began a bitter relationship between these rival editors, a confrontation that embodied the forces at work in the Dalton chenille campaign of 1955 and, in a larger sense, the dilemma of organized dissent in the age of McCarthy. After their first meeting, Pace made no public comment about West's arrival. Instead, he quietly asked Congressman Henderson Lanham to investigate the minister's record. By early May, Lanham had sent Pace a hefty package of information from the files of the House Un-American Activities Committee (HUAC) in Washington, D.C. Ammunition in hand, Pace bided his time and revealed nothing. Lanham, harboring other concerns, quickly contacted the CIO.

As a pro-labor congressman from northwest Georgia who owed his initial success to the CIO's Political Action Committee, Lanham was horrified that Dalton's unions were becoming involved with West. Having sent the deleterious information to Pace, he immediately informed David S. Burgess of the Georgia State Industrial Union Council about the events in Dalton. Lanham was worried that the "CIO will be damaged if the Textile locals continue their close collaboration with this publication," and he added, "I do hope that you and Charlie Gillman [CIO Region 5 director] can disengage the labor unions of Whitfield County from their entanglement with West and his paper." Burgess and Gillman, after briefly meeting and deciding not to confront the Dalton locals directly, both wrote to William Pollock, executive vice-president of TWUA, echoing Lanham's concerns and urging him to act on the situation. In response, Pollock contacted James O'Shea, manager of TWUA's Northwest Georgia Joint Board, asking him to meet with the Dalton locals and give them the HUAC information on West. O'Shea did so a few days later, but the Dalton leaders, being at the end of this bureaucratic loop, were the last to learn of Don West's reputation as a "Red."[10]

Dalton's union officials were upset by the news because they realized that West's past could mean trouble for the campaign, but they were also annoyed that TWUA's upper-level officials had been scheming behind their backs. Yet, they all recognized Dalton's dilemma. O'Shea put it clearly to Pollock in late May: "The people in Dalton knew nothing of [West's] background," and they recognized the need to distance themselves from him. He added that the locals had agreed to steer clear of *The Southerner*, at least in any official capacity. At the same time, though, O'Shea stressed that the Union Assembly was "a very influential and powerful Religious sect in this area, who [sic] urges its members to organize, [and] is greatly responsible for our organizing success in Dalton." There was the dilemma. The chenille campaign needed the Union Assembly, but West and his newspaper burdened the campaign with formidable problems.[11]

Although Communist Party members and fellow travelers had played critically important roles during the rapid rise of the CIO in the late 1930s and during World War II, top officials of the TWUA and the CIO had dealt with the issue of labor radicalism during the late 1940s and early 1950s by purging all Communists.[12] This solution, however, had its drawbacks. It damaged radical unionists who were not Party members while fueling the flames of anti-Communism in a manner that, ironically, aided McCarthyites and other red-baiters in their subsequent assaults on political opponents and the unions themselves. Indeed, as the CIO became increasingly centrist, its avidly anti-Communist leaders sometimes collaborated with the HUAC in smearing their radical union rivals. Nevertheless, the purges helped the CIO attain "mainstream" status, and in 1948 it vigorously attacked Henry Wallace, a presidential candidate strongly supported by Pratt and West. Naturally, top TWUA officials in 1955 disapproved the two ministers spearheading the carpet campaign. Dalton's union leaders understandably feared an anti-Communist assault from the International, which they resisted, arguing that "to make an issue [of West] publicly would hurt us greatly in this area, with many members pulling out of the Union." O'Shea also urged Pollock "to take no drastic action."[13] As it turned out, Dalton's unionists did have much to fear from anti-Communism, but the attack on West did not come from the International.

West's early efforts in Dalton produced both success and a severe backlash. By July, pro-union chenille workers had begun to stir. For the concerned manufacturers, there was little question where the trouble originated. In August, several chenille firms distributed questionnaires asking workers to state their religious affiliation. Dozens of employees who listed the Union Assembly as their church found themselves out of a job. West later reported that fifty-six chenille workers (which would have amounted to more than 10 percent of Pratt's Dalton congregation) had been fired on account of church membership. When these workers appealed to the TWUA for help, the union did step into the fray, but by that time the situation was becoming too messy to suit the TWUA's top officials. While the TWUA asked for a Senate investigation into firings on account of religious preference, its top officials were openly apologetic for the meddling influence of West and the Union Assembly in labor's affairs. By this time most TWUA leaders outside of Dalton viewed Pratt as a corrupt millionaire dodging taxes behind a facade of religion, and they saw West as a troublesome Red. Other potential allies soon turned away. West contacted the Anti-Defamation League of B'nai B'rith, hoping the organization would defend Dalton's workers. But the League recoiled from the Union Assembly's avid anti-Catholicism and veiled anti-Semitism. "It is our opinion," the League concluded, "that this is a good mess to stay away from at the present time."[14]

The chenille manufacturers and the local press were smart enough to downplay the issue of religion, even the issue of organized labor, and to hit the campaign in its most vulnerable spot: the alleged Communism of Don West. Criticizing white Protestants was a delicate matter, and it was awkward to disparage organized labor in a town with strong, civic-minded unions. But in 1955 anything smacking of Communism was all but doomed in the public arena. When the Dalton press launched an all-out campaign to smear Don West as a Communist, a firestorm erupted in the city. An early issue of *The Southerner* declared that "you are not worth a dime to any church or union until you get to where you can stand the fire." But the conflagration that soon engulfed Dalton overwhelmed not only Don West and the Union Assembly, but also the TWUA campaign to organize Dalton's chenille workers.[15]

The battle began with a bang. On 21 August 1955, the *Dalton News* published a full page of information on Don West taken (as boldly indicated) from "THE FILES OF THE COMMITTEE ON UN-AMERICAN ACTIVITIES, U.S. HOUSE OF REPRESENTATIVES." The article began with a government disclaimer that "it should be noted that the individual is not necessarily a Communist, a Communist sympathizer, or a fellow-traveler unless otherwise indicated." But "Communist" was written all over the report; that, of course, was the paper's point. "In answer to many questions . . . as to whether Don West . . . is really a Communist, we can merely say we don't know," Pace wrote. "However," he continued, "we can point you to the record, factual, uncolored, and absolutely untouched and non-edited, and you can arrive at your own conclusion." This tone and strategy was taken by the local press throughout the anti-West campaign: write as if objectivity were the rule and publish an avalanche of material that could only be interpreted one way.[16]

The same issue that carried the HUAC material also contained significant announcements from both the TTMA and the TWUA. The industry disclosed that chenille plants were raising wages 7 to 10 percent immediately and that "there undoubtedly will be another wage increase by late October or early November." The paper also revealed that the TTMA had voted to build a new national headquarters building in Dalton. These front-page stories sent clear messages: that workers could expect wage increases without union intervention and that chenille manufacturing was indispensable to Dalton's economic growth. Workers themselves might have disputed the first point, since the wage hikes were announced as preparations for chenille organizing were underway. The new union activity was no mere rumor. In the same issue, a TWUA advertisement announced: "ATTENTION ALL CHENILLE WORKERS! You are invited to attend a special organizing meeting sponsored by the Textile Workers Union of America, CIO. . . . Learn the facts." Few Daltonians could have missed the connections between the TWUA's chenille campaign, the TTMA's wage increase, and Marc Pace's attack on Don West.[17]

Pace had timed his release of the HUAC material carefully. He had received the committee's file several months earlier. When the HUAC material finally appeared in the *News* that August, any perceptive reader could have noticed that it was dated 3 May. It also seemed to be no small coincidence that the initial attack on West appeared in the very same issue in which the TWUA publicly announced its chenille campaign. Pace avoided explaining his delay in publishing the material, stating only that "because of matters which are private and which cannot be disclosed, we could not release that data any earlier." At the same time, he simply denied he was acting on behalf of the TTMA. Nevertheless, Pace was fully sympathetic to that group and doubtless opposed unions in Dalton's chenille plants, but as he understood very clearly, he did not have to fight the TWUA outright so long as he could link Don West to Communism.[18]

In any case, Pace withheld nothing after publishing the HUAC material. The following issue of the *Dalton Citizen* all but denounced West as a Communist and printed on the front page "a poem written some time ago by Don West" entitled "Listen, I'm a Communist," the opening lines of which read:

I am a Communist
  A Red
  A Bolshevik!
Do you, toilers of the South,
  Know Me?
Do you believe the lies,
  Capitalists say
  And print about me?
  You sharecroppers
  Renters,
  Factory Workers,

Negroes, poor whites
Do you understand me,
Do you see
That I am you.
That I, the Communist,
Am you—?[19]

West countered immediately, claiming the "Communist" poem was an inaccurate and malicious revision of a poem entitled "Listen, I'm an Agitator" that was published in his book *Clods of Southern Earth*. West even gave Pace a copy of the "Agitator" poem to publish. But the "Agitator" piece, while a better poem, was very similar to the "Communist" version and, in any case, clearly bespoke West's disdain of the status quo and his willingness to incite workers to fight against it. Those outraged by the "Communist" poem would hardly have been pacified by the "Agitator" version. To make matters worse for West, the *Citizen* soon branded him a liar by reprinting a section of a 1934 issue of the Communist *Daily Worker*, in which the "Communist" rendition of the poem was presented under Don West's name.[20]

West sought to turn attention to the chenille campaign, but Pace skillfully deflected the limelight back to the Communist issue. Pace always allowed the embattled minister to print rebuttals in the local papers, apparently believing that, if given enough rope, West would hang himself. In one of these pieces, West insisted, "I am not the issue. The real issue is wages and working conditions and organization of the unorganized." But Pace's responding editorial argued that "West would like to align the tufted textile industry with these [HUAC] releases . . . [but] we checked into his background for the sole purpose of letting our citizens know of it. At the time we hadn't even dreamed of any union connections." West wanted to know who paid for the full page of the HUAC information. Pace countered that "it was presented by the newspapers as a public service. . . . Certainly, we wouldn't ask any one to pay for a page advertisement of that nature which is our duty to publish." In a subsequent editorial in the *Citizen*, Pace wrote: "As far as we are concerned, the only issue right now is Don West and his background. . . . The fact that union organization movements are going on simultaneously with this series of West articles, editorials, etc, is something entirely out of our control."[21] Assuming that Pace was being entirely honest, he sought to obscure the obvious point that West and *The South-erner* were indispensable mobilizers of the chenille campaign and that attacking West amounted to an attack on the union.

Local antagonism toward West quickly surfaced. The Veterans of Foreign Wars (VFW) launched the first assault from the community. In an open letter to the *News,* its local commander demanded that West account for the HUAC reports and state openly whether he had been or was presently "a member of the Communist Party." "If you are a person who believes in our way of life," he wrote, "you will immediately respond to these questions." Other groups in Dalton had attacks of a more physical nature in mind, and Pace's weekly "Pipe Smoke" column warned against mob violence. The writer noted that "there were remarks about a group paying West a visit." Pace vowed that "this newspaper condemns such action" and warned that West had every right to defend himself: "[M]ob actions can be dangerous from either end—the attacked as well as the attackers." Pace then called forth a new and different assailant: "[W]e say leave it to the law and to legal channels, including the Whitfield County grand jury if it is interested." As it happened, the grand jury for the October term included several business leaders who were indeed interested.[22]

West responded to the VFW charge with a long, carefully argued letter in the *Citizen.* He began by questioning whether "any man or group should set themselves up as an inquisitorial body, assuming the authority to call citizens in question relative to religious or political beliefs." He considered at length the multiple meanings given the word "Communist," pointing out that the term had been used to slander reformers of all stripes, from non-Communist labor organizers to Franklin D. Roosevelt. Never one for modesty, West linked his own struggle for religious and political liberty to a long heritage of protest beginning with the Magna Charta and extending through the U.S. Constitution and the Dalton chenille campaign. As a prelude to answering the VFW's charges, West attacked all McCarthy-style interrogations. West claimed that he had often discussed his political views and would in the absence of duress gladly and openly air them again, but answering such questions on demand was another matter: "It would be nothing less than traitorous for me to accede to the demands of any group in matters of conscience, whether it be president, Pope or even a little volun-tary McCarthy Committee."

Nonetheless, West understood the difficulty his reputation posed for the chenille campaign, and he would oblige the VFW "for the benefit of many honest citizens who may be confused by what they've heard or read." Voicing his concern for underpaid workers, he said, "I believe in a living wage and decent working conditions for all who labor. If they call that being a Communist, then I could be called one along with many millions of other Americans!" But West stated explicitly, "I am NOT a Communist"; he concluded by emphasizing the points he most needed to convey: "I am not the issue. The real issue in the Dalton area is the rights of workers to organize and bargain collectively. The attack on me is only to confuse the issues. I do not believe the working people will allow this maneuver to succeed. In closing I want to say that I am an ordained minister in the Church of God of the Union Assembly and 100 percent American!" Although West's epistle amounted to a classic reply to the blunt anti-Communist interrogations of the 1950s, it doubtless won few converts to his point of view.[23]

The battle of the press continued throughout 1955. The patterns of editorial combat remained the same: Pace offered evidence to discredit West and Pratt and added stories demonstrating the sly tactics of Communists everywhere; the Union Assembly leaders followed with rejoinders, which Pace published and held up to ridicule. Community groups continued to commend Pace for his efforts. The American Legion (Dalton Post 112), for example, praised the anti-Communist campaign and condemned "those who in the name of religion and the church are undertaking to turn our people against each other and . . . are acting as a front for a foreign ideology seeking to destroy the very foundations of this Republic." After polling Daltonians informally as to whether Communism presently posed a threat to the United States, the *News* offered the thoughts of "Hershel Eaker: chenille worker" who stated that "Communism is worse than a threat. It will ruin young people in the world today if they get mixed up in it. Communism is against the Bible and its teachings. I have always been taught that Jesus Christ is the Son of God and it is a disgrace to any nation in the world to believe Communism which is contrary to these teachings." Whether or not these views were representative, Pace's message to Dalton's chenille workers was unmistakable in Eaker's comments.[24]

Outside the editorial room, the chenille campaign intensified. The TWUA focused its efforts on two mills, the General Latex and Chemical Corporation (Latex) and Belcraft Chenilles. Employees at both plants were trying to organize, and during the period from 31 August to 8 September, the companies laid off twenty-six workers (eighteen from Latex, eight from Belcraft). The TWUA charged that these workers were fired for trying to organize and filed suit with the National Labor Relations Board.[25] At Belcraft the campaign remained peaceful to the extent that no strike occurred and no physical violence was evident. But at Latex the workers went on strike, the court imposed an injunction limiting picketing, the company called upon the state to protect strikebreakers, the governor sent in state troopers, and violence began to rip the community and the chenille campaign apart. Pace's attacks on West, Pratt, and Communism in Dalton paralleled this conflict, helping to fuel local antagonisms and providing a powerful if only vaguely indirect force against chenille unionization.

As the strike that began at Latex in mid-September continued, the plant, which employed only about fifty workers, took on an importance beyond the size of the workforce. Almost all of the hands banded together to form TWUA Local 10, and they had the support of the national office when the strike vote was taken. The Whitfield County Superior Court quickly issued a highly restrictive injunction against picketing, but the strike continued amid Pace's further denunciation of Union Assembly leaders. Widely publicized violence, labeled "The Riot" by mainstream papers even though no one was injured, erupted near the plant gate on 29 September. At that time the factory was not running, although a few nonunion employees entered the plant as did company president G. B. Coit, an outsider from Massachusetts who came to investigate the labor situation. Coit ill-advisedly drove away from the plant with a well-known strikebreaker riding by his side. Union pickets quickly intercepted and stopped the vehicle not far from the factory. They tilted it high into the air before letting it drop and pelting it with rocks. The following day dynamite rocked the front yards at the homes of a Latex manager and a strikebreaker. Coit quickly called on the state for help, and Governor Marvin Griffin, aware of purported Communism in Dalton, quickly responded. Although the TWUA later complained of Griffin's "anti-labor attitude," the governor, by pointing out the Communist issue and by emphasizing his commitment to public safety, could appear to remain circumspect on the labor issue while helping Coit break the strike. Indeed, Griffin sent Coit a contingent of state troopers as well as several representatives of the Georgia Bureau of Investigation. On 11 October, a few local anti-union workers and outside "scabs" entered the mill escorted by members of the Georgia Highway Patrol.[26]

Meanwhile, a group of union workers and other local supporters, called the Whitfield County Citizens Committee, sought to change Griffin's mind. The Dalton Citizens' Council, previously organized to oppose racial integration, frantically announced that it had "no connection at all" with this pro-labor group. The Citizens Committee visited the governor personally, presented petitions, and urged him to remove the troopers, but Griffin informed the group he would do so only "as soon as the violence ceases." When the committee argued that no violence had occurred for two weeks, Griffin countered that "he had received a report of egg throwing" that very morning. The union committee also asked Griffin to serve as an arbitrator in settling the strike, but the governor refused this request as well. In response to the workers' claim that Latex paid its Massachusetts workers seventy-seven cents per hour more than those in Dalton and that Coit was looking for "slave labor," the state's chief executive stated that he had never "held out cheap labor [as] an inducement" to lure industry to Georgia. In a prepared statement to the press, Griffin announced that "State patrolmen were assigned to Dalton to preserve order after several breaches of the peace took place. They were sent to protect the lives and property of all citizens, both strikers and non-strikers alike, and will be kept there until all possibility of violence has subsided." The Citizens Committee had a different view of Griffin's decision. The chairman, Reverend J. B. Watters of the Olivia Baptist Church, pronounced it "an insult to our community," giving "a green light to scabs and strike-breakers all over the state." Violence continued, although by whom was a controversial issue, as a Latex truck was dynamited and the TWUA campaign headquarters was vandalized. TWUA organizer Robert Freeman strongly implied that the dynamite explosions in September and October were the work of anti-unionists trying to discredit the union: "It's an insult to organized labor and the community for anyone to think that the union would dynamite anybody's place of business or throw explosives into somebody's yard. We are trying to get a contract and trying to build up an atmosphere of decency. We certainly couldn't get a contract with a company by such methods." It was a logical argument, but not one that would compel Griffin to change his mind. The troopers stayed.[27]

Meanwhile, the local grand jury launched a powerful attack against West and the Latex workers. In effect, the October term's jury acted as a local HUAC. Superior Court Judge James Paschal chose the jurors with care, and

Pace hailed them as "business men" who were working hard "in the interest of the community." Paschal charged the grand jury to look into press allegations that "subversive organizations" were operating in Dalton. "You are free agents to investigate anything at anytime in the county," Paschal told the jury members, "and from recent reports there are some things that need investigating here in Dalton."[28]

The grand jury received added incentive to interrogate West after Edgar C. Bundy, an obscure anti-Communist crusader from Illinois, came to town. Bundy, according to the *Citizen*, "held leading positions with the Illinois American Legion's Americanism Committee and its Anti-Subversive Commission." Traveling north along the Dixie Highway from Miami, where he had attended the Legion's national convention, Bundy saw a Chattanooga, Tennessee, newspaper that reported Judge Paschal's concern over "Communist patterns" in Dalton. Bundy hurried to Dalton to warn the grand jury that he had heard Don West's name from undercover F.B.I agents who had infiltrated the Communist Party. West, he said, was "a dangerous man." Furthermore, "for every known Communist, there are 10 fellow travelers who are not known or identified [who] are equally dangerous." Received enthusiastically by both the grand jury and the business press, Bundy remained in town for several weeks, holding public meetings sponsored by the local American Legion and VFW and making speeches over local radio on the dangers of Communism and Don West. Infiltration, not direct and violent assault, Bundy said, was the Communist strategy for taking over America: "Under the guise of religion, education, and labor unions, the infiltrators are trying to obtain their goal." The worst infiltrators, the northerner warned, were "those people who claim to be for the working people." Lest this statement be misinterpreted, the *Citizen* explained that Bundy meant "those people [who] get their money off the laboring class people"—by no subtle implication, West and Pratt. Shortly thereafter, the grand jury sent West a subpoena.[29]

Bundy was not the only outsider relied on by the *News* to smear West and the chenille campaign. The paper also advertised a series of radio broadcasts by Allston Calhoun, Jr., an anti-Communist-for-hire who worked for the Foundation of Americanism Preferred, a privately sponsored group headquartered in Greenwood, South Carolina. Besides presenting his McCarthy-like message for radio audiences, Calhoun wrote full-page advertisements for the *Citizen* and *News*. To the consternation of Dalton's TWUA locals, Calhoun made explicit connections between Communism and unionism. Referring to a United Auto Workers' strike in Indiana, he spoke of the "CIO Communist-style dress parade revolution. . . . There is one big labor union in Russia to which all the workers must belong," he said, "[and] it is through this big labor union that the few men at the head of the Communist Party have a virtual life and death control over the unfortunate working people of that land." Calhoun praised Governor Griffin for his "splendid and courageous action" and damned the "CIO-promoted insurrection" in Dalton. He further warned of the old "Reds" who had "announced themselves as 'reverends' and started up their own so called church" as well as a "monthly sheet" (he never called it *The Southerner*) in which CIO representatives assailed his programs. Sometimes he signed his large ads, "Calhoun, 'The Working Man's Friend.'" Americanism Preferred ads always carried the same message and tone. One edition, printed in both papers, shrieked that the "CIO CONVERTS NORMAL HUMAN BEINGS TO READY AGENTS FOR MOB VIOLENCE" and, in a slightly more graphic assault, "CIO MAN SPITS TOBACCO JUICE INTO FACE OF HIS OWN MOTHER."[30]

Latex workers, still on strike at the end of October despite court injunctions and state troopers, sought to restore their tarnished image. In a full-page ad in the *News,* thirty-three workers signed a lengthy statement that explained "our side of the story." The strikers insisted, "You have not been told the truth. It has been made to appear that we are a bunch of hoodlums and gangsters. We want you to know we are decent law-abiding citizens." The company, they said, had made no effort to settle. Strikebreakers "who have never worked at General Latex" were brought in from surrounding counties. The workers also pointed to anti-union violence apparently overlooked by Pace's reporters. "We have been cursed by these strike-breakers, they have used their cars to run some of us off the road." Moreover, "the company has been before the Grand Jury and apparently told lies on us. The Grand Jury has indicted us without hearing our side of the story." "The only thing we have asked [the company] to do," said the workers, "is to put back the five employees they have fired, to recognize our union and to treat us as human beings. . . . So far, all the company has been willing to do is have us arrested, disgrace our names, lie on us, [and] bring in strike breakers." In a poignant concluding point the workers pleaded that "we are now and always have been law abiding citizens, we are hard working men who are trying to maintain a decent living for our family. We have lived here and around you most of our life."[31]

But the strike was doomed. The company filled virtually every position in the small plant with strikebreakers and upon doing so declared these workers permanent and eligible to vote in any upcoming NLRB election.[32] In a bitter statement in the *News*, the Latex workers lashed out at the treatment they had received. The manufacturers "deny we working people the right of assembly . . . freedom of speech . . . and they deny us the freedom of religion. They even try to deny us the privilege of calling ourselves American." If these rights had been taken away from the industrialists, "you would have said this is not America; this kind of crime can't go on in America. You would have said that's the way they do in China and Russia." But "Mr. Manufacturer, that has happened to us working people here in Whitfield County, who are trying to organize in the chenille industry."[33]

The older, well-established TWUA locals in Dalton watched the campaign with dismay. For several months they maintained a low profile while working behind the scenes to support the organizing effort. With the failure at Latex they threw themselves into the fray and defended unions as bastions of democracy and community improvement. TWUA Locals 185 and 134 jointly issued their own lengthy statement to the general public in the *News*, affirming that "unions, as a matter of public record, have fought an outstanding fight to rid themselves of Communist infiltration. There has never been and there is not now a single Communist in Local 185 or Local 134." Dalton's unions, the message continued, "stand for and work for . . . the things that make the community a better place in which to live," including higher standards of living for working people, which in turn meant better sales for local merchants. The statement explained union finances to demonstrate that no economic coercion was involved and to outline the impressive list of local and national charities to which the union contributed. Unions, the letter maintained, allowed workers in Dalton to "live and work as free people, free from the fear of unjust discharge or unjust treatment at the hands of their supervisors." The workers offered Allston Calhoun a particularly large serving of abuse. They derided him as a "paid parasite who produces nothing" except "hate and discord" and portrayed him as a cowardly stooge of anti-union chenille manufacturers. "What has Allston Calhoun done for Dalton?" the workers asked. "Has he lived and worked here for a better community?"[34] The TWUA locals voiced strong support for pro-union chenille workers and urged them to organize. "Cheap labor is the base for the high profits [in the chenille industry], and you furnish the labor," Dalton's union millhands warned. "Pay heed to Allston Calhoun and you will continue to furnish the cheap labor." Locals 185 and 134 called upon "the chenille workers in this area to join us in our unions to work for a better way of life."[35] Union leaders tried to shake off the Latex defeat and asserted that "we are confident and certain that when the election for the union is held the workers in the plant will vote union." This boast amounted to wishful thinking; but the TWUA soon received another chance, for at Belcraft Chenilles, a much larger plant, an election was on the horizon.[36]

The turmoil at Latex had obscured the numerically more important campaign proceeding simultaneously at Belcraft, which involved some two thousand workers, most of them in Dalton but some in Calhoun, a textile town thirty miles south. Belcraft workers had petitioned for a union election about the same time the Latex employees did, but no strike occurred at Belcraft to disrupt the normal process of the labor election. Two days after Locals 185 and 134 published their impassioned defense of unionization, the NLRB set the Belcraft election for 15 December. Everyone knew this day would be critical. "TWUA spokesmen have indicated," the *Citizen* noted, "that the outcome of the Belcraft vote will determine to a great extent whether they continue the current unionization effort in other plants."[37]

Dalton's union leaders threw themselves into a final frenzy to make the Belcraft election a success. Their hopes bloomed at an impressive labor rally held at the Whitfield County Courthouse on 11 December. Locals 185 and 134 sponsored the meeting and urged the attendance of all organized workers in Dalton, including those from the "railroad brotherhood, electricians, painters, brick-masons, [and] plumbers." As advertised in the local papers, the goal was to "work together as good honest people to make this area a better place in which to work and live." The timing of the meeting clearly indicated its purpose of redeeming the name of organized labor in Dalton and of encouraging chenille workers to vote for the union. "Our children and our friends," the advertisement insisted, "deserve the best effort we can possibly give to this end."[38] The meeting was an inspirational success for the city's union workers, who pledged support for the chenille campaign and condemned the manufacturers and local press for smearing Don West and the TWUA. The workers also expressed their commitment to a unionized Dalton and their optimism for the future. State and national labor leaders attended the meeting and made dramatic speeches, lending credibility to the resolutions and offering a show of national support for the chenille campaign. But it was anybody's guess whether such enthusiasm could counteract the deleterious effects of the anti-Communist campaign, the state troopers, and the defeat at Latex.[39]

When the votes were in on 15 December, the chenille campaign had suffered a crippling blow. Belcraft workers cast 840 votes (57 percent) against the union and only 625 votes for it. Pro-union workers and TWUA organizers tried to remain optimistic as they assembled in the American Thread union hall that evening. They unanimously resolved "to get the election set aside" as unfair. "We're going to keep right on till we get a union" said one leader. *The Southerner* insisted that "it's just the beginning. We'll win next time." In an editorial following the election, John Bunch contended that "we will have this better way of life in spite of the Allston Calhouns and those who pay them. This propaganda against unions and decent men will boomerang. When we all get organized there will be a better day for all."[40] Courageous assessments aside, it was nonetheless apparent that union leaders harbored serious doubts following the Belcraft election. No subsequent unionization drives ever took place. Belcraft was an ending, not a beginning.

Once the chenille campaign had faltered, Marc Pace resumed his "West campaign" with a flurry of attacks in late December and early January. The grand jury for the fall term finally closed out its lengthy session with a report that strongly warned against Communist activity in Dalton, called for federal authorities to investigate the situation, requested the next grand jury to continue the effort to root out Communism, and condemned Don West for refusing to answer its questions. The jury report also commended Marc Pace for his "alertness in this matter and [his] policy to expose such activity."[41] Noting a strong demand for back issues concerning Don West, Pace presented a special edition in the *Citizen* on 12 January, which reprinted five pages of "the more outstanding articles relative to Communism and the Don West campaign." Extra copies were available for five cents. Conspicuously absent in the special edition were stories relating to the TWUA chenille campaign. The implication, one not at all consonant with the reality of the local labor situation, was that the West campaign had no connection with the union effort.[42] The special edition was the last straw for West, who tendered his resignation to Pratt. The Union Assembly actually voted West out of the church, but speculation ran wild as to whether West and Pratt had a disagreement or were simply plotting a new strategy. Such speculation hardly mattered, for Pace had long since destroyed the public reputations of both men beyond the point of redemption.[43]

In the process, Pace also discredited the long-time union millhands of Dalton, and he had done so without once denying local unions access to his papers and without criticizing the TWUA or the cause of organized labor. Membership figures for TWUA Local 185 paint a picture of a once-thriving union withering on the vine. During the 1955 campaign, 94 percent of all workers at Crown Mill were members of Local 185; by 1967 that figure had fallen to 69 percent. This decline mirrored national trends, and numerous factors were involved; but the chenille-campaign disasters in 1955 appeared to dampen union enthusiasm among Dalton's younger millhands. The union workers at Crown and American Thread were aging, and retirement began to thin the ranks of their locals. Dalton's newer, younger millhands did not fill the void.

The trend in Dalton could be seen in 1962, when the TWUA won an unexpected victory at the Dixie Belle chenille mill in nearby Calhoun, Georgia. Unlike Dalton, Calhoun had never been a strong union town; but, ironically, in 1962 one of the key ingredients of the Calhoun campaign was the TWUA's efforts to hold an election in Calhoun with Dalton excluded. The national office, which in 1947 had hailed Dalton as a "Real Union Town," now viewed it as an anti-union city. Dixie Belle's executives apparently agreed, for they sought, unsuccessfully, to have their Dalton plants included in the election so as to thwart the union drive. The union won easily in Calhoun, with a comfortable two to one margin. The victory inspired talk of a new chenille campaign in the Dalton area, but it never materialized. The chenille campaign of 1955 and the Don West disaster that accompanied it had helped ensure that unionization would slowly fade from one of Dixie's important union enclaves. As the nonunion carpet industry boomed, Dalton's organized cotton mill workers found themselves isolated and embittered within their own city. The days of Dalton as a strong union town had passed.[44]

Ironically, as the TWUA suffered defeat at Belcraft, its international office was celebrating the AFL-CIO merger of December 1955 and proclaiming a new day for organized labor. In Dalton, that new day was a rather dark one. The International never gave any press to the Dalton campaign; top officials were probably glad it had ended. Dalton's business press had discovered the joys of McCarthyism; without ever attacking organized labor, Marc Pace devastated the local labor movement. By smearing Don West and the Union Assembly, Pace effectively paralyzed TWUA officials and frightened away labor's potential allies. Had the TWUA been able to tap the region's indigenous radicalism, the history of organized labor in the postwar South might not have been a tale of woe. Historians need not view West and Pratt as heroic martyrs to accept the point. National unions had already cast their lot with mainstream respectability, and there was no way to merge their efforts with groups like the Union Assembly. From the International's perspective, Pratt and West were loose wheels, and in all fairness this perspective was not always without merit. Working-class Protestant radicalism, spiced with some local bigotry, might have helped rally southern white millhands to the union cause, but it did not blend well with unionism in the 1950s. With red-baiting being all the rage, such radicalism was open to severe attacks from all levels of government and from the local community. So, Dalton in 1955 was another defeat for southern labor. But if this was Dixie, it was also McCarthy's America, and the TWUA's Dalton dilemma highlighted a larger problem for Big Labor in the postwar era. Unable to broaden the boundaries of dissent and unwilling to fight the anti-radical hysteria of the 1950s, the CIO could not capitalize on the energizing force of grass-roots movements. This state of affairs not only contributed to union failures in the South but also helped create an unresponsive labor bureaucracy that has watched all of America's industrial unions suffer a steady and irreversible decline.

13 ALAN DRAPER

George Wallace, Civil Rights, and the Alabama AFL-CIO

In March 1958, the recently merged Alabama American Federation of Labor-Congress of Industrial Organizations (AFL-CIO) prepared for its first Democratic primary. The state council gave a "favorable" evaluation to five of the thirteen candidates, and when only one of the five, George C. Wallace, made it to the runoff, the state council endorsed him. Wallace, a former circuit court judge, had compiled an impressive liberal record while serving in the Alabama state legislature. He opposed the "right to work" law, voted against regressive sales taxes, favored more liberal unemployment compensation laws, and remained loyal to the national Democratic Party in 1948 while other southerners bolted.[1] Indeed, his earlier progressive legislative stands had led the Alabama Chamber of Commerce to label him a "Radical."[2]

Wallace lost the Democratic primary runoff in 1958 but returned four years later in another bid for the governor's mansion. On 9 March 1962, the Alabama Committee on Political Education's (COPE) executive board met to evaluate Wallace and the other Democratic gubernatorial candidates. A screening committee reviewed their records and gave a "favorable" rating to three of the nine: former Governor James E. Folsom, state legislator Ryan deGraffenried, and Judge George C. Wallace.[3] In fact, the executive board briefly considered giving a favorable rating to a fourth contender, Birmingham Police Commissioner Eugene "Bull" Connor, but with his "states' rights" history this effort quickly died.[4] As the board finally settled upon its three preferences, however, it pondered whether to "single shot" one candidate or report out all three favorably. It left this decision to the full COPE Committee, which held its own internal version of a southern primary to determine whether any of the three had enough support to warrant a single endorsement. Wallace won the first COPE Committee "primary" against both Folsom and deGraffenried and then defeated Folsom 34–23 in its "runoff."[5] But this result still left Wallace three votes shy of the two-thirds majority needed for an endorsement under the AFL-CIO's central body rules. Despite the clear preference for Wallace, the COPE Committee forwarded three "favorable" ratings to the COPE convention, which voted to ratify by 314 to 211.[6]

The primary results in May failed to clarify the picture, because both Wallace and deGraffenried survived. Before the runoff, Wallace vigorously lobbied the Alabama AFL-CIO executive board, and in return for its support he reportedly promised to recommend a speaker of the House and chair of the House Business and Labor Committee acceptable to labor.[7] Wallace also clearly stated his views on racial matters: "I am for segregated schools." But this stand differed little from deGraffenried's assertion that he "would do everything in his power to preserve segregation" if elected governor.[8]

Wallace decisively defeated deGraffenried in the runoff, assuring his election as governor. When the Alabama AFL-CIO convention met in October, a victorious George Wallace showed his appreciation by attending and expressing his gratitude for the state council's faith and support over the course of his political career. He sympathized with the delegates' concerns and promised that his pro-labor record was a precursor of what could be expected from his administration.

The state council, however, never benefited from its investment in Wallace's career. Instead of access and influence, labor's political profile declined precipitously during Wallace's first term. When he emerged as the South's most popular and defiant defender of segregation, the council's opposition to him cost it dearly. Local unions disaffiliated, membership declined, and council political candidates suffered defeat. Despite promises that the "door of the Governor's office would be open," Wallace failed to consult the state council on bills pertinent to union members, refused to make traditional labor appointments to state commissions, and campaigned against council-endorsed candidates. The political career they so carefully nourished now threatened their survival.

Governor George Wallace's defense of white supremacy posed a challenge to the Alabama AFL-CIO in the 1960s. The state council was accountable to and depended financially upon local unions whose members believed in white supremacy and supported George Wallace. Yet, the Alabama AFL-CIO braved these threats and criticized Wallace's racial demagoguery. It endorsed loyal Democrats over candidates favored by Wallace and fought with Wallace supporters to ensure that the Alabama Democratic Party remained faithful to the national party.

The Alabama AFL-CIO opposed Wallace because its leaders sympathized with black demands for civil rights. In addition, Wallace's defense of white supremacy threatened the state council's political strategy, which depended on black enfranchisement. Black political participation, state council leaders believed, would increase the influence liberals exerted within the state legislature and the Alabama Democratic Party. Labor officials also believed that black enfranchisement would realign Alabama's party system, permitting voters at last to choose between conservative Republicans and liberal Democrats.

Their pursuit of these goals and their resistance to the Wallace juggernaut took a toll. The more the state council challenged the governor over civil rights, the more institutional and political costs it accumulated. As local unions disaffiliated, the state council lost political influence. A decade passed before the political courage it displayed in the 1960s bore fruit. The civil rights record it assembled in the 1960s laid the basis for the black-labor coalition that sustains the Alabama Democratic Party today.

The rank-and-file racism and anger of Alabama unionists appeared to be general. When AFL-CIO President George Meany reaffirmed labor's support for the *Brown* decision and condemned the segregationist White Citizens' Councils as a Ku Klux Klan without hoods, more angry protests came from Alabama unions than from any other state. Birmingham's Machinists Lodge 271 advised Meany that outsiders "who know little or nothing about the real situation" should not interfere while southern unionists solved their own problems.[9] The Iron City Lodge 60 of the Brotherhood of Railway Carmen, also in Birmingham, asked if Meany realized "how many thousands of Hoodless Ku Klux are members of the affiliate labor organizations of the AFL-CIO?" If the AFL-CIO planned to get rid of such unionists, the Carmen warned, it had better make haste, because "the White Citizens' Councils may purge themselves of the AFL-CIO."[10] Birmingham's United Steel Workers at the Tennessee Coal and Iron Division of U.S. Steel expressed similar loyalties when they threatened Meany, "If we have to choose between staying in the union or see our segregated way of life being destroyed we will pull out and form our own union."[11]

Meany's volume of mail from Alabama reflected the Citizens' Councils' success in recruiting union members there.[12] According to one Council estimate, three-quarters of its members in the Birmingham area held union cards. On the city's west side, 90 percent of the members from one very active Citizens' Council chapter belonged to unions.[13] They also voted for white supremacy. A 1955 "private school" constitutional amendment designed to circumvent the *Brown* decision carried every labor district except Gadsden, according to COPE Area Director Dan Powell.[14] Two years later, "Bull" Connor used openly racist appeals in white working-class wards to achieve insurmountable pluralities in defeating the incumbent candidate for Public Safety Commissioner of Birmingham.[15]

Trade unionists also voted with their feet. Union members from nearby rubber, steel, and paper plants stormed the University of Alabama campus seeking to prevent Autherine Lucy, a black woman, from matriculating. Acknowledging the presence of many union members in the campus protest, one local labor leader explained to a *New York Times* reporter, "These men believe in segregation and they believe that Northern leaders who have never been in the South have no right to intervene."[16] Morton T. Elder found similar sentiments during his tour of Alabama for the Southern Regional Council. Racial matters simmered among the 2,500 members of United Steel Workers (USWA) Local A. Elder reported, "This local union was considerably worked up over the Lucy case . . . and [they] also protested vigorously . . . President Meany's remarks on civil rights. This movement was led and supported by L. U. [local union] officers. . . . The situation here is quite explosive and would certainly respond to capable leadership by white supremacists."[17] Such leadership emerged soon enough as Birmingham segregationists achieved more success in organizing racist challenges to existing unions than any other group in the South.[18]

While the rank and file tried to save Jim Crow, the Alabama AFL-CIO remained as sympathetic and sensitive to black demands as its position in the Deep South would permit. The 1956 unity convention of its state councils took place in Mobile, due to its status as the most racially tolerant and least segregated city in Alabama. Mobile prevailed despite AFL executive board objections that its relative geographical isolation might discourage attendance. Board members preferred Montgomery, where the convention was originally scheduled, or Birmingham, located closer to most locals. But both cities could not qualify, having been the sites of recent racial turmoil.[19]

The state council exhibited other sensitivity to black unionists, including black representation on its executive board. In addition to district vice-presidents, the new Alabama AFL-CIO constitution provided for twelve vice-presidents-at-large. Four of these at-large posts were reserved for blacks and two for women,[20] according to a gentleman's agreement reached during the AFL-ClO merger negotiations. Regarding civil rights issues, however, the Alabama AFL-CIO remained silent, avoiding racial matters that so exorcised its members. Thus, it failed both to protest attempts to bar the National Association for the Advancement of Colored People from the state and to denounce Jim Crow. Preoccupied with reconciling local unions and local central bodies to the merger, the state council hesitated to antagonize them further.

Meanwhile, the AFL-CIO in Washington, D.C., pursued a more active course. In 1957, the AFL-CIO COPE funded a Birmingham black voter registration drive conducted by the Alabama State Coordinating Association for Registration and Voting (ASCARV).[21] Pleased with the results, COPE endowed ASCARV with a full-time position for voter registration. COPE also invested in similar voter registration activity conducted by the Montgomery Improvement Association (MIA). Under the dynamic, effective leadership of a young minister, Dr. Martin Luther King, Jr., MIA boycotted segregated buses in Montgomery, successfully organized an alternative transportation network, and maintained the spirit and solidarity of the black community in the face of threats and intimidation. When the boycott came to its successful conclusion, MIA turned its attention to electoral politics.[22] In 1958, COPE Minorities Director Philip Weightman and his assistant, Earl Davis, enlisted MIA's support for the Alabama, COPE-endorsed candidate, Wilbur B. Nolen, running in the Democratic primary against Representative George M. Grant. Davis found the MIA "most cooperative" in conducting the campaign. "But most significant," Davis wrote, "was the cooperation of MIA President Reverend Martin Luther King. He came through on every request that we made of him. His expressions of appreciation, at the mass meetings, of AFL-CIO's efforts in Montgomery, and the desire for complete cooperation between Labor and the Negro was most impressive."[23]

Ultimately and perhaps inevitably, the Alabama AFL-CIO became implicated in the activities of national AFL-CIO departments such as COPE, and the hostile reaction from its affiliates was predictable. When the 5,280 members of a United Steel Workers local learned of Weightman's work in

Alabama, they reduced their per capita payments to the Alabama AFL-CIO from $422 per month to an insulting $4.[24] Fortunately for the state council, few other local unions knew of COPE's ties to ASCARV or the MIA. Local unions, however, did not need specific details of COPE's connivance to punish the state council. COPE's identification with the national Democratic Party and the AFL-CIO's public support of civil rights enraged many rank-and-file unionists. In 1961, Local 211 of Montgomery's Printing Pressmen informed Alabama AFL-CIO President Barney Weeks that it would pay its regular assessment to the state council but not to the Dedicated Fund for COPE. As a local official explained, a majority of the members "refuse to support COPE because of their [sic] national views." Understanding that its failure to contribute to the Dedicated Fund for COPE would lead to suspension by the state council, the local viewed its exile as a small price for maintaining integrity in defense of segregation.[25] Jasper's Brotherhood of Painters Local 241 was more blunt. In 1964 it warned the state council that the enclosed check for per capita dues would be the last "unless someone shuts or closes Geo. Meany's mouth for he definitely does not speak for this body when he says that Labor is 100% behind the Civil Rights Bill. We are for George Wallace on this issue and think all of Alabama should get behind him."[26]

Another instance in which the Alabama AFL-CIO suffered in the crossfire between national and local policy disagreements occurred when the AFL-CIO Industrial Union Department (IUD) contributed five thousand dollars to the Congress of Racial Equality (CORE) to help defray costs incurred by the Freedom Rides. Plumbers Union 548 in Elmore, Alabama, asked Barney Weeks whether any of its dues went toward the CORE contribution. It is unknown whether Weeks's assurance that "not one penny of this money" came from the state council placated the angry plumbers, but Weeks did his best to portray IUD as a wayward relative over which even George Meany had little influence.[27] Despite Weeks's protests of innocence, the state council remained a convenient target as local unions sought someone to punish for the IUD contribution.

In addition to the "sins" of others, the Alabama AFL-CIO soon accumulated its own list of trespasses in the eyes of the membership, including its failure to endorse Wallace in the 1964 presidential primaries and its opposition to the governor's slate of unpledged electors in the Alabama Democratic primary.

Wallace announced his candidacy for the 1964 Democratic presidential nomination on 7 March and soon entered the Wisconsin primary. This action brought a swift response from the Wisconsin AFL-CIO, which sent letters to its affiliated locals accusing Wallace of being a "carpetbagger, a bigot, a racist, and one of the strongest anti-labor spokesmen in America." Wallace supporters in Alabama moved quickly to parry this charge and to portray the governor as a friend of workers. In a statement to the United Press International (UPI) wire service, H. L. Welch, business agent for the Carpenters and president of the Montgomery Building Trades Council, called the Wisconsin AFL-CIO statement "false and malicious. . . . The rank and file membership of the AFL-CIO in Alabama . . . is 100% behind Governor Wallace."[28] Weeks immediately alerted the news media that the writer of the wire service story had erred in implying that the Alabama AFL-CIO had endorsed Wallace. Welch spoke only for himself. Wallace's campaign aides then pressed Weeks for a statement to counter the attack by the Wisconsin state council. When Weeks refused, they recruited Alabama union officers to praise Wallace's pro-labor record.[29] In a letter to the Milwaukee Labor Council, Communication Workers Local 3902 urged support for Wallace in the Wisconsin primary.[30] William T. Thrash, business manager of Birmingham's Operating Engineers Local 312, telegrammed the Wisconsin AFL-CIO that the governor had a "perfect labor record in Alabama" and demanded a retraction of the Wisconsin state council's negative statement.[31] When Wallace spoke on Milwaukee's Polish southside, two Alabama union officials joined him on the stage of Serbian Memorial Hall. John Stone of the Bessemer Labor Council and Jack Pratt of the USWA received resounding applause as they unrolled a sixty-two-foot list with 1,734 names of Alabama union members who each contributed one dollar to Wallace's campaign. "Irregardless [sic] of what you have heard," Stone told the packed auditorium, "George Wallace is a friend of labor and we are behind him 100%."[32]

As Wallace returned to Alabama after a surprisingly strong showing in Wisconsin and prepared for the Indiana primary, an independent committee from the Tuscaloosa Rubber Workers greeted him, donated six hundred dollars to his campaign, and presented a petition signed by four hundred members urging that his fight against the 1964 Civil Rights Act continue. Papermakers Local 297 provided a letter of endorsement that praised Wallace's labor record and his defense of states' rights. That local along with

Pulp and Papermill Workers Local 157 then gave Wallace a check to help defray his campaign expenses.[33] An alarmed Barney Weeks warned Dallas Sells, president of the Indiana AFL-CIO, that Alabama union leaders would appear in Indiana to claim that Wallace had labor's support. "Needless to say," Weeks wrote, "no such statement is true nor are they authorized to make such statements."[34]

Friction between the governor and the state council also occurred over the selection of Alabama's presidential electors. Alabama COPE wanted a pledged slate of electors who would be loyal to the Democratic Party candidate. Wallace proposed instead that Alabamians elect a slate of un-pledged electors, thus permitting the state to bargain for civil rights relief in return for its electoral votes. In a letter urging delegates to the 1964 Ala-bama COPE convention to support his slate, Wallace advised that indepen-dent electors "would put them on notice in Washington, especially about the so-called Civil Rights Bill," which threatened "to destroy the seniority rights" of every union member.[35]

At the 1964 COPE convention, the state council and the governor crossed swords even before the question of presidential electors came up for consid-eration. Former Governor James E. Folsom opposed Birmingham Police Commissioner Eugene "Bull" Connor in two important races—one for national Democratic committeeman and the other for president of the Alabama Public Service Commission. Alabama COPE previously had en-dorsed Folsom for office twice—when he ran for governor in 1954 and again in 1962. But Connor also had rendered friendly service to organized labor. While serving in the state legislature, Connor had voted for a civil service bill, the creation of the Alabama Department of Labor, and a more liberal workmen's compensation law.[36] In 1957 the Joint Labor Committee of Jefferson County endorsed Connor for Birmingham police commissioner because his opponent had used the force to break strikes.[37] At the time, COPE Area Director Dan Powell described Connor to superiors in Washing-ton, D.C., as a "segregationist de luxe who was very friendly to labor while in office."[38] Thereafter, Connor enhanced his reputation as a staunch segre-gationist by using fire hoses and dogs on civil rights protesters in Bir-mingham. As the delegates voted to endorse Folsom for both positions, however, they seemed more disturbed over Connor's disloyalty to the Demo-cratic Party than his segregationist activities.

The Connor-Folsom contest served as a prelude to the main event, the endorsement of a slate of presidential electors. Earl Pippin, vice-president of the state council, spoke for the Alabama COPE Committee and recommended the loyalist slate of pledged electors. According to Pippin, Wallace's unpledged slate included right-to-work advocates, Dixiecrats, strikebreakers, and reactionaries. A delegate rose immediately in opposition, arguing that a vote for the pledged electors committed Alabama to President Lyndon B. Johnson, who had betrayed the South by supporting civil rights. A vote for the unpledged electors, however, meant an endorsement of George Wallace, "a true friend of labor," whom the state council leadership had recommended for governor in 1958 and 1962. Wallace, argued the delegate, had done nothing since then to forfeit labor's support. Applause greeted his conclusion: "How can we go against the best friend we have had in many a day?"[39] Another delegate, speaking for Alabama COPE, reminded his colleagues that civil rights was but one issue. None of the supporters of unpledged electors stood for the programs that labor advocated, including social security, better schools, or medical care for the needy. Rather than being swayed by one issue, he cautioned, delegates should consider the entire program when voting on the question.

As the convention delegates approved the pledged electors by a voice vote, Dan Powell congratulated them. He urged them to remind their local union members what was at stake in the 4 May Democratic primary. Support for the unpledged elector slate would isolate Alabama from the rest of the nation, relieve President Johnson of a sense of obligation to the state, and imperil the flow of federal funds.[40]

No sooner had delegates returned from the convention than the results were repudiated by local unions. Following lengthy and boisterous meetings, these local unions voted to endorse Wallace's slate of unpledged electors. Local central bodies and building trades councils violated their charters and endorsed candidates in opposition to the Alabama COPE-sanctioned slate, including "Bull" Connor. By early March, Weeks began sending distress signals to AFL-CIO COPE Director Al Barkan about Wallace's attempts to sow discord within the state council. "I don't know what you can do about this, but wanted you to know the present situation, which is steadily deteriorating."[41] Dan Powell also sounded the alarm at COPE headquarters. He wrote Barkan, "No elected state or municipal official, no large local union officer, city central body official or no state council officer in Alabama today can survive if Wallace actively opposes him. I know this statement sounds fantastic and almost unbelievable, but the situation in Alabama today is without parallel in the history of this nation. . . . From recent reports . . . there is every indication that Wallace intends to oppose Weeks and the other officers in October."[42]

Even George Meany intervened. In a strongly worded letter, he informed the international union presidents that some of their Alabama unions were "actually aiding and abetting the forces of race hatred." This action threatened Weeks and the state council, and Meany requested their assistance, presumably by disciplining the wayward locals.[43] In April, Weeks sent Powell several items that confirmed the success of Wallace's strategy of circumventing the state council and appealing directly to local union leaders of the rank and file: "The reason for sending you all this is to show you some small evidence of the total concentration on the race issue (because of George Wallace's activities) by so many of our members, which is costing us the loss of thousands of members in affiliations."[44]

Rebel locals attached to George Wallace disaffiliated from the state council to protest its failure to endorse the governor's slate of unpledged electors and his candidacy in the Democratic primaries. These defections further weakened the state council, which had been losing members even before the crisis broke. The Alabama AFL-CIO membership first began to decline in 1960 when it doubled its per capita tax. Membership declined further when twenty-five Steel Workers locals withdrew in a tiff over the removal of one of their members as secretary-treasurer of the state council. Just as this drama ended, the state council's conflict with Wallace brought even more defections. From a peak membership of 107,000 in 1958, or 58 percent of all Alabama AFL-CIO members, the state council's representation declined to 30 percent by 1965 when it collected per capita taxes on only 55,568 unionists. Its 485 affiliated local unions in 1958 dwindled to 349 by 1964 out of a total of 740 AFL-CIO local unions statewide.[45]

The disaffiliations had a devastating effect upon the state council, since 80 percent of its revenue derived from membership dues. The loss of members brought deficits and retrenchment, including the closing in 1963 of the Montgomery office and the dismissal of a full-time lobbyist in order to cut costs. The state council's political credibility also suffered from the reduced financial or organizational assistance to its endorsed candidates.

As the fate of Congressman Carl Elliot revealed, the outright political rejection the state council experienced hurt even more than the organizational decay. Elliot, the most liberal member of Alabama's House delegation, had compiled a COPE voting record of 82 percent, with nine "right" votes and only two "wrong" in the Eighty-eighth Congress. His district included the northern Alabama hills where during the Civil War pro-Union sentiment flourished and where in more recent times various federal projects, such as the Tennessee Valley Authority, dotted the landscape. Extraordinary circumstances in 1964, however, influenced the conditions under which candidates for the House would have to compete. Alabama lost a congressional seat as a result of the 1960 census, but the legislature refused to redistrict the state. Instead, it adopted the "8–9 plan," which forced Democratic candidates to run three times. The first test came in their old districts. Then the nine winners competed in an at-large statewide election, those with the fewest votes being dropped from the ticket. In November the surviving eight candidates competed against the Republicans in assigned districts.

In the first round, the Wallace camp entered Alabama House Floor Leader Tom Bevill in the district primary against Elliot. Bevill, who attracted money from national conservative pressure groups, attacked Elliot for being soft on integration. The AFL-CIO took an active interest in Elliot's future, and COPE Director Barkan asked Weeks to keep him apprised of Elliot's prospects. Weeks's reply proved discouraging. Local unions of the Bricklayers, Carpenters and Painters had deserted Elliot over segregation, while the Jasper Building Trades Council, disregarding Alabama COPE's endorsement of Elliot, supported Bevill in violation of its charter. In addition, local ILGWU and CWA unions that had campaigned for Elliot in the past now refused to do so.[46] At Weeks's request, union staff representatives joined Elliot's campaign when it became clear that the local unions would not help him. Elliot won the May primary, but following his victory, Weeks wrote Barkan, "Many of our members left us, because of their loyalty to Wallace, and their preoccupation with the race issue. Those who stuck with us were apathetic, and did not work in the campaign. . . . [The] full-time paid union representatives assigned to the campaign . . . in my judgment, was the one thing which meant the difference between victory or the defeat of Congressman Elliot."[47]

A month later, however, Elliot's candidacy floundered at the second hurdle when he received the lowest total in the statewide runoff of the nine district survivors. A mortified Barney Weeks wrote Barkan, "This is the worst blow we've suffered here in Alabama in a long time, and it will be some time before we recover from this."[48] The climate in Alabama "had gone from bad to worse."[49] The voting records of Alabama's congressmen and senators prepared for distribution by COPE could not be used in Alabama because they included civil rights votes, Weeks noted. Instead, the state council produced its own analysis that omitted such controversial material.[50]

The fratricide within the Alabama AFL-CIO even attracted the attention of the *New York Times*, which reported the exodus of dissatisfied union members from the state council.[51] A follow-up story disclosed opposition to President Johnson to be "greatest in Alabama where . . . Wallace has achieved great influence among the rank and file." With unionists deploring the Democratic Party's civil rights record, radical right-wing groups such as the Ku Klux Klan infiltrated and in some cases seized control of local unions.[52] Alabama Klansmen who held union cards included Imperial Wizard Robert Shelton, a member of the United Rubber Workers. Former Grand Dragon Robert Creel presided over a United Steel Workers local in Fairfield. Two of the three Klansmen accused in 1965 of the murder of civil rights marcher Viola Luizzo belonged to this union.[53] Whether or not direct organizational links to the Klan existed became largely irrelevant because the union members' views closely resembled Klan positions. Dan Powell reported to Al Barkan: "In several large locals in Mississippi and Alabama the presidents are either members of the John Birch Society or are cheating the society out of dues. . . . I am afraid that a majority of our union membership in the South today is more aware of and in sympathy with the program and policies of the John Birch Society than they are with the program and policies of the AFL-CIO."[54] Although Powell exaggerated, his report reflected the depth of the reaction to the civil rights movement.

Despite financial and organizational losses, the Alabama AFL-CIO continued to hold the line for the national Democratic Party. Speaker after speaker at the union's October 1964 convention urged delegates to vote the entire Democratic ticket. Senator John Sparkman reminded delegates that Alabama received funds from Washington three times the amount sent there in taxes. In his farewell address, defeated Congressman Elliot warned against "deceitful promises and false hopes." Both President Johnson and his opponent, Republican Senator Barry Goldwater, endorsed civil rights, although Goldwater would leave the matter up to the states. "The only issue" in November, according to Elliot, "is prosperity, and Johnson has a proven record on that." AFL-CIO Coordinator of State and Local Central Bodies Stanton Smith alerted delegates to the real meaning of states' rights: more regressive taxes and restrictive labor legislation. Finally, COPE Director Al Barkan on the last day of the convention gave a rousing speech that accused Goldwater of hypocrisy. He embraced the 1964 Civil Rights Act when speaking in the North and condemned it when appearing in the South. Barkan labeled Goldwater an integrationist as indicated by his NAACP membership. Delegates should not be duped by promises that Goldwater would keep blacks in their place, because he intended to put union members right beside them. They should not vote for Goldwater simply to protest civil rights; union members had to take the whole Goldwater, the one who had voted for Taft-Hartley and for Landrum-Griffin. Vote a straight Democratic ticket, Barkan urged, because more was at stake in November than the end of segregation under Lyndon Johnson. A Goldwater victory would destroy trade unionism.[55]

The final word belonged to the defecting rank and file, most of whom objected to the state council's fealty to the national Democratic Party. On 1 November, two days before the election, an advertisement in the *Mobile Press-Register* endorsed Goldwater. Over three hundred members from AFL-CIO unions signed petitions and paid for the ad.[56]

Alabama became one of six states lost by Johnson while accumulating a national margin of sixteen million votes. In addition to the Goldwater victory, Republicans won five congressional seats in Alabama. In 1960, Alabama's COPE-endorsed candidates had taken every statewide and congressional contest but one. The 1964 results reversed those of just four years earlier. Congressman Robert Jones, the sole COPE-endorsed candidate to survive the 1964 election, faced only meager competition in the primaries and ran unopposed in the general election. The story of another Birmingham legislator illustrated vividly how union members disregarded COPE's recommendations, thus undermining the state council's political credibility. When union leaders asked the legislator to vote for a particular bill, he noted their campaign in support of his union-endorsed opponent. "Yes," replied one of the union supplicants, "but you got most of our votes."[57]

By 1965 all contact between the Wallace administration and the state council had ceased. Wallace spokesmen no longer received invitations to speak at labor conferences, and the governor ignored the council when making appointments. He even excluded them from negotiations over proposed changes in the state's unemployment insurance law.[58] Disaffiliations continued to sap the state council's strength. Asked by COPE how Alabama labor proposed to take advantage of the 1965 Voting Rights Act, Weeks replied that "due to the loss of so many members because of the civil rights issue, the state council was unable to do anything financially at this time."[59] Meanwhile, Wallace continued to drive a wedge between the state council and its membership. "Interest in COPE has declined" due to the influence of Wallace and the "Radical Right," Alabama COPE Director William Mintz noted. A 1965 Oliver Quayle poll of the Alabama electorate confirmed Mintz's suspicions; no demographic, economic, or occupational group seemed more devoted to Wallace than members of organized labor.[60] When the Alabama AFL-CIO executive board opposed a bill permitting Wallace to succeed himself as governor, one participant confessed ruefully, "My members have got their minds made up and it would do no good to go back and tell them how we voted here."[61] Wallace became so influential that the Anniston central labor council in 1965 gave him a lifetime membership. The following year, as Weeks pressed charges seeking to have its charter lifted, the Anniston group disregarded state council wishes and endorsed Lurleen Wallace, George Wallace's wife, for governor. "We need action on this as quickly as possible," Weeks warned Stanton Smith; "several groups outside of Labor are watching to see what kind of discipline we have."[62]

Despite such setbacks, the Alabama AFL-CIO continued to defy Wallace and resolutely stood by the national Democratic Party. When the state council at its COPE convention in March 1966 endorsed a loyalist slate for the Alabama Democratic Party's executive committee, it rejected Birmingham Building Trades Council President William Thrash because he supported independent electors in 1964. Weeks explained that the office required someone with solid Democratic Party, not union, credentials.[63] Due to past party disloyalty, Speaker of the House Albert Brewer also forfeited state council support in his bid for lieutenant governor. Its previous good relations with Brewer (it had recommended him for his current legislative post) notwithstanding, the state council now shunned him because of his support of independent electors in 1964.[64] The council endorsed Ruth Owens for state treasurer, because she was a loyal Democrat who had joined President Johnson's wife aboard the Lady Bird Special when it came through Alabama in 1964. In the 1966 Democratic gubernatorial primary the COPE convention selected a loyal friend, former Congressman Carl Elliot. Although Dan Powell admired the planning that secured the Elliot endorsement over Lurleen Wallace, a surrogate for her husband who could not succeed himself, he recognized it, nevertheless, as a leadership decision with little rank-and-file support. "Indications are that a substantial portion of the rank-and-file membership . . . favor Mrs. Lurleen Wallace," he reported to AFL-CIO COPE. He then gave the example of the Hayes Aircraft local in Birmingham where the UAW representative and the local union officers could not release money to Elliot from the local's citizenship fund because of "strong Wallace sentiment among many of the rank-and-file members. Among many of the locals which are not affiliated," Powell continued, "the Wallace sentiment is even stronger."[65]

The 1966 COPE convention endorsements touched off a new wave of disaffiliations that the state council could ill-afford. One council executive board member broke ranks, charging that "the council meeting was turned into a National Democratic party meeting rather than a labor convention." To President Robert Lowe of the Mobile Building Trades Council the "endorsements definitely do not reflect those members of [my] council." The twenty-three locals in his organization would disaffiliate. Montgomery's Capital City Building Trades Council also repudiated the convention's endorsements and withdrew from the state council with Hatters Local 122 and IBEW Local 1998 following suit.[66] The Elliot endorsement split the local labor movement in Birmingham, its Building Trades Council defecting to Lurleen Wallace while its Labor Council remained loyal to Elliot. Conflict even erupted within local unions. Rank-and-file members of Rubber Workers Local 351 in Tuscaloosa challenged their leaders by ripping Elliot posters off the front door of the union hall on five occasions.

The 1966 Democratic primary results could not have been more disappointing. Every council-endorsed candidate for statewide office lost. Despite the "most support ever given a candidate for public office by organized labor in Alabama," Elliot, with a mere 8 percent of the vote, finished third behind Lurleen Wallace in a field of ten.[67] With each new election, the Wallace vote continued to attract more white working-class support.[68] Defeated in the primaries, the Alabama AFL-CIO, finding all alternatives in the November general elections objectionable, declined to endorse any state or federal candidate. The brevity of the state council's COPE Program Report on the 1966 elections could not hide its officers' discouragement.

"Racial hatred stirred by Governor Wallace and the Klan have badly divided
the ranks of Labor. . . . The state council conducts leadership week-end [sic]
institutes in political and legislative action each year in a not-too-successful
effort to unify the Labor Movement. State council is further weakened by
the non-affiliation of most of the Steel locals."[69]

"In sum, the salience of race in Alabama, by alienating the rank and file
from the leadership has done more to damage the efficacy of organized labor
as a political interest group than any other factor," concluded George Kundahl in his study of the state council.[70] The Alabama state council suffered
defections, lost revenue, closed offices, and laid-off staff. Politically, it became an outcast without influence. The candidates it endorsed lost elections, and its members openly repudiated it. Years later a UAW official from
Alabama confessed to Stanley Greenberg, "We couldn't get off the ground in
politics so long as that racial issue was there."[71] For Weeks and other state
council officers who drew on personal reserves of courage and fortitude, the
entire period drained and exhausted them. Wallace's appeal to white supremacy remained so powerful that the council struggled simply to maintain some organizational presence to say nothing of building a biracial
working-class coalition through the Alabama Democratic Party. The period
confirms one scholar's view that "the pre-eminence of the race question all
but negated the possibility of class-based politics in postwar Alabama."[72]
    Yet the Alabama AFL-CIO, for many reasons, persevered despite the
institutional and political pressures arrayed against it. Leadership became a
determining factor. A principled ideological commitment to civil rights
existed at the very top of the labor hierarchy. Alabama AFL-CIO President
Barney Weeks believed in the justice of black demands. But he had to be
circumspect in publicizing such views because open support of the civil
rights movement would have been political suicide. Even Weeks's support of
the national Democratic Party and his denunciation of segregationists
stretched the endurance and tolerance of his members. While framing his
civil rights position in indirect, muted tones out of political necessity,
Weeks still acted courageously, for in defying Wallace he tangled with both a
popular and a pro-labor governor. Weeks simply could not attack Wallace as
another southern demagogue who used race as a popular disguise to hide an
anti-labor agenda, because Wallace had relatively good credentials on labor

issues. A student of Alabama politics accurately suggests that Wallace's "great popularity among white unionists was based on more than a simple appeal to racial fear. On almost all issues important to labor, Wallace took the correct position."[73] That Weeks willingly opposed a governor with such a solid labor record underscores his strong commitment to racial justice.

Second, a black-labor coalition held for the state council the promise of political rewards as well as risks. In 1960, twenty out of Alabama's sixty-six counties had a black residency of 40 percent or more. Most were agricultural counties located in the Black Belt region that bisects the state. Their anti-labor legislators felt immune to political pressure from the state council, because few union members resided in those districts. Given the sizable black populations, however, these legislators could be defeated by enfranchised blacks. Consequently, the state council supported civil rights as a way of empowering blacks to challenge anti-labor legislators beyond the state council's reach.

Finally, the state council expected a black-labor coalition to do more than simply increase liberal influence within the state legislature and the Alabama Democratic Party. The Alabama AFL-CIO sought nothing less than a political realignment, creating a two-party system that could offer voters a choice between conservative Republicans and liberal Democrats. It would replace Alabama's personalized, transitory political coalitions with a responsible, polarized two-party system.[74] In pursuit of this larger vision, the state council remained loyal to the policies of the national Democratic Party, even endorsing its candidates on the basis of this test. After the disastrous 1964 elections, Weeks approached another group that had remained loyal to the national Democratic Party, the Young Democrats of Alabama. He requested their cooperation in creating the party realignment that Alabama politics required. The tenor of politics in Alabama could be changed, Weeks argued, only "if right-thinking, forward-looking, progressive people within the state join together in one party and welcome others of like mind into that party." Only those who adhered to the Democratic Party's platform and principles should run under the Democratic Party label. Weeks admonished that the party should accept no imposters, such as "Alabama Democrats, Southern Democrats, Conservative Democrats, Goldwater Democrats, or any other such camouflaged name for the Republican Party."[75]

Despite such sentiments, fewer and fewer white union members in Alabama cared whether candidates ran as Democrats regardless of classification. By 1968 only 39 percent identified themselves as Democrats, with fully half claiming to be Independents. Defecting from both parties and ignoring union recommendations, 83 percent of all white Alabama union members voted for Wallace in his third party presidential bid in 1968; Hubert Humphrey, the AFL-CIO-endorsed Democratic presidential candidate, received a paltry 6 percent of their votes.[76]

In the 1970s, a repentant Wallace led his flock back into the church of "Southern Democracy." Not as many white unionists returned as had departed, and their zealous devotion had diminished. Nevertheless, they took places beside blacks as mainstays of a reconstituted Alabama Democratic Party. To the delight of the state council, the Alabama Democratic Party now had a biracial working-class coalition that "dropped its old (racist) mind set and accepted much of the program of the programmatically liberal national Democratic party as its own."[77] Just as a chastened Wallace would apologize to blacks for his previous race-baiting, so did he try to repair relations with the state council. The Alabama AFL-CIO endorsed Wallace for governor in 1974 because he had adopted its views. Wallace accepted the principle of civil rights for blacks and led a biracial, liberalized Alabama Democratic Party that the state council had always envisioned.[78]

Notes

Part I: Introduction

1. Full citations to these works and others relating to southern textiles appear in Robert H. Zieger, "Textile Workers and Historians," in *Organized Labor in the Twentieth-Century South*, ed. Robert H. Zieger (Knoxville: University of Tennessee Press, 1991), 35–59.

2. This rich tradition of social investigation is the subject of an essay to appear in *Cultural Perspectives on the American South*, vol. 7 (forthcoming).

3. The work of Dale Newman and Edward Beardsley, however, carries on the traditional themes of victimization and debility. See Zieger, "Textile Workers and Historians," 57, n. 18.

4. Frederickson updated her findings in a paper entitled "Race Relations" as part of a session on "Race, Class, and Gender: Toward a New Synthesis in Southern Textile History," Southern Labor Studies Conference, Atlanta, 10–13 October 1991.

5. There have been several discrete, but overlapping, wings of the new social history. One, as recently exemplified in the work of such scholars as Darrett and Anita Rutman, Howard Chudacoff, and Eric Monkkonen, centers on the development and perfection of analytical methodology, often borrowing and adapting techniques from the harder social sciences and frequently deploying sophisticated quantitative techniques. Another, as exemplified in the labor history of Herbert Gutman and in the work of such scholars as Jesse Lemisch, Gary Nash, and James Green, makes few claims to methodological innovation but rather concentrates on bringing to historiographical life ordinary people as agents of their own lives and as neglected factors in the larger social, economic, and political landscape. Such pioneers of the new social history, notably Stephan Thernstrom and Michael Katz, integrated "hard" methodological concerns into an agenda that focused on the lives of ordinary people. Likewise, Gutman's work on slavery is a notable example of a book that brought together these two wings of the new social history.

6. See also David L. Carlton, "The Revolution from Above: The National Market and the Beginnings of Industrialization in North Carolina," *Journal of American History* 77 (September 1990): 445–75, and "The State and the Worker in the South: A

Lesson from South Carolina," in *The Meaning of South Carolina History: Essays in Honor of George C. Rogers, Jr.*, ed. David R. Chesnutt and Clyde N. Wilson (Columbia: University of South Carolina Press, 1991), 186–201.

7. The same is true of Linda Frankel's work on the Harriet-Henderson strike of 1958. See Linda Frankel, "'Jesus Leads Us, Cooper Needs Us, the Union Feeds Us': The 1958 Harriet-Henderson Textile Strike," in *Hanging by a Thread: Social Change in Southern Textiles*, ed. Jeffrey Leiter, Michael D. Schulman, and Rhonda Zingraff (Ithaca: ILR Press, 1991), 101–20.

8. Suggestive examples of the pivotal role of textile workers in shaping broad national or regional developments in other parts of the world include Peter Winn, *Weavers of Revolution: The Yarur Workers and Chile's Road to Socialism* (New York: Oxford University Press, 1986); and Padraic Jeremiah Kenney, "Working-Class Identity, Control, and the Question of Resistance in Pre-Stalinist Poland: The Poznanski Strike in Lodz, September, 1947," forthcoming in *Social History*.

1. Gender Relations in Southern Textiles

The author wishes to acknowledge the assistance of Jacquelyn Dowd Hall and Robert H. Zieger, who read and commented on an earlier draft of this essay.

1. George Makepeace to Webb and Douglass, 11 September 1851; James Webb Papers, Southern Historical Collection, University of North Carolina at Chapel Hill.

2. U.S. Bureau of Labor, *Report on the Condition of Women and Child Wage Earners in the United States*, Senate Document no. 645, 61st Cong., 1910, vol. 1; Mary Britt to Mark Morgan, n.d., Mark Morgan Papers, Duke University.

3. Quoted in Victoria Byerly, *Hard Times Cotton Mill Girls* (Ithaca: Cornell University Press, 1986), 64.

4. Anne Firor Scott, *Making the Invisible Woman Visible* (Urbana: University of Illinois Press, 1984).

5. Jean E. Friedman, *The Enclosed Garden: Women and Community in the Evangelical South, 1830–1900* (Chapel Hill: University of North Carolina Press, 1985).

6. David L. Carlton, *Mill and Town in South Carolina, 1880–1920* (Baton Rouge: Louisiana State University Press, 1982), 146–48.

7. Jacquelyn Dowd Hall, "Partial Truths," *Signs* 14 (Summer 1989), no. 4.

8. Catherine Clinton, *The Plantation Mistress: Women's World in the Old South* (New York: Pantheon Books, 1982), xv.

9. Anne Firor Scott, *The Southern Lady: From Pedestal to Politics, 1830–1930* (Chicago: University of Chicago Press, 1970).

10. Clinton, *Plantation Mistress*; Elizabeth Fox-Genovese, *Within the Plantation Household: Black and White Women of the Old South* (Chapel Hill: University of

North Carolina Press, 1988), 401–2, n. 9; Dolores Janiewski, *Sisterhood Denied: Race, Gender and Class in a New South Community* (Philadelphia: Temple University Press, 1985).

11. Leslie Woodcock Tentler, *Wage-Earning Women: Industrial Work and Family Life in the United States, 1900–1930* (New York: Oxford University Press, 1979), 71.

12. Broadus Mitchell, *The Rise of the Cotton Mills in the South* (Baltimore: Johns Hopkins University Press, 1921), 95, 188.

13. Liston Pope, *Millhands and Preachers: A Study of Gastonia* (New Haven: Yale University Press, 1942), 229.

14. Melton Alonzo McLaurin, *Paternalism and Protest: Southern Cotton Mill Workers and Organized Labor, 1875–1905* (Westport: Greenwood Press, 1971), 4.

15. Carlton, *Mill and Town*, 146–48.

16. Linda Frankel, "Southern Textile Women: Generations of Survival and Struggle," in *My Troubles Are Going to Have Trouble With Me: Everyday Trials and Triumphs of Women Workers*, ed. Karen Brodkin Sacks and Dorothy Remy (New Brunswick: Rutgers University Press, 1984), 39; Jeffrey Leiter, Michael D. Schulman, and Rhonda Zingraff, eds., *Hanging by a Thread: Social Change in Southern Textiles* (Ithaca: ILR Press, 1991).

17. Mary Frederickson, "'I Know Which Side I'm On': Southern Women in the Labor Movement in the Twentieth Century," in *Women, Work and Protest: A Century of Women's Labor History*, ed. Ruth Milkman (Boston: Routledge and Kegan Paul, 1985), 156.

18. Jacquelyn Dowd Hall, "Disorderly Women: Gender and Labor Militancy in the Appalachian South," *Journal of American History* 73 (September 1986): 354–82; Tom Tippett, *When Southern Labor Stirs* (New York: Jonathan Cape and Harrison Smith, 1931), 60, 69.

19. Jacquelyn Dowd Hall et al., *Like a Family: The Making of a Southern Cotton Mill World* (Chapel Hill: University of North Carolina Press, 1987), quotes on 70, 74.

20. I. A. Newby, *Plain Folk in the New South: Social Change and Cultural Persistence, 1880–1915* (Baton Rouge: Louisiana State University Press, 1989), quotes on 5, 80.

21. Allen Tullos, *Habits of Industry: White Culture and the Transformation of the Carolina Piedmont* (Chapel Hill: University of North Carolina Press, 1989), quotes on 205, 253.

22. Gay Gullickson, "Technology, Gender, and Rural Culture: Normandy and the Piedmont," and Gary R. Freeze, "Poor Girls Who Might Otherwise Be Wretched: The Origins of Paternalism in North Carolina's Mills, 1836–1880," in *Hanging by a Thread*, ed. Leiter et al., 33–58, 21–33; Jacquelyn Dowd Hall, "Private Eyes, Public Women: Images of Class and Sex in the Urban South, Atlanta, Georgia, 1913–1915," in *Work Engendered: Toward a New History of Men, Women, and Work*, ed. Eva

Baron (Ithaca: Cornell University Press, 1991), 243–72; Lee Ann Whites, "The De Graffenried Controversy: Class, Race, and Gender in the New South," *Journal of Southern History* 54 (August 1988): 449–78; Byerly, *Hard Times Cotton Mill Girls.*

23. Byerly, *Hard Times Cotton Mill Girls,* 202, 217.

2. Paternalism and Southern Textile Labor

1. Broadus Mitchell, *The Rise of Cotton Mills in the South* (Baltimore: Johns Hopkins University Press, 1921); Holland M. Thompson, *From the Cotton Field to the Cotton Mill: A Study of the Industrial Transition in North Carolina* (New York: Macmillan, 1906; reprint, 1971); see also Marjorie A. Potwin, *Cotton Mill People of the Piedmont: A Study in Social Change* (New York: Columbia University Press, 1927).

2. Frank Tannenbaum, *Darker Phases of the South* (New York: G. P. Putnam's Sons, 1924), 39–73; Lois MacDonald, *Southern Mill Hills* (New York: Alex L. Hillman, 1928); Liston Pope, *Millhands and Preachers: A Study of Gastonia* (New Haven: Yale University Press, 1942); Herbert J. Lahne, *The Cotton Mill Worker* (New York: Farrar and Rinehart, 1944); W. J. Cash, *The Mind of the South* (New York: Alfred A. Knopf, 1941), esp. 193–243.

3. Dwight B. Billings, Jr., *Planters and the Making of a "New South"* (Chapel Hill: University of North Carolina Press, 1979), 96–131; Philip J. Wood, *Southern Capitalism: The Political Economy of North Carolina, 1880–1980* (Durham: Duke University Press, 1986); I. A. Newby, *Plain Folk in the New South: Social Change and Cultural Persistence, 1880–1915* (Baton Rouge: Louisiana State University Press, 1989).

4. Robert H. Zieger, "Textile Workers and Historians," in *Organized Labor in the Twentieth-Century South,* ed. Robert H. Zieger (Knoxville: University of Tennessee Press, 1991), 35–59.

5. C. Vann Woodward, *Origins of the New South, 1877–1913* (Baton Rouge: Louisiana State University Press, 1951), 222–25; Bess Beatty, "Textile Labor in the North Carolina Piedmont: Mill Owner Images and Mill Workers Response, 1830–1900," *Labor History* 25 (Fall 1984): 485–503; Paul D. Escott, *Many Excellent People: Power and Privilege in North Carolina, 1850–1900* (Chapel Hill: University of North Carolina Press, 1986), 219–40; David L. Carlton, *Mill and Town in South Carolina, 1880–1920* (Baton Rouge: Louisiana State University Press, 1982), 82–128.

6. Woodward, *Origins of the New South,* 222–25.

7. Anthony F. C. Wallace, *Rockdale: The Growth of an American Village in the Early Industrial Revolution* (New York: W. W. Norton, 1977); Jonathan M. Prude, *The Coming of Industrial Order: Town and Factory Life in Rural Massachusetts, 1810–1860* (New York: Cambridge University Press, 1983); Barbara M. Tucker, *Samuel Slater and the Origins of the American Textile Industry, 1790–1860* (Ithaca: Cornell University Press, 1984).

8. James Michael Shirley, "From Congregation Town to Industrial City: Industrialization, Class and Culture in Nineteenth Century Winston and Salem, North Carolina" (Ph.D. diss., Emory University, 1986), and "Yeoman Culture and Millworker Protest in Antebellum Salem, North Carolina," *Journal of Southern History* 57 (August 1991): 427–52; Gary R. Freeze, "Model Mill Men of the New South: Paternalism and Methodism in the Odell Cotton Mills of North Carolina, 1877–1908" (Ph.D. diss., University of North Carolina at Chapel Hill, 1988), and "Poor Girls Who Might Otherwise Be Wretched: The Origins of Paternalism in North Carolina's Mills, 1836–1880," in *Hanging by a Thread: Social Change in Southern Textiles*, ed. Jeffrey Leiter, Michael D. Schulman, and Rhonda Zingraff (Ithaca: ILR Press, 1991), 21–32; Allen Tullos, *Habits of Industry: White Culture and the Transformation of the Carolina Piedmont* (Chapel Hill: University of North Carolina Press, 1989).

9. Philip Scranton, "Varieties of Paternalism: Industrial Structures and the Social Relations of Production in American Textiles," *American Quarterly* 36 (Summer 1984): 235–57; Cathy L. McHugh, *Mill Family: The Labor System in the Southern Cotton Textile Industry, 1880–1915* (New York: Oxford University Press, 1988).

10. Newby, *Plain Folk in the New South*; George S. Mitchell, *Textile Unionism and the South* (Chapel Hill: University of North Carolina Press, 1931); Melton Alonzo McLaurin, *Paternalism and Protest: Southern Cotton Mill Workers and Organized Labor, 1875–1905* (Westport: Greenwood Press, 1971).

11. On "day-to-day resistance" among mill workers, with specific comparisons to the historical literature on slavery, see Newby, *Plain Folk in the New South*, 520–22. Jacquelyn Dowd Hall et al., *Like a Family: The Making of a Southern Cotton Mill World* (Chapel Hill: University of North Carolina Press, 1987), 105–9, applies the model to workers' propensity for "moving about." On the problems of understanding the meaning of day-to-day resistance, see Eugene D. Genovese, *Roll, Jordan, Roll: The World the Slaves Made* (New York: Pantheon, 1974), 597–98; and Eugene D. Genovese and Elizabeth Fox-Genovese, *Fruits of Merchant Capital: Slavery and Bourgeois Property in the Rise and Expansion of Capitalism* (New York: Oxford University Press, 1983), 169–99.

12. Carlton, *Mill and Town*, and "The State and the Worker in the South: A Lesson From South Carolina," in *The Meaning of South Carolina History: Essays in Honor of George C. Rogers, Jr.*, ed. David R. Chestnutt and Clyde N. Wilson (Columbia: University of South Carolina Press, 1991), 186–201; Hall et al., *Like a Family*.

13. Hall et al., *Like a Family*, 131–39; Stuart D. Brandes, *American Welfare Capitalism, 1880–1940* (Chicago: University of Chicago Press, 1976).

14. Tamara Hareven, *Family Time and Industrial Time* (New York: Cambridge University Press, 1982). On workers and moral control, see Newby, *Plain Folk in the New South*, 325–51.

15. Gerald Zahavi, "Negotiated Loyalty: Welfare Capitalism and the Shoeworkers

of Endicott Johnson, 1920–1940," *Journal of American History* 71 (December 1983): 602–20, and *Workers, Managers, and Welfare Capitalism: The Shoeworkers and Tanners of Endicott Johnson, 1890–1950* (Urbana: University of Illinois Press, 1988).

16. Hall et al., *Like a Family*, 289–357; James A. Hodges, *New Deal Labor Policy and the Southern Cotton Textile Industry, 1933–1941* (Knoxville: University of Tennessee Press, 1986); Janet Irons, "Testing the New Deal: The General Textile Strike of 1934" (Ph.D. diss., Duke University, 1988); Barbara S. Griffith, *The Crisis of American Labor: Operation Dixie and the Defeat of the CIO* (Philadelphia: Temple University Press, 1988).

17. Irons, "Testing the New Deal"; Griffith, *Crisis of American Labor;* Paul David Richards, "The History of the Textile Workers Union of America, CIO, in the South, 1937 to 1945" (Ph.D. diss., University of Wisconsin, 1978).

18. Irons, "Testing the New Deal"; Linda Frankel, "'Jesus Leads Us, Cooper Needs Us, the Union Feeds Us': The 1958 Harriet-Henderson Textile Strike" in *Hanging by a Thread,* ed. Leiter et al., 101–20, and "Women, Paternalism and Protest in a Southern Textile Community: Henderson, North Carolina, 1900–1950" (Ph.D. diss., Harvard University, 1986); Carlton, "State and the Worker in the South"; Leon Fink, "Labor, Liberty, and the Law: Trade Unionism and the Problem of the American Constitutional Order," *Journal of American History* 74 (December 1987): 904–25; the quote is from p. 911.

19. Hall et al., *Like a Family*, 345–47; Douglas Flamming, *Creating the Modern South: Millhands and Managers in Dalton, Georgia, 1884–1984* (Chapel Hill: University of North Carolina Press, 1992); Carlton, "State and the Worker in the South."

20. David Brody, *Workers in Industrial America: Essays on the Twentieth-Century Struggle* (New York: Oxford University Press, 1980); John E. Bodnar, *Workers' World: Kinship, Community, and Protest in an Industrial Society, 1900–1940* (Baltimore: Johns Hopkins University Press, 1982); Flamming, *Creating the Modern South*, chaps. 7–10; Bryant Simon, "Choosing Between the Ham and the Union: Paternalism in the Cone Mills of Greensboro, 1925–1930," in *Hanging by a Thread,* ed. Leiter et al., 81–100.

21. Flamming, *Creating the Modern South;* Frankel, "Women, Paternalism and Protest," and "'Jesus Leads Us, Cooper Needs Us, the Union Feeds Us'"; Simon, "Choosing Between the Ham and the Union"; Daniel James Clark, "The TWUA in a Southern Mill Town: What Unionization Meant in Henderson, North Carolina" (Ph.D. diss., Duke University, 1989).

22. Nelson Fischbaum, "An Economic Analysis of the Southern Capture of the Cotton Textile Industry Progressing to 1910" (Ph.D. diss. in Economics, Columbia University, 1965), esp. 89–133; Gavin Wright, *Old South, New South: Revolutions in the Southern Economy Since the Civil War* (New York: Basic Books, 1986), 78–80, 124–25, 131–33; David L. Carlton, "The Revolution from Above: The National

Market and the Beginnings of Industrialization in North Carolina," *Journal of American History* 77 (September 1990): 445–75, esp. 467, 472–73.

23. Harriet Laura Herring, *The Passing of the Mill Village: Revolution in a Southern Institution* (Chapel Hill: University of North Carolina Press, 1949); Wright, *Old South, New South*, 269–74; Flamming, *Creating the Modern South*, chaps. 12, 14; John Gaventa and Barbara Ellen Smith, "The Deindustrialization of the Textile South: A Case Study," in *Hanging by a Thread*, ed. Leiter et al., 181–96.

3. Patriarchy Lost

1. Holland M. Thompson, "Some Effects of Industrialism in an Agricultural State," *South Atlantic Quarterly* 4 (1905): 72, and "Life in a Southern Mill Town," *Political Science Quarterly* 14 (1900): 2.

2. Thompson was a private school principal in Concord from 1895 to 1899 when he won a fellowship to Columbia University. The field work in Concord led to his monograph, *From the Cotton Field to the Cotton Mill: A Study of the Industrial Transition in North Carolina* (New York: Macmillan, 1906).

3. See Jacquelyn Dowd Hall et al., *Like a Family: The Making of a Southern Cotton Mill World* (Chapel Hill: University of North Carolina Press, 1987); I. A. Newby, *Plain Folk in the New South: Social Change and Cultural Persistence, 1880–1915* (Baton Rouge: Louisiana State University Press, 1989); and Allen Tullos, *Habits of Industry: White Culture and the Transformation of the Carolina Piedmont* (Chapel Hill: University of North Carolina Press, 1989).

4. Thompson, "Southern Mill Town," 9. The later paradigmatic work exploring this attitude is Broadus Mitchell, *The Rise of the Cotton Mills in the South* (Baltimore: Johns Hopkins University Press, 1921).

5. J. A. Baldwin, "Mills or Morals," *Southern and Western Textile Excelsior*, 17 December 1898. This Charlotte labor journal was read widely in Concord.

6. This argument is more fully elaborated in Gary R. Freeze, "Poor Girls Who Might Otherwise Be Wretched: The Origins of Paternalism in North Carolina's Mills, 1836–1880," in *Hanging by a Thread: Social Change in Southern Textiles*, ed. Jeffrey Leiter, Michael D. Schulman, and Ronda Zingraff (Ithaca: ILR Press, 1990), 21–32.

7. Data were aggregated from the manuscript of the Population Schedule, Ward Two, Concord, North Carolina, United States Census of 1900. The census was taken by an Odell overseer who listed every millhand by his or her specific task in the mill. Almost every Odell millhand lived in Ward Two.

8. Bill Cecil-Fronsman, *Common Whites: Class and Culture in Antebellum North Carolina* (Lexington: University Press of Kentucky, 1992), 137–41. The "poor girls" quotation is in Benson J. Lossing, *Pictorial Field Book of the Revolution* (New York: Harper, 1851), 2:594.

9. See Gary R. Freeze, "Model Mill Men of the New South: Paternalism and Methodism in the Odell Cotton Mills of North Carolina, 1877–1908" (Ph.D. diss., University of North Carolina at Chapel Hill, 1988), 233–39. The anecdotes are taken from *Concord Standard*, 31 May 1895, 7 January 1898.

10. Freeze, "Model Mill Men," 239–51; North Carolina Bureau of Labor Statistics, *The First Annual Report* (Raleigh: Edwards & Broughton, 1887), 102; *Stanly News*, reprinted in *Concord Standard*, 1 December 1893.

11. *Concord Standard*, 18 April 1894, 20 November 1895.

12. See Freeze, "Model Mill Men," 252–63, for a fuller analysis of the Stanly migrants. The records for Hall are in Crop Lien books, Stanly County Register of Deeds, Albemarle, N.C.

13. The records for Fry and Hall were also drawn from the Register of Deeds in Stanly County. See Freeze, "Model Mill Men," 257–61.

14. *First Annual Report*, 135, 102, 109.

15. *Concord Standard*, 28 January 1888.

16. Ibid., 10 February 1888; Board of Directors Minutes, Odell Manufacturing Company, 12 January 1892, typescript copy in the local history archives, Charles Cannon Memorial Library, Concord, N.C.; Thompson, "Effects of Industrialism," 72.

17. Manuscript Population Schedule, 1900 Census.

18. Thompson, "Southern Mill Town," 6.

19. Freeze, "Model Mill Men," 280–86. The backgrounds of the various mill-hands were compiled through genealogical and local history sources, most of which are in the Cannon Memorial Library.

20. Ibid. Caudle's comment was written on the census form in the occupation column.

21. Ibid.

22. The wage model was computed using wage figures, by occupation, from Odell reports given to the North Carolina Bureau of Labor Statistics. See *First Annual Report*, 142–43. Wages remained relatively constant from 1888 to 1900. The hypothetical wage each operative could have made, with adjustments for absenteeism, was computed, and then family wages were calculated. The wages made by boarders in each household were not factored into the model. For more details, see Freeze, "Model Mill Men," 287–91.

23. *Concord Standard*, 23 October 1893, 16 February 1895, 3 February, 8 March, 10 July 1893, 15 October 1897; *Concord Times*, 1 June 1899.

24. *Concord Standard*, 8 February 1893.

25. Ibid., 4 June 1897, 27 August 1898, 29 July, 25 September 1893, 17 May, 17 December 1895.

26. Married persons enumerated in the 1900 census listed the years they had been married. I omitted cases where I knew it was a second marriage. My assumption was

that marriages that predated 1890 were generally in the country, while the younger people who came with their parents to the mills had married in the mill village after 1890. I also consulted, where possible, the Marriage Register of Cabarrus County, 1868–1900, North Carolina State Archives, Raleigh.

27. J. W. Mahaffey to Zebulon B. Vance, 15 July 1890, Zebulon B. Vance Papers, Southern Historical Collection, University of North Carolina, Chapel Hill. Mahaffey, an antebellum worker on the North Carolina Railroad, was one of the few vocal critics of the New South changes taking place in Concord. He seems to have talked with the recent migrants at some length soon after the Odells doubled the size of the mill village.

28. J. M. Odell to the Commissioner of Labor, *Eighth Annual Report* (Raleigh: Bureau of Labor Statistics, 1895), 16.

29. Thompson, "Southern Mill Town," 5, and "Effects of Industrialism," 72.

30. "The almost extinct class of shouting Methodists has representatives here," Thompson noted. "Southern Mill Town," 8. For details of community life in Forest Hill, see Freeze, "Model Mill Men," 330–69.

31. The "Big Daddy" quotation came from John Dunn, interview with author, Charlotte, N.C., 10 April 1986. Dunn's father, a Charlotte drummer, worked the mill villages of Concord frequently in that period.

32. *Concord Standard*, 24 November 1896, 4 June, 13 September 1897.

33. *Textile Excelsior*, 27 April 1901.

34. Thompson, *From the Cotton Field to the Cotton Mill*, 9.

4. Prelude to the New Deal

1. Jack Irby Hayes, Jr., "South Carolina and the New Deal, 1932–1938" (Ph.D. diss., University of South Carolina, 1972), 314, 334–35; *Greenwood Index-Journal*, 18 July 1933; *The State* [Greenwood], 19 July 1933.

2. Lizabeth Cohen, *Making a New Deal: Industrial Workers in Chicago, 1919–1939* (Cambridge: Cambridge University Press, 1990), 2, 3.

3. The one notable exception would be the work of David L. Carlton, *Mill and Town in South Carolina, 1880–1920* (Baton Rouge: Louisiana State University Press, 1982), and "The State and the Worker in the South: A Lesson from South Carolina," in *The Meaning of South Carolina History: Essays in Honor of George C. Rogers, Jr.*, ed. David R. Chesnutt and Clyde N. Wilson (Columbia: University of South Carolina Press, 1991), 186–201.

4. In a recent survey of the literature, for example, Robert H. Zieger does not mention the subject of politics. This omission reflects more the orientation of the field than it does Zieger's own perspective. See Robert H. Zieger, "Textile Workers and Historians," in *Organized Labor in the Twentieth Century South*, ed. Robert H.

Zieger (Knoxville: University of Tennessee Press, 1991), 35–39. For a more general critique of the treatment of politics with the "new" social history, see Elizabeth Fox-Genovese and Eugene Genovese, "The Political Crisis of Social History: A Marxian Perspective," *Journal of Social History* 10 (Winter 1976): 205–20; Tony Judt, "The Clown in Regal Purple: Social History and Historians," *History Workshop* (Spring 1979): 667–94; and William E. Leuchtenburg, "The Pertinence of Political History: Reflections of the Significance of the State," *Journal of American History* 76 (December 1986): 585–600.

5. On industrial engineers, see Robert W. Dunn and Jack Hardy, *Labor and Textiles: A Study of Cotton and Wool Manufacturing* (New York: International Publishers, 1931), 121–27; Tom Terrill and Jerrold Hirsh, *Such as Us: Southern Voices of the Thirties* (New York: Norton, 1978), 182–83; Jacquelyn Dowd Hall et al., *Like a Family: The Making of a Southern Cotton Mill World* (Chapel Hill: University of North Carolina Press, 1987), 219; Daniel T. Rogers, *The Work Ethic in Industrial America, 1850–1920* (Chicago: University of Chicago, 1978), 166–68; and *Greenwood Index-Journal*, 18 March 1929.

6. For the timing and dates of managerial moves, see "Report on the Stretch-Out System for Board of Health," [South Carolina] Senate *Journal* 1933, pp. 70–71; Glen Gilman, *Human Relations in the Industrial Southeast: A Study of the Textile Industry* (Chapel Hill: University of North Carolina Press, 1956), 96; Gavin Wright, *Old South, New South: Revolutions in the Southern Economy Since the Civil War* (New York: Basic Books, 1986), 147–55; Phillip J. Wood, *Southern Capitalism: The Political Economy of North Carolina, 1880–1980* (Durham: Duke University Press, 1986), 59–93; and Hall et al., *Like a Family*, 198–99, 210.

7. For descriptions of the pre-stretch-out regimen, see Jesse Carter, interview by Allen Tullos, 5 May 1980, Piedmont Industrialization Project, Southern Oral History Project, Southern Historical Collection, University of North Carolina, Chapel Hill; "The Honest Card and Spinning Workers of the Watts Mill" to General Hugh Johnson, 24 February 1934, Watts Mill, Laurens, SC, folder, box 33, Record Group (RG) 9, series 398, National Recovery Administration Papers (NRA Papers), National Archives (NA).

8. Testimony of Charles Putnam before the Byrnes Stretch-Out Committee, Byrnes Papers, Clemson University. I have relied on several other sources to augment his story. See notes 9, 10; "Report on the Stretch-Out System for the Board of Health," [South Carolina] Senate *Journal*, 1933, pp. 60, 62; and Hall et al., *Like a Family*, 211–12.

9. On wages, see annual *Proceedings* of the South Carolina Federation of Labor (SCFL), 1928, George Meany Library, Silver Spring, Maryland (Meany Library); Abraham Berglund, George T. Starnes, and Frank deVyver, *Labor in the Industrial South: A Survey of Wages and Living Conditions in Three Major Industries of the Industrial South* (Charlottesville: University of Virginia Press, 1930), 88–90; and "Trends of

Annual Earnings of South Carolina Textile Workers 1909–1937," box 39, Olin D. Johnston Papers, Departmental Commissions, South Carolina Department of Archives and History, Columbia (SCDAH).

10. The employment situation is detailed in a variety of sources. For examples, see *Greenwood Index-Journal*, 28 June, 3 July 1929, 12 December 1930; *Textile Worker*, May 1930, pp. 61–63, June 1932, pp. 118–19, October 1931, pp. 301–3; *Greenville Observer*, 29 February 1932; *New York Times*, 13 August, 2 November 1930, 14 August, 15, 22, September 1932; Anne Belle Pittman to Wil Lou Grey, 19 April 1928, Wil Lou Grey Papers, South Carolinian Library (SCL), Columbia; F. E. Whitman, treasurer of the Union-Buffalo Mills Company, to Manning, 1 January 1928, folder 354, box 4, Manning Papers, SCL; and Paul Stroman Lofton, Jr., "A Social and Economic History of Columbia, South Carolina, During the Great Depression, 1929–1940" (Ph.D. diss., University of Texas, Austin, 1977), 33, 50–61, 67, 219. J. E. Hill and all of those who worked around him were laid off. Hill to Richards, 13 June 1930, box 65, Unemployment file, Richards Papers, SCDAH.

11. Mrs. C. M. Hogan to Blackwood, 24 February 1930, box 56, John G. Richards Papers, SCDAH.

12. W. H. Riddle to Governor John G. Richards, 15 January 1930, folder R, box 14, ibid.

13. Thomas Dubin defines the stretch-out as "the assignment of additional pieces of machinery to each operative." *Women at Work: The Transformation of Work and Community in Lowell, Massachusetts, 1826–1830* (New York: Columbia University Press, 1979), 109. For a broader interpretation, see Hall et al., *Like a Family*, 211–12.

14. Paul Eli Clark to Blackwood, n.d. [circa 1931], Current Subjects 1931 box, Blackwood Papers, SCDAH; speech by President Brookshire, Annual *Proceedings*, SCFL, 1931, Meany Library.

15. "Report on the Stretch-Out System," [South Carolina] Senate *Journal* 1933, p. 60. On workers, see, for example, J. M. Fletcher to Governor John G. Richards, 19 January 1930, State Agencies, Conciliation Board box, Blackwood Papers, SCDAH; C. M. Bissel (Saxon Mills) to Blackwood, 26 January 1931, General Correspondence folder, General Correspondence, Appointments, Petitions box, SCDAH; Anonymous to Huge [sic] Johnson, 9 August 1933, Wallace Mfg. Co. folder, box 33, RG 9, series 398, NRA Papers, NA; and P. M. Mooney to Dear Sir, 14 July 1933, Olympia Mills folder, box 24, ibid.

16. On the stretch-out and slavery, see Paul Eli Clark to Blackwood, n.d. [circa 1931], Current Subjects 1931 box, Blackwood Papers, SCDAH; G. L. Summer interview with "The Edward Fulmers," Newberry, 28 December 1938, WPA Files, A–3–7–9, SCL; Hall et al., *Like a Family*, 221, 296–97; unsigned letter, Langley to Frances Perkins, 12 November 1933, Horse Creek Valley folder, box 19, RG 9, series 398, NRA Papers, NA; Anonymous to FDR, 10 September 1934, Complaints of Workers-

Individuals folder, box 1, RG 9, series 401, ibid; and "A Mill Worker" to Gov. John G. Richards, 1 January 1930, box 56, Richards Papers, SCDAH.

17. Slavery had long served as a powerful image for white South Carolinians. See Lacy K. Ford, Jr., *Origins of Southern Radicalism: The South Carolina Upcountry, 1880–1960* (New York: Oxford University Press, 1988).

18. Eric Foner's discussion of the meaning of the phrase "wage slavery" to nineteenth-century laborers has shaped my own understanding of the stretch-out. See Eric Foner, *Politics and Ideology in the Age of the Civil War* (New York: Oxford University Press, 1980), 59–63. See also David R. Roediger, *The Wages of Whiteness: Race and the Making of the American Working Class* (New York: Verso, 1991).

19. *Textile Worker*, March 1932, pp. 243–44.

20. U.S. Department of Labor, Bureau of Labor Statistics, "Strikes in the United States, 1880–1936," comp. Florence Peterson (Washington, D.C.: Government Printing Office, 1958), 117. Probably the best single account of the 1929 strikes can be found in Irving Bernstein, *The Lean Years: A History of the American Worker, 1920–1933* (Boston: Houghton Mifflin, 1960), 1–44. See also Liston Pope, *Millhands and Preachers: A Study of Gastonia* (New Haven: Yale University Press, 1942); and Jacquelyn Dowd Hall, "Disorderly Women: Gender and Labor Militancy in the Appalachian South," *Journal of American History* 65 (September 1986): 354–82. On the South Carolina strikes, see Paul Blanchard, "One Hundred Percent Americans on Strike," *Nation*, 8 May 1929, p. 551; George Googe, "Textile Workers Organize," *American Federationist* 36 (July 1929): 793–99; Tom Tippett, *When Southern Labor Stirs* (New York: Jonathan Cape & Harrison Smith, 1931), 184–89; and George S. Mitchell, *Textile Unionism and the South* (Chapel Hill: University of North Carolina Press, 1931), 78–81.

21. *The State*, 2 April, 9, 10 May 1922; *Greenwood Index-Journal*, 15 April 1929; Blanchard, "One Hundred Percent Americans," 552.

22. Carlton, *Mill and Town*, 140; Janet Irons, "Testing the New Deal: The General Textile Strike of 1934" (Ph.D. diss., Duke University, 1988), 33–34.

23. On the importance of the textile industry in the state and the political power of its workforce, see Carlton, *Mill and Town*, and "State and the Worker in the South." Various other aspects of South Carolina's constitution and political structure are discussed in J. Morgan Kousser, *The Shaping of Southern Politics: Suffrage Restrictions and the Establishment of the One-Party South, 1880–1910* (New Haven: Yale University Press, 1974), 84–91, 145–52; and V. O. Key, Jr., *Southern Politics in State and Nation* (New York: Alfred A. Knopf, 1949), 131–55. For population figures for Spartanburg County, see *Fifteenth Census of the United States, 1930, Population*, vol. 1, pt. 812. On numbers of mill workers and mill village residents, see *Seventeenth Annual Report of the Commissioner of Agriculture, Commerce and Industries—Labor Division* (Columbia: State Department of Agriculture, Commerce and Industry, 1925), 32–35.

24. Rinnie Bishop to Governor Richards, 22 January 1930, folder B, Misc. Correspondence box, Richards Papers, SCDAH.

25. According to *Fifteenth Census*, vol. 3, pt. 2, p. 775, in 1930, there were 5,358 foreign-born residents of South Carolina or 0.3 percent of the state's total population. On immigration restriction, see *Labor*, 19 July 1932; and [Winnsboro] *News and Herald*, 9 September 1932, Ellison D. Smith Scrapbooks, scrapbooks 10, 12, SCL.

26. On women in the labor force during the depression, see William H. Chafe, *The American Woman: Her Changing Social, Economic, and Political Roles, 1920–1970* (New York: Oxford University Press, 1972), 103; Lois Scraf, *To Work and Wed: Female Employment, Feminism, and the Great Depression* (Westport: Greenwood Press, 1979), 157–80; Winifred D. Wandersee, *Women's Work and Family Values, 1920–1940* (Cambridge: Harvard University Press, 1981), 84, 101, 102; Alice Kessler-Harris, *Out of Work: A History of Wage-Earning Women in the United States* (New York: Oxford University Press, 1982), 257–59, 260–61; and Susan Ware, *Holding Their Own: American Women in the 1930s* (Boston: Twayne, 1982), 21–50.

27. Robert Battle, Jr. to Richards, 18 July 1927, Unemployment 1930 folder, box 16, Misc., box 65, Current Files, Richards Papers, SCDAH.

28. Public opinion polls, which first appeared in the 1930s, asked Americans whether married women should be permitted to work if their husbands had jobs. "No!" was the response of 82 percent of the nation in a 1936 Gallup poll. George Gallup said that he had never seen people "so solidly united in opposition as on any subject imaginable including sin and hay fever." Irving Bernstein, *A Caring Society: The New Deal, the Worker, and the Great Depression, A History of the American Worker, 1933–1941* (Boston: Houghton Mifflin, 1985).

29. J. C. S. to Governor Richards, 19 November 1930, Unemployment 1930 folder, box 65, Richards Papers, SCDAH; F. Chapman to Franklin D. Roosevelt, 24 August 1933, Poe Mills folder, box 26, RG 9, series 398, NRA Papers, NA.

30. Mrs. I. Campbell to Blackwood, 20 June 1932, General Correspondence C folder, General Subjects, 1931–35 box, Blackwood Papers, SCDAH; Hall et al., *Like a Family*, 310–12.

31. The percentage of women in the mills of South Carolina were:

Year	Percentage
1925	33.1
1935	33.8
1936	35.6
1937	34.9

Seventeenth Annual Report, 34; "Comparison of Textile Statistics," from the South Carolina Department of Labor, box 39, Olin D. Johnston Papers, SCDAH.

32. "Report on the Stretch-Out System," Senate *Journal* 1933, p. 60; C. M. Bissel (Saxon Mills) to Blackwood, 26 January 1931, General Correspondence Folder, General Correspondence, Appointments, Petitions box, Blackwood Papers, SCDAH.

33. Anonymous to Huge [*sic*] Johnson, 9 August 1933, Wallace Mfn. Co. folder, box 33, RG 9, series 398, NRA Papers, NA; P. M. Mooney to Dear Sir, 14 July 1933, Olympia Mills folder, box 24, ibid.

34. Interview with Old Man Dobbin in Federal Writers' Project, *These Are Our Lives* (1939; reprint, New York: Norton, 1975), 210.

35. "An Appeal to the Honorable General Assembly of South Carolina," signed by "Textile Workers," 21 January 1930, box 56, Richards Papers, SCDAH.

36. On the owners' views of their rights, see *Greenwood Index-Journal*, 30 March 1929; and *The State*, 7 May 1929.

37. Annual *Proceedings* of the SCFL, 1929–1935, Meany Library; [South Carolina] Senate *Journal* 1929, 1933; [South Carolina] House *Journal* 1929, 1932. On workers, see, for example, J. M. Fletcher to Governor John G. Richards, 19 January 1930, State Agencies, Conciliation Board box, Blackwood Papers, SCDAH.

38. *Spartanburg Herald*, 14 August—12 September 1932. See especially the 14 August issue "Legislation For Labor is Pledged." Precinct returns appear on 30 August and 11 September. For a vivid description of a South Carolina stump gathering, see "Jimmy Barnes," *Life* 14 (4 January 1944): 65.

39. *Spartanburg Herald*, 3, 24, 28 February, 13 March, 13 April, 12 May 1933. This year was not the first that such a measure was debated. See also [South Carolina] House *Journal*, 1932, 1933; [South Carolina] Senate *Journal*, 1932, 1933; *Greenville Observer*, 3 February 1932; and *Spartanburg Herald*, 7 February 1932.

40. A. P. Dewitt to Governor John G. Richards, 10 March 1927, box 16, Richards Papers, SCDAH; Y. P. Harrison to Governor Richards, 16 August 1927, box 3, ibid.

41. "An Appeal to the Honorable General Assembly of South Carolina."

42. Paul Eli Clark to Blackwood, n.d. [circa 1931], Current Subjects 1931 box, Blackwood Papers, SCDAH.

43. *Textile Worker*, April 1931, pp. 6–7; *Spartanburg Herald*, 5 February 1932, 22 January, 29 February 1933. The reduction of hours was a popular program within both the state and national labor movements. See Annual *Proceedings* of the SCFL, 1931, 1932, 1933, Meany Library; and Bernstein, *Lean Years*, 223–25.

44. [South Carolina] House *Journal*, 1929, 1930, 1931, 1932, 1933; [South Carolina] Senate *Journal*, 1932, 1933; *Greenville Observer*, 3 February 1932; *Spartanburg Herald*, 7 February 1932, 29 February, 13 April 1933.

45. This perspective on Blease has been put forth by W. J. Cash, *The Mind of the South* (New York: Alfred A. Knopf, 1941); and Francis Butler Simkins, *Pitchfork Ben Tillman: South Carolina* (Baton Rouge: Louisiana State University Press, 1944). Moreover, Key's *Southern Politics*, 143–45, and Kousser's *Shaping of Southern Poli-*

tics, 235–36, suggest that workers supported Blease because the candidate duped them with meaningless appeals to white supremacy.

46. This account of Bleasism relies heavily on David Carlton's *Mill and Town.* I. A. Newby, *Plain Folks in the New South: Social Change and Cultural Persistence, 1880–1915* (Baton Rouge: Louisiana State University Press, 1989) echoes this view. No published biography of Blease exists, primarily because his personal papers have not been located. Nonetheless, see Ronald Burnside, "The Governorship of Coleman Livingston Blease of South Carolina, 1911–1915" (Ph.D. diss., University of Indiana, 1963); Anthony Barry Miller, "Coleman Livingston Blease" (Master's thesis, University of North Carolina at Greensboro, 1971); and Daniel Hollis, "Cole L. Blease and the Senatorial Campaign of 1924," *Proceedings of the South Carolina Historical Association,* 1978, pp. 53–68.

47. On Blease, see James C. Derieux, "Crawling Toward the Promised Land," *The Survey* 48 (1922): 178; Osta L. Warr, "Mr. Blease of South Carolina," *American Mercury* 16 (1929): 25–32; Carlton, *Mill and Town,* 244–50; and Miller, "Coleman Livingston Blease," 37, 88, 89. For other suggestions on labor and the uses of political power, see Leon Fink, "The Uses of Political Power: Toward a Theory of the Labor Movement in the Era of the Knights of Labor," in *Working-Class America: Essays on Labor, Community, and American Society,* ed. Michael H. Frisch and Daniel J. Walkowitz (Urbana: University of Illinois Press, 1983), 104–22; and Michael Kazin, *Barons of Labor: The San Francisco Building Trades and Union Power in the Progressive Era* (Urbana: University of Illinois Press, 1989), 145–76.

48. On the 1930 campaign, see *Greenwood Index-Journal,* 2, 7, 9, 11 July 1930; *The State,* 20–28 August 1930; Winfred Bobo Moore, Jr., "New South Statesman: The Political Career of James Francis Byrnes, 1911–1941" (Ph.D. diss., Duke University, 1976), 84–91; Miller, "Coleman Livingston Blease," 166–67; and "Jimmy Byrnes," *Life* 14 (4 January 1944): 65.

49. The election was settled by little more than four thousand votes; Byrnes won 119,893 to Blease's 115,044. A comparison of the percentage of votes for Blease in 1924 and 1930 is as follows:

	1924	1930
Statewide	50.57	49.05
Average for Industrial Counties	56.63	51.63
Average for Mill Precincts	71.57	61.38

Anderson Independent, 10 September 1930; *Gaffney Ledger,* 11 September 1924, 11 September 1930; *Greenville News,* 10 September 1924, 10 September 1930; *Easley Progress,* 10 September 1924, 11 September 1930; *Spartanburg Herald,* 10 September 1924, 11 September 1930; *Rock Hill Evening Herald,* 10 September 1924, 10 September 1930; *Union Daily Times,* 10 September 1924, 10 September 1930.

50. For examples, see the views of Hugh Johnson quoted by Arthur M. Schlesinger, Jr., *The Coming of the New Deal* (Boston: Houghton Mifflin, 1959), 87, 88, and of Frances Perkins quoted by Steve Fraser, *Labor Will Rule: Sidney Hillman and the Rise of American Labor* (New York: Free Press, 1991), 330.

51. Many workers saw Roosevelt as a "god-sent man." For example, see J. A. Strickland of Ware Shoals to Robert Bruere, General Correspondence S folder, box 12, RG 9, series 397, NRA Papers, NA; *Carolina Free Press*, 7 September 1934; Martha Gellhorn, "Report to Mr. Hopkins," 11 November 1934, Gellhorn, Martha folder, box 66, Hopkins Papers, Franklin D. Roosevelt Library. Gellhorn was one of dozens of young people sent by Harry Hopkins to investigate political and economic conditions across the country. See their stories in John E. Bauman and Thomas H. Coode, *In the Eye of the Great Depression: New Deal Reporters and the Agony of the American People* (DeKalb: Northern Illinois University Press, 1990).

5. J. P. Stevens and the Union

1. James G. Maddox et al., *The Advancing South: Manpower Prospects and Problems* (New York: Twentieth Century Fund, 1967), 24.

2. *The State*, [Columbia, S.C.], 31 January 1988; John Gaventa and Barbara Ellen Smith, "The Deindustrialization of the Textile South: A Case Study," in *Hanging by a Thread: Social Change in Southern Textiles*, ed. Jeffrey Leiter, Michael D. Schulman, and Rhonda Zingraff (Ithaca: ILR Press, 1991), 182; Phillip J. Wood, *Southern Capitalism: The Political Economy of North Carolina, 1880–1980* (Durham: Duke University Press, 1986), 169.

3. David Avery and Gene D. Sullivan, "Changing Patterns: Reshaping the Southern Textile-Apparel Complex," Federal Revenue Board of Atlanta, vol. 70 pp. 34–38; Roger Penn and Jeffrey Leiter, "Employment Patterns in the British and U.S. Textile Industries: A Comparative Analysis of Recent Gender Changes," in *Hanging by a Thread*, ed. Leiter et al., 140. See also "Textile Plant Employment in the Southeast: 1990", U.S. Department of Labor news release, 27 June 1991. The South is defined as North Carolina, South Carolina, Alabama, Georgia, Tennessee, and Virginia.

4. James A. Hodges, *New Deal Labor Policy and the Southern Cotton Textile Industry, 1933–1941* (Knoxville: University of Tennessee Press, 1986), 178.

5. Paul David Richards, "The History of the Textile Workers Union of America, CIO, in the South, 1937 to 1945" (Ph.D. diss., University of Wisconsin, 1978), 209.

6. Barbara S. Griffith, *The Crisis of American Labor: Operation Dixie and the Defeat of the CIO* (Philadelphia: Temple University Press, 1988), 162.

7. Ibid., 12–21. 46–61, 161–76.

8. *Textile Labor*, 8 May 1948.

9. Ibid., 22 January 1949.

10. Ibid., July–August 1949; Stetin interview, five days in 1978, reel 7, side 2, 5:45 to 10:35, Textile Workers Union of America Oral History Project, Textile Workers Union of America Papers, State Historical Society of Wisconsin (hereafter cited as TWUA Papers).

11. "My Trip South—October 16–24, 1939," Solomon Barkin to Emil Rieve, 25 October 1939, TWUA Papers; Boyd Payton to William Pollock, 4 October 1953, ibid.

12. Payton to Pollock, 12 February 1958, ibid.

13. On the history of Stevens, see, among many sources, Lloyd Ferguson, *J. P. Stevens and Company, Inc.: From Family Firm to Corporate Giant* (Boston: Federal Reserve Bank, 1964); Richard Whalen, "The Durable Threads of J. P. Stevens," *Fortune* (April 1963): 3–12; and Jim Overton et al., "The Men at the Top: The Story of J. P. Stevens," *Southern Exposure* 6 (Spring 1978): 52–63. For the decision to target Stevens, see "Committee to Work on Selecting Targets for IUD Organizing Drive," 24 April 1963, and "Potential Targets for IUD Organizing Drives," 8 February 1963, ACTWU office files, New York City.

14. Sol Stetin, interview with author, New York City, 20 January 1988. See also Stetin interview, five days in 1978, TWUA Papers.

15. H. S. Williams to William Pollock, 14 August 1963, TWUA Papers.

16. Ibid., 13 February 1964.

17. Stetin interview, 20 January 1988. From the beginning to its end the campaign attracted considerable attention from the newspapers and magazines, particularly during the period 1976–1980. For three brief reflective treatments, see Barry E. Truchil, *Capital Labor Relations in the U.S. Textile Industry* (New York: Praeger Press, 1988), 139–42; Wood, *Southern Capitalism*, 182–86; and Richard Rowan and Robert E. Barr, *Employee Relations Trends and Practices in the Textile Industry* (Philadelphia: Wharton School, 1987), 79–82. For some representative contemporary journalist accounts, see Ed McConville, "The Southern Textile War," *The Nation*, 2 October 1976; Gloria Emerson, "The Union vs. J. P. Stevens: Organizing the Plantation," *Village Voice*, 16 July 1979; Walter Guzzardi, Jr., "How the Union Got the Upper Hand on J. P. Stevens," *Fortune*, 19 June 1978, pp. 86–98; Peter Kovler, "The South: Last Bastion of the Open Shop," *Politics Today* (March–April 1979): 26–31; and George Tucker, "The Struggle to Organize J. P. Stevens," *Political Affairs* 57 (May 1978): 2–9. There will also be an entry summarizing the campaign in the forthcoming *Encyclopedia of Labor Conflict*, edited by David Bensman, to be published by Rutgers University Press. The *New York Times* extensively covered the dispute. See, for example, the noted labor correspondent A. H. Raskin's article, "J. P. Stevens: Labor's Big Domino," *New York Times*, 15 August 1976. See also the union's account of the conflict in *Labor Unity*, December 1980.

18. Steven Brill, "Labor Outlaws," *American Lawyer* (April 1980): 16.

19. "Speech by G. G. Walker to Employees, Wallace, N.C.," 17 February 1975,

ACTWU Papers, ILRS Document Center, Cornell University (hereafter cited as ACTWU Papers). For Stevens's basic anti-union argument, see J. P. Stevens and Co., Inc., *Straightening Things Out*, undated pamphlet [circa late 1976 or early 1977], copy in ACTWU Papers.

20. "Election History at Stevens," Bill Somplatsky-Jarman to Del Mileski et al., 16 January 1979, ACTWU Papers.

21. Author interview with former Stevens worker, Piedmont, S.C., March 1988.

22. Brill, "Labor Outlaws," 17. The legal records of the Stevens cases are in disarray. Some remain in the possession of the union while Stevens I is in the TWUA Papers. Portions of others, including field hearing testimony, are available in the NLRB Library in Washington, D.C. The most accessible route to review the legal battle is through the many summaries of individual cases printed by the NLRB in *Decisions and Orders of the National Labor Relations Board* from the 1960s to the 1980s. The index entry "Stevens" leads to more than twenty case summaries.

23. For quick looks at decisions and quoted material, see *Textile Labor*, April 1966, April 1967, May 1967, December 1969, May 1979. For the Reis quote, see *Decisions and Orders of the National Labor Board* 239 (1977). See also J. Gary Dinunno, "J. P. Stevens: An Anatomy of an Outlaw," *American Federationist* (April 1976): 1–8.

24. See Alan E. Kraus, "Labor Law–J. P. Stevens: Search For a Remedy to Fit the Wrong," *North Carolina Law Review* 55 (April 1977): 696–708.

25. Joel Ax, interview with author, New York City, 19 June 1989.

26. *Charlotte Observer*, 20 August 1974.

27. "Survey of Bargaining Units Under TWUA Agreement by Region, State and Industry—February, 1976," reel 7, microfilm, Research Department Records, TWUA Papers.

28. *Textile Labor*, June 1976. Both Stetin and Scott Hoyman deny that the union was in crisis. Scott Hoyman, interview with author, Summerville, S.C., 5 June 1989.

29. Stetin interview, 20 January 1988; Hoyman interview, 15 May 1984, reel 3, side 2, 24:40 to 26:10, Textile Workers Union of America Oral History Project, TWUA Papers.

30. "Progress Report on Organizing J. P. Stevens Plants," 17 January 1977, ACTWU Papers; "J. P. Stevens Organizing Staff," 13 December 1978, ibid.

31. No good published study of the boycott strategy exists. ACTWU Papers have several staff analyses of the economic impact, and in general they support a mild impact on sales. The boycott was primarily a public relations weapon, not an economic one.

32. "The Real Norma Rae," fact sheet, ACTWU Papers.

33. The best account of the corporate campaign is Liz Savory, "Forced Off the Board: The ACTWU Corporate Campaign Against J. P. Stevens," *Director and Board* (Summer 1979): 16–43.

34. Bruce Raynor, interview with author, Atlanta, 29 June 1989. Hoyman also emphasized the importance of Whitney Stevens's rise to power. Hoyman interview, 5 June 1989.

35. *Daily News Record*, 20 October 1980; TWUA press release, 20 October 1980, ACTWU Papers; *Charlotte News*, 21 October 1980.

36. *Wall Street Journal*, 21 October 1983; *Labor Unity*, December 1989.

37. Harold McIver, interview with author, Atlanta, 28 June 1989.

38. Terry W. Mullins and Paul Leubke, "Symbolic Victory and Political Reality in the Southern Textile Industry: The Meaning of the J. P. Stevens Settlement for Southern Labor Relations," *Journal of Labor Research* (Winter 1982): 81–82; Rowan and Barr, *Employee Relations*, 81; interviews previously cited.

39. Raynor interview.

40. Michael D. Schulman and Jeffrey Leiter, "Southern Textiles: Contested Puzzles and Continuing Paradoxes," in *Hanging by a Thread*, ed. Leiter et al., 9. As an example of the more than twenty sociological studies that argue for a persistent anti-union southern worker culture, see Jeffrey Leiter, "Reaction to Subordinates: Attitudes of Southern Textile Workers," *Social Forces* 64 (1986): 948–77; and Michael D. Schulman et al., "Race, Gender, Class Consciousness and Union Support: An Analysis of Southern Textile Workers," *Sociological Quarterly* 26 (1985): 187–204. For an argument that southern textile workers had shed much of their southern distinctiveness by the 1980s, see J. Douglas Flamming, *Creating the Modern South: Millhands, Managers, and the Crown Cotton Mills of Dalton, Georgia, 1884–1984* (Chapel Hill: University of North Carolina Press, 1992).

Part II: Introduction

1. U. B. Phillips, *American Negro Slavery: A Survey of the Supply, Employment, and Control of Negro Labor as Determined by the Plantation Regime* (1918; reprint, Baton Rouge: Louisiana State University Press, 1966); Kenneth Stampp, *The Peculiar Institution: Slavery in the Ante-Bellum South* (New York: Alfred A. Knopf, 1956); Stanley Elkins, *Slavery: A Problem in American Institutional Life* (Chicago: University of Chicago Press, 1959).

2. Quoted in John Blassingame, *The Slave Community: Plantation Life in the Antebellum South*, rev. ed. (New York: Oxford University Press, 1979), 105. See also Lawrence Levine, *Black Culture and Black Consciousness: Afro-American Folk Thought from Slavery to Freedom* (New York: Oxford University Press, 1977); Herbert G. Gutman, *The Black Family in Slavery and Freedom, 1750–1925* (New York: Vintage Books, 1976); and Eugene Genovese, *Roll, Jordan, Roll: The World the Slaves Made* (New York: Vintage Books, 1972).

3. Nell Irvin Painter, *Exodusters: Black Migration to Kansas after Reconstruction*, rev. ed. (Lawrence: University of Kansas Press, 1986); Thomas Holt, *Black Over*

White: Negro Political Leadership in South Carolina during Reconstruction (Urbana: University of Illinois Press, 1977); Leon Litwack, *Been in the Storm So Long: The Aftermath of Slavery* (New York: Vintage Books, 1979); Barbara Jean Fields, *Slavery and Freedom on the Middle Ground: Maryland during the Nineteenth Century* (New Haven: Yale University Press, 1985); Armstead Robinson, "The Difference Freedom Made: The Emancipation of Afro-Americans," in *The State of Afro-American History: Past, Present, and Future,* ed. Darlene Clark Hine (Baton Rouge: Louisiana State University Press, 1986), 51–74; Eric Foner, *Reconstruction: America's Unfinished Revolution, 1863–1877* (New York: Harper and Row, 1988).

4. See essays by Lewis, Darlene Clark Hine, Grossman, and Gottlieb in *The Great Migration in Historical Perspective: New Dimensions of Race, Class, and Gender,* ed. Joe W. Trotter, Jr. (Bloomington: Indiana University Press, 1991).

5. For a close analysis of black historians during the segregationist era, see Francille R. Wilson, "The Segregated Scholars: Black Labor Historians" (Ph.D. diss., University of Pennsylvania, 1988). See also Herbert G. Gutman, *Work, Culture and Society in Industrializing America* (New York: Vintage Books, 1977).

6. Gutman, *Work, Culture and Society,* 121–208; Robert H. Zieger in *Organized Labor in the Twentieth-Century South,* ed. Robert H. Zieger (Knoxville: University of Tennessee Press, 1991), 9. For more detailed discussions of the state of African-American history, see Robert L. Harris, Jr., "Coming of Age: The Transformation of Afro-American Historiography," *Journal of Negro History* 57 (1982): 107–21; Darlene Clark Hine, ed., *State of Afro-American History;* August Meier and Elliott Rudwick, *Black History and the Historical Profession, 1915–1980* (Urbana: University of Illinois Press, 1986); Trotter, ed., *Great Migration in Historical Perspective,* and "Afro-American Urban History: A Critique of the Literature," in *Black Milwaukee: The Making of an Industrial Proletariat, 1915–45,* ed. Trotter (Urbana: University of Illinois Press, 1985); and Zieger, ed., *Organized Labor in the Twentieth-Century South.*

6. Black Workers in Antebellum Richmond

1. J. T. Trowbridge, *A Picture of the Desolated States, and the Work of Restoration, 1865–1868* (Hartford, 1888); Peter Rachleff, *Black Labor in Richmond, 1865–1890* (1984; reprint, Urbana: University of Illinois Press, 1989), 38, 50–51; John O'Brien, "From Bondage to Citizenship: The Richmond Black Community, 1865–1867" (Ph.D. diss., University of Rochester, 1974), 280–82.

2. Rachleff, *Black Labor,* 45.

3. Ibid., 6, 28, 32, 118–19; Leon Fink, "'Irrespective of Party, Color or Social Standing': The Knights of Labor and Opposition Politics in Richmond, Virginia," *Labor History* 19 (Summer 1978): 325–49, and *Workingman's Democracy: The Knights of Labor and American Politics* (Urbana: University of Illinois Press, 1983), 169, 222.

4. For purposes of clarity, in this essay the "owner" owns the slave; the "employer" hires the slave from an owner; the "master" can be either the owner or an employer. Owner, employer, and master all "use" or "hold" the slave. The subject of slave negotiation has been explicitly explored by many historians. See especially Philip Morgan, "Work and Culture: The Task System and the World of Lowcountry Blacks, 1700–1880," *William and Mary Quarterly* 39 (October 1982): 563–99; John Campbell, "Slaves' Market-Related Activities in South Carolina," *Slavery and Abolition* 12 (September 1991): 145–63; Oren Schweninger, "The Underside of Slavery: The Internal Economy, Self-Hire, and Quasi-Freedom in Virginia, 1780–1865," *Slavery and Abolition* 12 (September 1991): 1–22; John Schlotterback, "The Internal Economy of Slavery in Virginia," *Slavery and Abolition* 12 (September 1991): 164–81; and Roderick McDonald, "The Slaves' Economy: Louisiana Sugar Plantations," *Slavery and Abolition* 12 (September 1991): 183–209.

5. Here, "tobacco slave" means any slave who worked for an owner or employer in a chewing tobacco factory. Elizabeth Hafkin Pleck, *Black Migration and Poverty: Boston 1865–1900* (New York: Academic Press, 1979), 43–91, esp. 69, argues that freed blacks who migrated from urban Virginia to Boston after the Civil War demonstrated that "even in bondage, blacks in the Upper South had made the transition from feudalism to quasi-wage labor." She notes that the "growth of industrial manufacturing in southern cities and the large supply of slave labor created a slave proletariat." For discussions of black working-class activism during the late antebellum period in Richmond, see Philip Schwarz, "'A Sense of Their Own Power—Black Virginians, 1619–1989," *Virginia Magazine of History and Biography* 97 (July 1989): 281–99; O'Brien, "Bondage to Citizenship"; Rachleff, *Black Labor*; Philip Foner and Ronald Lewis, eds., *The Black Worker to 1869*, 2 vols. (Philadelphia: Temple University Press, 1974), vol. 1; Suzanne Schnittman, "Slavery in Virginia's Urban Tobacco Industry, 1840–1860" (Ph.D. diss., University of Rochester, 1986).

6. U. B. Phillips, "Slave Labor in the Charleston District," *Political Science Quarterly* 22 (September 1907): 416–39; Claudia Goldin, *Urban Slavery in the American South, 1820–1860: A Quantitative History* (Chicago: University of Chicago Press, 1976), esp. p. 25. Robert Fogel and Stanley Engerman, *Time on the Cross: The Economics of American Slavery* (Boston: Little, Brown, 1974), 38, suggest that about 6 percent of slaves lived in cities and towns of one thousand or more. Many authors have explored urban and industrial slavery in Virginia. See Marie Tyler-McGraw and Gregg D. Kimball, *In Bondage and in Freedom: Antebellum Black Life in Richmond, Virginia* (Richmond: Valentine Museum, 1988); Charles Dew, *Ironmaker to the Confederacy: Joseph R. Anderson and the Tredegar Iron Works* (New Haven: Yale University Press, 1966); Kathleen Bruce, *Virginia Iron Manufacture in the Slave Era* (London: Century Company, 1931); John Edmund Stealey III, "Slavery and the West Virginia Salt Industry," *Journal of Negro History* 59 (April 1974): 105–31; Robert Starobin, *Industrial Slavery in the Old South* (New York: Oxford Univer-

sity Press, 1970); Richard Wade, *Slavery in the Cities: The South, 1820–1860* (1964; reprint, New York: Oxford University Press, 1969); and Ronald Lewis, *Coal, Iron, and Slaves: Industrial Slavery in Maryland and Virginia, 1715–1865* (Westport: Greenwood Press, 1979).

7. Manufacturing Census, Schedule MSS, Henrico County, 1860; *The Eighth Census of the United States, 1860,* Population Tables for Virginia, I–VI (Washington, D.C.: Government Printing Office, 1864); Census Schedule of Slave Inhabitants MSS, Henrico County, 1860; Personal and Property Tax Records, Richmond, 1850–1864, Virginia State Library, Richmond. See also *Richmond Dispatch,* 11 July, 3 December 1857. The slave Henry "Box" Brown noted that the tobacco factory to which he was hired during the 1840s had "room for 200 people to work in, but only 150 persons were employed, 120 of whom were slaves and the remainder free colored people." Henry "Box" Brown, *The Narrative of Henry Box Brown, Written by Himself,* 2nd ed. (Bilston, England: S. Webb, 1852), 40–55.

8. Manufacturing Census, Henrico County, 1860; Goldin, *Urban Slavery,* 20, 25. Frederick Law Olmsted visited Virginia industries to provide further impressions about their slave labor; see *A Journey in the Seaboard Slave States* (New York: Dix and Edwards, 1856), 102–3, 127–28, 154. For further discussion of slave-hiring procedures, see Charles Dew, "Disciplining Slave Ironworkers in the Antebellum South: Coercion, Conciliation, and Accommodation," *American Historical Review* 79 (April 1974): 393–418; Clement Eaton, "Slave-Hiring in the Upper South: A Step toward Freedom," *Journal of American History* 46 (December 1960): 663–78; Richard B. Morris, "The Measure of Bondage in the Slave States," *Mississippi Valley Historical Review* 41 (September 1945): 219–40; and Schnittman, "Slavery in the Tobacco Industry," chap. 3.

9. Hiring procedures are discussed in *Richmond Dispatch,* 25, 27 October 1852; 21 December 1853, 20 December 1854; 1 January, 24 February 1855; 2, 4 January, 18 December 1856; *Richmond Enquirer,* 18 January 1855; and *Richmond Whig,* 24 December 1841. Slave agents charged 5 to 7 percent of the hiring fee. Joseph Robert, *The Tobacco Kingdom: Plantation, Market, and Factory in Virginia and North Carolina, 1800–1860* (Durham: Duke University Press, 1938), 198–201; Bruce, *Virginia Iron Manufacture,* 242–43; William Towles to James Thomas, Jr., 31 December 1853, James Thomas, Jr., Papers, Duke University (hereafter cited as Thomas Papers).

10. Benjamin Fleet to James Thomas, Jr., 24 January 1850; 1 June 1852; 28 February 1855, Thomas Papers; *Richmond Dispatch,* 18 December 1856; 9 December 1859.

11. Jane Guild, *Black Laws of Virginia: A Summary of the Legislative Acts of Virginia Concerning Negroes from Earliest Times to the Present* (New York: Negro University Press, 1936), 70.

12. *Richmond Dispatch,* 22 December 1852, 18 December 1856, 15, 29, 31 December 1859; Wade, *Slavery in the Cities,* 672.

13. *Richmond Dispatch,* 31 December 1859. See also *Richmond Enquirer,* 18 January 1855; and *Richmond Dispatch,* 2, 4 January 1856.

14. Census Schedule of Slave Inhabitants MSS, Henrico County, 1860, Thomas Papers; Stealey, "Slavery and the West Virginia Salt Industry," 107. On customary rights, see Eugene Genovese, *Roll, Jordan, Roll: The World the Slaves Made* (New York: Vintage Books, 1972, 1976), 5, 17, 30, 31, 49, 89, 91, 95, 125, 141–49, 535–40. For information on slave negotiations, see citations in n. 4, above.

15. Richmond Common Council Minutes, 22 December 1857; *Richmond Dispatch,* 29, 31 December 1859.

16. Genovese, *Roll, Jordan, Roll,* 408–9; contracts, Valentine Museum, Richmond; Tredegar Iron Works Papers, Virginia State Library, Richmond; Goldin, *Urban Slavery,* 36–37; Frederick Bancroft, *Slave-Trading in the Old South* (Baltimore: J. H. Furst Company, 1931), 117, 118, 156–57. The average price of male slaves ranged from $1,100 to $1,500 in 1860. *Richmond Enquirer,* 29 July 1859; U. B. Phillips, *American Negro Slavery: A Survey of the Supply, Employment, and Control of Negro Labor as Determined by the Plantation Regime* (New York: D. Appleton-Century, 1918; reprint 1940), 410; Kenneth Stampp, *The Peculiar Institution: Slavery in the Ante-Bellum South* (New York: Alfred A. Knopf, 1956), 414–15.

17. James Thomas, Jr., "List of Hands, Winter 1853," "Clothes for Summer, 1853," invoices from Alex Hill and Co., Peter Tinsley, and John Dooley, booteries and clothiers, 1850–1863, Thomas Papers; Personal and Property Tax Records, Richmond, 1853.

18. Brown, *Narrative:* invoices to James Thomas, Jr., from Dr. A. G. Wortham, 1850–1863, Thomas Papers. For folk remedies used by slaves, see Todd Savitt, *Medicine and Slavery: The Disease and Health Care of Blacks in Antebellum Virginia* (Urbana: University of Illinois Press, 1978), 150–71, 207–17, 239.

19. *Richmond Republican,* 1 January 1852, describes the board system in detail. See also Robert, *Tobacco Kingdom,* 204; and Wade, *Slavery in the Cities,* 62, 71. For estimated costs of room and board, see Robert Fogel and Stanley Engerman, *Time on the Cross: Evidence and Methods, A Supplement* (Boston: Little, Brown, 1974), 117; Roger Ransom and Richard Sutch, *One Kind of Freedom: The Economic Consequences of Emancipation* (Cambridge: Cambridge University Press, 1977), 3–7; *Richmond Dispatch,* 12 July 1857; Olmsted, *Journey in the Seaboard States,* 154; and Dismal Swamp Papers, Duke University.

20. 1857 Richmond Ordinance for Negroes, Virginia State Library, Richmond; Brown, *Narrative,* 40–55. Ira Berlin, *Slaves Without Masters: The Free Negro in the Antebellum South* (New York: Oxford University Press, 1974), finds important patterns of racial segregation as well as integration in Richmond.

21. E. P. Thompson, "Time, Work-Discipline, and Industrial Capitalism," *Past and Present* 38 (December 1967): 56–97; Brown, *Narrative,* 40–55; E. A. Randolph, *The Life of Reverend John Jasper* (Richmond, 1884), 7; Olmsted, *Journey in the*

Seaboard States, 58. In a poem, "Richmond Before Daylight," the 18 August 1853 *Richmond Dispatch* notes that "tobacco factory men are by this time astir, and you see them one after another, each with his own provision pail, proceeding to his labors."

22. *Charter and Ordinance of the City of Richmond* (Richmond: Common Council, 1859); Richmond Hustings Court Records, 1837–1860, Virginia State Library, Richmond (hereafter cited as Hustings); *Richmond Dispatch*, 12 March, 19 November 1852, 23 March 1853; Addendum to 28 September 1852 Ordinance, sec. 17, chap. 109 of Code, reported in *Richmond Dispatch*, 13 November 1856. See also *Richmond Dispatch*, 31 January, 18 August 1852, 2 February, 26 November 1853; *Richmond Enquirer*, 29 July 1858; Luther Jackson, *Free Negro and Property Holding in Virginia, 1830–1860* (New York: Russell and Russell, 1942); and Berlin, *Slaves Without Masters.*

23. *Richmond Republican*, January 1852; Common Council Minutes, esp. March 1852 and December 1857; Tyler-McGraw and Kimball, *In Bondage*, 23. For a brief narrative of the four votes the Common Council took before it finally revised the board system, and then only slightly, see *Richmond Dispatch*, 12 March, 18 November 1852, 7, 22, 24, 29 December 1857, 18 January, 20 March 1858.

24. Robert Starobin, "Disciplining Industrial Slaves in the Old South," *Journal of Negro History* 52 (April 1968): 119, 122, 124, and *Industrial Slavery in the Old South*, 157, 259. Lewis, *Coal, Iron, and Slaves*, argues that slave bonuses received in iron foundries were given in credit to company stores and those in mining were either credit or cash at the end of the year. Stealey, "Slavery and the West Virginia Salt Industry," argues that slaves in Kanawha salt mines received bonuses in cash only at the end of the year. See also Olmsted, *Journey in the Seaboard States*, 102–3, 127–28, 154; *Richmond Dispatch*, 5 January 1853; and Robert Russell quoted in Robert, *Tobacco Kingdom*, 204.

25. Robert, *Tobacco Kingdom*, 197–98; Schnittman, "Slavery in the Tobacco Industry," 23–24.

26. Schnittman, "Slavery in the Tobacco Industry," 208, n. 21.

27. Parke Godwin, ed., *The Prose Writings of William Cullen Bryant*, II (1884: reprint, New York: D. Appleton-Century, 1964), 25; Alexander MacKay, *The Western World: Travels in the U.S. 1846–1847* (Philadelphia: Lea, 1849), 2:74; Julia Lord Noyes' Journal, 26 April 1855, Duke University. Jacqueline Jones, *Labor of Love, Labor of Sorrow: Black Women, Work, and the Family from Slavery to the Present* (New York: Vintage Books, 1985), 140, argues that black women tobacco workers sang to "establish a rhythm to make the repetitious tasks more bearable even as they collectively expressed a hope and a protest." See also Dena Epstein, *Sinful Tunes and Spirituals: Black Folk Music to the Civil War* (Urbana: University of Illinois Press, 1977); and Lawrence Levine, *Black Culture and Black Consciousness: Afro-American Folk Thought from Slavery to Freedom* (New York: Oxford University Press, 1977), 17–18.

28. For the numerous incidents of slave altercations with overseers, see *Richmond Dispatch*, 27, 28 February, 3, 13 March, 7, 12 May, 23 September, 12, 14, 15 November 1852, 24 April 1855, 15, 20, 24, December 1859; and Brown, *Narrative*, 43–46, 58–62. Tyler-McGraw and Kimball, *In Bondage*, 23, suggest that "tobacco workers exercised a group sense of limits on how far discipline could go on the factory floor and most white overseers understood this. Successful overseers balanced rewards and punishments, and unsuccessful ones used the whip or paddle." See also Harrison Ethridge, "The Jordan Hatcher Affair of 1852: Cold Justice and Warm Compassion," *Virginia Magazine of History and Biography* 84 (October 1976): 446–63.

29. Philip J. Schwartz, *Twice Condemned: Slaves and the Criminal Laws of Virginia, 1705–1865* (Baton Rouge: Louisiana State University Press, 1988), 298–99; Brown, *Narrative*, 318–19. During the period of 1850–1860, the *Richmond Dispatch* reported an average of one tobacco factory fire every three to four months that could have been set by free whites or free blacks, but many of which were specifically blamed on slaves. For example, see *Richmond Dispatch*, 4, 24 March, 12 April, 29 September, 15 November 1853, 23, 31 January, 1, 2 February, 20 March, 24, 29, 30 August 1854, 12 January 1858. The W. Greanor case, in which his hired slave threatened to burn the factory unless he got a new overseer, was reported on 2 February 1854.

30. Incidents of slaves stealing tobacco from factories were reported in the *Richmond Dispatch*, 31 January, 28 February, 27 September 1852, 23 March 1853, 20 December 1854, 24 April 1855, 23 February 1856, 25 July 1857, 2, 21 May 1858. For related slave incidents, see *Richmond Dispatch*, 18, 22 December 1856, 29 March, 6, 13, 16 April, 18 December 1858. For incidents of whites trading illegally with slaves, see *Richmond Dispatch*, 6 October 1852, 20, 31 August, 1, 26 November 1853, 11, 13 November 1854, 13, 14 February, 24 April, 11 October 1855, 25 July, 18 December 1856, 25 July, 30 December 1857, 15, 17 May 1858, 1 January, 9 May, 17 August 1859, 9 May 1860; and *Richmond Enquirer*, 1, 10 December 1853.

31. *Richmond Enquirer*, 10, 18 August 1853; *Richmond Dispatch*, 9 May 1860. John O'Brien, "Factory, Church and Community: Blacks in Antebellum Richmond," *Journal of Southern History* 44 (November 1978): 54–56, 60, 68, argues that churches provided a haven in which blacks "were reminded less of their bondage" than they were "prepared for emancipation." See also O'Brien, "Bondage to Citizenship," 176; and Luther Jackson, "Religious Development of the Negro in Virginia, 1760–1860," *Journal of Negro History* 16 (April 1931): 236–39.

32. The importance of private life in the formation of working-class identity has been found by many historians. See Herbert G. Gutman, *The Black Family in Slavery and Freedom, 1750–1925* (New York: Vintage Books, 1976); and Roy Rosenzweig, *Eight Hours for What We Will: Workers and Leisure in An Industrial City, 1879–1920* (Cambridge: Cambridge University Press, 1983). Patricia Click, *The Spirit of the*

Times: Amusements in Nineteenth-Century Baltimore, Norfolk, and Richmond (Charlottesville: University Press of Virginia, 1989), 5–6, 14, 17–18, 38, 43, 57–63, 77–97, argues that the wide participation of slaves and free blacks, as well as lower-class whites, in public amusements encouraged the upper and middle ruling classes to regulate those amusements.

33. Manufacturing Census MSS, Henrico County 1870, 1880; David Goldfield, "Communities and Regions: The Diverse Cultures of Virginia," *Virginia Magazine of History and Biography* 95 (October 1987): 444; Rachleff, *Black Labor;* Howard N. Rabinowitz, *Race Relations in the Urban South, 1865–1890* (Urbana: University of Illinois Press, 1980), 15–18, 329–40; O'Brien, "Bondage to Citizenship," chaps. 1, 2.

7. Overseers and the Nature of Southern Labor Contracts

1. T. S., "Overseers," *Southern Planter* 3 (December 1843): 271.

2. Morton J. Horwitz, *The Transformation of American Law, 1780–1860* (Cambridge: Harvard University Press, 1977), 186–88, 333n; Wythe Holt, "Recovery by the Worker Who Quits: A Comparison of the Mainstream, Legal Realist, and Critical Legal Studies Approaches to a Problem of Nineteenth Century Contract Law," *Wisconsin Law Review* (1986): 677–732; Christopher Tomlinson, "The Ties That Bind: Master and Servant in Massachusetts, 1800–1850," *Labor History* 30 (Spring 1989): 193–227. For a rebuttal to the position taken by these scholars, see Peter Karsten, "'Bottomed on Justice': A Reappraisal of Critical Legal Studies Scholarship Concerning Breaches of Labor Contracts by Quitting or Firing in Britain and the U.S., 1630–1880," *American Journal of Legal History* 34 (July 1990): 211–61.

3. James D. Schmidt, "'Neither Slavery nor Involuntary Servitude': Free Labor and American Law, ca. 1815–1880" (Ph.D. diss., Rice University, 1992), 36–67.

4. Both Holt and Karsten do note the existence of overseers' contracts in passing. Holt, "Recovery by the Worker Who Quits," 701–2; Karsten, "'Bottomed on Justice,'" 240–41.

5. Mark Tushnet, *The American Law of Slavery, 1810–1860: Considerations of Humanity and Interest* (Princeton: Princeton University Press, 1981), 169–88. For a quick summary of the practice of slave hiring, see Eugene D. Genovese, *Roll, Jordan, Roll: The World the Slaves Made* (New York: Vintage Books, 1972), 390–92; Ira Berlin, *Slaves Without Masters: The Free Negro in the Antebellum South* (New York: Oxford University Press, 1974), 217–49, esp. 223–24; and Ira Berlin and Herbert Gutman, "Natives and Immigrants, Free Men and Slaves: Urban Workingmen in the Antebellum American South," *American Historical Review* 88 (December 1983): 1175–1200.

6. The only full-length study of overseers is William Kauffman Scarborough, *The Overseer: Plantation Management in the Old South* (Baton Rouge: Louisiana State

University Press, 1966). Scarborough contends that overseers were not the rogues often pictured in older versions of plantation life. Three classes of overseers existed: sons of planters, a small band of "floaters," and a class of semi-professional managers. An older book-length study is John Spencer Bassett, *The Southern Plantation Overseer as Revealed in His Letters* (Northampton: Smith College, 1925). Genovese, *Roll, Jordan, Roll*, 12–25, is a useful discussion of the relationship between planter and overseer.

7. *Saunders v. Anderson*, 2 Hill 487 (South Carolina, 1834).

8. For examples of share contracts, see *Cochran v. Tatum*, 19 Kentucky 405 (1826); *Anderson v. Rice, adm'x*, 20 Alabama 240 (1852); *Lambert v. King*, 12 Louisiana Ann. 662 (1856); *Steed v. McRae*, 18 North Carolina 57 (1836); *Dillard v. Wallace*, 1 McMul. 482 (South Carolina, 1837); *Graham v. Lewis*, 2 Hill 478 (South Carolina, 1834); *Hassell v. Nutt*, 14 Texas 260 (1855); and *Rogers v. Parham*, 8 Georgia 191 (1850). See also *Southern Planter* 1 (April 1841): 58, and 3 (October 1843): 234. For contracts with supply clauses, see *Seal v. Earwin*, 2 Mart. (North Carolina) 245 (Louisiana, 1824); *Walworth v. Pool*, 9 Arkansas 395 (1849); *Nolan v. Danks*, 1 Rob. 332 (Louisiana, 1842); and *Coursey v. Covington*, 5 H. & J. 46 (Maryland, 1820). For examples of contracts with wages only, see *Wright v. Falkner*, 37 Alabama 274 (1861); *Johnson v. Gorham*, 30 Georgia 613 (1860); *Anderson v. Wales*, 22 Kentucky 324 (1827); *McDaniel v. Parks*, 19 Arkansas 673 (1858); *Hays v. Marsh*, 11 Louisiana 369 (1837); and *Hendrickson v. Anderson*, 50 North Carolina 246 (1858).

9. Robert A. Jones Account Book, 1817–1828, pp. 129–30, 309–10, 341–42, 385–86, Manuscripts Department, Southern Historical Collection, University of North Carolina, Chapel Hill.

10. *Roberts v. Brownrigg*, 9 Alabama 108 (1846); *Whitley v. Murray*, 34 Alabama 157 (1859); Ulrich B. Phillips, *Plantation and Frontier Documents: 1649–1863*, 2 vols. (Cleveland: Arthur C. Clark Company, 1909), 1:112–30, quote at p. 128. See also *Hariston v. Sale*, 14 Mississippi 635 (1846); *Nolan v. Danks*, 1 Rob. 333 (Louisiana, 1842); Scarborough, *Overseer*, 68–70; Bassett, *Southern Plantation Overseer*, 24–32; John Hebron Moore, ed., "Two Documents Relating to Plantation Overseers of the Vicksburg Region, 1831–1832," *Journal of Mississippi History* 16 (January 1954): 35; Lucille Griffith, ed., "The Plantation Record Book of Brookdale Farm, Amite County, 1856–1857," *Journal of Mississippi History* 7 (January 1945): 23–27; and "Overseers' Rules," *Southern Planter* 18 (July 1858): 410–11.

11. *Hariston v. Sale*, 14 Mississippi 635 (1846). See also *Nolan v. Danks*, 1 Rob. 333 (Louisiana, 1842); and Sarah McCulloh Lemon, ed., *The Pettigrew Papers, Volume II: 1819–1843* (Raleigh: North Carolina Department of Cultural Resources, 1988), 172. Such bonus arrangements were fairly common. See Scarborough, *Overseer*, 30.

12. *Craig v. Pride*, 2 Speers 122 (South Carolina, 1843); *McDaniel v. Parks*, 19 Arkansas 674 (1858); Whatley and Jones contract reprinted in Bassett, *Southern*

Plantation Overseer, 33; Scarborough, *Overseer*, 112–16, quotation on 114. See also *Steed v. McRae*, 18 North Carolina 57 (1836); *Word v. Winder*, 16 Louisiana Ann. 112 (1861); and Kenneth Stampp, *The Peculiar Institution: Slavery in the Ante-Bellum South* (New York: Alfred A. Knopf, 1956), 38. Scarborough, *Overseer*, 20–47, discusses violability and many other factors in overseer contracts. On at-will clauses generally, see Jay M. Feinman, "The Development of the Employment of the at Will Rule," *American Journal of Legal History* 20 (April 1976): 118–35.

13. *Pettigrew v. Bishop*, 3 Alabama 440 (1842); *Hays v. Marsh*, 11 Louisiana 369 (1837). See also *Roberts v. Brownrigg*, 9 Alabama 106 (1846); and *Whitley v. Murray*, 34 Alabama 155 (1859). In the few cases involving common laborers, southern courts usually upheld entirety as strongly as their northern counterparts. For example, see *Wright v. Turner*, 1 Stew. 35 (Alabama, 1827).

14. *Byrd v. Boyd*, 4 McCord 246 (South Carolina, 1827). It is unclear when the case was actually decided. It appears that it was in 1825. However, the case was lost for a time and not reported until 1827. The court used this rule in several subsequent cases: *McClure v. Pyatt*, 4 McCord 26 (1826); *Eaken v. Harrison*, 4 McCord 249 (1827); *Saunders v. Anderson*, 2 Hill 486 (1834); and *Suber v. Vanlew*, 2 Speers 126 (1843).

15. *Hariston v. Sale*, 14 Mississippi 634–40 (1846); affirmed in *Robinson v. Sanders*, 24 Mississippi 391 (1852); *Jones v. Jones*, 32 Tennessee 605–9 (1853); *Steed v. McRae*, 18 North Carolina 435 (1836); and *Meade v. Rutledge*, 11 Texas 50 (1853). For the doctrinal development in Louisiana, see *Nolan v. Danks*, 1 Rob. 333 (Louisiana, 1842); *Youngblood v. Dodd*, 2 Louisiana Ann. 187 (1847); *Lambert v. King*, 12 Louisiana Ann. 662 (1856); and *Kessee v. Mayfield*, 14 Louisiana Ann. Reports 90 (1859). For Alabama, see *Martin v. Everett*, 11 Alabama 375 (1847). Arkansas formed a similar rule, but it was not based on *Byrd v. Boyd*. See *McDaniel v. Parks*, 19 Arkansas 671 (1858). South Carolina also passed an act in 1747 to regulate overseers' contracts, but it was not enforced. *Dillard v. Wallace*, 1 McMul. 484 (South Carolina, 1837).

16. *Ford v. Danks*, 16 Louisiana Ann. 119 (1861).

17. Bassett, *Southern Plantation Overseer*, 24; Phillips, *Plantation and Frontier Documents*, 1:113; Genovese, *Roll, Jordan, Roll*, 17–22; John Blassingame, *The Slave Community: Plantation Life in the Antebellum South*, rev. ed. (New York: Oxford University Press, 1979), 273, 276; Scarborough, *Overseer*, 120–21.

18. *Fly v. Armstrong*, 50 North Carolina 340 (1858).

19. Ibid., 342. For other complaints about absence, see *McCracken v. Hair*, 2 Speers 258 (South Carolina, 1843); and *Martin v. Everett*, 11 Alabama 375 (1847). The latter case also involved cruelty to slaves.

20. *Meade v. Rutledge*, 11 Texas 50 (1853); *Prichard v. Martin*, 27 Mississippi 308 (1854); *Johnson v. Gorman*, 30 Georgia 613 (1860); *Harper v. Ray*, 27 Mississippi 623 (1854); *Lane v. Phillips*, 51 North Carolina 443 (1859); *Kessee v. Mayfield*, 14 Louisiana Ann. 90–91 (1859); Scarborough, *Overseer*, passim. In the last case, the planter

wanted the black drivers or other slaves to perform the task, but the overseer flogged the slaves himself. See also *Dillard v. Wallace*, 1 McMul. 480 (South Carolina, 1837); and *Saunders v. Anderson*, 2 Hill 486 (South Carolina, 1834).

Agricultural reformers favored creating a professional class of overseers, as did those overseers aspiring to achieve such a status. See "Overseers," *Southern Planter* 5 (August 1845): 172; "Overseers," *Southern Planter* 5 (September 1845): 209–11; M. W. Phillips, "Domestic Economy—Overseers—A Few Thoughts on the Subject," *Southern Cultivator* 14 (November 1856): 339; and A. T. Goodloe, "Overseers," *Southern Cultivator* 18 (September 1861): 287.

21. *Dwyer v. Cane*, 6 Louisiana Ann. 707 (1851). For other cases involving allegations of sexual misconduct, see *Fowler v. Waller*, 25 Texas 697 (1860); and *Suber v. Vanlew*, 2 Speers 126 (South Carolina, 1843).

22. *Wilson v. Bossier*, 11 Louisiana Ann. 640 (1856); *Brunson v. Martin*, 17 Arkansas 274 (1856); *Posey v. Garth*, 7 Missouri 97 (1841); *Hendricks v. Phillips*, 8 Louisiana Ann. 618 (1848); *Kennedy v. Mason*, 10 Louisiana Ann. 519 (1855). See also *McCracken v. Hair*, 2 Speers 258 (South Carolina, 1843); *Jones v. Jones*, 32 Tennessee 608 (1853); and *Miller v. Stewart*, 12 Louisiana Ann. 170 (1857).

23. Harris S. Evans, "Rules for the Government of the Negroes, Plantation &c. at Float-Swamp, Wilcox County South Alabama," *Southern Agriculturist* 5 (May 1832): 231–34, in *Advice Among Masters: The Ideal in Slave Management in the Old South*, ed. James O. Breeden (Westport: Greenwood Press, 1980), 292; Scarborough, *Overseer*, 112–16, 131–32. See also Little River, South Carolina, "Overseers," *Soil of the South* 6 (August 1856): 233–34, in *Advice Among Masters*, ed. Breeden, 317; Charles S. Sydnor, "A Slave Owner and His Overseers," *North Carolina Historical Review* 14 (January 1937): 35; James C. Bonner, "The Plantation Overseer and Southern Nationalism as Revealed in the Career of Garland D. Harmon," *Agricultural History* 19 (January 1945): 1–2; Moore, "Two Documents," 33; and James Oakes, *The Ruling Race: A History of American Slaveholders* (New York: Alfred A. Knopf, 1982), 174–75.

24. *Byrd v. Boyd*, 4 McCord 246 (South Carolina, 1827); *Suber v. Vanlew*, 2 Speers 127 (South Carolina, 1843); *Talbert v. Stone*, 10 Louisiana Ann. 537 (1855); *Nations v. Cudd*, 22 Texas 551 (1858). On the honor ethic generally, see Bertram Wyatt-Brown, *Southern Honor: Ethics and Behavior in the Old South* (New York: Oxford University Press, 1982).

25. *Prichard v. Martin*, 27 Mississippi 308, 313 (1854); *Boone v. Lyde*, 3 Strob. 78 (South Carolina, 1848); *Henderson v. Stiles*, 13 Georgia 136–37 (1853); *Youngblood v. Dodd*, 2 Louisiana Ann. 187 (1847); *Darden v. Nolan*, 4 Louisiana Ann. 374 (1849). On the idea of personal independence in republican ideology, see Richard L. Bushman, " 'This New Man': Dependence and Independence, 1776," in *Uprooted Americans: Essays in Honor of Oscar Handlin*, ed. Richard L. Bushman et al. (Boston: Little, Brown, 1979), 91–93; Rowland Bertoff, "Independence and Attachment, Virtue and

Interest: From Republican Citizen to Free Enterpriser, 1787–1837," in *Uprooted Americans*, ed. Bushman et al., 100, 117–18; and Gordon Wood, "Interests and Disinterestedness in the Making of the Constitution," in *Beyond Confederation: Origins of the Constitution and American National Character*, ed. Richard Beeman, Stephen Botein, and Edward C. Carter II (Chapel Hill: University of North Carolina Press, 1987), 83–85.

26. "Overseers," *Southern Planter* 16 (February 1856): 48–49; "Overseers," *Southern Planter* 4 (August 1844): 184; "Overseers," *Southern Planter* 5 (July 1845): 166. See also "Virginia Overseers," *Southern Planter* 5 (June 1845): 136–37; and "Overseers—Their Duties," *Southern Cultivator* 12 (July 1854): 270.

27. *Walworth v. Pool*, 9 Arkansas 398 (1849); *Meade v. Rutledge*, 11 Texas 52 (1853).

28. This point affirms the conclusions of Kermit Hall and James Ely about the relationship between modes of production and regional distinctiveness in law. See Kermit L. Hall and James W. Ely, Jr., "The South and the American Constitution," in *Uncertain Tradition: Constitutionalism and the History of the South*, ed. Kermit L. Hall and James W. Ely, Jr. (Athens: University of Georgia Press, 1989), 4, 7. It also supports Lawrence Friedman's suggestion that looking closely at southern legal history often complicates theories of legal, social, and economic change that are based on research primarily in northeastern sources. Lawrence Friedman, "The Law Between the States: Some Thoughts on Southern Legal History," in *Ambivalent Legacy: A Legal History of the South*, ed. James W. Ely, Jr., and David J. Bodenhamer (Jackson: University Press of Mississippi, 1984), 43. This latter argument is especially relevant with regard to the relationship between the law and capitalism. Southern courts started with the same English doctrines but derived a considerably different law of contracts. Yet they did so for essentially the same "capitalist" purpose that northern courts pursued in establishing the entirety doctrine: discipline of nonslave workers.

8. Hope versus Reality

1. Hollis Lynch, *The Black Urban Condition: A Documentary History, 1866–1971* (New York: Thomas Crowell, 1973), 421–22; Leon Litwack, *Been in the Storm So Long: The Aftermath of Slavery* (New York: Alfred A. Knopf, 1979), 311–14.

2. Gerald Capers, *The Biography of a River Town, Memphis: Its Heroic Age* (New Orleans: Hauser-American, 1966), 44–49, 151–61.

3. General Stephen Hulbut to Abraham Lincoln, 27 March 1863, *The War of the Rebellion: A Compilation of the Official Records of the Union and Confederate Armies* (Washington, D.C.: Government Printing Office, 1890–1901), ser. II, vol. 1, 149–50 (hereafter cited as *OR*).

4. *Memphis Bulletin*, 7 July 1862, 2 January 1863; Louis Gerteis, *From Contraband to Freedmen* (Westport: Greenwood Press, 1973), 15, 20, 30, 51–52.

5. Sherman to John Rawling, 4 September 1862, *OR*, ser. II, vol. 1, 201.

6. Military Order No. 60, 22 July 1862, ibid., 113.

7. Military Order No. 67, 8 August 1862, ibid., 158–60.

8. *Memphis Bulletin*, 18 July 1863.

9. Special Order No. 15, 11 November 1862, quoted in John Eaton and Ethel Mason, *Grant, Lincoln and the Freedmen: Reminiscences of the Civil War* (1909; reprint, New York: Longmans Green, 1970), 5.

10. Ibid., 18–22.

11. General Order No. 13, 17 December 1862, ibid., 26–44.

12. Ibid., 31–32.

13. Ibid., 126–28.

14. Ibid., 56–58.

15. Ibid., 59–60.

16. Ibid., 60.

17. Ibid., 59.

18. Ibid., 60.

19. Selected Records of the Tennessee Field Office of the Bureau of Refugees, Freedmen and Abandoned Lands, reel 42, pt. II, Record Group 105, National Archives, Washington, D.C. (hereafter cited as *BRFAL*).

20. *Reports of Superintendent of Freedmen for the State of Arkansas and the District of West Tennessee* (Memphis: Freedmen Press Print, 1865), 13; John Cimprich, *Slavery's End in Tennessee, 1861–1865* (Tuscaloosa: University of Alabama Press, 1985), 48–50, 52.

21. *Reports of Superintendent*, 14.

22. Ibid.

23. A. C. Swatzwelder to S. B. Varney, head of Freedmen's Hospital on President's Island, 27 September 1865, vol. 159, reel 21, *BRFAL*; J. H. Grove to A. C. Swatzwelder, 3 October 1865, ibid.; *Reports of Superintendent*, 13–17.

24. Eaton and Mason, *Grant, Lincoln and the Freedmen*, 164–65; James T. Currie, *Enclave: Vicksburg and Her Plantations, 1863–1870* (Jackson: University Press of Mississippi, 1980), 83.

25. Eaton and Mason, *Grant, Lincoln and the Freedmen*, 145.

26. Ibid., 146–53; Janet Hermann, *The Pursuit of a Dream* (New York: Oxford University Press, 1981), 48–49.

27. *Memphis Argus*, 25 May 1865. On the continuing tendency of local blacks to celebrate certain holidays and white reaction thereto, see *Memphis Post*, 24, 26 May, 7 June 1866; and William Wiggins, *O'Freedom: Afro-American Emancipation Celebrations* (Knoxville: University of Tennessee Press, 1989).

28. Cimprich, *Slavery's End*, 118–31; William Cohen, *At Freedom's Edge: Black Mobility and the Southern White Quest for Racial Control, 1861–1915* (Baton Rouge: Louisiana State University Press, 1991), 17–21.

29. On the antebellum North, see Morton J. Horwitz, *The Transformation of American Law, 1780–1860* (Cambridge: Harvard University Press, 1977); and Harry Scheiber, "Regulation of Property Rights, and Definition of 'The Market': Law and the American Economy," *Journal of Economic History* 41 (March 1981): 101–5.

30. *Memphis Argus*, 24 August 1865.

31. Ibid., 9 August, 3 September 1865.

32. John Sproat, "Blueprint for Radical Reconstruction," *Journal of Southern History* 23 (February 1957): 25–44; James McPherson, *The Struggle for Equality: Abolitionists and the Negro in the Civil War and Reconstruction* (Princeton: Princeton University Press, 1964), 178–91; Herman Belz, *A New Birth of Freedom: The Republican Party and Negro Rights* (Westport: Greenwood Press, 1976), 69–112.

33. *Memphis Daily Appeal*, 16 November 1865; Donald Nieman, *To Set the Law in Motion: The Freedmen's Bureau and the Legal Rights of Blacks, 1865–1868* (New York: KTO Press, 1979), 13–14.

34. "Labor Contracts Received," Shelby County, 22 February 1865, reels 70–71, *BRFAL*. It should be noted that the 2,189 contracts referred to in this analysis and discussion represent only those contracts that have survived. Many more contracts, though the number is unknown, were arranged between freedmen and planters during the fall and winter of 1865. In his farewell address Tennessee's Assistant Commissioner of the Bureau, for example, claimed that "over 10,000 [freedmen] in one month went to the plantations in the vicinity of Memphis." Fiske's successor, Colonel J. R. Lewis, maintained that for the entire state in the fall and winter of 1865 the bureau "registered for the last season about 20,000 contracts, including about 50,000 persons, adults and children." *Nashville Daily Press and Times*, 3 September 1866; *Senate Executive Documents*, no. 6, 39th Cong., 2d sess. 1866, p. 130.

35. Tables 1, 2.

36. A. A. Taylor, *The Negro in Tennessee, 1865–1880* (Washington, D.C.: Associated Publishers, 1941), 128–29.

37. To its credit the bureau refused to initiate an official policy of "specific performance" to which freedmen had to adhere. Nieman, *To Set the Law in Motion*, 174–75.

38. Contract A was first used by the Memphis subdistrict office in June 1865. "Labor Contracts Received," Shelby County, June–September 1865, reel 70, *BRFAL*.

39. Ibid., reels 70–72.

40. Whitelaw Reid, *After the War* (New York: Little, Brown, 1956), 414–15.

41. Editorial by J. D. B. DeBow, *DeBow's Review*, 8 February 1866, p. 332.

42. Harold Woodman, *King Cotton and His Retainers* (Lexington: University of Kentucky Press, 1968), 249–51; Alfred Stone, "The Cotton Factorage System of the Southern States," *American Historical Review* 20 (April 1915): 95–102.

43. For contrasting interpretations of the efficiency of work gangs, see Robert Fogel and Stanley Engerman, *Time on the Cross: The Economics of American Slavery* (Boston: Little, Brown, 1974), 203–5; and Roger Ransom and Richard Sutch, *One Kind of Freedom: The Economic Consequences of Emancipation* (Cambridge: Cambridge University Press, 1977), 75–76.

44. *Memphis Argus*, 9 February 1866. With the approval of the Freedmen's Bureau another employment agency was organized that same year. *Memphis Daily Post*, 12 June 1866.

45. *Memphis Argus*, 9 February 1866; Gerald Jaynes, *Branches Without Roots: Genesis of the Black Working Class in the American South, 1862–1882* (New York: Oxford University Press, 1986), 301–8.

46. Although this explanation is generally accepted as the reason blacks so despised the gang labor arrangements, Jaynes has raised questions concerning its veracity. Specifically, he argues that the prevailing interpretation "seldom distinguishes among an inherent dislike for gang labor, overseers, and drivers." He concludes that the disdain felt by blacks was a "reaction to inept management of freed people on the part of a particular foreman," not foremen in general. Jaynes, *Branches Without Roots*, 180. See also *Memphis Daily Post*, 1 February 1866; and Eric Foner, *Nothing But Freedom: Emancipation and Its Legacy* (Baton Rouge: Louisiana State University Press, 1988), 186–87.

47. For a discussion of postwar violence against blacks in Tennessee, see Stephen Ash, *Middle Tennessee Society Transformed, 1860–1870* (Baton Rouge: Louisiana State University Press, 1988), 220–23.

48. *Colored Tennessean*, 11 August 1865; Sheldon Van Aukin, "A Century of the Southern Plantation," *Virginia Magazine of History and Biography* 59 (July 1950): 345–65; George Arerlof, "The Market for Lemons: Qualitative Uncertainty and the Market Mechanism," *Quarterly Journal of Economics* 84 (February 1970): 125–47; Harold Woodman, "Post-Civil War Southern Agriculture and the Law," *Agricultural History* 53 (June 1979): 331–33; Ralph Shlomowitz, "The Squad System on Postbellum Cotton Plantations," in *Toward a New South? Studies in Postbellum Civil War Southern Communities*, ed. Orville Burton and Robert McMath, Jr. (Westport: Greenwood Press, 1982), 65–89; J. William Harris, "Plantation and Power," in *Toward a New South*, ed. Burton and McMath, 103–10.

49. Based on analysis of "Labor Contracts Received," Shelby County, June 1865–May 1868, reels 70–72, BRFAL; Tables 1, 3.

50. Claudia Goldin, "Female Labor Force Participation: The Origin of Black and White Differences, 1870 and 1880," *Journal of Economic History* 37 (March 1977): 87–108; Frances Loring and C. F. Atkinson, *Cotton Culture and the South Considered with Reference to Emigration* (Boston: A. Williams, 1869), 4. An 1868 survey of economic and labor conditions in the South constitute the primary data base for this study. Ransom and Sutch, *One Kind of Freedom*, 52–65.

51. Janice Reiff, Michel Dahlim, and Daniel Scott Smith, "Rural and Urban Pull: Work and Family Experiences of Older Black Women in Southern Cities, 1880–1900," *Journal of Social History* 16 (May 1983): 39–48; Jacqueline Jones, *Labor of Love, Labor of Sorrow: Black Women, Work, and the Family From Slavery to the Present* (New York: Vintage Books, 1985), 58–59.

52. Tables I.3–5.

53. Eaton and Mason, *Grant, Lincoln and the Freedmen*, 237–38; *New York Times*, 26 May 1865; for an account less critical of the bureau's activities in another southern state, see Richard Lowe, "The Freedmen's Bureau and Local Black Leadership," *Journal of American History* 80 (December 1993): 989–98.

54. For some sense of local labor unrest, see *Memphis Post*, 20, 22–23 May, 9, 12 June 1866; Nieman, *To Set the Law in Motion*, 162–68.

55. "Complaint Books of the Freedmen's Court in the Memphis District, 24 July 1865–2 June 1866," vols. 169–72, reel 24, *BRFAL*.

56. For a discussion of the phenomenon of whitecapping, see William Holmes, "Whitecapping: Agrarian Violence in Mississippi, 1902–1906," *Journal of Southern History* 35 (May 1969): 165–85, "Whitecapping in Mississippi: Agrarian Violence in the Populist Era," *Mid-America* 55 (1973): 134–48, and "Whitecapping in Late Nineteenth-Century Georgia," in *From the Old South to the New: Essays on the Transitional South*, ed. Walter Fraser and Winfred Moore (Westport: Greenwood Press, 1981), 121–32; "Report on Outrages Against Freedmen" April 1868, reel 39, *BRFAL*. On Memphis area Ku Klux Klan violence, see *Memphis Post*, 11, 18 March, 7, 8 April 1868; and *Memphis Appeal*, 16 April, 20, 21 July 1868.

57. *New York Times*, 14 February 1865; United States, *Statutes at Large*, 12:508.

58. Nieman, *To Set the Law in Motion*, 220–21.

59. Ibid., 157–66.

60. Claude Oubre, *Forty Acres and a Mule: The Freedmen's Bureau and Black Land Ownership* (Baton Rouge: Louisiana State University Press, 1978), 86–89, 185–90; Warren Hofnagle, "The Southern Homestead Act: Its Origin and Operation," *The Historian* 32 (August 1970): 612–29; Edward Magdol, *A Right to the Land: Essays on the Freedmen's Community* (Westport: Greenwood Press, 1977), 188–90; Michael Lanza, *Agrarianism and Reconstruction Politics* (Baton Rouge: Louisiana State University Press, 1990), 80–96.

61. J. B. Killebrew, *Resources of Tennessee* (Nashville: Hardman, 1874), 350–59.

9. Black Workers Remember

1. Neil R. McMillen, *Dark Journey: Black Mississippians in the Age of Jim Crow* (Urbana: University of Illinois Press, 1989), provides an in-depth treatment of the workings of southern segregation. On politics, economics, and the racial system, see

V. O. Key, Jr., *Southern Politics in State and Nation* (New York: Random House, 1949); and Paul Lewinson, *Race, Class and Party: A History of Negro Suffrage and White Politics in the South* (New York: Grosset and Dunlap, 1932, 1959, 1965).

2. For an interesting discussion of the psychological and perceived economic benefits of racism to white workers, see David R. Roediger, *The Wages of Whiteness: Race and the Making of the American Working Class* (New York: Verso, 1991). For details on Memphis labor, see Michael Honey, *Southern Labor and Black Civil Rights: Organizing Memphis Workers* (Urbana: University of Illinois Press, 1993).

3. White labor organizers, among others, commented on the commitment of blacks to unions. William E. Davis, interview with author, St. Louis, Mo., 26–28 January 1983; Morton Davis, interview with author, St. Louis, Mo., 28 January 1983; Forrest Dickenson, interview with author, Memphis, Tenn., 20 February 1983; Dan Powell, interview with author, Memphis, Tenn., 4 March 1983; Robert Tillman, interview with author, Memphis, Tenn., 24 February 1983. *Fifteenth Census of Populations* (Washington, D.C.: Government Printing Office, 1933); and *Sixteenth Census of Populations* (Washington, D.C.: Government Printing Office, 1943) provide employment statistics. Also consulted were the files of the Mississippi Valley Collection, Brister Library, Memphis State University, on organizing in the 1960s and 1970s.

4. Robert J. Norrell, "Caste in Steel: Jim Crow Careers in Birmingham, Alabama," *Journal of American History* 73 (December 1986): 669–94. Herbert Hill makes his argument in numerous articles; for one example, see "Race and Ethnicity in Organized Labor: The Historical Sources of Resistance to Affirmative Action," *Journal of Intergroup Relations* 12 (Winter 1984): 5–50.

5. Honey, *Southern Labor and Black Civil Rights; Fifteenth Census of Populations.* Blacks composed nearly 47 percent of Memphis blue-collar workers in 1970. "Summary Manpower Indicators, 1975 Memphis," U.S. Department of Labor, 1.

6. Laura and Hilley Pride, interview with author, Memphis, Tenn., 26 May 1989.

7. Ibid.

8. Matthew Davis, interview with author, Memphis, Tenn., 29 October 1984; Eddy Harrel, interview with author, Memphis, 29 October 1984; Pride Interview.

9. Richard Routon, interview with author, Memphis, Tenn., 18 February 1983; Matthew Davis, interview with author, Memphis, Tenn., 28 May 1989; Clarence Coe, interview with author, Memphis, Tenn., 28 May 1989.

10. George Holloway, interview with author, Baltimore, Md., 23 March 1990.

11. Ibid.

12. Stanley Denlinger, General Counsel for URW, to Sherman Dalrymple, President, 11 December 1940, Mediation file 199–6048, Federal Mediation and Conciliation Service records, Record Group 280, National Archives; Holloway interview.

13. Holloway interview.

14. Coe interview.

15. Ibid.; Routon interview.

16. Routon interview.

17. Holloway interview; Coe interview.

18. Coe interview; Evelyn Bates, interview with author, Memphis, Tenn., 25 May 1989.

19. Holloway interview.

20. Ibid.

21. Carl Moore, interview with author, Memphis, Tenn., 7 February 1983; Holloway interview; Local 988 UAW files, boxes 1, 2, ser. VI, Walter Reuther Papers, Records of the UAW, Walter Reuther Library of Labor and Urban Affairs, Wayne State University, Detroit, Mich.

22. Routon interview; George Clark, telephone interview with author, Memphis, Tenn., 17 February, 30 October 1984; Coe interview.

23. George Isabell, interview with author, Memphis, Tenn., 8 February 1983; Leroy Boyd, interview with author, Memphis, Tenn., 6 February 1983.

24. W. E. Davis, interview with author, Nashville, Tenn., 17 October 1982; Morton Davis, interview with author, Nashville, Tenn., 17 October 1982; Ed McCrea, interview with author, Nashville, Tenn., 17 October 1982; Lawrence McGurty, interview with author, Hometown, Ill., 17 January 1983.

25. W. E. Davis interview; Morton Davis interview; McCrea interview; Karl Korstad, interview with author, Greensboro, N.C., 20 May 1981. For details on the red scare, see Michael Honey, "Industrial Unionism and Racial Justice in Memphis," in *Organized Labor in the Twentieth-Century South*, ed. Robert H. Zieger (Knoxville: University of Tennessee Press, 1991), 135–57, and "Labor, the Left, and Civil Rights in the South: Memphis during the CIO Era, 1937–1955," in *Anti-Communism: The Politics of Manipulation*, ed. Judith Joel and Gerald M. Erickson (Minneapolis: MEP Publications, 1987), 57–86. See also Robert R. Korstad, "Daybreak of Freedom: Tobacco Workers and the CIO, Winston-Salem, North Carolina, 1943–1950" (Ph.D. diss., University of North Carolina, 1987); and Horace Huntley, "Iron Ore Miners and Mine Mill in Alabama: 1933–1952" (Ph.D. diss., University of Pittsburgh, 1977).

26. Josh Tools, telephone interview with author, Memphis, Tenn., 3 March 1983; Coe interview.

27. Coe interview.

28. Ibid.; Holloway interview.

29. Matthew Davis interview; Tools interview; Leroy Clark, interview with author, Memphis, Tenn., 27 March 1983; Alzeda Clark, interview with author, Memphis, Tenn., 24 May 1989; Isabell interview; Bates interview; Irene Branch, interview with author, Memphis, Tenn., 25 May 1989.

30. Routon, George Clark, W. E. Davis, Morton Davis, McCrea, Korstad, Powell and Dickenson acknowledged similar attitudes among most white industrial workers in Memphis. See interviews cited above.

31. Holloway interview.

32. Branch interview.

33. Ibid.; Pride interview.

34. Pride interview.

35. Coe interview; Pride interview.

36. Coe interview.

Part III: Introduction

1. Robin D. G. Kelley, " 'We Are Not What We Seem': Towards a Black Working-Class Infrapolitics in the Twentieth Century South," unpublished paper presented at the Southern Labor Studies Conference, Atlanta, October 1991; James C. Scott, *Domination and the Arts of Resistance: The Hidden Transcript* (New Haven: Yale University Press, 1990).

2. See, for example, Mercer Griffin Evans, "A History of the Organized Labor Movement in Georgia" (Ph.D. diss., University of Chicago, 1929); and Thomas M. Deaton, "Atlanta during the Progressive Era" (Ph.D. diss., University of Georgia, 1969).

3. Donald H. Grubbs, *Cry from the Cotton: The Southern Tenant Farmers' Union and the New Deal* (Chapel Hill: University of North Carolina Press, 1971); James A. Hodges, *New Deal Labor Policy and the Southern Cotton Textile Industry, 1933–1941* (Knoxville: University of Tennessee Press, 1986); J. Wayne Flynt, "The New Deal and Southern Labor," in *The New Deal and the South*, ed. James C. Cobb and Michael Namorato (Jackson: University Press of Mississippi, 1984), 63–96.

4. Douglas L. Smith, *The New Deal in the Urban South* (Baton Rouge: Louisiana State University Press, 1988); Aaron J. Nurick, *Participation in Organizational Change: The TVA Experiment* (New York: Praeger Press, 1985); Nancy Grant, *TVA and Black Americans: Planning for the Status Quo* (Philadelphia: Temple University Press, 1990).

5. Roger Biles, *Memphis in the Great Depression* (Knoxville: University of Tennessee Press, 1986); John Dean Martin, *The New Deal in Tennessee, 1932–1938* (New York: Garland Publishers, 1979); George T. Blakey, *Hard Times and the New Deal in Kentucky, 1929–1939* (Lexington: University Press of Kentucky, 1986); Michael S. Holmes, *The New Deal in Georgia: An Administrative History* (Westport: Greenwood Press, 1975), and "The Blue Eagle as 'Jim Crow Bird': The NRA and Georgia's Black Workers," *Journal of Negro History* 57 (July 1972): 276–83; Douglas L. Fleming, "Atlanta, the Depression and the New Deal" (Ph.D. diss., Emory University, 1984); Anthony J. Badger, *Prosperity Road: The New Deal, Tobacco and North Carolina* (Chapel Hill: University of North Carolina Press, 1980).

6. Carl Elliot and Michael D'Orso, *The Cost of Courage: The Journey of the American Congressman Carl Elliot, Sr.* (New York: Doubleday, 1992); Julian M.

Pleasants and Augustus M. Burns III, *Frank Porter Graham and the 1950 Senate Race in North Carolina* (Chapel Hill: University of North Carolina Press, 1990); Carl Grafton and Anne Permaloff, *Big Mules and Branchheads: James E. Folsom and Political Power in Alabama* (Athens: University of Georgia Press, 1985); Virginia Van der Veer Hamilton, *Lister Hill: Statesman for the South* (Chapel Hill: University of North Carolina Press, 1987); Nell I. Painter, *The Narrative of Hosea Hudson: His Life as a Negro Communist in the South* (Cambridge: Harvard University Press, 1979).

7. Daniel A. Powell, "PAC to COPE: Thirty-Two Years of Southern Labor in Politics," in *Essays in Southern Labor History: Selected Papers, Southern Labor History Conference, 1976*, ed. Gary M Fink and Merl E. Reed (Westport: Greenwood Press, 1977); Wayne Flynt, "A Vignette in Southern Labor Politics: The 1936 Mississippi Senatorial Primary," *Mississippi Quarterly* 26 (Winter 1972–73): 89–99; Robert J. Norrell, "Labor at the Ballot Box: Alabama Politics from the New Deal to the Dixiecrat Movement," *Journal of Southern History* 57 (May 1991): 201–34; Bryant Simon, "A Fabric of Defeat: The Politics of South Carolina Textile Workers in State and Nation, 1920–1938" (Ph.D. diss., University of North Carolina, 1992).

8. Karin A. Shapiro, "The Tennessee Coal Miners' Revolts of 1891–92: Industrialization, Politics and Convict Labor in the Late Nineteenth Century South" (Ph.D. diss., Yale University, 1991); Matthew J. Mancini, "Race, Economics, and the Abandonment of Convict Leasing," *Journal of Negro History* 63 (Fall 1978): 339–52; David C. Berry, "Free Labor He Found Unsatisfactory: James W. English and Convict Lease Labor at the Chattahoochee Brick Company" (Master's thesis, Georgia State University, 1991).

9. Michael Goldfield, *The Decline of Organized Labor in the United States* (Chicago: University of Chicago Press, 1989).

10. Patricia Ann Sullivan, "Gideon's Southern Soldiers: New Deal Politics and Civil Rights, 1933–1948" (Ph.D. diss., Emory University, 1983); Robert Korstad and Nelson Lichtenstein, "Opportunities Found and Lost: Labor, Radicals, and the Early Civil Rights Movement," *Journal of American History* 75 (December 1988): 786–811; Clifford M. Kuhn, "Two Small Windows of Opportunity: Black Politics in Georgia during the 1940s and the Pertinent Oral History Sources Today," unpublished paper presented at the joint meeting of the Georgia Political Science Association and Georgia Association of Historians, Savannah, February 1992.

11. For additional information on the events in Dalton, see the reminiscences of activist Don West in *Refuse to Stand Silently By: An Oral History of Grass Roots Social Activism in America, 1921–64*, ed. Eliot Wiggington (New York: Doubleday, 1992), 196–99.

10. Twice the Work of Free Labor?

1. Telegrams from John Towers to Governor Henry McDaniel, 9:40 A.M., 11:43 A.M, 1:30 P.M., 13 July 1886, and 9:17 A.M., 4:50 P.M., 14 July 1886, Convicts subject

file, box 64, file II, Georgia Department of Archives and History (GDAH); *Atlanta Constitution,* 13, 14, 15 July 1886; *Atlanta Journal,* 13 July 1886.

2. Georgia Penitentiary, Principal Keeper, *Report, 1884–1886,* p. 10; Georgia General Assembly, *Journal of the House of Representatives, 1886* (Atlanta: State Printer, 1886), 429, 432.

3. Report to Governor Gordon, December 1886, and "Special Report," E. T. Shubrick to Governor, 18 January 1887, E. T. Shubrick file, box 215, Names file, file II, GDAH; *State of Dade News,* 26 June 1891, p. 2; *Investigation of Charges Against Penitentiary Companies One, Two and Three,* 2 vols., *Evidence for the State,* vol. 1, *Evidence for Julius Brown, Receiver,* vol. 2, 10–21 February 1896, box 4, Julius L. Brown Papers, Atlanta Historical Society (AHS), vol. 1, pp. 474–75, 567, 570–71, 668 (hereafter cited as *Investigation, 1896);* Minutes of Stockholders Meeting, Dade Coal Company, 2 February 1892, Joseph E. Brown Papers, AHS; Principal Keeper, *Report, 1890–1892,* p. 7; *Atlanta Constitution,* 23, 25 June 1891; Report to Governor William J. Northen from Assistant Keeper R. F. Wright, 6 July 1891, p. 2; and Julius L. Brown to Governor William J. Northen, 26 October 1891, box 102, Governor's Correspondence, Executive Department Papers, GDAH.

4. "Original Petition of Georgia Iron and Coal Co.," *Hamby and Toomer v. Georgia Iron and Coal Company,* 5, Case File A–29478, box 510, Supreme Court Case Files, GDAH: Georgia Supreme Court, *Reports, Hamby and Toomer v. Georgia Iron and Coal Company,* 127 Ga. 792 (1907), 794–95; "Affidavit of Joel Hurt," and "Affidavit of George Hurt," *Georgia Iron and Coal v. Hamby and Toomer,* Case File A–29479, box 510, Supreme Court Case files, GDAH.

5. *State of Dade News,* 19 June 1891, p. 3; Georgia General Assembly, *Proceedings of the Joint Committee of the Senate and House to Investigate the Convict Lease System of Georgia, 1908,* 5 ms. vols., microfilm, GDAH, vol. 5, pp. 1562–63 (hereafter cited as *Proceedings).* On difficulty in recruiting mine labor, see Ronald Eller, *Miners, Millhands and Mountaineers* (Knoxville: University of Tennessee Press, 1982), 165–68, 193.

6. *Proceedings,* vol. 4, pp. 1220–21; Georgia Penitentiary, Prison Commission, *Report, 1901–02,* pp. 18–20.

7. Prison Commission, *Report, 1906–07,* p. 6; Principal Keeper, *Report, 1872–73,* pp. 8–9, 26; Georgia General Assembly, *Acts and Resolutions, 1876,* p. 42.

8. All figures are tabulated from a list of convicts assigned to Penitentiary Company No. 1, which in 1882 was identical to the Dade Coal Company. Principal Keeper, *Report, 1880–1882,* pp. 12–22. By 1890, of the 300 convicts that can be identified as coal mine workers, 84 were sentenced to life. Principal Keeper, *Report, 1888–1890,* pp. 12–22. The ever-increasing proportion of life-term convicts was a penitentiary-wide process: from 18 percent in 1897 to 29 percent by the time the lease came to an end in 1908. Principal Keeper, *Report, 1896–97,* p. 30; Prison Commission, *Report, 1907–08,* p. 22.

9. Georgia Penitentiary, Principal Physician, *Report, 1892–1893,* pp. 13–20.

10. Manuscript Census, 1880, Dade County, Georgia; Principal Keeper, *Report, 1888–1890*, pp. 12–22; Prison Commission, *Report, 1901–02*, p. 8, 1908–09, p. 13.

11. *Acts, 1876*, pp. 40–43; Principal Keeper, *Report, 1895–96*, pp. 9, 104.

12. See, for example, Georgia Geological Survey, *A Preliminary Report on the Coal Deposits of Georgia*, bulletin no. 12 (Atlanta: State Printer, 1904), 35, 38; U.S. Department of the Interior, United States Geological Survey (USGS), *Mineral Resources of the United States, 1886* (Washington, D.C.: Government Printing Office, 1886), 252, 394; and USGS, *Mineral Resources, 1907*, pt. 2, pp. 106–7.

13. *Investigation, 1896*, vol. 1, pp. 106–7; "Report of Receiver," 4 February 1895, *Sibley Manufacturing Co. v. Georgia Mining & Manufacturing Co.*, and "Hearing on Receivership," 24 January 1895, p. 5, Fulton Superior Court, Joseph Mackey Brown Papers II (restricted collection), Special Collections, University of Georgia (UGA).

14. Keith Dix, *Work Relations in the Coal Industry: The Hand-Loading Era, 1880–1930* (Morgantown: Institute for Labor Studies, West Virginia University, 1977), xi–xvii, 12–16, 50–51, 105–6; Curtis Seltzer, *Fire in the Hole: Miners and Managers in the American Coal Industry* (Lexington: University Press of Kentucky, 1985), 10–12. Carter Goodrich, *The Miner's Freedom: A Study of the Working Life in a Changing Industry* (Boston: Marshall Jones Company, 1925), is the classic tale of the persistence of the independent labor process into the twentieth century, written in the twilight of the "hand-loading era." For a wide-ranging discussion of nineteenth-century coal mining, see Priscilla Long, *Where the Sun Never Shines: A History of America's Bloody Coal Industry* (New York: Paragon House, 1989), pt. 1.

15. See, for example, U.S. Bureau of Labor, *Convict Labor, 20th Annual Report of the Commissioner of Labor* (Washington, D.C.: Government Printing Office, 1905), 30–31.

16. Philip Morgan, "Task and Gang Systems: The Organization of Labor on New World Plantations," in *Work and Labor in Early America*, ed. Stephen Innes (Chapel Hill: University of North Carolina Press, 1988), 189–220, offers the most complete summary of research on antebellum task work, with some allusions to piecework. See also Philip Morgan, "Work and Culture: The Task System and the World of Lowcountry Blacks," *William and Mary Quarterly* 39 (October 1982): 563–99; and Thomas Armstrong, "From Task Labor to Free Labor: The Transition Along Georgia's Rice Coast," *Georgia Historical Quarterly* 64 (Winter 1980): 432–47. Leslie Rowland offered a critique of this approach in a paper presented at the Culture and Cultivation in Slave Societies Conference at the University of Maryland, College Park, April 1989, emphasizing exploitation over autonomy. For a discussion of the exploitative function of task work in antebellum industry, see Robert S. Starobin, *Industrial Slavery in the Old South* (New York: Oxford University Press, 1970), 99–104; and Alex Lichtenstein, "In Retrospect: Industrial Slavery and the Tragedy of Robert Starobin," *Reviews in American History* 19 (December 1991): 604–17.

17. Principal Keeper, *Report, 1874*, pp. 7–8.

18. Testimony for Zeke Archey, U.S. Congress, Senate Committee on Education and Labor, *Report of the Committee of the Senate Upon the Relations Between Labor and Capital* (4 vols., 1885), vol. 4, pp. 435–37.

19. *Investigation, 1896*, vol. 1, pp. 100, 115, 315.

20. President's Report to Stockholders of the Georgia Mining and Manufacturing Co., 3 May 1893, folder 1, box 1, Julius L. Brown Papers, AHS.

21. "Report of the Investigating Committee," Georgia General Assembly, *Acts and Resolutions, 1908*, Extraordinary Session, p. 1082 (hereafter cited as General Assembly, "Report," 1908); *Proceedings*, vol. 3, pp. 873–74.

22. *Proceedings*, vol. 1, p. 170. See also ibid., vol. 3, pp. 877, 895, vol. 4, p. 1304.

23. For example, see *Proceedings*, vol. 1, pp. 146–47, 150, 177.

24. Hearing before the Prison Commission, Prison Commission folder, box 19, Hoke Smith Collection, Richard B. Russell Memorial Library, UGA (emphasis added).

25. *Investigation, 1896* vol. 2, p. 461.

26. By law, after 1879, county grand juries had to inspect the condition of the convict camps in their jurisdiction and report thereon along with their evaluations of other county matters. General Assembly, *Acts, 1878–1879*, pp. 140–41.

27. "The Georgia Convict Lease System," letter from Joseph E. Brown to *The Christian Union*, 24 December 1879, p. 549; House, *Journal*, 1881, p. 74; Dade County Grand Jury Presentments, March Term 1897, Dade County Superior Court Minutes, Book F (1896–1906), p. 66, microfilm, GDAH; Dade County Grand Jury Presentments, March Term 1898, Dade County Superior Court Minutes, Book F, p. 165, GDAH; Dade County Grand Jury Presentments, September Term 1901, Superior Court Minutes, Book F, p. 35, GDAH.

28. House, *Journal*, 1890, pp. 722–23.

29. Ibid., 1908, Extraordinary Session, p. 53; General Assembly, "Report," 1908, p. 1084. Task work for convicts also prevailed in the turpentine and brick industries. See, for example, *Proceedings*, vol. 1, pp. 90–92, 105, vol. 2, pp. 471, 529–31, 655. On convict coal mines in Alabama and Tennessee, see, for example, Alabama General Assembly, *Journal of the House of Representatives, 1896–97* (Montgomery: State Printer, 1897), pp. 627–29; and T. J. Hill, "Experience in Mining Coal with Convicts," *Proceedings of the Annual Congress of the National Prison Association, 1897* (Pittsburgh: Shaw Brothers, 1898), 393.

30. House, *Journal*, 1908, Extraordinary Session, p. 54; *Proceedings*, vol. 1, p. 179.

31. *Proceedings*, vol. 3, p. 800.

32. *Investigation, 1896*, vol. 2, pp. 462, 470–71.

33. Ibid., vol. 1, pp. 220–26, vol. 2, pp. 462, 967; "Declaration," 14 July 1888, *Dade Coal Company v. Haslett*, 83 Ga. 549 (1889), Case File A–15904, box 252, Supreme Court Case Files, Office of the Clerk of the Court, Records of the Supreme Court of Georgia, GDAH; House, *Journal*, 1886, pp. 433–34.

34. *Proceedings*, vol. 4, p. 1556.

35. On free miners, see, for example, U.S. Industrial Commission, *Report on Trusts and Industrial Combinations* (Washington, D.C.: Government Printing Office, 1901), vol. 13, p. 508; USGS, *Mineral Resources, 1889–1890*, pp. 170–71; and Alfred M. Shook to James T. Woodward, 22 June 1897, A. M. Shook Papers, Birmingham Public Library. On convicts, see "Declaration," 14 July 1888, *Dade Coal Company v. Haslett*, box 252, Supreme Court Case Files, GDAH; and *Proceedings*, vol. 1, pp. 28, 147, vol. 4, p. 1244.

36. *Proceedings*, vol. 1, p. 171.

37. Ibid.

38. *Investigation, 1896*, vol. 1, pp. 278, 405.

39. *Proceedings*, vol. 1, pp. 28, 147, 386, vol. 3, pp. 789–90.

40. Ibid., vol. 1, p. 195.

41. Ibid., vol. 1, pp. 63, 156.

42. Georgia Penitentiary, Principal Physician, *Report, 1895–96*, p. 111. See also Weekly Register of Convicts in Prison Camp Hospitals, Cole City, vols. 1891–92 and 1892–1895, Records of the Georgia Prison Commission, GDAH; Principal Physician, *Report, 1888–90*, pp. 13–14, and *1890–92*, pp. 12–13; and USGS, *Mineral Resources, 1900*, pp. 276–79, 451, and *1909*, pt. 2, pp. 47, 52. The national fatality rate in bituminous mining in 1896 was approximately 230,000 tons per fatality.

43. Dade County Grand Jury Presentments, March Term 1897, Superior Court Minutes, Book F, p. 66, GDAH; *Proceedings*, vol. 3, p. 779; House, *Journal*, 1908, Extraordinary Session, p. 53; *Proceedings*, vol. 4, pp. 1501, 1509. On the racial division of labor, see, for example, *Proceedings*, vol. 1, pp. 148, 170; and *Investigation, 1896*, vol. 2, pp. 450, 675.

44. *Proceedings*, vol. 1, pp. 157, 180–81.

45. House, *Journal*, 1908, Extraordinary Session, p. 52.

46. *Proceedings*, vol. 4, p. 1556; Warden E. D. Brock to George Hurt, 22 January 1902, in *Proceedings*, vol. 3, p. 863.

47. *Investigation, 1896*, vol. 2, pp. 693, 788. There is evidence of this practice in the Tennessee convict mines as well. See USGS, *Mineral Resources, 1894*, p. 189.

48. *Proceedings*, vol. 3, p. 783; *Investigation, 1896*, vol. 2, p. 643.

49. *Investigation, 1896*, vol. 2, pp. 617–18.

50. Monthly Reports of Convicts Punished ("Whipping Reports"), vol. 1, Cole City Camp, 1901–1904, Records of the Prison Commission, GDAH.

51. *Investigation, 1896*, vol. 2, pp. 462, 469–70, 474. On difficulty of task due to work place in mine, see ibid., vol. 1, pp. 314, 951. For further evidence of homosexuality in the mines, see ibid., vol. 1, pp. 281–82; and House, *Journal*, 1892, p. 655.

52. Dade County Grand Jury Presentments, September Term 1901, Superior Court Minutes, Book F, p. 351, GDAH; *Proceedings*, vol. 1, pp. 155, 386–87; *Investigation, 1896*, vol. 1, pp. 679–80.

53. House, *Journal*, 1895, p. 830; *The Code of the State of Georgia, Adopted*

December 15th, 1895 (Atlanta: Foote & Davies, 1896), vol. 3, p. 331. See also Pamphlet, folder 11, box 1, Joseph E. Brown Papers, AHS, pp. 11–12; Principal Physician, *Report, 1896–97*, pp. v–vi; and William D. Grant, "Georgia Penitentiary Company No. 3 and the Convicts," pamphlet, circa 1881, Georgia Room, UGA. The grand jury reports, legislative investigations, and "special investigations" commissioned by the governor and cited throughout this paper are fine examples of scrutiny of convict food, clothing, quarters, sanitation, labor conditions, and overall treatment. See also House, *Journal*, 1897, pp. 1264–72, 1903, pp. 885–91. Grant, "Georgia Penitentiary Company No. 3," contains several excerpts from investigations, as do the "Exhibits" in Benjamin G. Lockett, "Memorial to the Senate and House of Representatives . . . of the State of Georgia," circa 1881, Georgia Room, UGA, 7–12. For rules guaranteeing oversight and inspection, see *Code of the State of Georgia*, vol. 3, pp. 334 (inspectors), 335 (grand juries), 336 (physician), 338 (principal keeper and assistant principal keepers). The relationship among lessee, convict, and the state was expressed well by Georgia's Supreme Court: "Of course a [leased] convict is not property. He is a human being and the State owes to him the same duty it would owe to any other human being under the same unfortunate circumstances. . . . His labor, however, during his term of service, is a property right which may be the basis of a valid contract." *Hamby and Toomer v. Georgia Iron and Coal Company*, 127 Ga. 792 (1906), 801.

54. House, *Journal*, 1881, pp. 66–76 (quotes, p. 76). See House, *Journal*, 1892, p. 657, for a similar recommendation by Joseph S. Turner, Chairman of the Committee on the Penitentiary. Turner was appointed chair of the Prison Commission in 1897 when this form of direct supervision was passed into law.

55. Julius L. Brown to Governor William J. Northen, 30 May 1894, box 105, Governor's Correspondence, GDAH.

56. General Assembly, *Acts, 1880–81*, p. 107.

57. *Investigation, 1896*, vol. 1, p. 824. For a whipping boss who doubled as "Superintendent" at the Dade mines, see House, *Journal*, 1895, p. 829. On Governor Gordon, see Georgia Executive Minutes, 23 September 1887, 8 November 1887, pp. 488–90, GDAH.

58. W. O. Reese to Joseph E. Brown, 24 October 1889, and Joseph E. Brown to Governor John B. Gordon, 30 October 1889, box 98; Julius L. Brown to Governor William J. Northen, 26 October 1891, box 102; Julius L. Brown to Governor W. Y. Atkinson, 28 March 1896, box 112; all in Governor's Correspondence, GDAH.

59. General Assembly, *Acts, 1897*, pp. 71–78.

60. Ibid., pp. 75–76. The terms "lease," "hire," "bidder," and "paying . . . for the annual labor of the convicts" (perhaps "labor" was the operative word here) were all explicit in the act. "There is no lease law in Georgia, nor a lease system, nor lease contracts," claimed the prison commission (*Report, 1901–02*, p. 17); also *Report, 1899–1900*, p. 4. See also Prison Commission, *Report, 1907–08*, for repetition of this myth on the eve of abolition of leasing: "no convicts are in the custody or control of

any company" (pp. 5–6). On "good and faithful labor," see Prison Commission, *Report, 1898–99,* pp. 46–47. See also *Proceedings,* vol. 2, p. 660. The U.S. Bureau of Labor, however, in its report on convict labor in 1905, had no doubt that Georgia was one of the states that still leased convicts. U.S. Bureau of Labor, Convict Labor, 236.

61. General Assembly, "Report," 1908, pp. 1082–83; *Proceedings,* vol. 3, p. 800.

62. General Assembly, "Report," 1908, p. 1079; *Proceedings,* vol. 1, pp. 159, 180, vol. 3, pp. 782, 788–90.

63. *Proceedings,* vol. 2, pp. 614–15, 660–61, 719, 726, vol. 3, pp. 1114, 1156.

64. The evidence of this practice, which was apparently endemic, is widespread and conclusive. See General Assembly, "Report," 1908, pp. 1063–70; and *Proceedings,* vol. 1, pp. 38, 117, 152, 163, 168, vol. 2, pp. 459 (quote), 522, 549, 581, 589, 623, 651, 674, 678, vol. 3, pp. 776, 931, 1099.

65. See *Proceedings,* vol. 1, p. 678, vol. 2, pp. 804, 878, on its "customary" nature. See also ibid., vol. 2, pp. 547–48; General Assembly, "Report," 1908, p. 1069; Petitioners Amendment, Transcript of Record, 28 April 1909, *Chattahoochee Brick Company v. Goings,* Case File A–31445, box 558, Supreme Court Case Files, GDAH; Proceedings, vol. 1, p. 170; and Joel Hurt in *Proceedings,* vol. 2, pp. 438, 457.

66. *Proceedings,* vol. 2, p. 589, vol. 3, p. 772, vol. 4, pp. 1231–32.

67. Ibid., vol. 3, pp. 739–40, 1158–59, vol. 4, pp. 1298–301, 1306.

68. Ibid., vol. 1, pp. 91–92, 129–31; U.S. Bureau of Labor, *Convict Labor,* 30.

69. George Washington Cable, *The Silent South, together with the Freedmen's Case in Equity and the Convict-Lease System* (1883; reprint, New York: Charles Scribner's Sons, 1907), 177–78.

70. Prison Commission, *Report, 1901–02,* p. 8; USGS, *Mineral Resources,* selected years.

71. On days worked, see USGS, *Mineral Resources, 1900,* pp. 301–2. In 1890, Alabama recorded 217 days worked, Tennessee, 263, and Georgia, 313. J. J. Ormsbee, "The Coal Interests of the South," *Tradesman* 36 (1 January 1897): 120–23.

72. Report to Stockholders, 3 May 1893, folder 1, box 1, Julius L. Brown Papers, AHS; *Investigation, 1896,* vol. 1, p. 750; USGS, *Mineral Resources, 1896,* p. 482, *1906,* p. 659.

73. USGS, *Mineral Resources, 1886,* p. 252; Charles Willard Hayes, *The Southern Appalachian Coal Field,* in USGS, *22nd Annual Report* (Washington, D.C.: Government Printing Office, 1902), pt. 3, p. 243.

74. USGS, *Mineral Resources, 1905,* p. 561, *1900,* pp. 309, 372, *1910,* pt. 2, pp. 9–10, 113, *1907,* pt. 2, pp. 50–52, 106. On the impact of mechanization on the coal industry, see Keith Dix, *What's a Coal Miner to Do? The Mechanization of Coal Mining* (Pittsburgh: University of Pittsburgh Press, 1988).

75. *Dixie* 12 (March 1896): 37.

76. See USGS, *Mineral Resources, 1888,* p. 207, for a summary of factors bearing on productivity in the bituminous coal industry.

77. Prison Commission, *Report, 1901–02*, p. 18, *1897–98*, pp. 12–14, 44–45, *1900–01*, p. 7, *1901–02*, pp. 19–20, *1903–04*, pp. 7–9, *1907–08*, p. 4.

78. On the abolition of leasing in Georgia, see A. Elizabeth Taylor, "The Abolition of the Convict Lease System in Georgia," *Georgia Historical Quarterly* 26 (June 1942): 273–87; Matthew J. Mancini, "Race, Economics, and the Abandonment of Convict Leasing," *Journal of Negro History* 63 (Fall 1978): 339–52; Dewey Grantham, *Hoke Smith and the Politics of the New South* (Baton Rouge: Louisiana State University Press, 1958), 172–75; and Alex Lichtenstein, "Good Roads and Chain Gangs in the Progressive South: 'The Negro Convict Is a Slave,'" *Journal of Southern History* 59 (February 1993): 85–110.

79. Principal Physician, *Report, 1896–97*, pp. v–vi.

80. Harold Courlander, *Negro Folk Music, U.S.A.* (New York: Columbia University Press, 1963), 106–7.

11. The Failure of Operation Dixie

1. CIO Executive Board Minutes, 15 March 1946, Wayne State University Archives of Labor and Urban Affairs; *American Federationist*, May 1946. See also the April–May 1946 issue of *Labor and Nation* focusing on the South, especially the article by Allan S. Haywood, CIO vice-president and director of organizing, "We Propose to Unionize Labor in the South," 35.

2. *CIO News*, 18 December 1939. Among the early resolutions and commitments of support to southern organizing were those recorded at AFL conventions in 1915, 1919, 1927, and 1928. See various AFL Convention *Proceedings*. Recognition of the importance of organizing all workers in a national industry, thus removing the reduction of wages as a tactic in employer competition, is a readily apparent necessity. As Frank deVyver notes, "Strictly speaking, no labor movement, with the exception, perhaps, of those very few trades whose product is both produced and sold locally, can afford to be a regional movement." Frank T. deVyver, "The Present Status of Unions in the South," *Southern Economic Journal*, 5 (April 1939): 485–98.

3. "Labor Drives South," *Fortune* 34 (November 1946): 140.

4. The October 1948 issue of ibid., vol. 35, p. 150, observed that "The C.I.O. southern drive . . . [was] now grinding to a halt."

5. In an assessment with which I concur, Barbara Griffith states: "For American labor, Operation Dixie was, quite simply, a moment of high tragedy from which it has yet to recover." Barbara S. Griffith, *The Crisis of American Labor: Operation Dixie and the Defeat of the CIO* (Philadelphia: Temple University Press, 1988), 176. For detailed statistics and analysis of the decline of the organized labor movement in the post-World War II period, see Michael Goldfield, *The Decline of Organized Labor in the United States* (Chicago: University of Chicago Press, 1987).

6. For an incisive analysis of the anti-labor thrust of southern Democratic conservatism, see Ira Katznelson, Kim Geiger, and Daniel Kryder, "The Democratic Party and the Southern Veto: Congressional Coalitions, 1933–1952," unpublished manuscript, New School, 1992.

7. See the similar assessment in Robert Korstad and Nelson Lichtenstein, "Opportunities Found and Lost: Labor, Radicals, and the Early Civil Rights Movement," *Journal of American History* 75 (December 1988): 786–811.

8. V. O. Key, Jr., *Southern Politics in State and Nation* (New York: Alfred A. Knopf, 1949), 329–44.

9. Edmund S. Morgan, *American Slavery, American Freedom* (New York: Norton, 1975); Arthur Meier Schlesinger, Jr., *The Age of Jackson* (Boston: Little, Brown, 1950); W. E. B. Du Bois, *Black Reconstruction in America, 1860–1880* (Cleveland: Harcourt, Brace, 1935); Lawrence Goodwyn, *Democratic Promise: The Populist Moment in America* (New York: Oxford University Press, 1976); Stephen Skowronek, *Building a New American State* (New York: Cambridge University Press, 1982).

10. James L. Sundquist, *Dynamics of the Party System* (Washington, D.C.: Brookings Institute, 1983); Richard Hofstader, *Age of Reform* (New York: Vintage Books, 1955), 308; Richard E. Neustadt, *Presidential Power* (New York: John Wiley and Sons, 1980).

11. For further description and detailed references, see Michael Goldfield, "Worker Insurgency, Radical Organization, and New Deal Labor Legislation," *American Political Science Review* 83 (December 1989): 1257–82.

12. Max Weber, *The Methodology of the Social Sciences* (New York: Free Press, 1949), 164–88; John Elster, *Logic and Society: Contradictions and Possible Worlds* (New York: John Wiley and Sons, 1978); David Lewis, *Counterfactuals* (Cambridge: Harvard University Press, 1973).

13. See, for example, Key, *Southern Politics.*

14. Liston Pope, *Millhands and Preachers: A Study of Gastonia* (New Haven: Yale University Press, 1942); Griffith, *Crisis of American Labor.*

15. F. Ray Marshall, "The Development of Organized Labor," *Monthly Labor Review* 91 (March 1968): 67; Frederic Meyers, "The Growth of Collective Bargaining in Texas—A Newly Industrialized Area," in *Proceedings of the Seventh Annual Industrial Relations Research Association* (Madison: Industrial Relations Research Association, 1955), 288–89.

16. Meyers, "Growth of Collective Bargaining in Texas," 288–89.

17. F. Ray Marshall, "Some Factors Influencing the Growth of Unions in the South," in *Proceedings of the Thirteenth Annual Meeting of the Industrial Relations Research Association, St. Louis, Missouri, December 28, 29, 1960,* ed. Gerald G. Somers (Madison, Wis.: IRRA, 1960), 169; Nelson N. Bortz and James F. Walker, "Extent of Collective Bargaining Agreements in 17 Labor Markets," *Monthly Labor Review* 78 (January 1955): 64–68; Goldfield, *Decline of Organized Labor,* 149–52.

18. Marjorie A. Potwin, *Cotton Mill People of the Piedmont: A Study in Social Change* (New York: Columbia University Press, 1927), 48; F. Ray Marshall, *Labor in the South* (Cambridge: Harvard University Press, 1967), 80.

19. Marshall, "Some Factors," 175.

20. Ibid.; Marshall, "Development of Organized Labor," 67, and *Labor in the South*, 306.

21. Pope, *Millhands and Preachers*, 61; H. M. Douty, "Development of Trade Unionism in the South," *Monthly Labor Review* 63 (October 1946): 560–66; Frank T. deVyver, "The Present Status of Unions in the South," *Southern Economic Journal*, 16 (July 1949): 14.

22. Among others, see Jennings J. Rhyne, *Some Southern Cotton Mill Workers and Their Villages* (Chapel Hill: University of North Carolina Press, 1930), 205; Broadus Mitchell, *The Rise of the Cotton Mills in the South* (Baltimore: Johns Hopkins University Press, 1921); Melton Alonzo McLaurin, *Paternalism and Protest: Southern Cotton Mill Workers and Organized Labor, 1875–1905* (Westport: Greenwood Press, 1971); John Kenneth Morland, *The Millways of Kent* (Chapel Hill: University of North Carolina Press, 1958); Harry Boyte, "The Textile Industry, Keel of Southern Industrialization," *Radical America* 6 (March–April 1972): 4–49; and Jeffrey Leiter, "Continuity and Change in the Legitimation of Authority in Southern Mill Towns," *Social Problems* 29 (June 1982): 540–50.

23. Pope, *Millhands and Preachers*, 11.

24. Joseph A. McDonald and Donald A. Clelland, "Textile Workers and Union Sentiment," *Social Forces* 63 (December 1984): 512.

25. Robert Blauner, *Alienation and Freedom: The Factory Worker and His Industry* (Chicago: University of Chicago Press, 1964), 80, 87; John Shelton Reed, *The Enduring South: Subcultural Persistence in Mass Society* (Chapel Hill: University of North Carolina Press, 1986), 45–55.

26. Pope, *Millhands and Preachers*, 11.

27. *American Federationist* 35 (November 1928): 1327, 1329.

28. Irving Bernstein, *The Lean Years: A History of the American Worker, 1920–1933* (Boston: Houghton Mifflin, 1960), 40.

29. George B. Tindall, *The Emergence of the New South, 1913–1945* (Baton Rouge: Louisiana State University Press, 1967), 350.

30. Marshall, *Labor in the South*, 333.

31. W. J. Cash, *The Mind of the South* (New York: Alfred A. Knopf, 1941), 249–50, 353. On southern labor militancy in the nineteenth century, see, for example, Peter Rachleff, *Black Labor in Richmond, 1865–1890* (Philadelphia: Temple University Press, 1984); Leon Fink, *Workingman's Democracy: The Knights of Labor and American Politics* (Urbana: University of Illinois Press, 1983); and McLaurin, *Paternalism and Protest*. George Googe's remarks are in *American Federationist* 35 (November 1928): 1326.

32. Pope, *Millhands and Preachers*. For descriptions of anti-union violence, see the historical novel by Denise Giardina, *Storming Heaven* (New York: Norton, 1987).

33. Griffith, *Crisis of American Labor*, 174–75; Dennis R. Nolan and Donald E. Jonas, "Textile Unionism in the Piedmont," 1901–1932," in *Essays in Southern Labor History: Selected Papers, Southern Labor History Conference, 1976*, ed. Gary M Fink and Merl E. Reed (Westport: Greenwood Press, 1977), 50, 68.

34. William E. Regensburger, " 'Ground Into Our Blood': The Origins of Working Class Consciousness and Organization in Durably Unionized Southern Industries, 1930–1946" (Ph.D. diss., University of California, Los Angeles, 1987).

35. For the former view, see Marshall, *Labor in the South*, 133; Bert Cochran, *Labor and Communism* (Princeton: Princeton University Press, 1977), 55; Theodore Draper, "Communists and Miners," *Dissent* 19 (Spring 1972): 371–92; Philip Taft, *Organizing Dixie: Alabama Workers in the Industrial Era* (Westport: Greenwood Press, 1981), 129; and Walter Galenson, *The CIO Challenge to the AFL: A History of the American Labor Movement, 1935–1941* (Cambridge: Harvard University Press, 1960), 63. For the latter view, see Frank Emspak, "The Breakup of the Congress of Industrial Organizations (CIO), 1945–1950" (Ph.D. diss., University of Wisconsin, 1972), 321; Philip S. Foner, *Organized Labor and the Black Worker, 1619–1973* (New York: Praeger Press, 1974), 280; James R. Greene, *The World of the Worker: Labor in the Twentieth Century America* (New York: Hill and Wang, 1980), 193; and Regensburger, " 'Ground Into Our Blood,' " 14.

36. See, for example, Griffith, *Crisis of American Labor*, 72–73; Goldfield, *Decline of Organized Labor*, 134–35.

37. Herbert R. Northrup, "The Tobacco Workers International Union," *Quarterly Journal of Economics* 56 (August 1942): 606–7.

38. Morris Hillquit, *Loose Leaves from a Busy Life* (New York: Rand School Press, 1934), 130–31.

39. John F. Burton, Jr., and Terry Thomason, "The Extent of Collective Bargaining in the Public Sector," in *Public Sector Bargaining*, ed. Benjamin Aaron, Joyce M. Najita, and James L. Stern (Washington, D.C.: Bureau of National Affairs, 1988), 14–15; Michael Goldfield, "Public Sector Union Growth and Public Policy," *Policy Studies Journal* 18 (Winter 1989–1990): 404–20.

40. Jack Barbash, "The Elements of Industrial Relations," *British Journal of Industrial Relations* (1964): 105; Harvey O'Connor, *History of Oil Workers International Union-CIO* (Denver: Oil Workers International Union, 1950). For further discussion and references, see Goldfield, *Decline of Organized Labor*, 135–37.

41. Regensburger, " 'Ground Into Our Blood,' " 176, 188, 200.

42. Clyde Johnson, "CIO Oil Workers' Organizing Campaign in Texas, 1942–1943," in *Essays in Southern Labor History*, ed. Fink and Reed, 173–87; O'Connor, *History of Oil Workers International Union*.

43. Griffith, *Crisis of American Labor*, 23, 203.

44. *New York Times*, 19 April 1946.

45. Suggestions by some (e.g., Richard L. Simpson) that Operation Dixie had a large percentage of northern organizers would seem to be wrong. Richard L. Simpson, "Labor Force Integration and Southern U.S. Textile Unionism," in *Research in the Sociology of Work* (Greenwich: JAI Press, 1981), vol. 1.

46. Griffith, *Crisis of American Labor*, 164.

47. Jerry Lembcke, *Capitalist Development and Class Capacities* (Westport: Greenwood Press, 1988).

48. James Patterson, *Congressional Conservatism and the New Deal* (Lexington: University of Kentucky Press, 1967).

49. This latter question is answered affirmatively as a working hypothesis in the last chapter of Goldfield, *Decline of Organized Labor*.

12. Christian Radicalism, McCarthyism, and the Dilemma of Organized Labor in Dixie

1. Arguments for continuity, with varying complexity, are in John Kenneth Morland, *The Millways of Kent* (Chapel Hill: University of North Carolina Press, 1958), and "Kent Revisited: Blue-Collars Aspirations and Achievements," in *Blue-Collar World: Studies of the American Worker*, ed. Arthur B. Shostak and William Bomberg (Englewood Cliffs: Prentice-Hall, 1964), 134–43; Barbara S. Griffith, *The Crisis of American Labor: Operation Dixie and the Defeat of the CIO* (Philadelphia: Temple University Press, 1988); James A. Hodges, *New Deal Labor Policy and the Southern Cotton Textile Industry, 1933–1941* (Knoxville: University of Tennessee Press, 1986), chap. 12. Jacquelyn Dowd Hall et al., *Like a Family: The Making of a Southern Cotton Mill World* (Chapel Hill: University of North Carolina Press, 1987), esp. 354, stress the enduring impact of the General Textile Strike of 1934. Michael Goldfield, *The Decline of Organized Labor in the United States* (Chicago: University of Chicago Press, 1987), 239–40, suggests that postwar organizing in Dixie faltered because of the CIO's own shortcomings in dealing with the race issue and with the anti-labor Taft-Hartley Act.

2. Douglas Flamming, *Creating the Modern South: Millhands and Managers in Dalton, Georgia, 1884–1984* (Chapel Hill: University of North Carolina Press, 1992).

3. See Griffith, *Crisis of American Labor*; Lanham speech in *Congressional Record* of the House of Representatives, 11 June 1957, p. 7823; Gary M Fink, *Labor Unions* (Westport: Greenwood Press, 1977), 385, and *Biographical Dictionary of American Labor Leaders* (Westport: Greenwood Press, 1974), 12.

4. (Dalton) *The Southerner: A Voice of the People*, July 1955; *Dalton Citizen*, 25 March 1948; Anthony P. Dunbar, *Against the Grain: Southern Radicals and Profits, 1929–1959* (Charlottesville: University Press of Virginia, 1981), 245–47; Flamming, *Creating the Modern South*, chap. 11.

5. John M. Glen, *Highlander: No Ordinary School, 1932–1962* (Lexington: University Press of Kentucky, 1988), offers a fine analysis of reform movements in the southern upcountry. On West, see ibid., 16–20, 26; and Dunbar, *Against the Grain*, 52–58, 211–13, 228–29, passim. West's radicalism was actually exposed and publicized in papers near Dalton as early as 1940; and later it was dredged up to smear Highlander years after the Dalton campaign when West had retired to obscurity on a north Georgia farm. See, for example, the following items in the F.B.I. file on Highlander Folk School [microfilm ed.]: newsclipping from *Chattanooga News-Free Press*, 13 November 1940, roll 1, sect. 9, frame 1247; and a pamphlet issued by the Georgia Commission on Education [an anti-integration group headed by Governor Marvin Griffin], roll 1, sect. 5, frame 794ff. On the issue of West's membership in the Communist party, Dunbar, *Against the Grain*, 54. Robin D. G. Kelley, *Hammer and Hoe: Alabama Communists during the Great Depression* (Chapel Hill: University of North Carolina Press, 1990), 126, states that West "joined the Communist Party in 1934." Assuming West did join the party in 1934, his explicit denial of being a Communist in 1955 indicates that he had dropped out of the party by the mid-1950s or that he lied in an open letter to the public (*Dalton Citizen*, 1 September 1955).

6. Few issues of *The Southerner* have survived. The author has located only three issues: May 1955, available at Georgia State University's Southern Labor Archives in Atlanta; July 1955, a copy of which is housed at the Crown Gardens and Archives in Dalton; and January 1956, on microfilm at the University of Georgia Libraries in Athens.

7. All quotations here from *The Southerner*, May 1955; but similar phrases can be found in any surviving issue of the paper and in Pratt's statements in the local business press.

8. *The Southerner*, May 1955; John W. Edelman [TWUA's Washington, D.C. representative] to Very Reverend Msgr. George G. Higgins [National Catholic Welfare Conference], 9 September 1955, folder 49, box 1563; Donald L. West to James O'Shea, 23 May 1955, folder 49, box 1559, Ramsey Papers, Southern Labor Archives (SLA), Georgia State University, Atlanta.

9. *The Southerner*, May 1955.

10. "Statement of David Burgess, Executive Secretary, Georgia State CIO Council," 10 May 1955; C. H. Gillman to William Pollock, 10 May 1955; David S. Burgess to William Pollock, 11 May 1955 [attached to this letter is the HUAC report on West requested by Lanham]; William Pollock to James O'Shea, 13 May 1955; William Pollock to David S. Burgess, 16 May 1955; William Pollock to Charles H. Gillman, 16 May 1955; James O'Shea to William Pollock, 17 May 1955; all in folder 49, box 1559, Ramsey Papers, SLA.

11. James O'Shea to William Pollock, 17 May 1955, folder 49, box 1559, Ramsey Papers, SLA.

12. For a useful discussion of the CIO's Communist purges, see Robert H. Zieger, *American Workers, American Unions* (Baltimore: Johns Hopkins University Press, 1986), 123–34.

13. James O'Shea to William Pollock, 17 May 1955; James O'Shea to Donald L. West, 19 May 1955; Donald L. West to James O'Shea, 23 May 1955; James O'Shea to William Pollock, 31 May 1955; William Pollock to James O'Shea, 6 June 1955; all in folder 49, box 1559, Ramsey Papers, SLA.

14. See John G. Ramsey to Victor Reuther et al., 12 October 1955; John W. Edelman to Very Reverend Msgr. George G. Higgins, 9 September 1955; John W. Edelman to "Dear Mr. Senator" [for release], 8 September 1955; Ramsey to Rev. S. Wilkes Dendy [Presbyterian Church, Dalton], 21 October 1955; Milton Ellerin, Southeastern Office, Anti-Defamation League of B'nai B'rith, Atlanta to [John Ramsey?], 14 September 1955; and news release for *Atlanta Journal*, 9 September 1955; all in folder 99, box 1563, Ramsey Papers, SLA. For West's contact with B'nai B'rith, see Dunbar, *Against the Grain*, 246.

15. *The Southerner*, January 1956.

16. *Dalton News*, 21 August 1955. *Dalton Citizen*, 12 January 1956, pp. 17–22, offered a special "review of some of the more outstanding articles relative to Communism and the Don West campaign" (hereafter cited as "West Edition"), which also reprinted the *News'* HUAC Report.

17. *Dalton News*, 21 August 1955.

18. Ibid., 28 August 1955.

19. *Dalton Citizen*, 25 August 1955.

20. For the poems and the controversy surrounding them, see *Dalton Citizen*, 25 August, 1 September 1955; *Dalton News*, 28 August 1955. The *Daily Worker* reprint is in *Dalton Citizen*, 8 September 1955. The "Agitator" version is also in Dunbar, *Against the Grain*, 55–56.

21. *Dalton News*, 28 August 1955; *Dalton Citizen*, 1 September 1955.

22. *Dalton News*, 28 August 1955; *Dalton Citizen*, 1 September 1955.

23. *Dalton Citizen*, 1 September 1955.

24. *Dalton News*, 11, 18 September 1955; *Dalton Citizen*, 15, 22 September 1955. See also the "West Edition" for a recapitulation of the campaign, which adequately reflects the tone of the editorial battle.

25. *Dalton Citizen*, 8 September 1955; *Dalton News*, 18 September 1955. The mainstream papers spelled it "Latex" (except for *Dalton Citizen*, 8 September, which used "Lawtex"); *The Southerner* sometimes spelled it "Lawtex."

26. The action may be followed in *Dalton Citizen*, 15, 22, 29 September, 6, 13, 20 October, 17 November 1955; *Dalton News*, 18, 25 September, 2, 16, 23 October 1955.

27. *Dalton News*, 6 November 1955; *Dalton Citizen*, 10 November 1955. Little is known about Watters or the Olivia Baptist Church. The 1948 *City Directory* lists one

W. P. Waters as an employee of the Crown Cotton Mills. The Olivia Baptist is not listed therein. No city directory is available for 1955.

28. *Dalton Citizen*, 6, 13 October 1955.

29. Ibid., 6, 20 October 1955; *Dalton News*, 16, 23 October 1955. West feared a "frame up effort" and wrote friends in New York to express his concerns. Pace got hold of an issue of the *National Guardian*, in which West's concerns were aired, and used it to smear West by linking him to northerners and by portraying him as disloyal to Dalton for trying to give the city and its leaders a bad name. That anti-Communist Edgar C. Bundy was from Illinois never seemed to matter. See *Dalton News*, 3 November 1955.

30. *Dalton News*, 18 September 1955; *Dalton Citizen*, 17, 24 November, 11 December 1955.

31. *Dalton News*, 30 October 1955.

32. *Dalton Citizen*, 17 November 1955; *Dalton News*, 20 November 1955.

33. *Dalton News*, 4 December 1955.

34. Ibid.

35. Ibid.

36. *Dalton Citizen*, 17 November 1955; *Dalton News*, 20 November 1955.

37. *Dalton Citizen*, 6 December 1955.

38. Ibid., 8 December 1955.

39. *The Southerner*, January 1956.

40. *Dalton News*, 18 December 1955; *The Southerner*, January 1956.

41. *Dalton Citizen*, 29 December 1955, 5 January 1956. The grand jury also questioned the trustworthiness of the police department in connection with the Latex violence. See ibid., 22, 29 December 1955. The Civil Service Commission, a three-person body appointed by the city council, was responsible for the operation of both the police and fire departments in Dalton and had been, since the late 1940s, a group generally considered sympathetic to organized labor. The commission was often composed of leaders of TWUA Locals 185 and 134. See *Textile Labor*, 3 May 1947.

42. *Dalton Citizen*, 5, 12 January 1956.

43. According to Dunbar, *Against the Grain*, 246–47, anti-West vigilantes tried to force West's car off the road on his way out of town, but West was carrying Pratt's pistol and was able to shoot out one of the attacker's tires and proceed without incident. *Dalton Citizen*, 26 January 1956, recounts the alleged confrontation between West and Pratt.

44. *Textile Labor*, December 1962, January 1963. For union membership in Local 185, see Flamming, *Creating the Modern South*, table 13.1. On national trends in organized labor, see Goldfield, *Decline of Organized Labor*.

13. George Wallace, Civil Rights, and the Alabama AFL-CIO

1. Alabama Labor Council *Newsletter*, 26 May 1958. For Wallace's remarks to the Alabama CIO, see Philip Taft, *Organizing Dixie: Alabama Workers in the Industrial Era* (Westport: Greenwood Press, 1981), 132.

2. Marshall Frady, *Wallace* (New York: World Publishing, 1968), 98.

3. Minutes of the Executive Board Meeting, 9 March 1962, p. 5, Alabama AFL-CIO Files, Birmingham.

4. Ibid.

5. Minutes of the COPE Committee Meeting, 9 March 1962, p. 5, Alabama AFL-CIO Files.

6. Alabama AFL-CIO 1962 COPE Convention *Proceedings*, 48.

7. George Kundahl, "Organized Labor in Alabama State Politics" (Ph.D. diss., University of Alabama, 1967), 149.

8. Minutes of the Executive Board Meeting, 28 October 1962, Alabama AFL-CIO Files.

9. C. A. Cardwell to The Honorable George Meany, 10 March 1956, "White Citizens' Councils, January–March, 1956" folder, box 4, AFL-CIO Civil Rights Collection, George Meany Memorial Archives, Silver Spring, Md. (hereafter cited as Meany Archives).

10. Recording Secretary to Mr. George Meany, 21 February 1956, ibid.

11. *Birmingham News*, 23 February 1956.

12. For information on the success the Citizens' Councils had in recruiting union members in the Birmingham area, see H. L. Mitchell to Boris Shiskin, 7, 12 March 1956, "National Agricultural Workers Union, 1956 & 1960" folder, box 4, AFL-CIO Civil Rights Collection, Meany Archives. See also Numan V. Bartley, *The Rise of Massive Resistance: Race and Problems in the South during the 1960s* (Baton Rouge: Louisiana State University Press, 1969), 309; Neil R. McMillen, *The Citizens' Councils: Organized Resistance to the Second Reconstruction, 1954–64* (Urbana: University of Illinois Press, 1971), 203; and Kundahl, "Organized Labor in Alabama," 47. For an excellent review of Jim Crow in the Birmingham steel mills and how tenaciously whites defended it, see Robert J. Norrell, "Caste in Steel: Jim Crow Careers in Birmingham, Alabama," *Journal of American History* 73 (December 1986): 669–94.

13. Robert Corley, "The Quest for Racial Harmony: Race Relations in Birmingham, Alabama, 1947–63" (Ph.D. diss., University of Virginia, 1979), 106.

14. Daniel Powell to Jack Kroll and Jim McDevitt, 2 September 1956, folder 2, box 1, lot 1A, AFL-CIO COPE Research Department Files, Meany Archives.

15. Corley, "Quest for Racial Harmony," 161.

16. *New York Times*, 26 February 1956.

17. Morton T. Elder, "Labor and Race Relations in the South," October 1956, box 108, Fund for the Republic Papers, Princeton University Library.

18. Ray Marshall, "Union Racial Problems in the South," *Industrial Relations* (May 1962): 117–29; "Southern Tension Seizes Labor," *Business Week,* 14 April 1956, pp. 47–50; Henry L. Trewitt, "Southern Unions and the Integration Issue," *The Reporter,* 14 October 1956, pp. 25–28.

19. Alabama AFL 1956 Convention *Proceedings,* 48. See also Taft, *Organizing Dixie,* 163. Prior to the merger, the Alabama CIO Industrial Union Council held three of its last five conventions in Mobile because of that city's racial tolerance.

20. Alabama AFL 1956 Convention *Proceedings,* 48. But the state council did receive a request from the AFL-CIO that it no longer distinguish its "Colored Vice-Presidents at Large" from the other vice-presidents on its official letterhead.

21. Report of National Director to COPE Operating Committee, 13 August 1957, folder 31, box 3, lot 1, AFL-CIO COPE Research Department Files, Meany Archives. See also "Alabama-Local" and "Alabama-State" folders, Philip Weightman Collection (where arrangements for COPE to assist ASCARV are discussed), Robert F. Wagner Labor Archives, Tamiment Library, New York University. Fannie Neal from the Clothing Workers was chosen for the position with ASCARV. For more details on Neal's employment with ASCARV, see Fannie Neal Oral History, 40–52, Bentley Historical Library, University of Michigan, Ann Arbor; and Philip Weightman to W. C. Patton, 15 September 1959, "Alabama-Local" folder, box 2, Philip Weightman Collection.

22. David J. Garrow, *Bearing the Cross: Martin Luther King, Jr., and the Southern Christian Leadership Conference* (New York: William Morrow, 1986), 75–77, provides a good account of MIA's electoral activity.

23. Earl W. Davis to Director James L. McDevitt, 15 May 1958, folder 3, Daniel Powell Papers, Southern Historical Collection, University of North Carolina Library, Chapel Hill (hereafter cited as SHC).

24. Barney Weeks to Mr. Philip Weightman, 22 March 1959, Alabama AFL-CIO Files.

25. Paul E. Golson to Mr. Leroy Lindsey, 22 June 1961, Alabama AFL-CIO Files.

26. Joseph M. Hood to Alabama Labor Council, 28 March 1964, folder 5, Daniel Powell Papers, SHC.

27. Jack W. Cook to Mr. Barney Weeks, 24 June 1961, and Weeks' reply to Cook, 26 June 1961, Alabama AFL-CIO Files.

28. Newspaper accounts dated 11 March 1964, folder 5, Daniel Powell Papers, SHC. See also the letter from Barney Weeks to Mr. Al Barkan, 13 March 1964, Alabama AFL-CIO Files.

29. Barney Weeks to Mr. Daniel A. Powell, 7 July 1964, Alabama AFL-CIO Files.

30. "Wallace's Labor Stand Defended," newspaper clipping, folder 5, Daniel Powell Papers, SHC.

31. "Wisconsin Labor Criticism of Wallace Irks Leader Here," ibid.

32. *Birmingham News*, 2 April 1964, ibid. See also Kundahl, "Organized Labor in Alabama," 354, for more evidence of Wallace support among the rank and file.

33. *Tuscaloosa News*, 13 April 1964, Alabama AFL-CIO Files.

34. Barney Weeks to Mr. Dallas W. Sells, 21 April 1964, ibid.

35. George C. Wallace to Delegate, 11 March 1964, folder 5, Daniel Powell Papers, SHC.

36. William A. Nunnelley, *Bull Connor* (Tuscaloosa: University of Alabama Press, 1991), 14.

37. Daniel A. Powell to James L. McDevitt, 17 May 1957, folder 3, box 1, lot 1A, AFL-CIO Research Department Files, Meany Library. On labor's friendly relations with Connor, see also Ben Segal, "The Educational Implications of Labor's Public Responsibility in Public Affairs: Civil Rights, Civil Liberties, and International Affairs," November 1959, p. 172, in Ben Segal's personal papers, Washington, D.C. In the special election to replace Birmingham's commissioner form of government with a mayor-council system, the commissioner alternative drew its votes "from precincts where Connor had done well in the past, the predominantly white, blue collar neighborhoods of Ensley, West End, Central Park, and East Lake." In the 1963 Birmingham mayoral contest, the Birmingham Labor Council endorsed Albert Boutwell over Connor, who despite the endorsement again polled very well from white working-class wards. See Corley, "Quest for Racial Harmony," 228–46.

38. Alabama, AFL-CIO 1964 COPE Convention *Proceedings*, 23.

39. Ibid., 25.

40. Ibid., 37–38. For a description of this convention, see Taft, *Organizing Dixie*, 174.

41. Barney Weeks to Mr. Al Barkan, 13 March 1964, Alabama AFL-CIO Files.

42. Dan Powell to Al Barkan, 12 July 1964, folder 201, Daniel Powell Papers, SHC.

43. President to Mr. William Burnell, 4 May 1964, Alabama AFL-CIO Files.

44. Barney Weeks to Mr. Daniel A. Powell, 3 April 1964, folder 5, Daniel Powell Papers, SHC.

45. These figures on membership in the Alabama AFL-CIO are from Kundahl, "Organized Labor in Alabama," 90–105.

46. Barney Weeks to Mr. Al Barkan, 3 April 1964, Alabama AFL-CIO Files.

47. Barney Weeks to Mr. Al Barkan, 6 May 1964, folder 5, Daniel Powell Papers, SHC.

48. Barney Weeks to Mr. Al Barkan, 4 June 1964, Alabama AFL-CIO Files.

49. Ibid., 5 June 1964.

50. Ben Albert to Daniel Powell, 8 July 1964, folder 201, Daniel Powell Papers, SHC.

51. *New York Times*, 14 June 1964.

52. Ibid., 29 September 1964.

53. Kundahl, "Organized Labor in Alabama," 77.

54. Daniel Powell to Mr. Al Barkan, 12 July 1964, folder 201, Daniel Powell Papers, SHC. Taft mentions sympathy for the Ku Klux Klan among the members of the old Alabama CIO that created problems for the CIO leadership similar to those Weeks faced. Taft, *Organized Dixie*, 129.

55. Alabama AFL-CIO 1964 Convention *Proceedings*, 29–34, 73–87, 109–17, 198–203. See also Taft, *Organizing Dixie*, 175, for another description of this convention.

56. Barney Weeks to Mr. Al Barkan, 2 December 1964, folder 5, Daniel Powell Papers, SHC.

57. Quoted in Kundahl, "Organized Labor in Alabama," 437.

58. Taft, *Organizing Dixie*, 176.

59. Fannie Neal to Philip Weightman, n.d., in possession of the author.

60. Robert J. Norrell, "Labor Trouble: George Wallace and Union Politics in Alabama," in *Organized Labor in the Twentieth-Century South*, ed. Robert H. Zieger (Knoxville: University of Tennessee Press, 1991), 264.

61. Executive Board Minutes, 9 September 1965, Alabama AFL-CIO Files.

62. Barney Weeks to Mr. Stanton Smith, 28 March 1966, ibid.

63. Actually, Weeks made this argument against endorsing Thrash at a meeting of the executive board that preceded the COPE convention where questions as to why Thrash was not being endorsed were raised. Executive Council Meeting, 18 March 1966, ibid.

64. See the debate on whether to endorse Brewer in the Alabama 1966 COPE Convention *Proceedings*, 32–39.

65. Field Report, 20 April 1966, folder 12, Daniel Powell Papers, SHC.

66. Reactions from the building trades to the Alabama 1966 COPE convention are reported in the *Birmingham News*, 27 March 1966. See also Kundahl, "Organized Labor in Alabama," 134–74.

67. The quote is from Kundahl, "Organized Labor in Alabama," 171. Voting patterns in the 1966 Alabama gubernatorial race are analyzed in Daniel A. Powell to Al Barkan, 20 May 1966, folder 12, Daniel Powell Papers, SHC.

68. Earl Black and Merle Black, "The Wallace Vote in Alabama: A Multiple Regression Analysis," *Journal of Politics* 35 (1973): 730–37.

69. Alabama C.O.P.E. Program 1966, folder 206, Daniel Powell Papers, SHC.

70. Kundahl, "Organized Labor in Alabama," 397.

71. Stanley Greenberg, *Race and State in Capitalist Development* (New Haven: Yale University Press, 1980), 340.

72. Robert J. Norrell, "Labor at the Ballot Box: Alabama Politics from the New Deal to the Dixiecrat Movement," *Journal of Southern History* 57 (May 1991): 234.

73. Norrell, "Labor Trouble," 263.

74. This description of Alabama politics is drawn from V. O. Key, Jr., *Southern Politics in State and Nation* (New York: Alfred A. Knopf, 1949), 36–58.

75. Speech by Barney Weeks to the Young Democrats of Alabama, n.d., Alabama AFL-CIO Files.

76. David M. Kovenock et al., *Explaining the Vote: Presidential Choices in Individual States* (Chapel Hill: Institute for Research in Social Sciences, 1973), 483–87.

77. William H. Stewart, "Alabama," in *The 1984 Presidential Election in the South*, ed. Robert P. Steed, Laurence W. Moreland, and Tod A. Baker (New York: Praeger Press, 1986), 76.

78. Jack Bass and Walter DeVries, *The Transformation of Southern Politics* (New York: Basic Books, 1976), 68–69.

Editors and Contributors

Editors

GARY M FINK, professor of history at Georgia State University, earned the Ph.D. at the University of Missouri. His most recent book, *The Fulton Bag and Cotton Mill Strike, 1914–15*, will be published by the ILR Press, Cornell University, in 1993. Fink is currently working on a study of Jimmy Carter and organized labor and a history of labor espionage in the United States.

MERL E. REED earned his doctorate at Louisiana State University and currently is professor of history at Georgia State University. His latest book, *Seedtime of the Modern Civil Rights Movement*, was published by the Louisiana State University Press in 1991. He is currently completing a history of Georgia State University as a case study of the role of urban universities in the New South.

Associate Editors

LESLIE S. HOUGH earned his Ph.D. at the University of Virginia. He currently serves as director of the Archives of Labor and Urban Affairs, Walter P. Reuther Library, Wayne State University. In addition to having published numerous articles in historical and archival journals, he is the author of *The Turbulent Spirit: Violence and Coaction Among Cleveland Workers, 1877–1899.*

CLIFFORD M. KUHN, who holds the Ph.D. from the University of North Carolina, Chapel Hill, is a co-author of *Living Atlanta: An Oral History of the City, 1914–1948.* He currently serves as the director of the Georgia Government Documentation Project, Georgia State University.

JOE W. TROTTER, JR., is a professor of history at Carnegie-Mellon University. His many publications include *Coal, Class, and Color: Blacks in Southern West Virginia, 1915–32; Black Milwaukee: The Making of an Industrial Proletariat, 1914–45;* and *The Great Migration in Historical Perspective: New Dimensions of Race and Class in Industrial America.*

ROBERT H. ZIEGER, a University of Maryland Ph.D., currently serves as professor of history at the University of Florida. His most recent books include *John L. Lewis: Labor Leader; American Workers, American Unions;* and *Organized Labor in the Twentieth Century South.* His newest study, a sweeping history of the Congress of Industrial Relations, will be published by the University of North Carolina Press.

Contributors

BESS BEATTY, who holds the Ph.D. in history from Florida State University, is an associate professor of history at Oregon State University. Her book, *A Revolution Gone Backward: The Black Response to National Politics, 1876–1896,* was published by Greenwood Press in 1987. She has also published articles in the *North Carolina Historical Review* and the *Journal of Southern History.* She is now working on a book on the Edwin Holt family in Almanac County, North Carolina, 1837–1900.

DAVID L. CARLTON earned his doctorate at Yale University and is currently an associate professor of history at Vanderbilt University. His highly acclaimed first book, *Mill and Town in South Carolina, 1880–1920,* was published by the Louisiana State University Press in 1982. His most recent article, "The Revolution from Above: The National Market and the Beginnings of Industrialization in North Carolina," was published in the *Journal of American History* (September 1990). Currently, Professor Carlton is completing a study of the process of industrialization in North Carolina, 1865–1940.

DERNORAL DAVIS, an assistant professor of history at Jackson State University, holds the Ph.D. in history from New York University. His articles have appeared in the *Tennessee Historical Quarterly* and in an anthology, *Black Exodus: The Great Migration from the American South,* published by the

University Press of Mississippi in 1989. Dr. Davis is now completing a book-length manuscript entitled, "Urban Journey: Black Memphians Between the Crucibles of Emancipation and the Nadir."

ALAN DRAPER holds the Ph.D. in political science from Columbia University and currently serves as an associate professor of government at St. Lawrence University. His book, *A Rope of Sand: The AFL-CIO Committee on Political Education, 1955–67,* was published by Praeger in 1989. His study of labor in the modern civil rights movement will be published by the ILR Press in 1994.

DOUGLAS FLAMMING earned his Ph.D. from Vanderbilt University and currently serves as an assistant professor of history at the California Institute of Technology. His first book, *Creating the Modern South: Millhands and Managers in Dalton, Georgia, 1884–1984,* was published by the University of North Carolina Press in 1992. His current research focuses on the origins and development of the African-American community in Los Angeles, 1900–1940. An article based on that research will appear in a volume entitled, *California Progressivism Revisited and Revised* (1993).

GARY R. FREEZE is chair of the Department of History and Government at Erskine College. He earned his doctoral degree at the University of North Carolina and is currently revising his dissertation for publication. His essay, "God, Cotton Mills, and New South Myths: A New Perspective on Salisburg, N.C., 1887–88," appeared in *The Adaptable South: Essays in Honor of George Brown Tindall,* ed. Elizabeth Jacoway et al. (1991). Dr. Freeze is also working on a social history of Catawba County, North Carolina.

MICHAEL GOLDFIELD earned his graduate degrees in political science at the University of Chicago. An associate professor of political science at Wayne State University, his major publications include "Worker Insurgency, Radical Organization and New Deal Labor Legislation," *American Political Science Review* (1991), "Class, Race and Politics in the United States," *Research in Political Economy* (1990), and *The Decline of Organized Labor in the United States* (1987). Professor Goldfield is working on a book on the failure of Operation Dixie and its impact on contemporary American politics.

JAMES A. HODGES is a professor of history at the College of Wooster. He is the author of *New Deal Labor Policy and the Southern Cotton Textile Industry, 1933–41* (1986). Professor Hodges is currently writing a book-length study of the union organizing efforts at J. P. Stevens.

MICHAEL HONEY is an assistant professor at the University of Washington, Tacoma. He earned his graduate degrees at Howard University (MA) and Northern Illinois University (Ph.D.). He is the author of *Southern Labor and Black Civil Rights: Organizing Memphis Workers* and currently is conducting a study of Martin Luther King, Jr., Civil Rights, and the American Labor Movement.

ALEX LICHTENSTEIN earned his Ph.D. from the University of Pennsylvania and currently serves as an assistant professor of history at Florida International University. His recent article, " 'The Negro Convict is a Slave': Chain Gangs and Good Roads in the Progressive South," appeared in the *Journal of Southern History.*

JAMES D. SCHMIDT recently completed work for the doctor's degree in history at Rice University. He now serves as an instructor at Mercer University—University College. His current research focuses on vagrancy and labor contracts, 1815–1880.

SUZANNE SCHNITTMAN wrote her dissertation at the University of Rochester under the advisement of Stanley Engerman and Eugene Genovese. She is an adjunct instructor at State University of New York at Brockport and is completing a book on industrial slavery in urban Virginia.

BRYANT SIMON earned his Ph.D. at the University of North Carolina, Chapel Hill, and now serves as an assistant professor of history at the California Institute of Technology.

Index

Alabama American Federation of Labor-Congress of Industrial Organization (AFL-CIO), 212, 213, 214, 216, 217, 223, 225, 226, 227, 228, 229; opposed Wallace on segregation, 213–14; affiliated unions threaten to bolt, 214, 217, 221, 222, 223; sensitive to the needs of black unionists, 215, 216, 217; union members join White Citizens' Councils, 214–15; contributes funds to CORE, 217; refused to endorse Wallace's 1964 presidential bid, 217; helped defray costs of Freedom Riders, 217; local unions revolt and endorse Wallace for president, 220–21; drastic decline in union affiliation during 1960s, 221; local unions endorse Goldwater for president, 224. See also AFL-CIO; Committee on Political Education (COPE, AFL-CIO)

Alabama State Coordinating Association for Registration and Voting (ASCARV), 216, 217

Amalgamated Clothing and Textile Workers Union of America (ACTWUA), 53, 59; campaign against J. P. Stevens Company, 53–64; litigation before the NLRB, 58; campaign strategy, 60–61; national boycott of J. P. Stevens, 61; "corporate campaign," 61–62; settlement with J. P. Stevens, 62; assessment of the campaign, 63–64

American Federation of Labor (AFL), 166, 180, 181, 184, 186, 188

American Federation of Labor-Congress of Industrial Organization (AFL-CIO), 56, 122, 126, 127, 128, 145, 210, 215, 216, 218, 229, 315, 317, 318. See also Alabama AFL-CIO; Committee on Political Education (COPE, AFL-CIO)

Ax, Joel, 59, 63

Baldanzi, George, 55, 186, 192
Barkan, Al, 220, 222, 223, 324
Beatty, Bess, xv, 7, 9, 19
Bernstein, Irving, 3, 5, 177–78
Bittner, Van, 186, 187, 267
Black workers in antebellum Richmond, 72–86; advantages as hired urban slaves, 73, 74–76; slave hiring period brought Christmas holiday and freedom, 77; contract provisions for tobacco factory slaves, 78–79; medical care, 79; independent living arrangements (board system), 80; pass system, 81; board system attacked by *Richmond Republican*, 82; cash and bonuses, 82; the factory task system, 82–83; work pace and singing, 83–84; slave arsonists and physical punishment, 84; theft by slaves, 84–85; slave class formation, 85; slave "cookshops," 85; tighter restrictions in Richmond after emancipation, 85–86

Black workers in Memphis: remembering unionism during Jim Crow, 121–37; and segregation, 121–22, 125; and the CIO, 122, 125; and the Great Depression, 123–24; paid low wages and denied promotions, 125

Black workers in the South: historiography, 67–71. See also Black workers in antebellum Richmond; Black workers in Memphis